CONTENTS

page **16**

page **10**

page **08**

HOME PLANS

RESOURCES

Find thousands of plans on-line, visit our website **www.familyhomeplans.com**

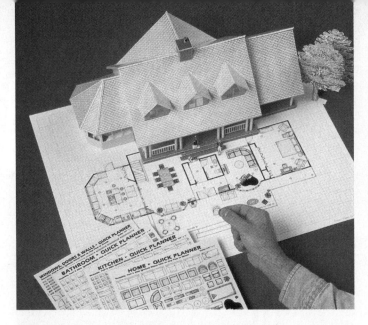

Camps, Cabins & Cottages

An Active Interest Media Publication

GARLINGHOUSE, LLC

Art Director	Christopher Berrien
Managing Editor	Debra Cochran
Art Production Manager	Debra Novitch
Production Artist	Cindy King
Exec. Director of Operations	Wade Schmelter
Senior Accountant	Angela West
Director of Home Plan Sales	Sue Lavigne
Director of Sales	Tom Valentino
Accounts Receivable/Payable	Monika Jackson
Telesales Manager	Helene Crispino
Telesales Team	Julianna Blamire
	Randolph Hollingsworth
	Renee Johnson
	Barbara Neal
	Carol Patenaude
	Robert Rogala
	Alice Sonski
Fulfillment Supervisor	Audrey Sutton

Advertising Sales
1-800-279-7361

For Plan Orders in Canada
The Garlinghouse Company
102 Ellis Street, Penticton, BC V2A 4L5
1-800-361-7526

For Designer's Submission Information,
e-mail us at dcochran@aimmedia.com

CAMPS, CABINS & COTTAGES
Library of Congress: 2004104787   ISBN: 1-893536-14-9

At Garlinghouse, you're buying more than a set of plans.

You're buying a history of exceptional customer service and understanding.

In addition to our experienced staff of sales professionals, The Garlinghouse Company maintains an expert staff of trained house design professionals to help guide you through the complex process of customizing your plans to meet all your needs and expectations.

We don't just want to sell you a plan, we want to partner with you in building your dream home. Some of the many services we offer our customers include:

Answers to Your Questions
If you have technical questions on any plan we sell, give us a call toll-free at 1-800-235-5700.

Customizing Your Stock Plan
Any plan we sell can be modified to become your custom home. For more information, see page 32 and page 407.

Information for Budgeting Your New Home's Construction
A very general cost of building your new home can be arrived at using the so-called National Average Cost to Build, which is $110 per square foot. Based on that average, a 2,400-square-foot home would cost $264,000, including labor and materials, but excluding land, site preparation, windows, doors, cabinets, appliances, etc.

For a more inclusive rough estimate, Garlinghouse offers a Zip Quote estimate for every plan we sell. Based on current prices in your zip code area, we can provide a rough estimate of material and labor costs for the plans you select. See page 408 to learn more.

However, for a more accurate estimate of what it will cost to build your new home, we offer a full materials list, which lists the quantities, dimensions, and specifications for the major materials needed to build your home including appliances. Available at a modest additional charge, the materials list will allow you to get faster, more accurate bids from your contractors and building suppliers—and help you avoid paying for unused materials and waste. Due to differences in regional requirements and homeowner or builder preferences, electrical, plumbing, and heating/air conditioning equipment specifications are not designed specifically for each plan. See page 409 for additional information.

Garlinghouse blueprints have helped create a nation of homeowners, beginning back in 1907. Over the past century, we've made keeping up with the latest trends in floor plan design for new house construction our business. We understand the business of home plans and the real needs and expectations of the home plan buyer. To contact us, call 1-800-235-5700, or visit us on the web at www.familyhomeplans.com.

For America's best home plans.
Trust, value, and experience. Since 1907.

Woodland
Retreat

At first glance, it's a simple design—a single-floor cabin with a rustic look. But the interior is an open floor plan, created for an easy traffic flow and access to all conveniences. Ideal for a weekend getaway, this home manages to include all the basic conveniences, while maintaining a cozy, country feel. A hall runs along the first floor, leading to a large living room with double doors to the back screen porch. Beside the porch, you'll find a raised deck, the ideal spot for all your outdoor gatherings. Tall windows in the living room create a special spot from which to enjoy the view. L-shape counters give the kitchen ample workspace, while double doors open to a convenient laundry closet. In the opposite wing, two bedrooms flank a full bath. This home is designed with basement and crawlspace foundation options. ◗

Photography: James Salomon

MAIN FLOOR

Screen Porch

Deck

UP

LIVING
15x16

BEDROOM
15x11

HALL

W
D

R

KITCHEN
15x8

ENTRY

BEDROOM
16x10

ABOVE, LEFT: Cottage-style cabinetry lends form and function to the kitchen.

ABOVE: Natural light streams into the front bedroom. The planked ceiling carries through the pleasing elements of the cabin's refined country interior.

BELOW: The screen porch offers a comfortable retreat within a retreat.

Design 32122

Price Code	A
Total Finished	1,112 sq. ft.
Main Finished	1,112 sq. ft.
Basement Unfinished	484 sq. ft.
Deck Unfinished	280 sq. ft.
Porch Unfinished	152 sq. ft.
Dimensions	47'x45'6"
Foundation	Basement Crawlspace
Bedrooms	2
Full Baths	1

Please note: The photographed home may have been modified to suit homeowner preferences. If you order plans, have a builder or design professional check them against the photographs to confirm construction details.

Cape Cod
Cottage

ABOVE: A steeply gabled roof with low eaves and a central chimney hark back to the eighteenth-century design origins of the Cape, one of the country's most popular cottage-style homes.

An efficient design puts every square foot of space to good use in this classic American cottage. The left side of the home is given over to the more utilitarian spaces, such as the kitchen—complete with pantry and breakfast area—the utility room, two-car garage, and storage space. The long great room forms the core of the home, while the master suite is secluded in a wing of its own. Two secondary bedrooms, a full bath, and a large bonus space comprise the second floor. This home is designed with a combination basement and crawlspace foundation. ◗

Design 57000

Price Code	Please call for pricing
Total Finished	2,076 sq. ft.
First Finished	1,540 sq. ft.
Second Finished	536 sq. ft.
Bonus Unfinished	502 sq. ft.
Dimensions	62'8"x61'
Foundation	Basement/ Crawlspace
Bedrooms	3
Full Baths	2
Half Baths	1

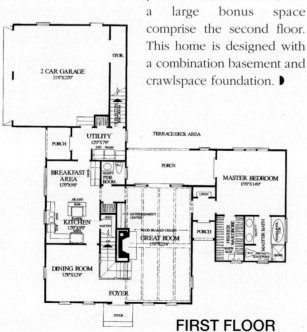

FIRST FLOOR

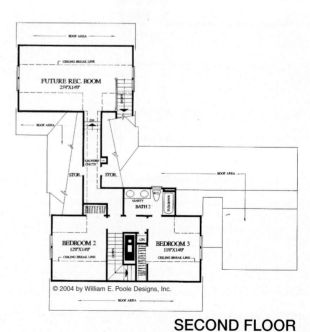

© 2004 by William E. Poole Designs, Inc.

SECOND FLOOR

To order blueprints, call **800-235-5700** or visit us on the web, **familyhomeplans.com**

Photography: Chris A. Little

ABOVE: A split staircase comes together at a landing and leads up to the covered porch, offering a warm welcome from all sides.

Design 94658

Price Code	D
Total Finished	2,205 sq. ft.
First Finished	1,552 sq. ft.
Second Finished	653 sq. ft.
Dimensions	60'x50'
Foundation	Pier/Post
Bedrooms	3
Full Baths	2

Please note: The photographed home may have been modified to suit homeowner preferences. If you order plans, have a builder or design professional check them against the photographs to confirm construction details.

Distinct
Spaces

This home is divided into two very distinct spaces: the private and the common areas. The foyer leads directly into the combined living/dining room, which is well-lit by walls of windows and warmed by a center fireplace. L-shape counters define the kitchen, while a hexagonal island services all three areas. A hall in the right wing connects the two secondary bedrooms to a full bath. The master suite fills the entire second floor and includes a five-piece bath, walk-in closet, and private balcony. A porch jutting onto a wood deck rounds out the plan. This home is designed with a pier/post foundation. ◗

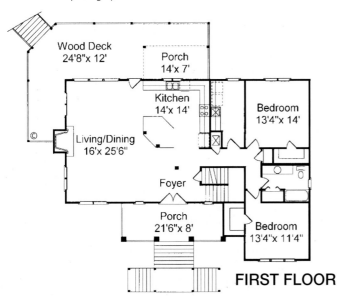

FIRST FLOOR

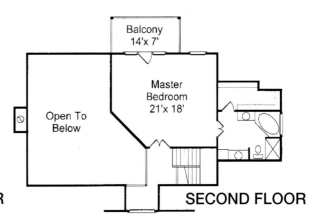

SECOND FLOOR

Photography: Chris A. Little

A Part of the
Scenery

ABOVE: A lattice porch gable lets light flood onto the porch and into the house through tall windows.

BELOW: The front of this bright and open cottage features a gracious symmetry.

Ideal for waterfront property, this home features rooms designed to take in the scenery. The dining room, kitchen, and living area form the core of the first floor, where a central cooktop island also serves as a snack bar. The living room ceiling soars two stories and tops a wall of windows and two doors that open onto a porch, which leads out to a deck to extend comfortable living outdoors. The left and right wings are filled with the bedrooms. Each secondary bedroom offers generous closet space and two of them have direct access to a four-piece bath. The third is steps away from a full bath. In the right rear corner, the master suite has its own full bath and a walk-in closet. A fifth bedroom encompasses the entire second floor. A three-piece bath and walk-in closet complete the space, which is lit by twin dormers. This home is designed with a pier/post foundation. ◗

Design 94664

Price Code	G
Total Finished	2,977 sq. ft.
First Finished	2,061 sq. ft.
Second Finished	464 sq. ft.
Lower Finished	452 sq. ft.
Garage Unfinished	780 sq. ft.
Deck Unfinished	197 sq. ft.
Porch Unfinished	312 sq. ft.
Dimensions	50'x63'
Foundation	Pier/Post
Bedrooms	5
Full Baths	4

Please note: The photographed home may have been modified to suit homeowner preferences. If you order plans, have a builder or design professional check them against the photographs to confirm construction details.

ABOVE: The living room, with its wall of windows, opens out onto the porch.

BELOW: This is just one of the five bedrooms in this spacious design, four of which have private baths.

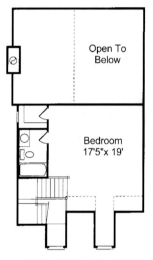

SECOND FLOOR

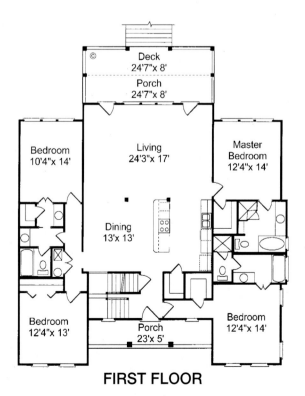

FIRST FLOOR

Photography: James Salomon

New England
Classic

ABOVE: Traditional clapboard siding is beautifully set off by the white trim that outlines the screen porch, windows, and arched entry.

BELOW: Informality reigns in the relaxed dining area, which is open to the great-room.

Built for great family times and hearty entertaining, this cottage retreat pays homage to the coastal homes of Maine. The moment guests pass through the barrel-vaulted entry and set foot on the porch, they feel a welcoming presence. The great-room is warmed by a corner fireplace and illuminated by floor-to-ceiling windows that provide light from two directions. The deck and screen porch provide places to relax while enjoying outdoor views. Both have direct access to the eating nook and kitchen.

The master suite, which features another corner fireplace, rounds out the 1,508-square-foot main level. The 947-square-foot upper level features an elevated study surrounded by windows. This level also has two bedrooms with separate baths. A staircase in the garage leads to a large office that can be converted into a suite. This home is designed with a basement foundation. ▶

Design 32189

Price Code	E
Total Finished	2,455 sq. ft.
First Finished	1,508 sq. ft.
Second Finished	947 sq. ft.
Basement Unfinished	1,508 sq. ft.
Garage Unfinished	735 sq. ft.
Dimensions	60'4"x60'
Foundation	Basement
Bedrooms	3
Full Baths	1
3/4 Baths	2
Half Baths	1

Please note: The photographed home may have been modified to suit homeowner preferences. If you order plans, have a builder or design professional check them against the photographs to confirm construction details.

ABOVE: A window, framed by cabinets and a shelf, brightens up the kitchen. Instead of a peninsula counter, the owners of this home added a central opening that maintains the connection to the living areas while hiding any cooking mess.

LEFT: Large picture windows offer uninterrupted views and fill the interior with light.

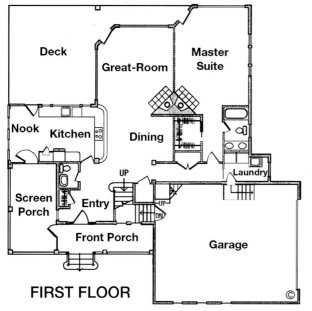

FIRST FLOOR

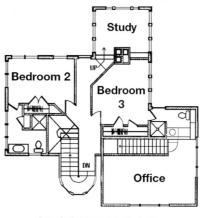

SECOND FLOOR

ABOVE: An abundance of windows, including a greenhouse window and clerestories, bring the outdoors in.

Light-Filled
Home

This elegant home is filled with natural light. A wraparound deck outside the living and dining area is directly accessible through sliding-glass doors. A fireplace warms the living room on long winter evenings. An efficient kitchen, adjacent to the dining area, has such amenities as a double sink, generous counter space, and a pantry. The first-floor master suite features a walk-in closet and a full bathroom with convenient laundry facilities. Upstairs, two bedrooms share a full bath. A mezzanine overlooks the living area and provides room for an open study or a sitting area. The unfinished basement is ideal for storage or for expanding to meet a family's growing needs. This home is designed with a basement foundation. ◗

Design 65141

Price Code	B
Total Finished	1,550 sq. ft.
First Finished	946 sq. ft.
Second Finished	604 sq. ft.
Dimensions	37'x30'8"
Foundation	Basement
Bedrooms	3
Full Baths	2

SECOND FLOOR

FIRST FLOOR

ABOVE: This rustic beauty offers views and abundant natural light throughout.

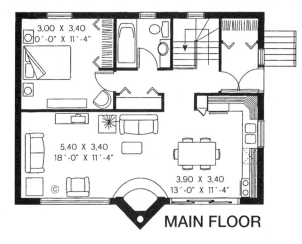

3,00 X 3,40	
10'-0" X 11'-4"	
5,40 X 3,40	3,90 X 3,40
18'-0" X 11'-4"	13'-0" X 11'-4"

MAIN FLOOR

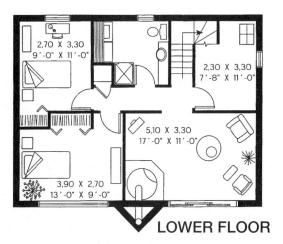

2,70 X 3,30	2,30 X 3,30
9'-0" X 11'-0"	7'-8" X 11'-0"
3,90 X 2,70	5,10 X 3,30
13'-0" X 9'-0"	17'-0" X 11'-0"

LOWER FLOOR

Mountain
Getaway

This chalet-style home is designed with entertaining and comfort in mind. In the 787-square-foot first floor, a sunny family room and kitchen share a fireplace. The casual eat-in kitchen provides access to the wraparound deck through sliding doors. The back of the first floor is devoted to the master suite and a full bath. On the 787-square-foot lower floor, family members and guests have plenty of room to relax. Two additional bedrooms, an area well suited for storage space, and a full bath with laundry facilities nearby round out the lower floor. A downstairs family room features its own fireplace and sliding glass doors. This home is designed with a basement foundation. ◗

Design 65007

Price Code	B
Total Finished	1,574 sq. ft.
Main Finished	787 sq. ft.
Lower Finished	787 sq. ft.
Dimensions	32'4"x24'4"
Foundation	Basement
Bedrooms	3
Full Baths	1
3/4 Baths	1

Photography: Tria Giovan

ABOVE & BELOW: Exposed rafter tails, shingle siding and latticed gables create interesting texture.

Maximum
Views

From the outside looking in, this home offers a splendid sight to all passers by. But this home's winding deck and panoramic windows give residents inside a view as well. Sliding doors in the dining room and a front door to the entry let everyone enter from either end of the deck. A built-in snack bar in the kitchen provides easy meal service. An intimate living room features a fireplace between windows. One bedroom enjoys access to its own full bath, while both have ample closet space. The upper level loft is perfect for accommodating a house full of weekend guests in bunk-house style. There are 988 square feet on the main level and 182 square feet on the upper level. This home is designed with a pier/post foundation. ❱

ABOVE, LEFT: A fireplace warms the bright, window-filled living room.

ABOVE: Windows on both sides of the loft offer light and cross-ventilation.

LEFT: The kitchen snack bar is an ideal place to prepare or serve meals.

Design 32611

Price Code	B
Total Finished	1,170 sq. ft.
First Finished	988 sq. ft.
Second Finished	182 sq. ft.
Dimensions	26'x38'
Foundation	Pier/Post
Bedrooms	2
Full Baths	2

Please note: The photographed home may have been modified to suit homeowner preferences. If you order plans, have a builder or design professional check them against the photographs to confirm construction details.

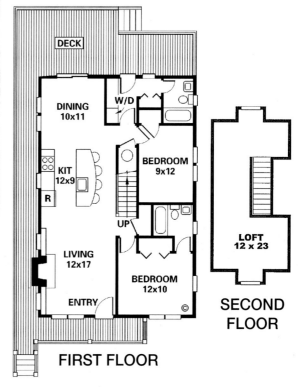

DECK

DINING
10x11

W/D

KIT
12x9

R

BEDROOM
9x12

UP

LIVING
12x17

BEDROOM
12x10

ENTRY

FIRST FLOOR

LOFT
12 x 23

SECOND FLOOR

Photography: Beth Singer

ABOVE: The back of this home is designed to maximize the views and the enjoyment of the outdoors.

BELOW: An enclosed porch that spans the rear of the home offers a comfortable transition between the great-room and the outdoors.

Life of
Leisure

Built on a lakefront lot, this home provides grand backyard views from every room. Although designed as a weekend retreat, the carefully planned layout makes this design suitable for year-round living. A walk-in pantry serves the kitchen, which looks out over the wide-open great-room and beyond to the rear porch. A fireplace on an interior wall preserves the great-room's rear wall for floor-to-ceiling windows and French doors topped by transoms. The master suite also has a fireplace. On the opposite side of the main level, an enclosed porch is wrapped in glass so that it feels like part of both the outdoor and the indoor spaces. This home is designed with a crawlspace foundation. ❯

To order blueprints, call **800-235-5700** or visit us on the web, **familyhomeplans.com**

ABOVE: At the front of the home, bump-outs for the pantry and laundry room shelter a welcoming entry.

LEFT: The light decor of the open great-room makes the already generous space seem larger. The open stairway adds to the feeling of spaciousness.

Design 32338

Price Code	H
Total Finished	3,054 sq. ft.
First Finished	1,990 sq. ft.
Second Finished	1,064 sq. ft.
Deck Unfinished	388 sq. ft.
Porch Unfinished	713 sq. ft.
Dimensions	68'8"x48'4"
Foundation	Crawlspace
Bedrooms	4
Full Baths	1
3/4 Baths	2
Half Baths	1

Please note: The photographed home may have been modified to suit homeowner preferences. If you order plans, have a builder or design professional check them against the photographs to confirm construction details.

FIRST FLOOR

SECOND FLOOR

ABOVE: Unique window detailing and prominent gables dominate the exterior design.

All-Season
Entertaining

This all-season vacation home is designed for entertaining and relaxation. The combined family room/dining areas share a wood-burning stove. Both rooms have direct access to the front deck through sliding glass doors. The generous kitchen occupies almost the entire length of the home and features a breakfast bar at the center island, two sinks, and a large pantry. A guest bath with laundry facilities and an entry closet complete the first floor. All of the upstairs living space is devoted to the master suite, which has a walk-in closet and a luxurious private bathroom. A mezzanine overlooks the family room below. The unfinished lower floor can be converted into two bedrooms, a family room, and a bathroom. This home is designed with a basement foundation. ▶

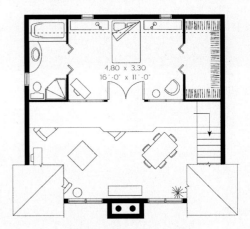

SECOND FLOOR

Design 65365

Price Code	A
Total Finished	1,146 sq. ft.
First Finished	726 sq. ft.
Second Finished	420 sq. ft.
Basement Unfinished	728 sq. ft.
Dimensions	28'x26'
Foundation	Basement
Bedrooms	1
Full Baths	1
Half Baths	1

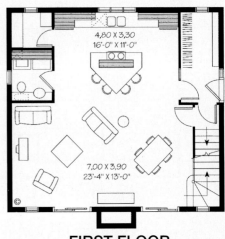

FIRST FLOOR

ABOVE & BELOW: A basic square with a gable-roof makes an affordable retreat. The screen porch opens up off the kitchen making it ideal for casual entertaining.

One-Bedroom
Getaway

This cozy little compact charmer blends indoor and outdoor spaces with a generous amount of windows and French doors. This plan starts with a basic square, making it very cost-effective to build, while the blending of indoor and outdoor spaces packs a lot of scale into its modest three-room plan. The living room and bedroom open up to a pergola-covered patio while the kitchen offers access to a screen porch. A large bathroom houses a convenient closet laundry that's just steps away from a big walk-in clothes closet. This home is designed with a slab foundation. ▶

Design 32347

Price Code	A
Total Finished	980 sq. ft.
Main Finished	980 sq. ft.
Porch Unfinished	172 sq. ft.
Dimensions	40'x35'
Foundation	Slab
Bedrooms	1
Full Baths	1

Please note: The photographed home may have been modified to suit homeowner preferences. If you order plans, have a builder or design professional check them against the photographs to confirm construction details.

MAIN FLOOR

Photography: Courtesy of William E. Poole Architects, Inc.

Eastern Shore
Cottage

Careful planning and attention to detail are evident throughout this traditional cottage-style home, which offers every space a growing family might need. A deep, comfortable front porch leads into the home through a spacious foyer. Arched doorways open to the formal dining room at the front of the home and the vaulted great room at the rear. On the right side of the first floor, two secondary bedrooms share a hall bath. On the left side of the home, the master suite includes a sumptuous bath and two walk-in-closets. Utilitarian areas such as the kitchen pantry and laundry room are cleverly incorporated into the plan to be both convenient and unobtrusive. A large recreation room on the optional second floor shares space with a fourth bedroom, full bath, and plenty of attic storage. This home is designed with a combination basement and crawlspace foundation. ◗

ABOVE: A wide front porch with tapered columns and gabled dormers with working shutters embellish the facade of this classic cottage.

BELOW: A gracefully arched doorway separates the bay-windowed breakfast area from the great room.

To order blueprints, call **800-235-5700** or visit us on the web, **familyhomeplans.com**

Design 57001

Price Code	Please call for pricing
Total Finished	2,151 sq. ft.
First Finished	2,151 sq. ft.
Optional Second Finished	814 sq. ft.
Dimensions	61'x55'8"
Foundation	Basement/ Crawlspace
Bedrooms	4
Full Baths	3

Please note: The photographed home may have been modified to suit homeowner preferences. If you order plans, have a builder or design professional check them against the photographs to confirm construction details.

ABOVE: Natural light floods the two-story great room from every level with dormers above and a wall of windows below. The built-in bookcase designed to look like a piece of furniture and the heavy mantel over the fireplace add rustic cottage charm to this soaring space.

RIGHT: The use of large arched doorways throughout the public spaces creates the sense of a traditional, well-crafted home, as illustrated by the elegant dining room.

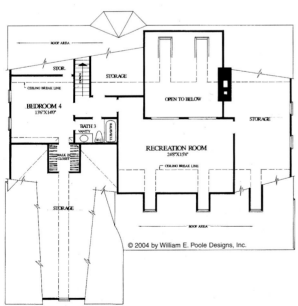

OPTIONAL SECOND FLOOR

FIRST FLOOR

Photography: James Yochum Photography

Bungalow
Update

ABOVE: Traditional tapered columns, eave brackets, forward sloping roof, and a dormer mix with the less traditional garage design to create a more efficient bungalow update.

BELOW: From the rear it's still a bungalow, but what a difference in appearance. Here, 2½-stories create a dramatic elevation on the downhill side, including a deep rear porch.

Sloped lots are problems for most homeowners. But, for some designers, such steep lots are a creative challenge that can bring out their best work. This home is an example of such a challenge met. The architect who designed it owned the narrow, steep lot and solved his dilemma by designing a bungalow that appears to be 1½-stories from the front but is 2½-stories at the rear, thanks to a walk-out basement. While maintaining the flavor of a 1930s bungalow, the architect made a few improvements to the original concept. The floor plan accommodates the needs of a large family or a family that entertains a lot. A fireplace, an 18-foot ceiling, and adjacency to the porch and deck make the living room a favorite gathering spot. Sleeping quarters offer the same flexibility; two bedrooms are designed for bunk beds, allowing for plenty of guests. This house is designed with a basement foundation. ◗

ABOVE: A loft overlooks the two-story living room, which features a large stone fireplace.

ABOVE, RIGHT: The lower-level den offers a quiet retreat with a traditional stone hearth and sliding glass doors that lead out to the rear covered patio.

RIGHT: The sunny four-season porch off the living room is also convenient to the kitchen.

Design 32332

Price Code	E
Total Finished	3,705 sq. ft.
First Finished	1,311 sq. ft.
Second Finished	1,214 sq. ft.
Lower Finished	1,180 sq. ft.
Garage Unfinished	553 sq. ft.
Deck Unfinished	346 sq. ft.
Porch Unfinished	180 sq. ft.
Dimensions	38'8"x70'9"
Foundation	Basement
Bedrooms	6
Full Baths	1
3/4 Baths	2
Half Baths	1

Please note: The photographed home may have been modified to suit homeowner preferences. If you order plans, have a builder or design professional check them against the photographs to confirm construction details.

SECOND FLOOR

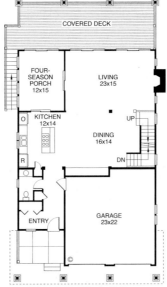

FIRST FLOOR

LOWER FLOOR

Photography: Chris A. Little

ABOVE: Tall windows, a large deck, and a balcony off the master suite make this home a perfect ocean-front getaway.

Decked
Out

This plan packs a lot of living into less than 2,000 square feet. The front deck wraps around a covered porch, which leads into the living room. This area blends into the dining room and L-shape kitchen, which are separated by an island. Two bedrooms fill the right wing and share a full hall bath. Two more bedrooms, including the master suite, are on the second floor. Each has two walk-in closets and a private bath. This home is designed with a pier/post foundation. ▶

Design 94653

Price Code	A
Total Finished	1,863 sq. ft.
First Finished	1,056 sq. ft.
Second Finished	807 sq. ft.
Dimensions	35'6"x54'
Foundation	Pier/Post
Bedrooms	4
Full Baths	3

Please note: The photographed home may have been modified to suit homeowner preferences. If you order plans, have a builder or design professional check them against the photographs to confirm construction details.

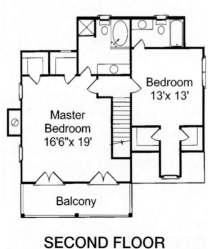

Master Bedroom 16'6"x 19'

Bedroom 13'x 13'

Balcony

SECOND FLOOR

Dining 11'x 11'

Bedroom 13'x 11'

Living 16'6"x 21'

Bedroom 13'x 11'

Porch

Deck

FIRST FLOOR

Photography: James Salomon

ABOVE: A wraparound porch, open deck, second floor balcony, and lots of windows open up this cottage for comfortable enjoyment of the outdoors.

Design 32182

Price Code	C
Total Finished	1,913 sq. ft.
First Finished	1,209 sq. ft.
Second Finished	704 sq. ft.
Basement Unfinished	685 sq. ft.
Garage Unfinished	524 sq. ft.
Dimensions	37'x49'
Foundation	Basement
Bedrooms	2
Full Baths	1
3/4 Baths	2

Coastal
Retreat

This timeless cottage design offers an attractive retreat no matter where it's built, although the wraparound porch, open deck, and numerous windows are perfect for catching those welcome breezes off the lake or ocean. The great room with its large bow window and central fireplace, is a light-filled space for lazy afternoons and evening entertaining. At the core of the first floor is a highly functional kitchen. A den at the front of the home can be used as a third bedroom. On the second floor, the master bedroom includes a full bath and has access to a large private balcony. A secondary bedroom with ¾ bath completes the upstairs. This home is designed with a basement foundation. ▶

Please note: The photographed home may have been modified to suit homeowner preferences. If you order plans, have a builder or design professional check them against the photographs to confirm construction details.

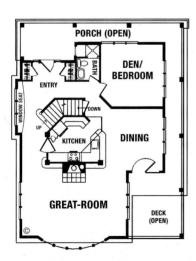

FIRST FLOOR

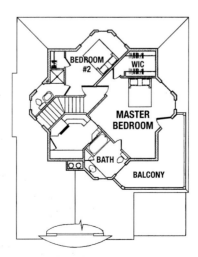

SECOND FLOOR

Gulf Coast
Cottage

ABOVE: Tall windows and a deep porch with Victorian trim lend old house appeal to this up-to-date plan.

BELOW: The kitchen and breakfast area are open to the great room where a vaulted ceiling provides visual separation between the spaces.

The best of both worlds meet in this plan, which offers the beautiful curb appeal of a century-old southern cottage combined with a modern floor plan designed with the needs of a modern family in mind. From the two-story foyer, a center hall leads beyond the stairs straight back to the vaulted great room where a fireplace and built-in bookshelves lend a traditional touch to this open, contemporary space. An eating bar separates the great room from the kitchen, which features a built-in pantry and an adjoining breakfast bay. The master bedroom takes up the left side of the main floor with a spacious bath and deep walk-in closet. On the second floor, two comfortable bedrooms share a full bath. Beyond the great room on the first floor lies a utility room and a two-car garage as well as a separate staircase to the bonus space above the garage. This home is designed with a combination basement and crawlspace foundation. ▶

To order blueprints, call **800-235-5700** or visit us on the web, **familyhomeplans.com**

ABOVE LEFT: The vaulted great room provides a large, inviting space at the heart of the home for family gatherings. The room adjoins the kitchen and breakfast area, making it convenient for entertaining.

ABOVE RIGHT: The master bedroom is a bright, light-filled space thanks to two tall windows and a set of French doors that lead out onto a rear patio.

Design 57002

Price Code	Please call for pricing
Total Finished	2,457 sq. ft.
First Finished	1,819 sq. ft.
Second Finished	638 sq. ft.
Bonus Unfinished	385 sq. ft.
Dimensions	47'4"x82'8"
Foundation	Basement/ Crawlspace
Bedrooms	3
Full Baths	2
Half Baths	1

Please note: The photographed home may have been modified to suit homeowner preferences. If you order plans, have a builder or design professional check them against the photographs to confirm construction details.

© 2004 by William E. Poole Designs, Inc.

SECOND FLOOR **FIRST FLOOR**

Southern Style

Photography: Courtesy of William E. Poole Architects, Inc.

ABOVE: A red standing-seam metal roof with small gabled dormers over a deep covered porch gives authentic Southern cottage appeal to this spacious home.

BELOW: The efficient design packs a lot of counter space and storage into the sunny kitchen.

This attractive home wraps modern amenities within a classic southern farmhouse-style exterior. The foyer is flanked by a coat closet on one side and a powder room on the other. A wide arched doorway opens from the foyer into the soaring two-story great room. To the left of the great room, an open staircase rises to a balcony where a sitting area separates two secondary bedrooms, each with its own full bath. The luxurious master suite takes up the left side of the first floor. To the right of the great room, at the front of the home, is the dining room. Behind that lies the kitchen where every wall is lined with counters or cabinets—or both. The kitchen sink and dishwasher are tucked into a bay window, providing a pleasant and sunny work area. A utility wing stretches out behind the right side of the house to include a large laundry room, screen porch and two car garage. An apartment with dormered kitchen/dining area and a full bath is above the garage. This home is designed with a crawlspace foundation. ▶

Design 57003

Price Code	Call for pricing
Total Finished	2,438 sq. ft.
First Finished	1,704 sq. ft.
Second Finished	734 sq. ft.
Bonue Unfinished	479 sq. ft.
Dimensions	50'x82'6"
Foundation	Crawlspace
Bedrooms	3
Full Baths	4
Half Baths	1

Please note: The photographed home may have been modified to suit homeowner preferences. If you order plans, have a builder or design professional check them against the photographs to confirm construction details.

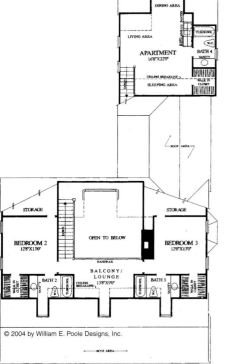

© 2004 by William E. Poole Designs, Inc.

SECOND FLOOR

FIRST FLOOR

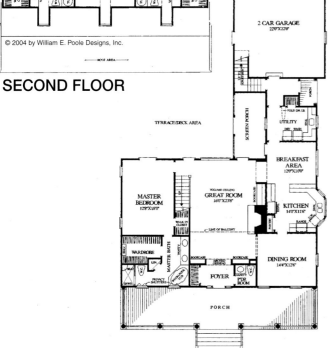

ABOVE & BELOW: A great room that lives up to the name. The large space features built-ins, a fireplace, a volume ceiling, and a second floor overlook. The casual look of the exposed brick and natural wood nicely complements the elegant white trim and molding.

LEFT & BELOW: This charming little retreat offers four bedrooms within its modest footprint. The homeowner modified the plan by adding a masonry fireplace to the large living room.

Year Round
Vacation

Whether intended as a year-round home or a vacation getaway, this home offers much within its 1,174 square feet. A large deck fronts the dwelling and leads directly into the living/dining room. From here, the kitchen is easily accessible, right past the snack bar/work area. Two bedrooms share the back of the floor plan and have easy access to the full bath. A spiral staircase leads to the second floor, which is divided into two bedrooms. Inhabitants of the upper-level bedrooms enjoy the view from their own private balcony. This home is designed with a basement foundation. ◗

Photography: John Ehrenclou

Design 10054

Price Code	A
Total Finished	1,174 sq. ft.
First Finished	768 sq. ft.
Second Finished	406 sq. ft.
Dimensions	24'x32'
Foundation	Basement
Bedrooms	4
Full Baths	1

Please note: The photographed home may have been modified to suit homeowner preferences. If you order plans, have a builder or design professional check them against the photographs to confirm construction details.

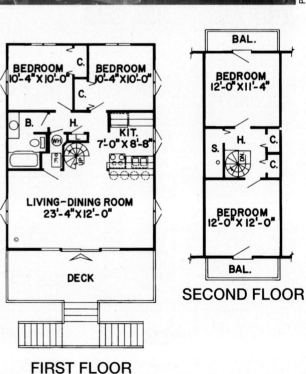

FIRST FLOOR

SECOND FLOOR

Photography: John Ehrenclou

ABOVE: From the front, visitors have no idea of the dramatic scale and scope of this hillside home. Skylights take advantage of natural lighting on the second floor.

BELOW: From the rear, three levels of deck and masses of windows add drama.

Design 10396

Price Code	D
Total Finished	2,228 sq. ft.
First Finished	886 sq. ft.
Second Finished	456 sq. ft.
Lower Finished	886 sq. ft.
Dimensions	38'x40'
Foundation	Basement
Bedrooms	3
Full Baths	3

A Hillside
Home

From the front, this 2,228-square-foot home simply looks like a very nice 1½-story residence. Its hillside site, however, allows for a full walk-out lower floor with enough windows to make you forget you're in a basement. A secondary bedroom shares the efficient first floor with a kitchen/dining area and large living room. A deck wraps around the rear and one side. The master bedroom occupies the entire second floor and includes a dressing area, walk-in closet, and wide balcony. The lower floor contains a big recreation room, another secondary bedroom, and ample space for a shop, plus storage room. The owner of this home modified the plan to include clerestory windows and a fireplace against the back wall in the living room. This home is designed with a basement foundation. ▶

Please note: The photographed home may have been modified to suit homeowner preferences. If you order plans, have a builder or design professional check them against the photographs to confirm construction details.

LOWER FLOOR

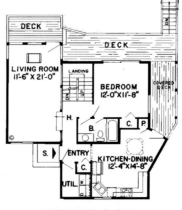

FIRST FLOOR

SECOND FLOOR

Quick and Easy Customizing
Make Changes to Your Home Plan in 4 Easy Steps

Here's an affordable and efficient way to make custom changes to your home plan.

1 Select the house plan that most closely meets your needs. Purchase of a reproducible master (vellum) is necessary to make changes to a plan.

2 Call 800-235-5700 to place your order. Tell the sales representative you're interested in customizing a plan. A $50 refundable consultation fee will be charged. Then you'll need to complete a customization checklist indicating all the changes you wish to make to your plan, attaching sketches if necessary. If you proceed with the custom changes, the $50 will be credited to the total amount charged.

3 Fax the completed customization checklist to our design consultant at 1-866-477-5173 or e-mail blarochelle@drummonddesigns.com. Within 24 to 48* business hours you will be provided with a written cost estimate to modify your plan. Our design consultant will contact you by phone if you wish to discuss any of your changes in greater detail.

4 Once you approve the estimate, a 75% retainer fee is collected and customization work gets underway. Preliminary drawings can usually be completed within 5 to 10* business days. Following approval of these preliminary drawings, your design changes are completed within 5 to 10* business days. Your remaining 25% balance due is collected prior to shipment of your completed drawings. You will be shipped five sets of revised blueprints, or a reproducible master.

*Terms are subject to change without notice.

BEFORE

AFTER

Sample Modification Pricing Guide

CATEGORIES	AVERAGE COST
Adding or removing living space (square footage)	Quote required
Adding or removing a garage	$400—$680
Garage: Front entry to side load or vice versa	Starting at $300
Adding a screened porch	$280—$600
Adding a bonus room in the attic	$450—$780
Changing full basement to crawlspace or vice versa	Starting at $220
Changing full basement to slab or vice versa	Starting at $260
Changing exterior building material	Starting at $200
Changing roof lines	$360—$630
Adjusting ceiling height	$280—$500
Adding, moving, or removing an exterior opening	$55 per opening
Adding or removing a fireplace	$90—$200
Modifying a non-bearing wall or room	$55 per room
Changing exterior walls from 2"x4" to 2"x6"	Starting at $200
Redesigning a bathroom or a kitchen	$120—$280
Reverse plan right reading	Quote required
Adapting plans for local building code requirements	Quote required
Engineering stamping only	Quote required
Any other engineering services	Quote required
Adjust plan for handicapped accessibility	Quote required
Interactive Illustrations (choices of exterior materials)	Quote required
Metric conversion of home plan	$400

Note: Prices are subject to change according to plan size and style. Please remember that figures shown are average costs. Your quote may be higher or lower depending upon your specific requirements.

Design 10306

Units	Single
Price Code	A
Total Finished	408 sq. ft.
Main Finished	408 sq. ft.
Dimensions	16'x28'
Foundation	Pier/Post
Bedrooms	1
3/4 Baths	1

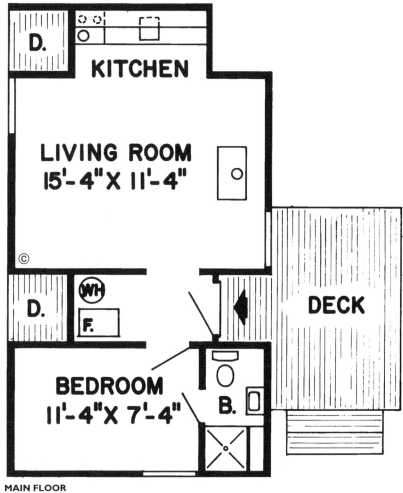

KITCHEN

LIVING ROOM
15'-4" X 11'-4"

D.

WH

F.

DECK

BEDROOM
11'-4" X 7'-4"

B.

MAIN FLOOR

Units	Single
Price Code	A
Total Finished	576 sq. ft.
Main Finished	576 sq. ft.
Dimensions	24'x24'
Foundation	Crawlspace
	Slab
Bedrooms	2
3/4 Baths	1
Max Ridge Height	14'
Roof Framing	Truss
Exterior Walls	2x4, 2x6

Br 1
9-8 x 8-8

Br 2
10-8 x 7-10

Living Rm
8-10 x 11-8

U

Kit / Dining
10-5 x 9-3

lin.

©

MAIN FLOOR

Design 32317

PHOTOGRAPHY: JOHN FULKER

Units	Single
Price Code	A
Total Finished	610 sq. ft.
Main Finished	610 sq. ft.
Porch Unfinished	162 sq. ft.
Dimensions	31'4"×40'
Foundation	Pier/Post
Bedrooms	1
3/4 Baths	1
Max Ridge Height	23'4"
Roof Framing	Stick
Exterior Walls	2×6

Hot New Design

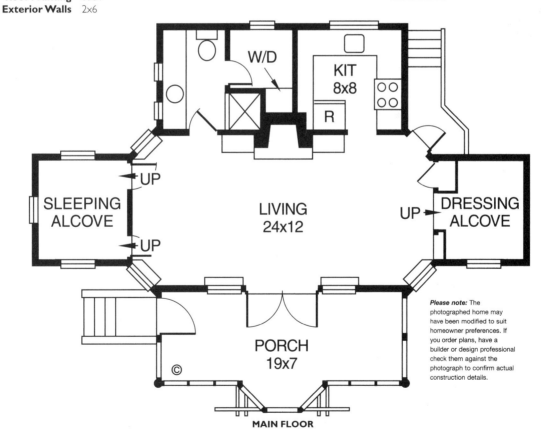

Please note: The photographed home may have been modified to suit homeowner preferences. If you order plans, have a builder or design professional check them against the photograph to confirm actual construction details.

MAIN FLOOR

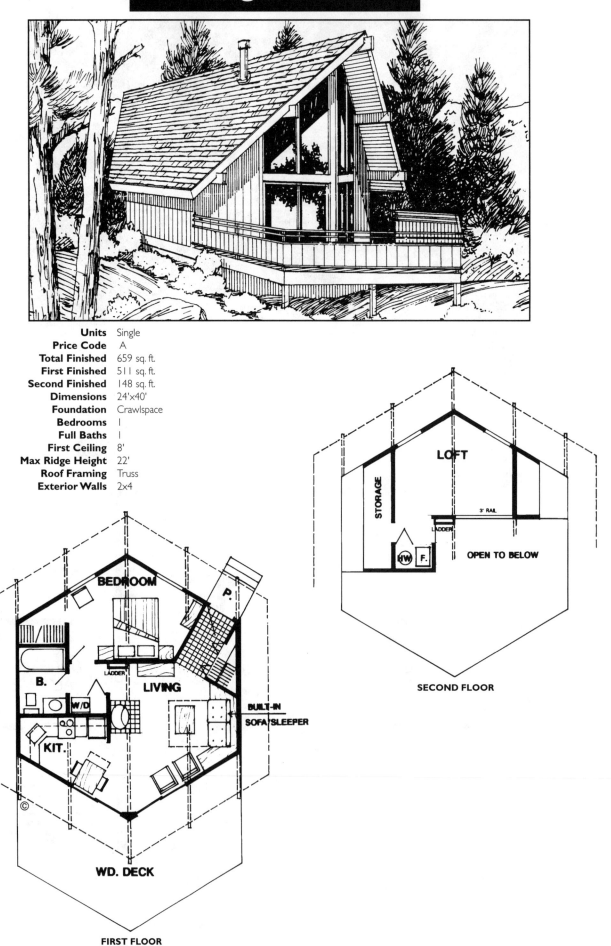

Units	Single
Price Code	A
Total Finished	659 sq. ft.
First Finished	511 sq. ft.
Second Finished	148 sq. ft.
Dimensions	24'x40'
Foundation	Crawlspace
Bedrooms	1
Full Baths	1
First Ceiling	8'
Max Ridge Height	22'
Roof Framing	Truss
Exterior Walls	2x4

SECOND FLOOR

LOFT

STORAGE

OPEN TO BELOW

3' RAIL

LADDER

HW F.

FIRST FLOOR

BEDROOM

P.

B.

W/D

LIVING

BUILT-IN SOFA/SLEEPER

LADDER

KIT.

WD. DECK

Design 32018

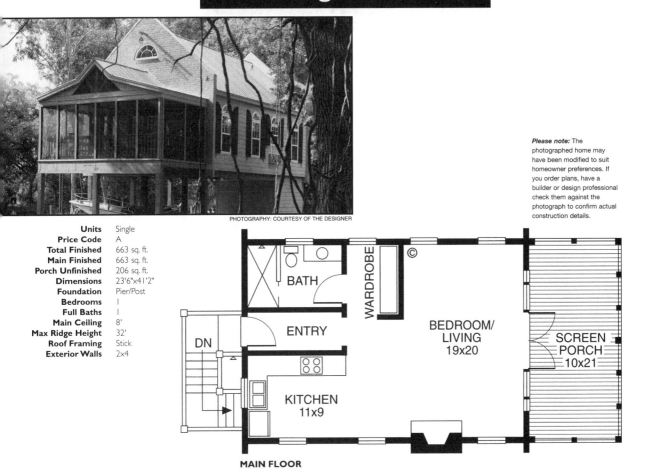

PHOTOGRAPHY: COURTESY OF THE DESIGNER

Please note: The photographed home may have been modified to suit homeowner preferences. If you order plans, have a builder or design professional check them against the photograph to confirm actual construction details.

Units	Single
Price Code	A
Total Finished	663 sq. ft.
Main Finished	663 sq. ft.
Porch Unfinished	206 sq. ft.
Dimensions	23'6"x41'2"
Foundation	Pier/Post
Bedrooms	I
Full Baths	I
Main Ceiling	8'
Max Ridge Height	32'
Roof Framing	Stick
Exterior Walls	2x4

BATH

WARDROBE

ENTRY

DN

KITCHEN 11x9

BEDROOM/ LIVING 19x20

SCREEN PORCH 10x21

MAIN FLOOR

Design 84020

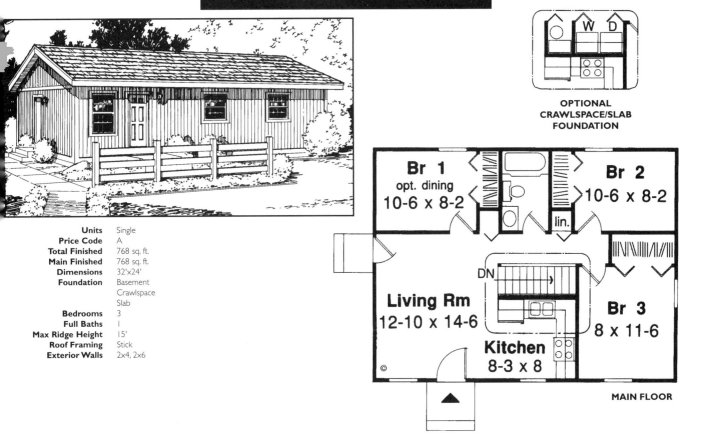

OPTIONAL CRAWLSPACE/SLAB FOUNDATION

Units	Single
Price Code	A
Total Finished	768 sq. ft.
Main Finished	768 sq. ft.
Dimensions	32'x24'
Foundation	Basement
	Crawlspace
	Slab
Bedrooms	3
Full Baths	I
Max Ridge Height	15'
Roof Framing	Stick
Exterior Walls	2x4, 2x6

Br 1 opt. dining 10-6 x 8-2

Br 2 10-6 x 8-2

lin.

DN

Living Rm 12-10 x 14-6

Br 3 8 x 11-6

Kitchen 8-3 x 8

MAIN FLOOR

Units	Single
Price Code	A
Total Finished	784 sq. ft.
Main Finished	784 sq. ft.
Dimensions	28'x28'
Foundation	Slab
Bedrooms	1
Full Baths	1
Main Ceiling	8'
Max Ridge Height	18'
Roof Framing	Truss

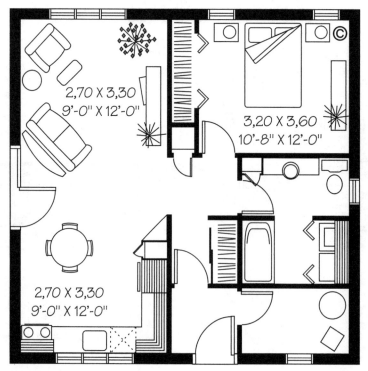

2,70 X 3,30
9'-0" X 12'-0"

3,20 X 3,60
10'-8" X 12'-0"

2,70 X 3,30
9'-0" X 12'-0"

MAIN FLOOR

Design 94307

Units	Single
Price Code	A
Total Finished	786 sq. ft.
Main Finished	786 sq. ft.
Deck Unfinished	580 sq. ft.
Dimensions	46'x22'
Foundation	Crawlspace
Bedrooms	2
3/4 Baths	2
Main Ceiling	8'
Vaulted Ceiling	16'
Max Ridge Height	18'6"
Roof Framing	Truss
Exterior Walls	2x6

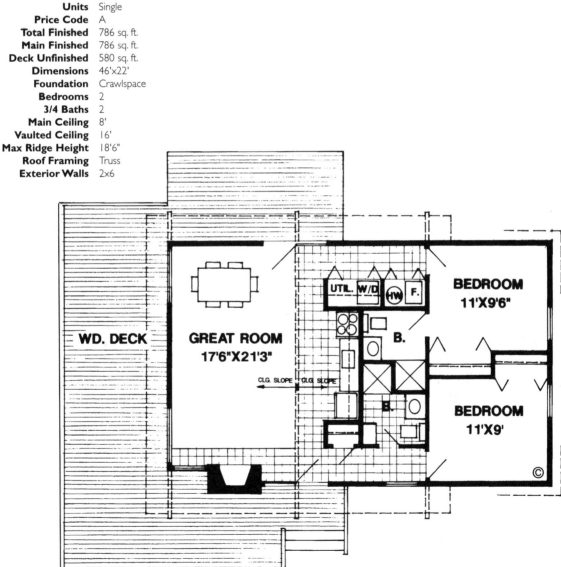

WD. DECK

GREAT ROOM
17'6"X21'3"

CLG. SLOPE   CLG. SLOPE

UTIL. W/D HW F.

B.

BEDROOM
11'X9'6"

B.

BEDROOM
11'X9'

MAIN FLOOR

Design 19709

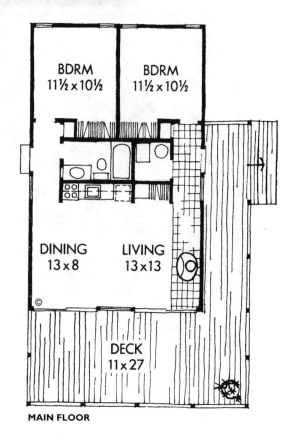

MAIN FLOOR

Units	Single
Price Code	A
Total Finished	792 sq. ft.
Main Finished	792 sq. ft.
Deck Unfinished	588 sq. ft.
Dimensions	22'x36'
Foundation	Crawlspace
Bedrooms	2
Full Baths	1
Max Ridge Height	19'
Roof Framing	Stick
Exterior Walls	2x4

Design 90821

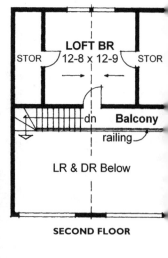

SECOND FLOOR

FIRST FLOOR

Units	Single
Price Code	A
Total Finished	796 sq. ft.
First Finished	616 sq. ft.
Second Finished	180 sq. ft.
Basement Unfinished	796 sq. ft.
Dimensions	22'x28'
Foundation	Basement Crawlspace
Bedrooms	2
Full Baths	1
First Ceiling	7'6"
Second Ceiling	7'6"
Max Ridge Height	20'6"
Roof Framing	Stick
Exterior Walls	2x6

Design 24308

Units	Single
Price Code	A
Total Finished	823 sq. ft.
First Finished	660 sq. ft.
Second Finished	163 sq. ft.
Dimensions	22'x33'
Foundation	Crawlspace
Bedrooms	1
3/4 Baths	1
Max Ridge Height	23'
Roof Framing	Stick
Exterior Walls	2x6

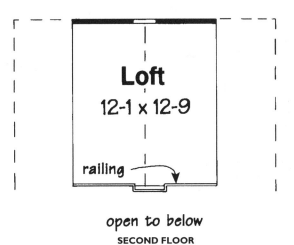

Loft
12-1 x 12-9

railing

open to below
SECOND FLOOR

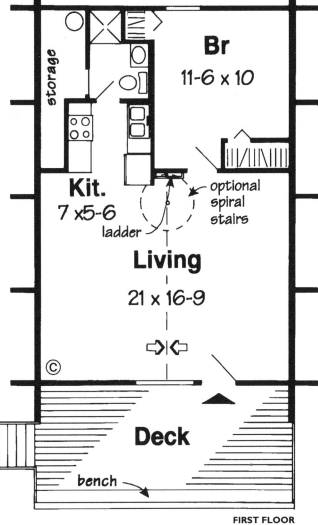

storage

Br
11-6 x 10

Kit.
7 x5-6

optional spiral stairs

ladder

Living
21 x 16-9

Deck

bench

FIRST FLOOR

Units	Duplex
Price Code	A
Total Finished	834 sq. ft. (per unit)
Main Finished	834 sq. ft. (per unit)
Garage Unfinished	208 sq. ft. (per unit)
Dimensions	48'x44'
Foundation	Basement
Bedrooms	2 (per unit)
Full Baths	1 (per unit)
Main Ceiling	8'
Max Ridge Height	20'5"
Exterior Walls	2x6

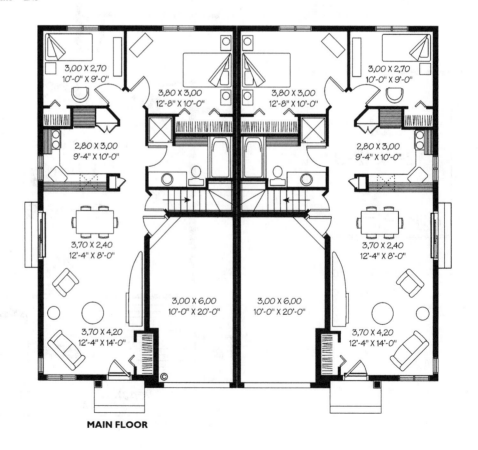

MAIN FLOOR

Design 65263

Units	Single
Price Code	A
Total Finished	840 sq. ft.
Main Finished	840 sq. ft.
Porch Unfinished	466 sq. ft.
Dimensions	33'x31'
Foundation	Basement
Bedrooms	1
Full Baths	1
Main Ceiling	8'
Max Ridge Height	22'11"
Roof Framing	Truss
Exterior Walls	2x6

4.80 X 4.80
16'-0" X 16'-0"

4.40 X 3.30
14'-8" X 11'-0"

2.70 X 3.90
9'-0" X 13'-0"

2.40 X 3.90
8'-0" X 13'-0"

3.60 X 3.50
12'-0" X 11'-8"

MAIN FLOOR

Design 92026

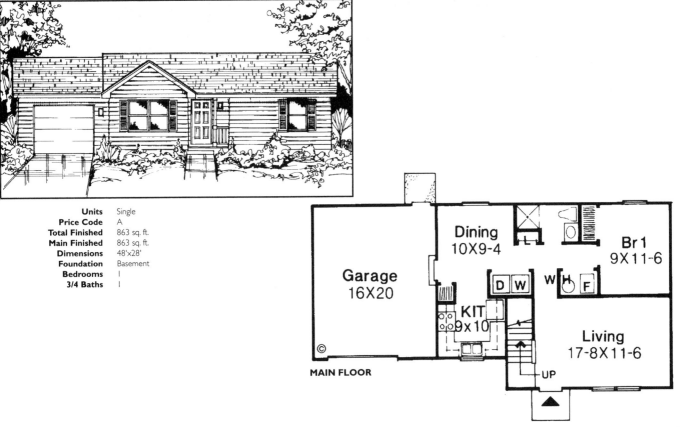

Units	Single
Price Code	A
Total Finished	863 sq. ft.
Main Finished	863 sq. ft.
Dimensions	48'x28'
Foundation	Basement
Bedrooms	1
3/4 Baths	1

Garage
16X20

Dining
10X9-4

Br 1
9X11-6

KIT
9X10

D W

W H F

Living
17-8X11-6

UP

MAIN FLOOR

Units	Single
Price Code	A
Total Finished	880 sq. ft.
First Finished	572 sq. ft.
Second Finished	308 sq. ft.
Dimensions	22'x26'
Foundation	Crawlspace
Bedrooms	2
3/4 Baths	I
Max Ridge Height	20'
Roof Framing	Stick
Exterior Walls	2x6

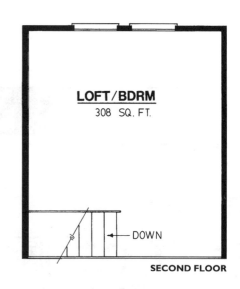

LOFT / BDRM
308 SQ. FT.

DOWN

SECOND FLOOR

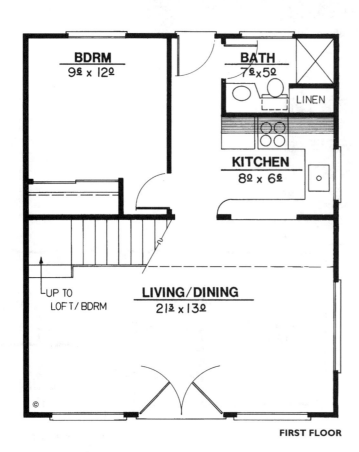

FIRST FLOOR

Design 90934

Units	Single
Price Code	A
Total Finished	884 sq. ft.
Main Finished	884 sq. ft.
Deck Unfinished	170 sq. ft.
Dimensions	34'x31'
Foundation	Crawlspace
	Slab
Bedrooms	2
Full Baths	1
Main Ceiling	8'
Max Ridge Height	15'6"

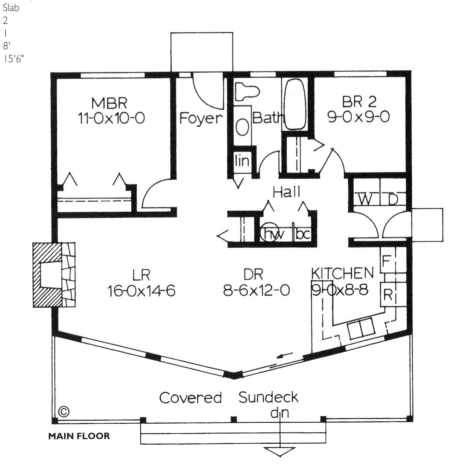

MBR
11-0x10-0

Foyer

Bath

BR 2
9-0x9-0

lin

Hall

W D

hw bc

LR
16-0x14-6

DR
8-6x12-0

KITCHEN
9-0x8-8

F

R

Covered Sundeck
dn

MAIN FLOOR

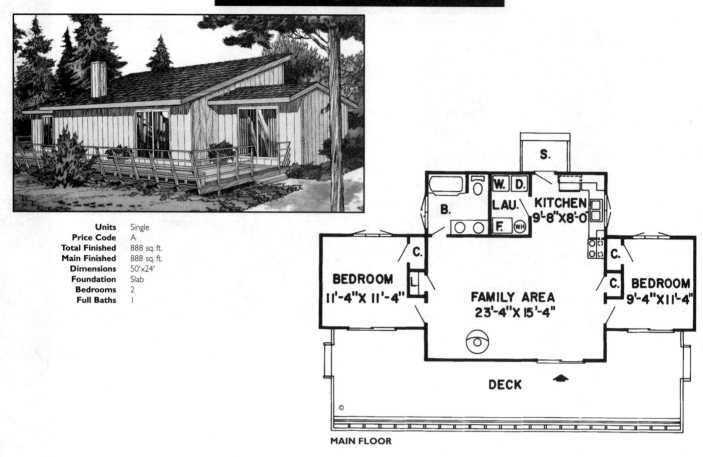

Units	Single
Price Code	A
Total Finished	888 sq. ft.
Main Finished	888 sq. ft.
Dimensions	50'x24'
Foundation	Slab
Bedrooms	2
Full Baths	1

MAIN FLOOR

Design 24310

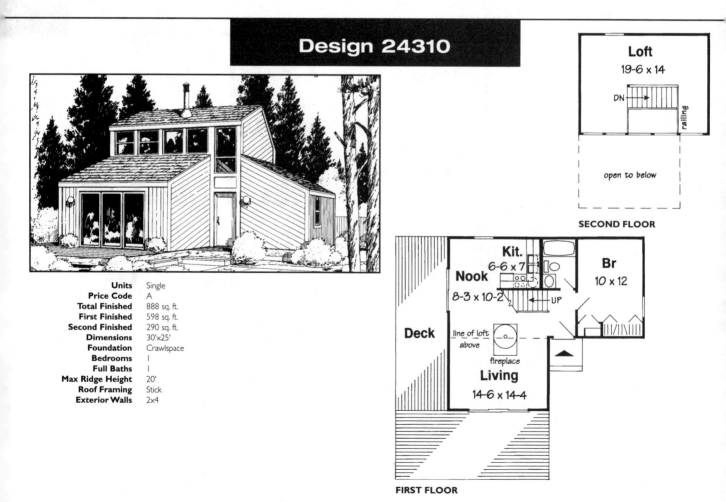

Units	Single
Price Code	A
Total Finished	888 sq. ft.
First Finished	598 sq. ft.
Second Finished	290 sq. ft.
Dimensions	30'x25'
Foundation	Crawlspace
Bedrooms	1
Full Baths	1
Max Ridge Height	20'
Roof Framing	Stick
Exterior Walls	2x4

SECOND FLOOR

FIRST FLOOR

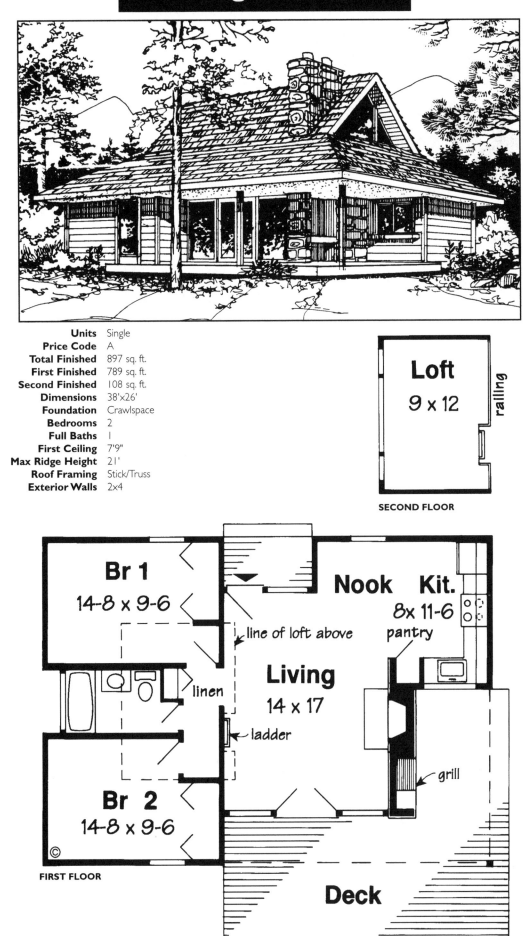

Units	Single
Price Code	A
Total Finished	897 sq. ft.
First Finished	789 sq. ft.
Second Finished	108 sq. ft.
Dimensions	38'×26'
Foundation	Crawlspace
Bedrooms	2
Full Baths	1
First Ceiling	7'9"
Max Ridge Height	21'
Roof Framing	Stick/Truss
Exterior Walls	2x4

Loft
9 x 12

railing

SECOND FLOOR

Br 1
14-8 x 9-6

line of loft above

Nook **Kit.**
8x 11-6

pantry

linen

Living
14 x 17

ladder

grill

Br 2
14-8 x 9-6

FIRST FLOOR

Deck

Design 69030

Units	Single
Price Code	A
Total Finished	914 sq. ft.
Main Finished	914 sq. ft.
Dimensions	28'x28'
Foundation	Basement
Bedrooms	2
Full Baths	1

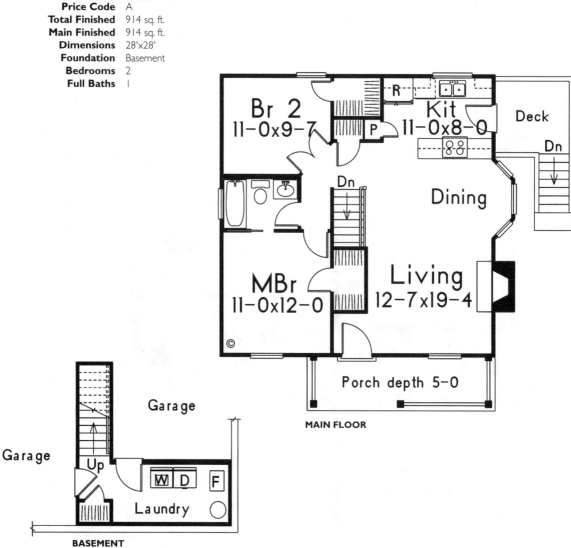

MAIN FLOOR

BASEMENT

Design 65006

Units	Single
Price Code	A
Total Finished	920 sq. ft.
Main Finished	920 sq. ft.
Porch Unfinished	152 sq. ft.
Dimensions	38'x28'
Foundation	Basement
Bedrooms	2
Full Baths	1
Main Ceiling	8'
Max Ridge Height	20'6"
Roof Framing	Truss
Exterior Walls	2x6

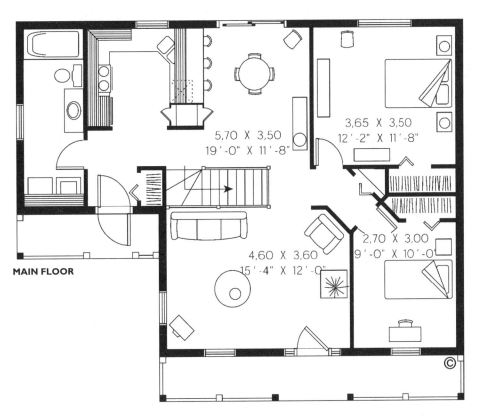

5,70 X 3,50
19'-0" X 11'-8"

3,65 X 3,50
12'-2" X 11'-8"

4,60 X 3,60
15'-4" X 12'-0"

2,70 X 3,00
9'-0" X 10'-0"

MAIN FLOOR

Design 91324

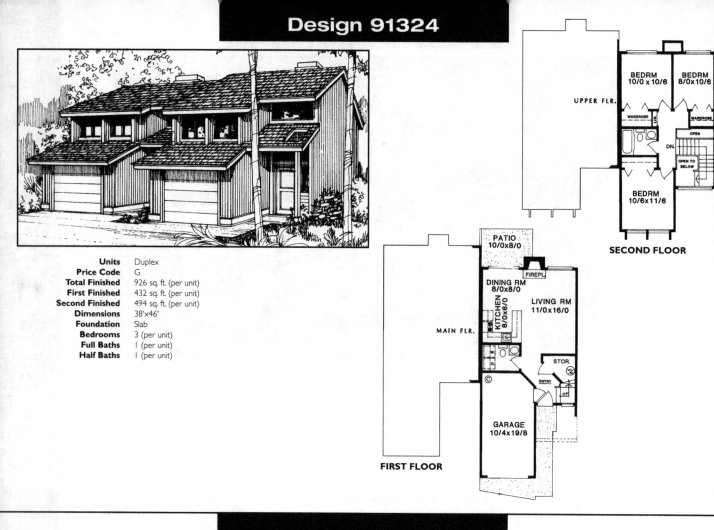

SECOND FLOOR

BEDRM 10/0 x 10/6
BEDRM 8/0x10/6
WARDROBE
WARDROBE
UPPER FLR.
OPEN
DN.
OPEN TO BELOW
BEDRM 10/6x11/6

PATIO 10/0x8/0
FIREPL
DINING RM 8/0x8/0
LIVING RM 11/0x16/0
KITCHEN 8/0x6/0
MAIN FLR.
STOR.
W.
ENTRY
UP
GARAGE 10/4x19/8

FIRST FLOOR

Units	Duplex
Price Code	G
Total Finished	926 sq. ft. (per unit)
First Finished	432 sq. ft. (per unit)
Second Finished	494 sq. ft. (per unit)
Dimensions	38'x46'
Foundation	Slab
Bedrooms	3 (per unit)
Full Baths	1 (per unit)
Half Baths	1 (per unit)

Design 90433

Units	Single
Price Code	A
Total Finished	928 sq. ft.
Main Finished	928 sq. ft.
Porch Unfinished	230 sq. ft.
Dimensions	32'x29'
Foundation	Crawlspace
	Slab
Bedrooms	2
Full Baths	1
Half Baths	1
Roof Framing	Stick

BATH
CLOSET
BEDROOM 12'x16'
BEDROOM 10'6"x16'
BATH
LINEN
STOR.
PANTRY
CLOSET
KITCHEN 8'x10'
EATING 23'x12'
LIVING
SCREEN PORCH 23'x10'

MAIN FLOOR

Design 65026

Units	Duplex
Price Code	C
Total Finished	946 sq. ft. (per unit)
First Finished	946 sq. ft. (per unit)
Dimensions	48'x40'
Foundation	Basement
Bedrooms	2 (per unit)
Full Baths	1 (per unit)

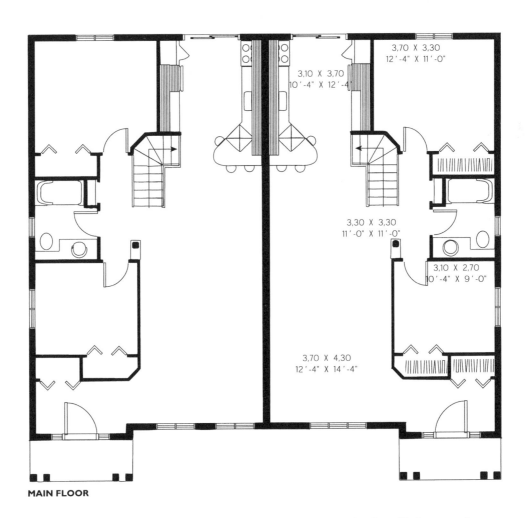

3,70 X 3,30
12'-4" X 11'-0"

3,10 X 3,70
10'-4" X 12'-4"

3,30 X 3,30
11'-0" X 11'-0"

3,10 X 2,70
0'-4" X 9'-0"

3,70 X 4,30
12'-4" X 14'-4"

MAIN FLOOR

Design 65387

Units	Single
Price Code	A
Total Finished	948 sq. ft.
Main Finished	948 sq. ft.
Dimensions	30'x34'
Foundation	Basement
Bedrooms	2
Full Baths	1
Roof Framing	Stick

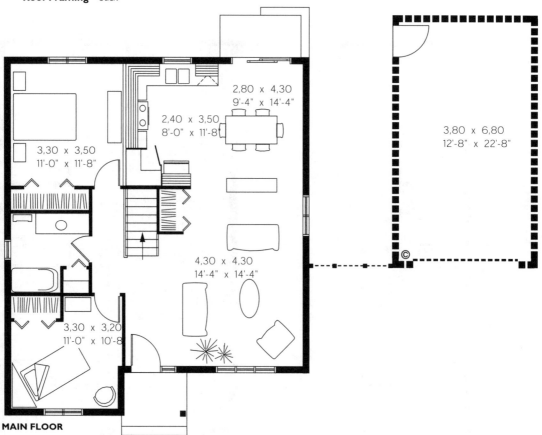

MAIN FLOOR

Design 94300

Units	Single
Price Code	A
Total Finished	950 sq. ft.
Main Finished	950 sq. ft.
Dimensions	40'x53'
Foundation	Crawlspace
Bedrooms	2
3/4 Baths	2

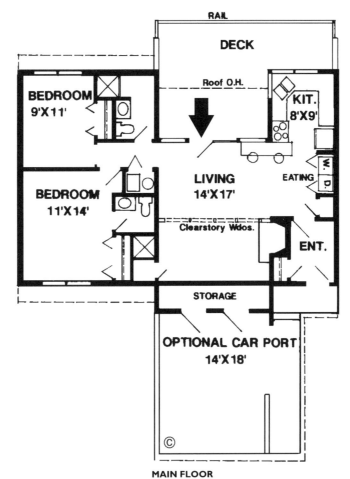

RAIL

DECK

Roof O.H.

KIT.
8'X9'

BEDROOM
9'X11'

W. D.

EATING

LIVING
14'X17'

BEDROOM
11'X14'

Clearstory Wdos.

ENT.

STORAGE

OPTIONAL CAR PORT
14'X18'

©

MAIN FLOOR

Units	Single
Price Code	A
Total Finished	964 sq. ft.
Main Finished	964 sq. ft.
Dimensions	28'x52'
Foundation	Crawlspace
Bedrooms	2
Full Baths	1
3/4 Baths	1
Max Ridge Height	23'
Roof Framing	Stick
Exterior Walls	2x4

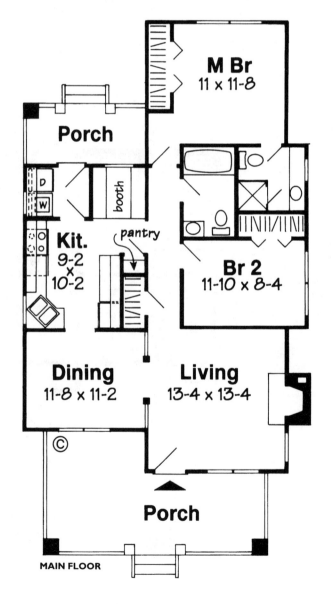

Porch

M Br
11 x 11-8

booth

pantry

Kit.
9-2
x
10-2

Br 2
11-10 x 8-4

Dining
11-8 x 11-2

Living
13-4 x 13-4

Porch

MAIN FLOOR

Design 99904

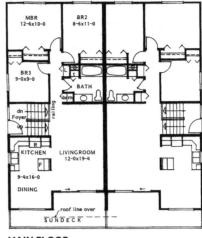

MAIN FLOOR

Units	Duplex
Price Code	H
Total Finished	964 sq. ft. (per unit)
Main Finished	964 sq. ft. (per unit)
Lower Unfinished	772 sq. ft. (per unit)
Garage Unfinished	292 sq. ft. (per unit)
Deck Unfinished	136 sq. ft. (per unit)
Dimensions	44'x50'
Foundation	Basement
Bedrooms	3 (per unit)
Full Baths	1 (per unit)
Max Ridge Height	22'
Roof Framing	Truss
Exterior Walls	2x6

LOWER FLOOR

Design 65005

Units	Single
Price Code	A
Total Finished	972 sq. ft.
Main Finished	972 sq. ft.
Basement Unfinished	972 sq. ft.
Dimensions	30'x35'
Foundation	Basement
Bedrooms	2
Full Baths	1
Main Ceiling	8'2"
Max Ridge Height	17'6"
Exterior Walls	2x6

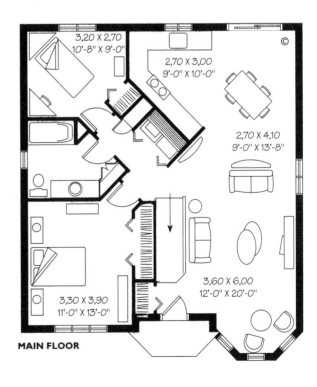

MAIN FLOOR

Design 65003

Units	Single
Price Code	A
Total Finished	976 sq. ft.
First Finished	593 sq. ft.
Second Finished	383 sq. ft.
Basement Unfinished	593 sq. ft.
Dimensions	22'8"x26'8"
Foundation	Crawlspace
Bedrooms	2
Full Baths	1
3/4 Baths	1
First Ceiling	8'
Second Ceiling	8'
Max Ridge Height	22'8"
Roof Framing	Truss
Exterior Walls	2x6

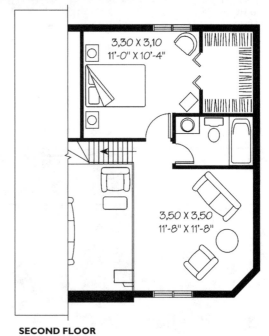

SECOND FLOOR

FIRST FLOOR

Design 19984

PHOTOGRAPHY: COURTESY OF THE DESIGNER

Units	Single
Price Code	A
Total Finished	982 sq. ft.
Main Finished	982 sq. ft.
Garage Unfinished	208 sq. ft.
Dimensions	28'x51'4"
Foundation	Slab
Bedrooms	2
Full Baths	2
Main Ceiling	9'6"-8"
Max Ridge Height	15'
Roof Framing	Stick
Exterior Walls	2x6

Hot New Design

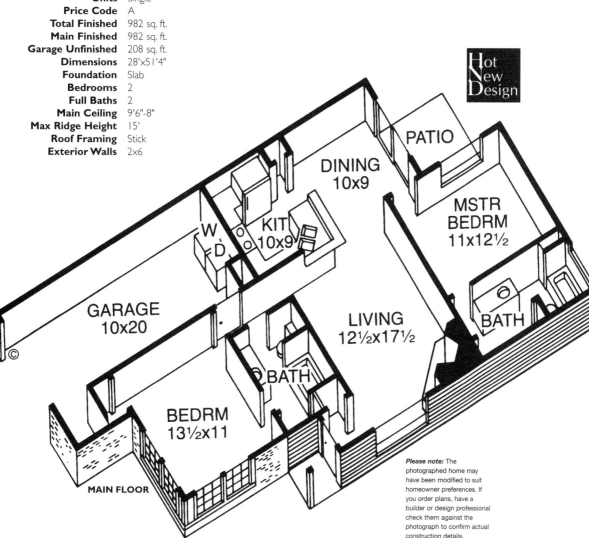

MAIN FLOOR

Please note: The photographed home may have been modified to suit homeowner preferences. If you order plans, have a builder or design professional check them against the photograph to confirm actual construction details.

Design 24303

**OPTIONAL
BASEMENT STAIR
LOCATION**

Units	Single
Price Code	A
Total Finished	984 sq. ft.
Main Finished	984 sq. ft.
Basement Unfinished	960 sq. ft.
Garage Unfinished	280 sq. ft.
Dimensions	54'x28'
Foundation	Basement
	Crawlspace
Bedrooms	3
Full Baths	1
3/4 Baths	1
Max Ridge Height	15'
Roof Framing	Stick
Exterior Walls	2x4

Mstr. Br. 13-7 x 11-8

Kitchen 8-0 x 8-3

Dining 8-10 x 8-3

Covered Patio

Br 2 9-8 x 11-8

Br 3 11-0 x 10-2

Living Rm 15-8 x 11-7

Garage 13-9 x 19-5

MAIN FLOOR

Design 24302

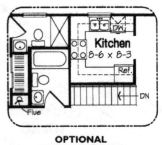

**OPTIONAL
BASEMENT STAIR
LOCATION**

Units	Single
Price Code	A
Total Finished	988 sq. ft.
Main Finished	988 sq. ft.
Basement Unfinished	988 sq. ft.
Garage Unfinished	280 sq. ft.
Dimensions	54'x28'
Foundation	Basement
	Crawlspace
Bedrooms	3
Full Baths	1
3/4 Baths	1
Main Ceiling	8'
Max Ridge Height	18'
Roof Framing	Stick
Exterior Walls	2x4

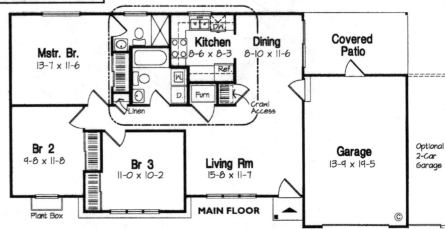

Mstr. Br. 13-7 x 11-6

Kitchen 8-6 x 8-3

Dining 8-10 x 11-6

Covered Patio

Br 2 9-8 x 11-8

Br 3 11-0 x 10-2

Living Rm 15-8 x 11-7

Garage 13-9 x 19-5

Optional 2-Car Garage

Plant Box

MAIN FLOOR

Design 10751

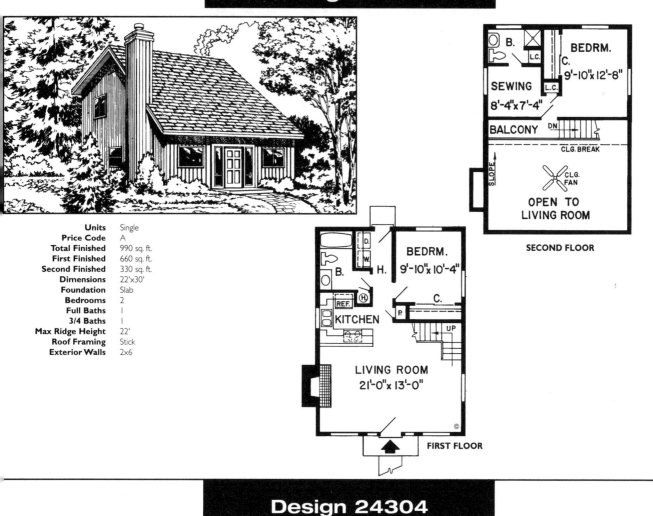

SECOND FLOOR

B.
L.C.
SEWING
8'-4"x7'-4"
BEDRM.
9'-10"x12'-8"
L.C.
C.
BALCONY
DN
CLG. BREAK
SLOPE
CLG. FAN
OPEN TO
LIVING ROOM

SECOND FLOOR

FIRST FLOOR

D.
W.
H.
B.
BEDRM.
9'-10"x10'-4"
REF.
H
C.
P.
KITCHEN
UP
LIVING ROOM
21'-0"x13'-0"

Units	Single
Price Code	A
Total Finished	990 sq. ft.
First Finished	660 sq. ft.
Second Finished	330 sq. ft.
Dimensions	22'x30'
Foundation	Slab
Bedrooms	2
Full Baths	I
3/4 Baths	I
Max Ridge Height	22'
Roof Framing	Stick
Exterior Walls	2x6

under 1,000 sq.ft. HOME PLANS

Design 24304

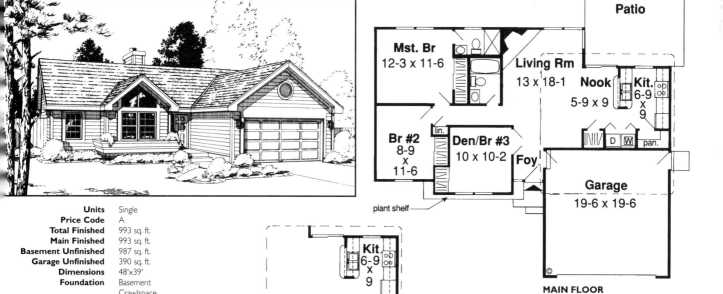

MAIN FLOOR

Patio
Mst. Br
12-3 x 11-6
Living Rm
13 x 18-1
Nook
5-9 x 9
Kit.
6-9 x 9
Br #2
8-9 x 11-6
Den/Br #3
10 x 10-2
Foy
D W pan.
Garage
19-6 x 19-6
plant shelf

OPTIONAL BASEMENT STAIR LOCATION

Kit
6-9 x 9
DN
pan.

Units	Single
Price Code	A
Total Finished	993 sq. ft.
Main Finished	993 sq. ft.
Basement Unfinished	987 sq. ft.
Garage Unfinished	390 sq. ft.
Dimensions	48'x39'
Foundation	Basement Crawlspace
Bedrooms	3
Full Baths	I
3/4 Baths	I
Max Ridge Height	18'
Roof Framing	Truss
Exterior Walls	2x4

To order blueprints, call **800-235-5700** or visit us on the web, **familyhomeplans.com**   59

Units	Single
Price Code	A
Total Finished	996 sq. ft.
Main Finished	896 sq. ft.
Lower Finished	100 sq. ft.
Garage Unfinished	796 sq. ft.
Dimensions	28'×32'
Foundation	Slab
Bedrooms	2
3/4 Baths	I
Half Baths	I
Main Ceiling	8'2"
Max Ridge Height	26'10"
Roof Framing	Truss
Exterior Walls	2x6

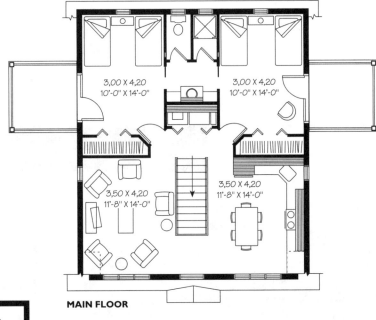

MAIN FLOOR

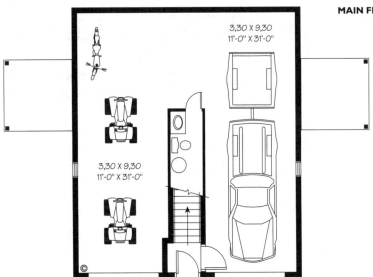

LOWER FLOOR

Design 92426

Units	Single
Price Code	A
Total Finished	997 sq. ft.
Main Finished	997 sq. ft.
Dimensions	49'6"x33'6"
Foundation	Crawlspace
Bedrooms	3
Full Baths	2
Max Ridge Height	16'
Roof Framing	Stick
Exterior Walls	2x4

DECK
14'0" x 11'8"

OPTIONAL BAY

MASTER BDRM
13'6" x 10'10"

FAMILY ROOM
14'0" x 20'0"
VLT
VLT

BRKFST
7'3" x 8'0"

KITCH
7'3" x 8'0"

DW

WH

OPT. LAUNDRY

W   D

BEDRM 2
9'6" x 9'6"

BEDRM 3
9'6" x 9'6"

PORCH
11'8" x 5'0"

GARAGE
14'10" x 24'6"

MAIN FLOOR

OPT. BEDRM 3 EXPANSION

©

Design 35009

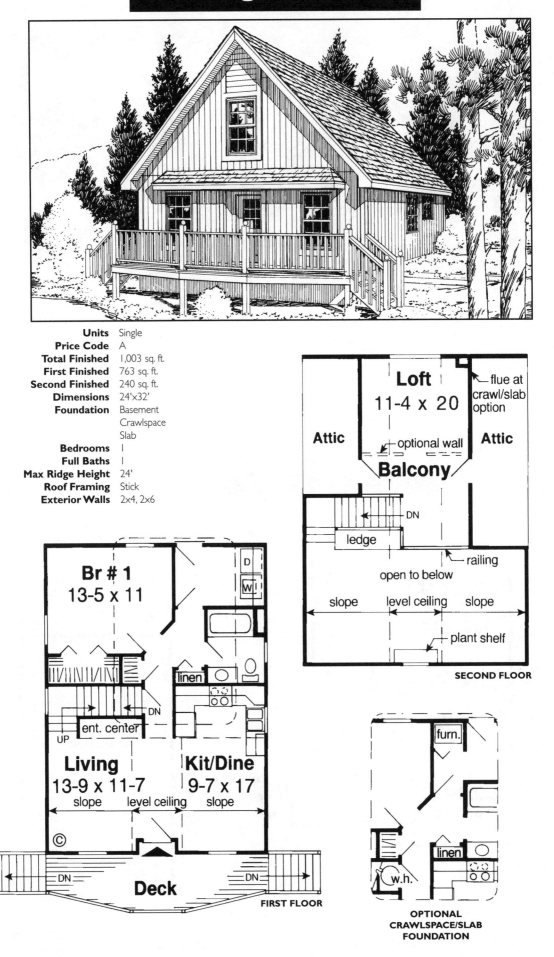

Units	Single
Price Code	A
Total Finished	1,003 sq. ft.
First Finished	763 sq. ft.
Second Finished	240 sq. ft.
Dimensions	24'x32'
Foundation	Basement
	Crawlspace
	Slab
Bedrooms	1
Full Baths	1
Max Ridge Height	24'
Roof Framing	Stick
Exterior Walls	2x4, 2x6

Loft
11-4 x 20

flue at crawl/slab option

Attic

optional wall

Attic

Balcony

DN

ledge

railing

open to below

slope   level ceiling   slope

plant shelf

SECOND FLOOR

Br # 1
13-5 x 11

D

W

linen

ent. center

DN

UP

Living
13-9 x 11-7

slope   level ceiling   slope

Kit/Dine
9-7 x 17

©

Deck

DN   DN

FIRST FLOOR

furn.

linen

w.h.

OPTIONAL CRAWLSPACE/SLAB FOUNDATION

Design 90995

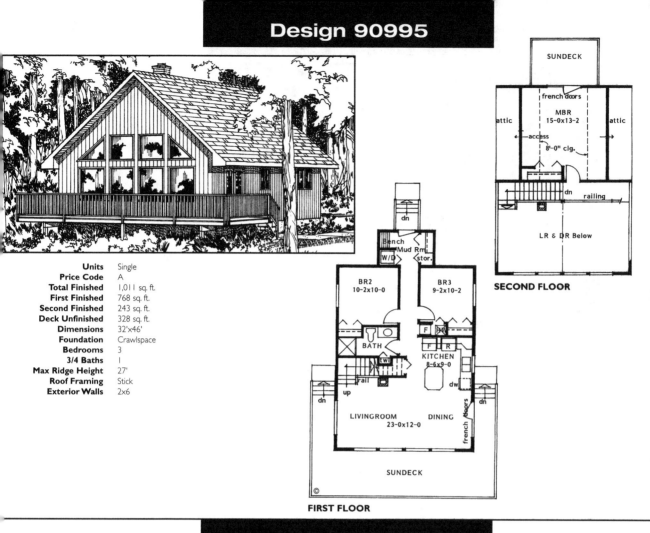

SUNDECK

french doors

MBR
15-0x13-2

attic   attic

access

8'-0" clg.

dn   railing

LR & DR Below

SECOND FLOOR

Bench   Mud Rm.
W/D   stor.

BR2
10-2x10-0

BR3
9-2x10-2

dn

F   W

BATH   F   R

KITCHEN
8-6x9-0

tw

dw

dn   up

rail   dn

LIVINGROOM
23-0x12-0   DINING

french doors

SUNDECK

FIRST FLOOR

Units	Single
Price Code	A
Total Finished	1,011 sq. ft.
First Finished	768 sq. ft.
Second Finished	243 sq. ft.
Deck Unfinished	328 sq. ft.
Dimensions	32'x46'
Foundation	Crawlspace
Bedrooms	3
3/4 Baths	1
Max Ridge Height	27'
Roof Framing	Stick
Exterior Walls	2x6

Design 94306

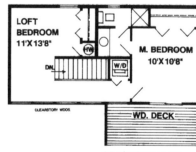

LOFT
BEDROOM
11'X13'8"

M. BEDROOM
10'X10'8"

HW

DN   W/D

CLEARSTORY WDOS

WD. DECK

SECOND FLOOR

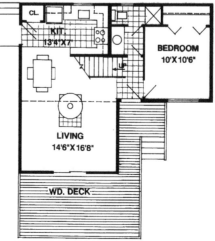

CL.

KIT
13'4"X7'

BEDROOM
10'X10'6"

up

LIVING
14'6"X16'8"

WD. DECK

FIRST FLOOR

Units	Single
Price Code	A
Total Finished	1,012 sq. ft.
First Finished	598 sq. ft.
Second Finished	414 sq. ft.
Dimensions	30'x35'
Foundation	Basement Crawlspace
Bedrooms	3
3/4 Baths	2
Max Ridge Height	23'
Roof Framing	Truss
Exterior Walls	2x6

Units	Duplex
Price Code	A
Total Finished	2,029 sq. ft.
First Finished	1,011 sq. ft. (unit A)
Second Finished	1,018 sq. ft. (unit B)
Dimensions	32'x32'
Foundation	Basement
Bedrooms	2 (per unit)
Full Baths	1 (per unit)

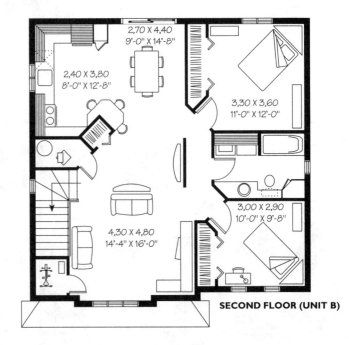

SECOND FLOOR (UNIT B)

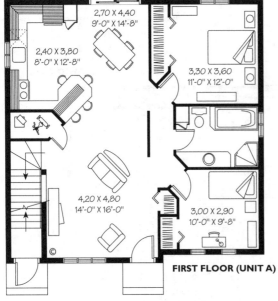

FIRST FLOOR (UNIT A)

Design 65056

Units	Single
Price Code	A
Total Finished	1,019 sq. ft.
Main Finished	1,019 sq. ft.
Dimensions	32'x37'
Foundation	Basement
Bedrooms	2
Full Baths	1

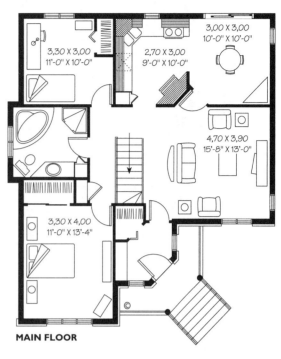

3,30 X 3,00
11'-0" X 10'-0"

2,70 X 3,00
9'-0" X 10'-0"

3,00 X 3,00
10'-0" X 10'-0"

4,70 X 3,90
15'-8" X 13'-0"

3,30 X 4,00
11'-0" X 13'-4"

MAIN FLOOR

Design 94312

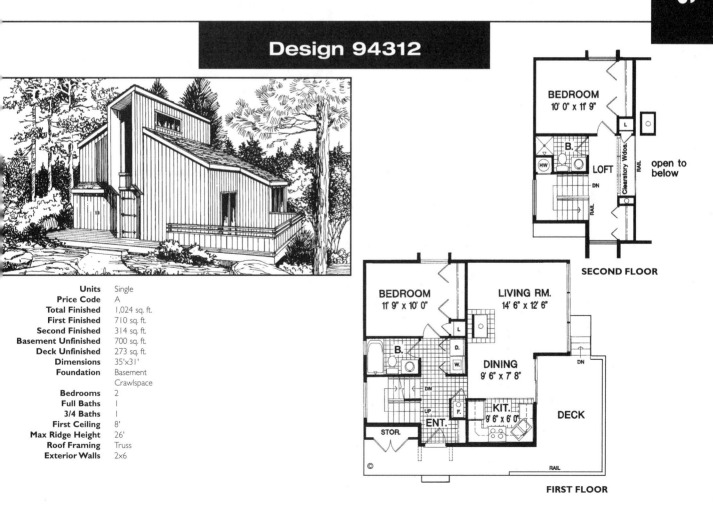

Units	Single
Price Code	A
Total Finished	1,024 sq. ft.
First Finished	710 sq. ft.
Second Finished	314 sq. ft.
Basement Unfinished	700 sq. ft.
Deck Unfinished	273 sq. ft.
Dimensions	35'x31'
Foundation	Basement
	Crawlspace
Bedrooms	2
Full Baths	1
3/4 Baths	1
First Ceiling	8'
Max Ridge Height	26'
Roof Framing	Truss
Exterior Walls	2x6

BEDROOM
10' 0" x 11' 9"

LOFT

open to below

Clearstory Wdos.

SECOND FLOOR

BEDROOM
11' 9" x 10' 0"

LIVING RM.
14' 6" x 12' 6"

DINING
9' 6" x 7' 8"

KIT.
9' 6" x 6' 0"

DECK

ENT.

STOR.

FIRST FLOOR

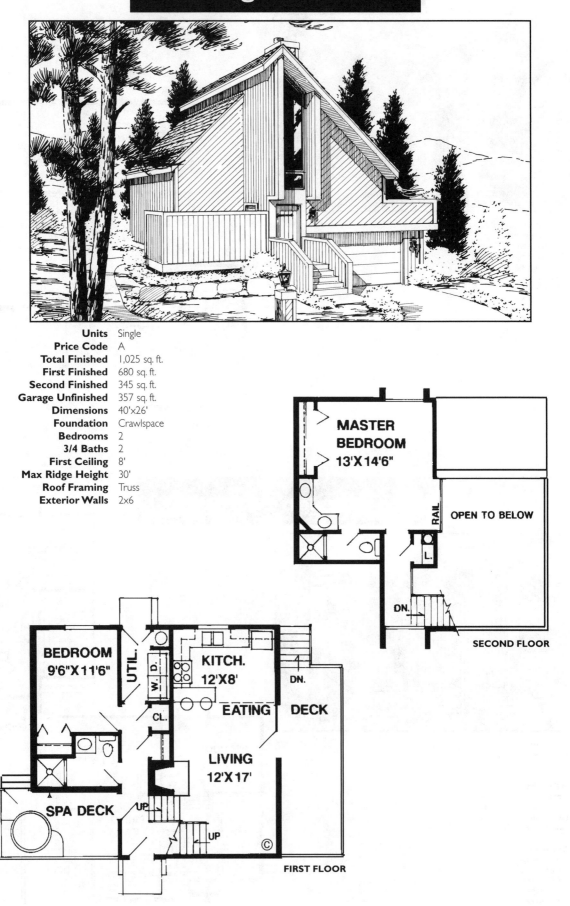

Units	Single
Price Code	A
Total Finished	1,025 sq. ft.
First Finished	680 sq. ft.
Second Finished	345 sq. ft.
Garage Unfinished	357 sq. ft.
Dimensions	40'x26'
Foundation	Crawlspace
Bedrooms	2
3/4 Baths	2
First Ceiling	8'
Max Ridge Height	30'
Roof Framing	Truss
Exterior Walls	2x6

MASTER BEDROOM 13'X14'6"

OPEN TO BELOW

RAIL

DN.

SECOND FLOOR

BEDROOM 9'6"X11'6"

UTIL.

W. D.

CL.

KITCH. 12'X8'

EATING

DN.

DECK

LIVING 12'X17'

SPA DECK

UP

UP

FIRST FLOOR

Design 35007

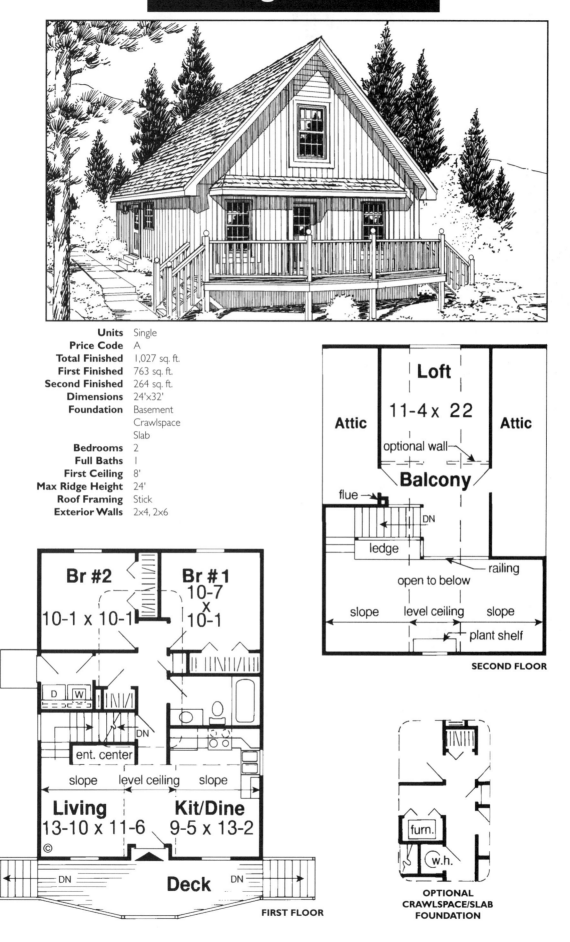

Units	Single
Price Code	A
Total Finished	1,027 sq. ft.
First Finished	763 sq. ft.
Second Finished	264 sq. ft.
Dimensions	24'x32'
Foundation	Basement
	Crawlspace
	Slab
Bedrooms	2
Full Baths	1
First Ceiling	8'
Max Ridge Height	24'
Roof Framing	Stick
Exterior Walls	2x4, 2x6

Loft

11-4 x 22

Attic   **Attic**

optional wall

Balcony

flue

DN

ledge

railing

open to below

slope   level ceiling   slope

plant shelf

SECOND FLOOR

Br #2

10-1 x 10-1

Br #1

10-7 X 10-1

D   W

DN

ent. center

slope   level ceiling   slope

Living

13-10 x 11-6

Kit/Dine

9-5 x 13-2

DN   DN

Deck

FIRST FLOOR

furn.

w.h.

OPTIONAL CRAWLSPACE/SLAB FOUNDATION

Design 90309

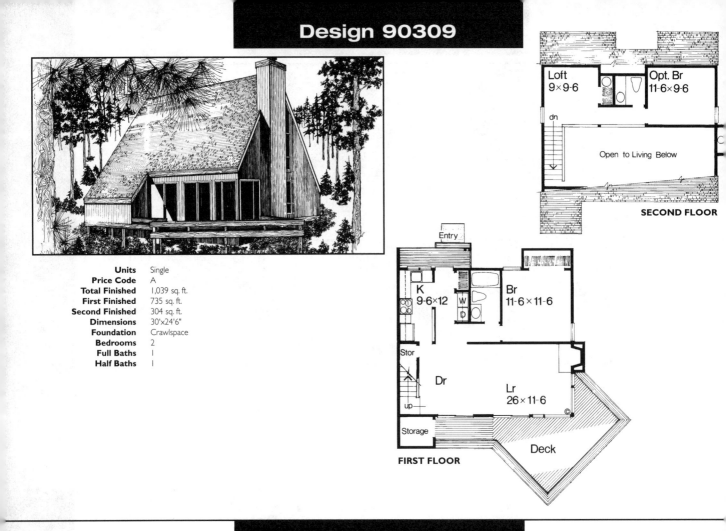

Units	Single
Price Code	A
Total Finished	1,039 sq. ft.
First Finished	735 sq. ft.
Second Finished	304 sq. ft.
Dimensions	30'x24'6"
Foundation	Crawlspace
Bedrooms	2
Full Baths	1
Half Baths	1

Loft 9×9-6

Opt. Br 11-6×9-6

dn

Open to Living Below

SECOND FLOOR

Entry

K 9-6×12

Br 11-6 × 11-6

W D

Stor

Dr

up

Lr 26 × 11-6

Storage

Deck

FIRST FLOOR

Design 90638

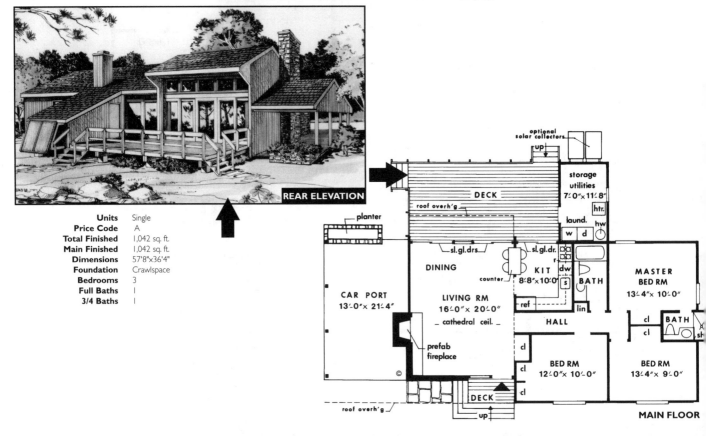

REAR ELEVATION

Units	Single
Price Code	A
Total Finished	1,042 sq. ft.
Main Finished	1,042 sq. ft.
Dimensions	57'8"x36'4"
Foundation	Crawlspace
Bedrooms	3
Full Baths	1
3/4 Baths	1

optional solar collectors

up

DECK

roof overh'g

storage utilities 7'-0"x11'-8"

htr.

laund.

hw

planter

sl. gl. drs

sl. gl. dr.

w d

r

BATH

MASTER BED RM 13'-4"x 10'-0"

DINING

KIT 8'-8"x 10'-0"

dw

counter

ref

s

lin

cl

cl

BATH

LIVING RM 16'-0"x 20'-0"
cathedral ceil.

HALL

st

prefab fireplace

cl

cl

BED RM 12'-0"x 10'-0"

BED RM 13'-4"x 9'-0"

CAR PORT 13'-0"x 21'-4"

DECK

up

roof overh'g

MAIN FLOOR

Design 92400

Units	Single
Price Code	A
Total Finished	1,050 sq. ft.
Main Finished	1,050 sq. ft.
Garage Unfinished	261 sq. ft.
Dimensions	36'×42'
Foundation	Basement
	Slab
Bedrooms	3
Full Baths	2
Max Ridge Height	16'
Roof Framing	Stick
Exterior Walls	2x4

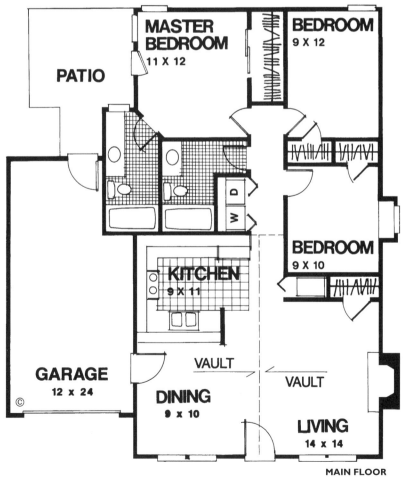

MAIN FLOOR

Units	Single
Price Code	A
Total Finished	1,059 sq. ft.
Main Finished	1,059 sq. ft.
Garage Unfinished	300 sq. ft.
Dimensions	38'x46'8"
Foundation	Basement
Bedrooms	2
Full Baths	1
Main Ceiling	8'
Max Ridge Height	17'1"
Roof Framing	Truss
Exterior Walls	2x6

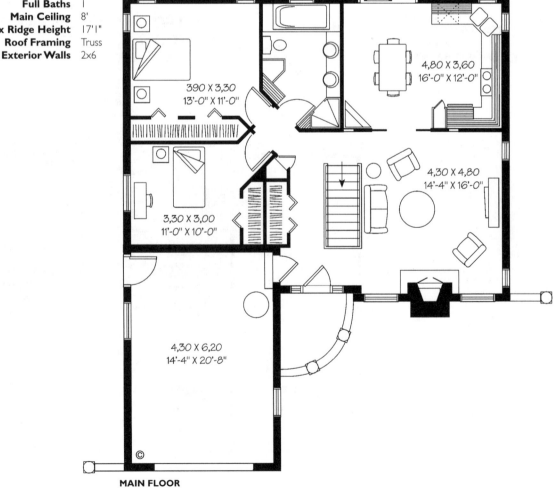

390 X 3,30
13'-0" X 11'-0"

4,80 X 3,60
16'-0" X 12'-0"

3,30 X 3,00
11'-0" X 10'-0"

4,30 X 4,80
14'-4" X 16'-0"

4,30 X 6,20
14'-4" X 20'-8"

MAIN FLOOR

Design 65241

Units	Single
Price Code	A
Total Finished	1,068 sq. ft.
Main Finished	1,068 sq. ft.
Basement Unfinished	1,068 sq. ft.
Garage Unfinished	245 sq. ft.
Dimensions	30'8"x48'
Foundation	Basement
Bedrooms	2
Full Baths	1
Main Ceiling	8'
Max Ridge Height	22'1"
Roof Framing	Truss
Exterior Walls	2x6

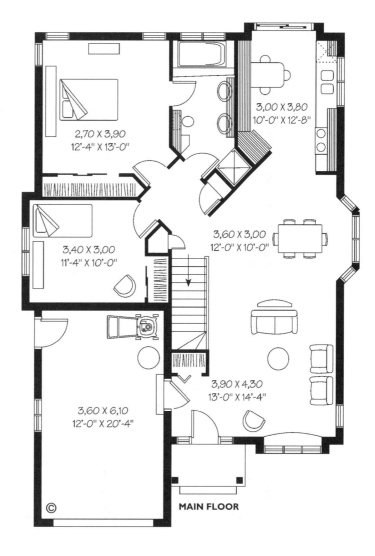

MAIN FLOOR

Units	Single
Price Code	A
Total Finished	1,079 sq. ft.
Main Finished	1,079 sq. ft.
Dimensions	34'x34'
Foundation	Basement
Bedrooms	2
Full Baths	1
Max Ridge Height	22'6"
Roof Framing	Truss
Exterior Walls	2x6

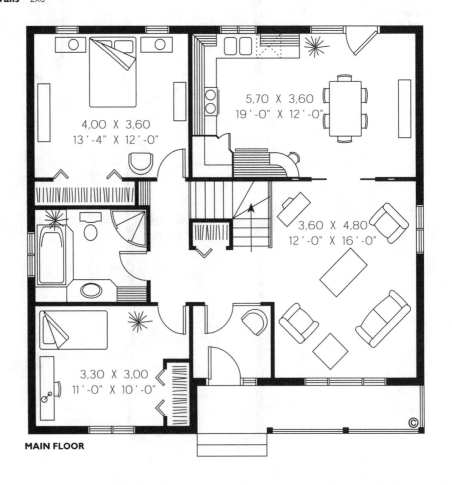

MAIN FLOOR

Design 98805

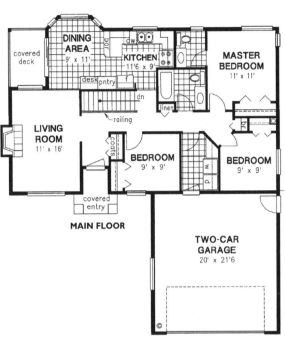

DINING AREA
9' x 11'

KITCHEN
11'6 x 9'

covered deck

desk

pntry

dn

railing

linen

MASTER BEDROOM
11' x 11'

LIVING ROOM
11' x 16'

BEDROOM
9' x 9'

BEDROOM
9' x 9'

covered entry

MAIN FLOOR

TWO-CAR GARAGE
20' x 21'6

Units	Single
Price Code	A
Total Finished	1,089 sq. ft.
Main Finished	1,089 sq. ft.
Basement Unfinished	1,089 sq. ft.
Garage Unfinished	462 sq. ft.
Deck Unfinished	54 sq. ft.
Dimensions	44'x50'
Foundation	Basement
Bedrooms	3
Full Baths	1
Half Baths	1
Max Ridge Height	16'2"
Roof Framing	Truss
Exterior Walls	2x6

Design 34328

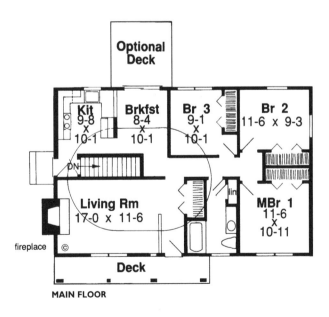

Optional Deck

Kit
9-8 x 10-1

Brkfst
8-4 x 10-1

Br 3
9-1 x 10-1

Br 2
11-6 x 9-3

DN

Living Rm
17-0 x 11-6

MBr 1
11-6 x 10-11

fireplace

lin

Deck

MAIN FLOOR

OPTIONAL CRAWLSPACE/SLAB FOUNDATION

Units	Single
Price Code	A
Total Finished	1,092 sq. ft.
Main Finished	1,092 sq. ft.
Basement Unfinished	1,092 sq. ft.
Dimensions	42'x26'
Foundation	Basement
	Crawlspace
	Slab
Bedrooms	3
Full Baths	1
Max Ridge Height	15'
Roof Framing	Stick
Exterior Walls	2x4, 2x6

Units	Single
Price Code	A
Total Finished	1,092 sq. ft.
Main Finished	1,092 sq. ft.
Dimensions	42'x26'
Foundation	Basement
Bedrooms	3
Full Baths	I

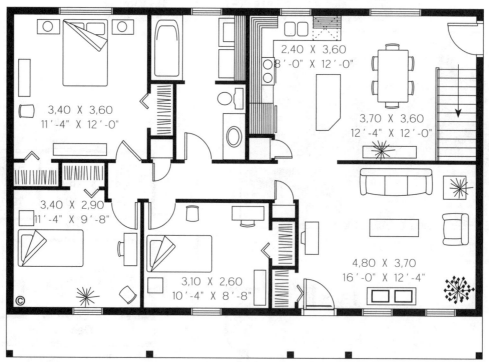

MAIN FLOOR

Design 24740

Units	Single
Price Code	A
Total Finished	1,093 sq. ft.
First Finished	792 sq. ft.
Second Finished	301 sq. ft.
Basement Unfinished	301 sq. ft.
Porch Unfinished	220 sq. ft.
Dimensions	22'x46'
Foundation	Crawlspace
Bedrooms	2
Full Baths	1
3/4 Baths	1
First Ceiling	8'
Second Ceiling	8'
Vaulted Ceiling	16'
Max Ridge Height	22'6"
Roof Framing	Truss
Exterior Walls	2x4

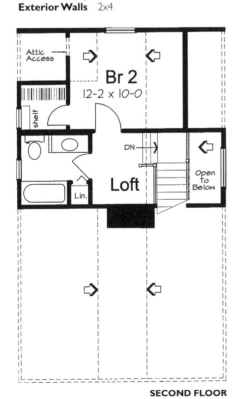

SECOND FLOOR

FIRST FLOOR

Design 91002

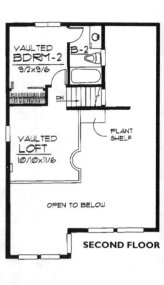

SECOND FLOOR

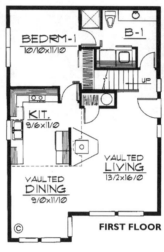

FIRST FLOOR

Units	Single
Price Code	A
Total Finished	1,096 sq. ft.
First Finished	808 sq. ft.
Second Finished	288 sq. ft.
Dimensions	24'x32'
Foundation	Crawlspace
Bedrooms	2
Full Baths	1
3/4 Baths	1
Max Ridge Height	25'
Roof Framing	Stick
Exterior Walls	2x6

Design 91340

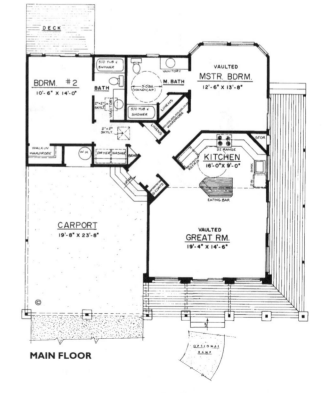

MAIN FLOOR

OPTIONAL BATH

Units	Single
Price Code	A
Total Finished	1,111 sq. ft.
Main Finished	1,111 sq. ft.
Dimensions	46'x44'
Foundation	Crawlspace
	Slab
Bedrooms	2
Full Baths	2
Max Ridge Height	18'
Roof Framing	Stick
Exterior Walls	2x4

Design 26114

Units	Single
Price Code	A
Total Finished	1,112 sq. ft.
First Finished	696 sq. ft.
Second Finished	416 sq. ft.
Basement Unfinished	696 sq. ft.
Dimensions	32'x24'
Foundation	Basement
Bedrooms	3
Full Baths	1
Half Baths	1
Max Ridge Height	32'
Roof Framing	Stick
Exterior Walls	2x6

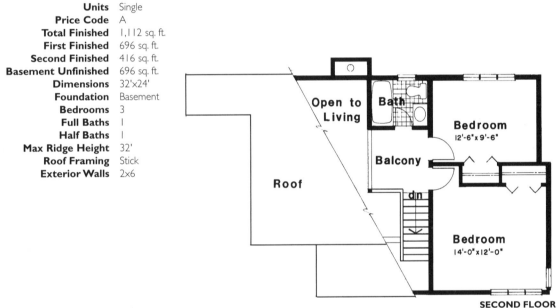

SECOND FLOOR

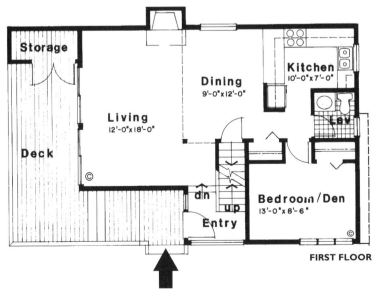

FIRST FLOOR

Design 24723

Units	Single
Price Code	A
Total Finished	1,112 sq. ft.
Main Finished	1,112 sq. ft.
Garage Unfinished	563 sq. ft.
Dimensions	64'x33'
Foundation	Crawlspace
	Slab
Bedrooms	3
Full Baths	2
Main Ceiling	8'-9'
Max Ridge Height	21'6"
Roof Framing	Stick
Exterior Walls	2x4

MBr
13-8 x 11-0
Clg. @ 9'

Br 2
10-3 x 9-2

Br 3
10-11x 10-8

Flat Clg. @ 8'

Broom

T.V. Built-In

Flat Clg. @ 9'

Kitchen
9-0 x 11-0

D.W.

Ref.

Skylt

Skylt

Fan/Light

12"
Serving
Cntr.

Dining
10-5 x 11-7

Util.

Furn

WH

Storage

Living
16-9 x 14-2

Fan/Light

Garage
21-9 x 20-2

MAIN FLOOR

Porch

To order blueprints, call **800-235-5700** or visit us on the web, familyhomeplans.com

Design 84330

Units	Single
Price Code	A
Total Finished	1,114 sq. ft.
Main Finished	1,114 sq. ft.
Dimensions	42'x26'
Foundation	Basement
	Crawlspace
	Slab
Bedrooms	3
Full Baths	1
Max Ridge Height	16'
Roof Framing	Stick
Exterior Walls	2x4, 2x6

OPTIONAL CRAWLSPACE/SLAB FOUNDATION

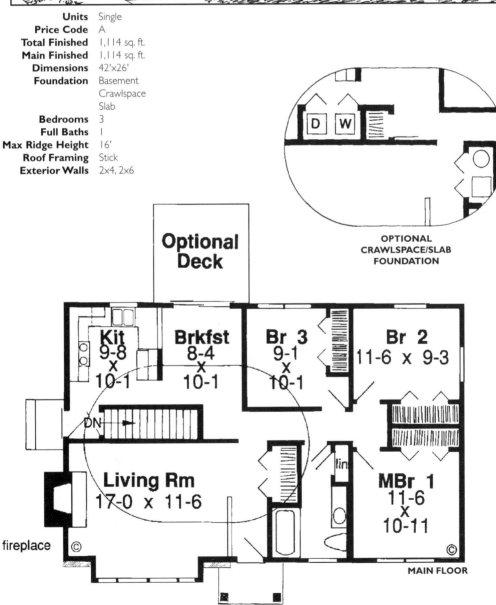

Optional Deck

Kit 9-8 X 10-1

Brkfst 8-4 X 10-1

Br 3 9-1 X 10-1

Br 2 11-6 x 9-3

DN

Living Rm 17-0 x 11-6

MBr 1 11-6 X 10-11

lin

fireplace ©

© **MAIN FLOOR**

Design 65016

Units	Single
Price Code	A
Total Finished	1,120 sq. ft.
Main Finished	1,120 sq. ft.
Basement Unfinished	1,120 sq. ft.
Garage Unfinished	208 sq. ft.
Dimensions	36'x48'
Foundation	Basement
Bedrooms	2
Full Baths	1
Main Ceiling	8'2"
Roof Framing	Truss
Exterior Walls	2x6

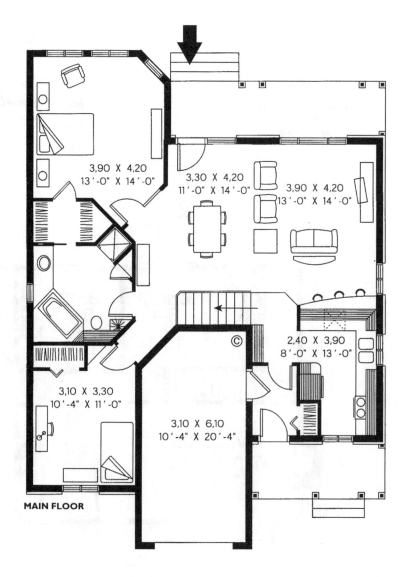

3,90 X 4,20
13'-0" X 14'-0"

3,30 X 4,20
11'-0" X 14'-0"

3,90 X 4,20
13'-0" X 14'-0"

2,40 X 3,90
8'-0" X 13'-0"

3,10 X 3,30
10'-4" X 11'-0"

3,10 X 6,10
10'-4" X 20'-4"

MAIN FLOOR

To order blueprints, call **800-235-5700** or visit us on the web, **familyhomeplans.com**

Design 24311

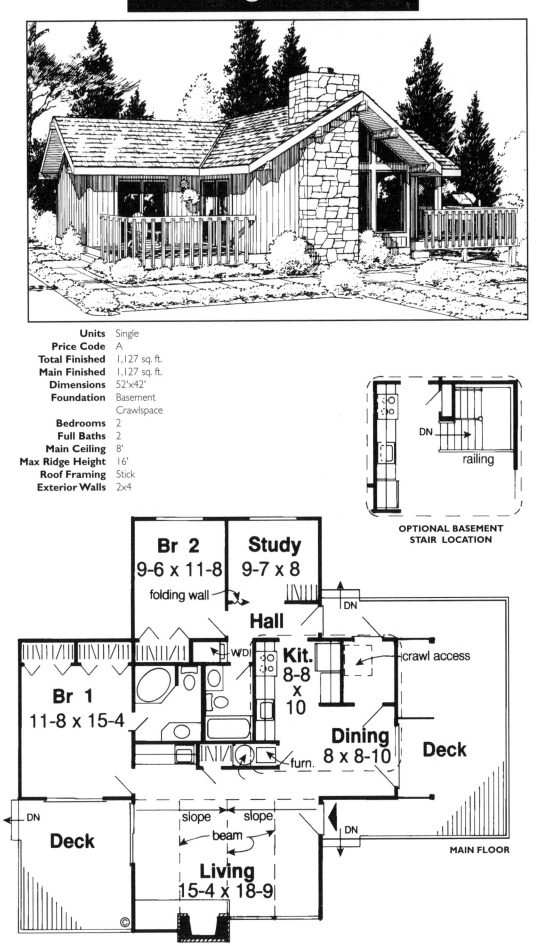

Units	Single
Price Code	A
Total Finished	1,127 sq. ft.
Main Finished	1,127 sq. ft.
Dimensions	52'x42'
Foundation	Basement
	Crawlspace
Bedrooms	2
Full Baths	2
Main Ceiling	8'
Max Ridge Height	16'
Roof Framing	Stick
Exterior Walls	2x4

DN

railing

**OPTIONAL BASEMENT
STAIR LOCATION**

Br 2
9-6 x 11-8

folding wall

Study
9-7 x 8

DN

Hall

WD

Kit.
8-8
x
10

crawl access

Br 1
11-8 x 15-4

furn.

Dining
8 x 8-10

Deck

DN

Deck

slope   slope

beam

DN

MAIN FLOOR

Living
15-4 x 18-9

Design 65376

Units	Single
Price Code	A
Total Finished	1,142 sq. ft.
Main Finished	1,142 sq. ft.
Garage Unfinished	400 sq. ft.
Dimensions	46'x38'
Foundation	Basement
Bedrooms	2
Full Baths	1

3,70 X 3,00
12'-0" X 10'-0"

4,20 X 3,40
14'-0" X 11'-4"

4,20 X 3,30
14'-0" X 11'-0"

3,00 X 3,30
10'-0" X 11'-0"

4,50 X 7,40
15'-0" X 24'-8"

3,60 X 4,50
12'-0" X 15'-0"

MAIN FLOOR

Design 34003

Units	Single
Price Code	A
Total Finished	1,146 sq. ft.
Main Finished	1,146 sq. ft.
Dimensions	44'x28'
Foundation	Basement
	Crawlspace
	Slab
Bedrooms	3
Full Baths	2
Main Ceiling	8'
Max Ridge Height	16'
Roof Framing	Stick
Exterior Walls	2x4, 2x6

W

D

**OPTIONAL
CRAWLSPACE/SLAB
FOUNDATION**

Br 2
10 x 12-8

Br 3
10 x 9-4

PANTRY

Kit
10 x 11

Dining
9 x 11

DN

linen

slope slope

MBr 1
13-4 x 12

Living Rm
19 x 12-4

Deck

MAIN FLOOR

Design 65014

Units	Single
Price Code	A
Total Finished	1,148 sq. ft.
First Finished	728 sq. ft.
Second Finished	420 sq. ft.
Basement Unfinished	728 sq. ft.
Dimensions	28'x26'
Foundation	Basement
Bedrooms	1
Full Baths	1
Half Baths	1
First Ceiling	8'
Second Ceiling	8'
Max Ridge Height	25'4"
Roof Framing	Truss
Exterior Walls	2x6

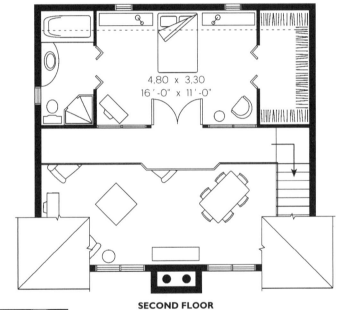

4,80 x 3,30
16'-0" x 11'-0"

SECOND FLOOR

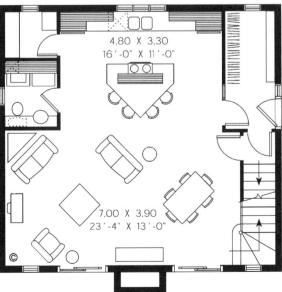

4,80 X 3,30
16'-0" X 11'-0"

7,00 X 3,90
23'-4" X 13'-0"

FIRST FLOOR

Design 90348

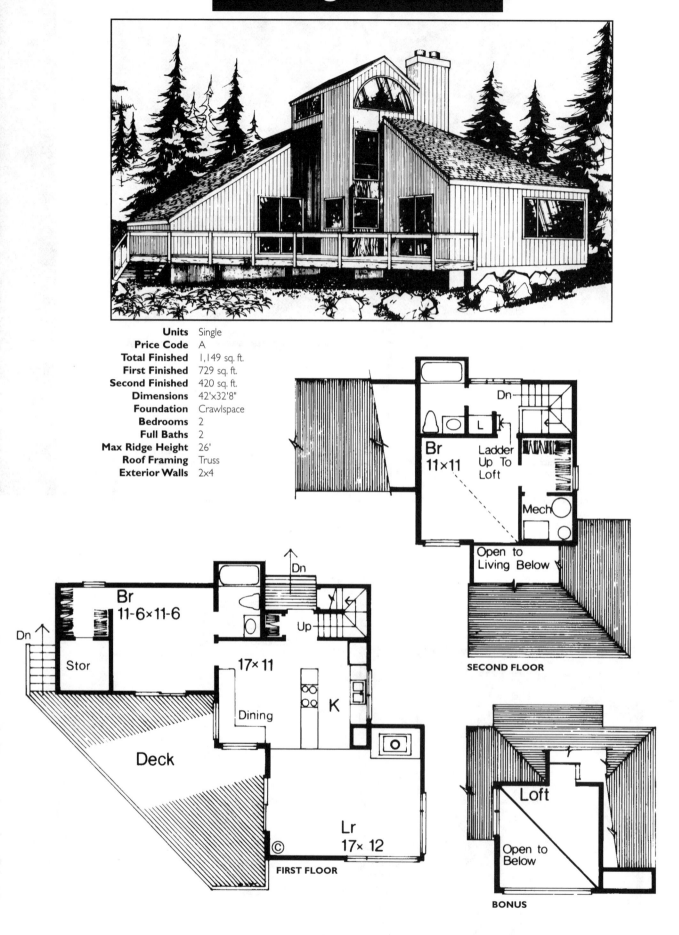

Units	Single
Price Code	A
Total Finished	1,149 sq. ft.
First Finished	729 sq. ft.
Second Finished	420 sq. ft.
Dimensions	42'×32'8"
Foundation	Crawlspace
Bedrooms	2
Full Baths	2
Max Ridge Height	26'
Roof Framing	Truss
Exterior Walls	2x4

Dn

Br
11×11

Ladder
Up To
Loft

Mech

Open to
Living Below

SECOND FLOOR

Dn

Br
11-6×11-6

Stor

Up

17×11

Dining

K

Deck

Lr
17×12

©

FIRST FLOOR

Loft

Open to
Below

BONUS

Design 82040

Units	Single
Price Code	A
Total Finished	1,172 sq. ft.
Main Finished	1,172 sq. ft.
Garage Unfinished	213 sq. ft.
Porch Unfinished	127 sq. ft.
Dimensions	37'x53'
Foundation	Crawlspace
	Slab
Bedrooms	2
Full Baths	2
Main Ceiling	9'
Roof Framing	Stick
Exterior Walls	2x4

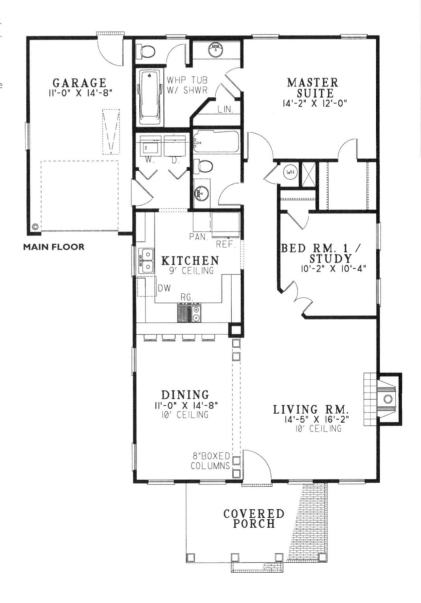

GARAGE
11'-0" X 14'-8"

WHP TUB
W/ SHWR

LIN.

MASTER
SUITE
14'-2" X 12'-0"

W. D.

MAIN FLOOR

WH

PAN. REF.

KITCHEN
9' CEILING

DW RG.

BED RM. 1 /
STUDY
10'-2" X 10'-4"

DINING
11'-0" X 14'-8"
10' CEILING

LIVING RM.
14'-5" X 16'-2"
10' CEILING

8" BOXED
COLUMNS

COVERED
PORCH

Units	Single
Price Code	A
Total Finished	1,174 sq. ft.
Main Finished	1,174 sq. ft.
Dimensions	28'x54'
Foundation	Crawlspace
Bedrooms	3
Full Baths	2
Max Ridge Height	21'
Roof Framing	Stick
Exterior Walls	2x4

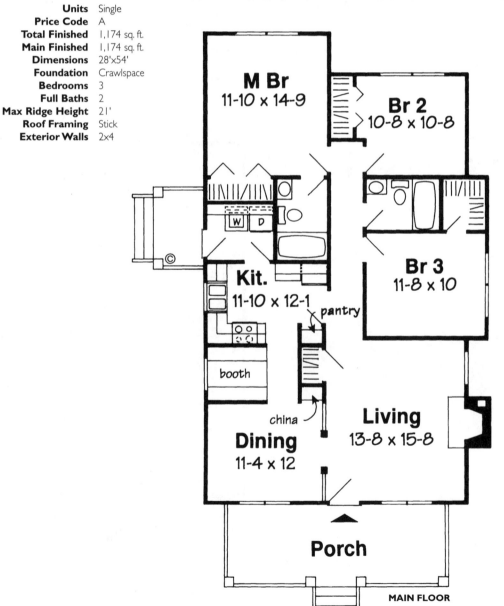

M Br
11-10 x 14-9

Br 2
10-8 x 10-8

Br 3
11-8 x 10

Kit.
11-10 x 12-1

pantry

Living
13-8 x 15-8

booth

china

Dining
11-4 x 12

Porch

MAIN FLOOR

Design 62114

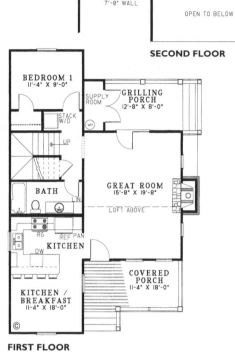

SECOND FLOOR

- BEDROOM 2 / LOFT 15'-8" X 15'-10"
- BATH
- 5' WALL
- 8' LINE
- VAULTED CEILING
- OPEN TO BELOW
- 7'-0" WALL
- DN
- LIN

FIRST FLOOR

- BEDROOM 1 11'-4" X 9'-0"
- SUPPLY ROOM
- GRILLING PORCH 12'-8" X 8'-0"
- STACK W/D
- WH
- UP
- BATH
- LIN
- GREAT ROOM 15'-8" X 19'-8"
- LOFT ABOVE
- RG
- REF PAN
- KITCHEN
- DW
- COVERED PORCH 11'-4" X 18'-0"
- KITCHEN / BREAKFAST 11-4" X 18'-0"

Hot New Design

Units	Single
Price Code	A
Total Finished	1,178 sq. ft.
First Finished	859 sq. ft.
Second Finished	319 sq. ft.
Dimensions	30'4"x44'6"
Foundation	Crawlspace
	Slab
Bedrooms	2
Full Baths	2
First Ceiling	8'
Second Ceiling	8'
Max Ridge Height	22'
Exterior Walls	2x6

Design 90855

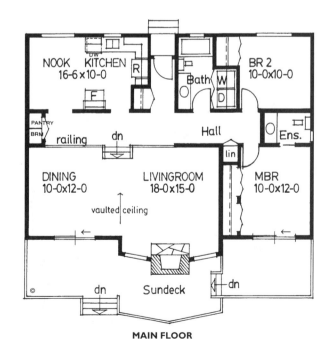

MAIN FLOOR

- NOOK
- KITCHEN 16-6 x 10-0
- R
- DW
- F
- BR 2 10-0x10-0
- Bath
- W D
- PANTRY
- BRM
- railing
- dn
- Hall
- Ens.
- lin
- DINING 10-0x12-0
- LIVINGROOM 18-0x15-0
- vaulted ceiling
- MBR 10-0x12-0
- dn
- Sundeck
- dn

Units	Single
Price Code	A
Total Finished	1,186 sq. ft.
Main Finished	1,186 sq. ft.
Dimensions	41'x40'
Foundation	Crawlspace
Bedrooms	2
Full Baths	1
Half Baths	1

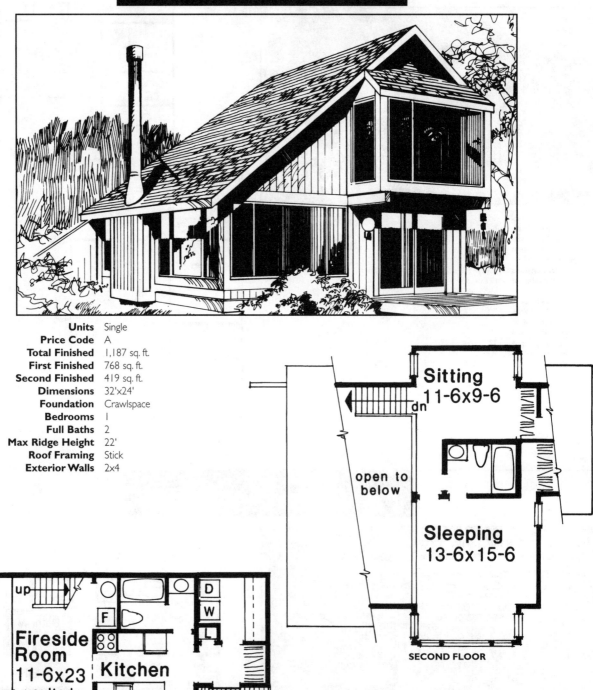

Units	Single
Price Code	A
Total Finished	1,187 sq. ft.
First Finished	768 sq. ft.
Second Finished	419 sq. ft.
Dimensions	32'x24'
Foundation	Crawlspace
Bedrooms	1
Full Baths	2
Max Ridge Height	22'
Roof Framing	Stick
Exterior Walls	2x4

Sitting
11-6x9-6

dn

open to
below

Sleeping
13-6x15-6

SECOND FLOOR

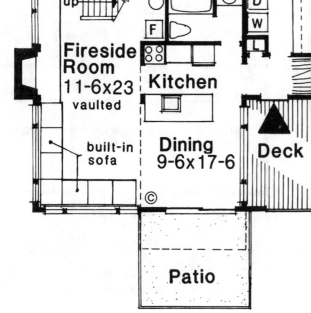

up

**Fireside
Room**
11-6x23
vaulted

F

D

W

Kitchen

built-in
sofa

Dining
9-6x17-6

Deck

©

Patio

FIRST FLOOR

Design 65064

Units	Single
Price Code	A
Total Finished	1,191 sq. ft.
Main Finished	1,191 sq. ft.
Basement Unfinished	1,191 sq. ft.
Porch Unfinished	21 sq. ft.
Dimensions	31'6"x38'8"
Foundation	Basement
Bedrooms	2
Full Baths	1
Main Ceiling	8'
Max Ridge Height	22'3"
Roof Framing	Truss
Exterior Walls	2x6

2,70 X 3,60
9'-0" X 12'-0"

3,30 X 4,20
11'-0" X 14'-0"

3,80 X 4,10
12'-8" X 13'-8"

5,10 X 3,00
17'-0" X 10'-0"

5,10 X 3,60
17'-0" X 12'-0"

MAIN FLOOR

Design 93073

Units	Single
Price Code	A
Total Finished	1,202 sq. ft.
Main Finished	1,202 sq. ft.
Garage Unfinished	482 sq. ft.
Porch Unfinished	147 sq. ft.
Dimensions	51'x43'10"
Foundation	Crawlspace
	Slab
Bedrooms	3
Full Baths	2
Max Ridge Height	21'6"
Roof Framing	Stick
Exterior Walls	2x4

OPTIONAL GARAGE DOOR LOCATION

MSTR BDRM 11–0x13–8 10 FT CLG
LIVING 13–0x17–8 10 FT CLG
GARAGE
MSTR BATH
BATH 2
STOR
BDRM 3 10–10x11–6
FOYER 9 FT CLG
STORAGE
BDRM 2 10–4x10–2
COVERED PORCH
DINING 11–0x9–2 9 FT CLG
DESK
KITCH 11–6x 8–0 9 FT CLG
LIN

MAIN FLOOR

Design 90630

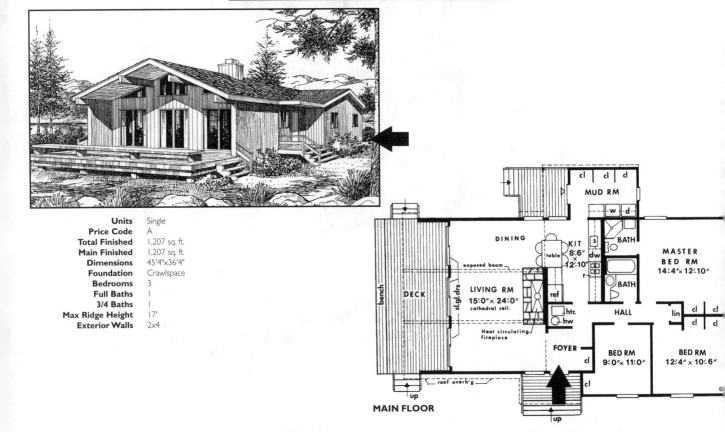

Units	Single
Price Code	A
Total Finished	1,207 sq. ft.
Main Finished	1,207 sq. ft.
Dimensions	45'4"x36'4"
Foundation	Crawlspace
Bedrooms	3
Full Baths	I
3/4 Baths	I
Max Ridge Height	17'
Exterior Walls	2x4

MUD RM
DINING
KIT 8'6" x 12'10"
BATH
MASTER BED RM 14'4" x 12'10"
exposed beam
bench
DECK
sl.gl.drs
LIVING RM 15'0" x 24'0" cathedral ceil.
ref
BATH
HALL
lin
Heat circulating fireplace
htr.
hw
FOYER
BED RM 9'0" x 11'0"
BED RM 12'4" x 10'6"
up
roof overh'g
up

MAIN FLOOR

Design 24313

Units	Single
Price Code	A
Total Finished	1,210 sq. ft.
First Finished	781 sq. ft.
Second Finished	429 sq. ft.
Dimensions	28'x30'
Foundation	Crawlspace
Bedrooms	2
Full Baths	1
3/4 Baths	1
Max Ridge Height	25'
Roof Framing	Truss
Exterior Walls	2x4

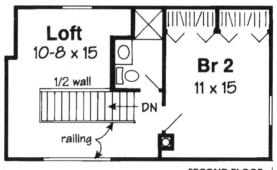

Loft
10-8 x 15

1/2 wall

DN

railing

Br 2
11 x 15

SECOND FLOOR

open to below

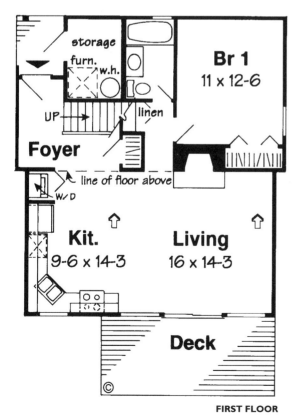

storage

furn.

w.h.

UP

linen

Foyer

W/D

line of floor above

Br 1
11 x 12-6

Kit.
9-6 x 14-3

Living
16 x 14-3

Deck

FIRST FLOOR

Design 32192

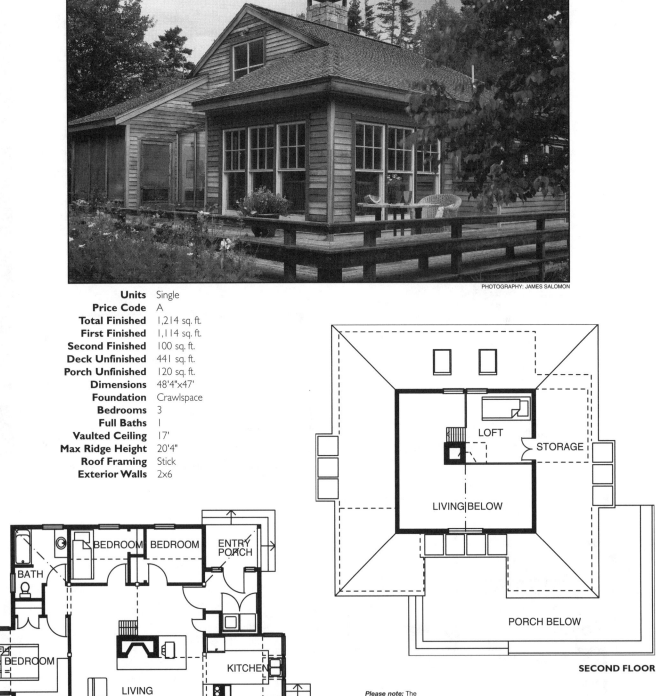

PHOTOGRAPHY: JAMES SALOMON

Units	Single
Price Code	A
Total Finished	1,214 sq. ft.
First Finished	1,114 sq. ft.
Second Finished	100 sq. ft.
Deck Unfinished	441 sq. ft.
Porch Unfinished	120 sq. ft.
Dimensions	48'4"×47'
Foundation	Crawlspace
Bedrooms	3
Full Baths	1
Vaulted Ceiling	17'
Max Ridge Height	20'4"
Roof Framing	Stick
Exterior Walls	2x6

SECOND FLOOR

LOFT
STORAGE
LIVING BELOW
PORCH BELOW

Please note: The photographed home may have been modified to suit homeowner preferences. If you order plans, have a builder or design professional check them against the photograph to confirm actual construction details.

FIRST FLOOR

BEDROOM BEDROOM
ENTRY PORCH
BATH
BEDROOM
LIVING
KITCHEN
SCREEN PORCH
DINING
PORCH

Design 94309

Units	Single
Price Code	A
Total Finished	1,215 sq. ft.
Main Finished	1,028 sq. ft.
Loft Finished	187 sq. ft.
Dimensions	40'x32'
Foundation	Crawlspace
Bedrooms	2
Full Baths	1
3/4 Baths	1
Main Ceiling	8'
Max Ridge Height	24'
Roof Framing	Truss
Exterior Walls	2x6

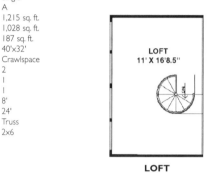

LOFT
11' X 16'8.5"

LOFT

DECK 23'X27'

W.I.C.

MASTER BEDROOM 12'X14'

LIVING 12'X18'

LOFT ABOVE

GRILLE

UP

BEDROOM 12'X9'6"

DINING

KIT. 8'6"X11'

D. W.

MAIN FLOOR

OPTIONAL GARAGE

Design 65188

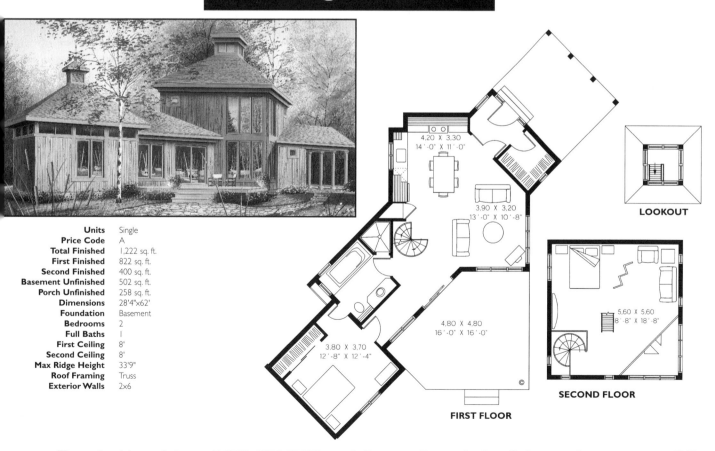

Units	Single
Price Code	A
Total Finished	1,222 sq. ft.
First Finished	822 sq. ft.
Second Finished	400 sq. ft.
Basement Unfinished	502 sq. ft.
Porch Unfinished	258 sq. ft.
Dimensions	28'4"x62'
Foundation	Basement
Bedrooms	2
Full Baths	1
First Ceiling	8'
Second Ceiling	8'
Max Ridge Height	33'9"
Roof Framing	Truss
Exterior Walls	2x6

4.20 X 3.30
14'-0" X 11'-0"

3.90 X 3.20
13'-0" X 10'-8"

LOOKOUT

4.80 X 4.80
16'-0" X 16'-0"

5.60 X 5.60
18'-8" X 18'-8"

3.80 X 3.70
12'-8" X 12'-4"

FIRST FLOOR

SECOND FLOOR

Design 32022

Units	Single
Price Code	A
Total Finished	1,230 sq. ft.
First Finished	750 sq. ft.
Second Finished	480 sq. ft.
Dimensions	28'x30'
Foundation	Crawlspace
Bedrooms	2
Full Baths	2
First Ceiling	8'
Second Ceiling	8'
Vaulted Ceiling	17'
Max Ridge Height	26'
Roof Framing	Stick
Exterior Walls	2x6

Hot New Design

SECOND FLOOR

Please note: The photographed home may have been modified to suit homeowner preferences. If you order plans, have a builder or design professional check them against the photograph to confirm actual construction details.

FIRST FLOOR

Design 34625

Units	Single
Price Code	A
Total Finished	1,231 sq. ft.
First Finished	780 sq. ft.
Second Finished	451 sq. ft.
Basement Unfinished	780 sq. ft.
Dimensions	26'x30'
Foundation	Basement
	Crawlspace
	Slab
Bedrooms	2
Full Baths	2
Max Ridge Height	24'
Roof Framing	Stick
Exterior Walls	2x4, 2x6

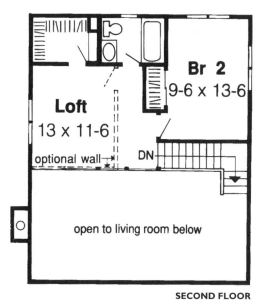

Loft
13 x 11-6

optional wall →

Br 2
9-6 x 13-6

DN

open to living room below

SECOND FLOOR

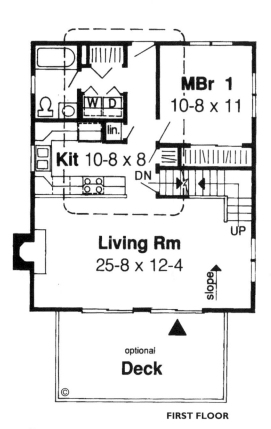

MBr 1
10-8 x 11

Kit 10-8 x 8

W D

lin.

DN

UP

Living Rm
25-8 x 12-4

slope

optional

Deck

©

FIRST FLOOR

W D

lin.

**OPTIONAL
CRAWLSPACE/SLAB
FOUNDATION**

Units	Single
Price Code	A
Total Finished	1,231 sq. ft.
Main Finished	1,231 sq. ft.
Dimensions	42'8"x50'8"
Foundation	Basement
Bedrooms	3
Full Baths	2

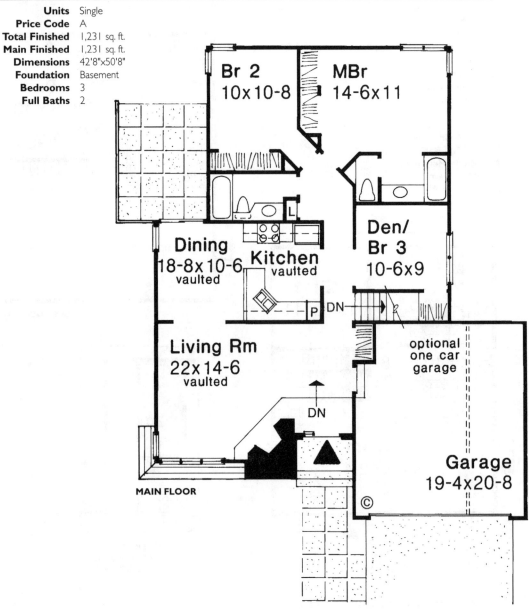

Br 2
10x10-8

MBr
14-6x11

Dining
18-8x10-6
vaulted

Kitchen
vaulted

Den/
Br 3
10-6x9

Living Rm
22x14-6
vaulted

P   DN

DN

optional
one car
garage

Garage
19-4x20-8

MAIN FLOOR

Design 65017

1,001-1,500 sq. ft. HOME PLANS

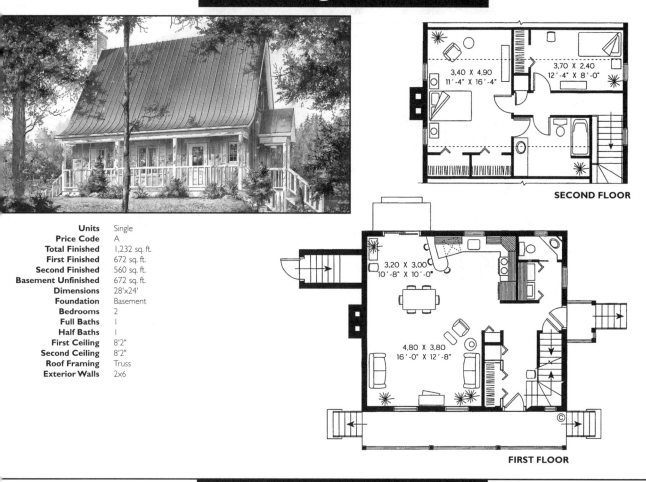

SECOND FLOOR

3,40 X 4,90
11'-4" X 16'-4"

3,70 X 2,40
12'-4" X 8'-0"

3,20 X 3,00
10'-8" X 10'-0"

4,80 X 3,80
16'-0" X 12'-8"

FIRST FLOOR

Units	Single
Price Code	A
Total Finished	1,232 sq. ft.
First Finished	672 sq. ft.
Second Finished	560 sq. ft.
Basement Unfinished	672 sq. ft.
Dimensions	28'x24'
Foundation	Basement
Bedrooms	2
Full Baths	1
Half Baths	1
First Ceiling	8'2"
Second Ceiling	8'2"
Roof Framing	Truss
Exterior Walls	2x6

Design 65638

Units	Single
Price Code	A
Total Finished	1,244 sq. ft.
Main Finished	1,244 sq. ft.
Dimensions	44'x62'
Foundation	Crawlspace
	Slab
Bedrooms	3
Full Baths	2
Main Ceiling	8'
Max Ridge Height	26'
Roof Framing	Stick
Exterior Walls	2x6

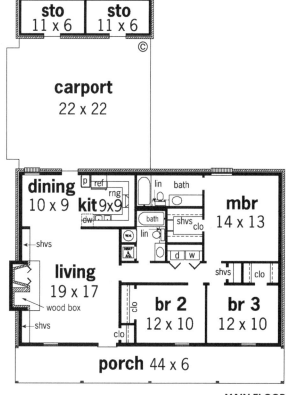

sto
11 x 6

sto
11 x 6

carport
22 x 22

dining
10 x 9

kit 9x9

bath

mbr
14 x 13

living
19 x 17

wood box

br 2
12 x 10

br 3
12 x 10

porch 44 x 6

MAIN FLOOR

Units	Single
Price Code	A
Total Finished	1,249 sq. ft.
First Finished	952 sq. ft.
Second Finished	297 sq. ft.
Dimensions	34'x28'
Foundation	Basement
	Crawlspace
Bedrooms	2
Full Baths	2
First Ceiling	8'
Max Ridge Height	24'
Roof Framing	Stick
Exterior Walls	2x6

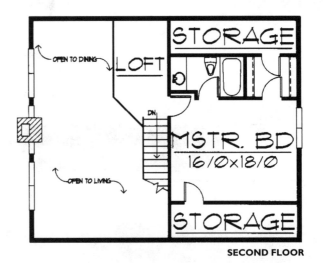

SECOND FLOOR

STORAGE

LOFT

OPEN TO DINING

DN

MSTR. BD
16/0x18/0

OPEN TO LIVING

STORAGE

OPTIONAL BASEMENT STAIR LOCATION

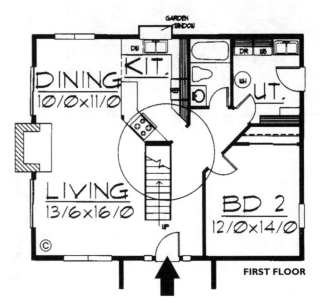

FIRST FLOOR

GARDEN WINDOW

DINING
10/0x11/0

KIT.

UT.

LIVING
13/6x16/0

BD 2
12/0x14/0

Design 91722

Units	Single
Price Code	A
Total Finished	1,249 sq. ft.
First Finished	972 sq. ft.
Second Finished	277 sq. ft.
Dimensions	24'x42'
Foundation	Crawlspace
Bedrooms	3
Full Baths	1
Max Ridge Height	26'
Roof Framing	Stick
Exterior Walls	2x6

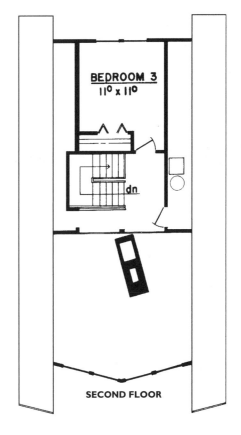

SECOND FLOOR

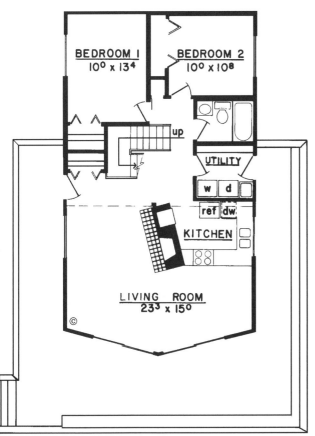

FIRST FLOOR

Design 20001

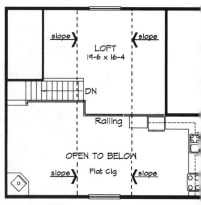

SECOND FLOOR

LOFT
19-6 x 16-4

slope   slope

DN

Railing

OPEN TO BELOW

slope   Flat Clg   slope

Units	Single
Price Code	A
Total Finished	1,255 sq. ft.
First Finished	960 sq. ft.
Second Finished	295 sq. ft.
Deck Unfinished	422 sq. ft.
Dimensions	32'x30'
Foundation	Crawlspace
	Slab
Bedrooms	2
Full Baths	1
First Ceiling	8'
Second Ceiling	7'6"
Max Ridge Height	22'6"
Roof Framing	Stick
Exterior Walls	2x6

BEDROOM 13-2 x 10-11

BEDROOM 13-2 x 10-11

Crawl Access

BATH

UP

Furn

LIVING 20-0 x 18-0

WH

Loft Above

Wood Stove

Flat Clg Above

slope

KITCHEN 11-7 x 12-6

slope

Wood Storage

DECK

FIRST FLOOR

Design 65285

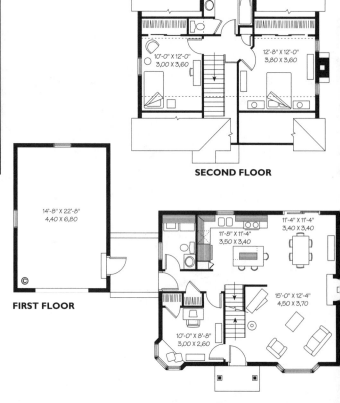

10'-0" X 12'-0"
3,00 X 3,60

12'-8" X 12'-0"
3,80 X 3,60

SECOND FLOOR

14'-8" X 22'-8"
4,40 X 6,80

11'-8" X 11'-4"
3,50 X 3,40

11'-4" X 11'-4"
3,40 X 3,40

15'-0" X 12'-4"
4,50 X 3,70

10'-0" X 8'-8"
3,00 X 2,60

FIRST FLOOR

Units	Single
Price Code	A
Total Finished	1,257 sq. ft.
First Finished	753 sq. ft.
Second Finished	504 sq. ft.
Garage Unfinished	384 sq. ft.
Dimensions	54'x35'8"
Foundation	Basement
Bedrooms	2
Full Baths	1
Half Baths	1
Roof Framing	Stick
Exterior Walls	2x6

Design 65140

Units	Single
Price Code	A
Total Finished	1,258 sq. ft.
First Finished	753 sq. ft.
Second Finished	505 sq. ft.
Basement Unfinished	753 sq. ft.
Dimensions	30'x28'
Foundation	Basement
Bedrooms	3
Full Baths	1
Half Baths	1
First Ceiling	8'
Second Ceiling	8'
Max Ridge Height	24'10"
Roof Framing	Truss
Exterior Walls	2x6

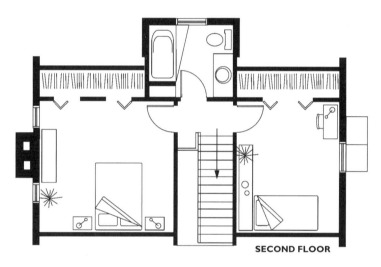

SECOND FLOOR

3,70 x 3,40
12'-4" x 11'-4"

3,20 x 2,60
10'-8" x 8'-8"

4,50 x 3,70
15'-0" x 12'-4"

3,00 x 2,70
10'-0" x 9'-0"

FIRST FLOOR

Units	Single
Price Code	A
Total Finished	1,260 sq. ft.
First Finished	864 sq. ft.
Second Finished	396 sq. ft.
Dimensions	24'x36'
Foundation	Crawlspace
Bedrooms	3
Full Baths	2
Max Ridge Height	18'
Roof Framing	Stick
Exterior Wall	2x6

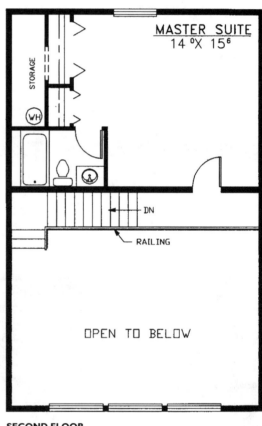

SECOND FLOOR

MASTER SUITE
14 ⁰X 15 ⁶

STORAGE

WH

DN

RAILING

OPEN TO BELOW

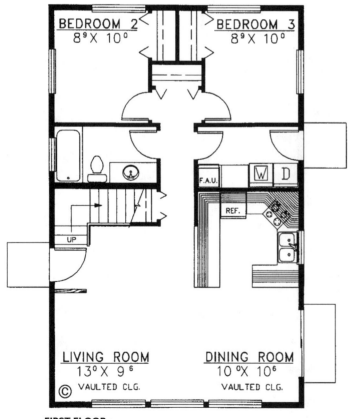

FIRST FLOOR

BEDROOM 2
8⁹X 10⁰

BEDROOM 3
8⁹X 10⁰

F.A.U.

W   D

REF.

UP

LIVING ROOM
13⁰X 9⁶
© VAULTED CLG.

DINING ROOM
10⁰X 10⁶
VAULTED CLG.

Design 90822

Units	Single
Price Code	A
Total Finished	1,263 sq. ft.
First Finished	925 sq. ft.
Second Finished	338 sq. ft.
Basement Unfinished	864 sq. ft.
Dimensions	33'x47'
Foundation	Basement
Bedrooms	3
Full Baths	1
Half Baths	1
Roof Framing	Stick
Exterior Walls	2x6

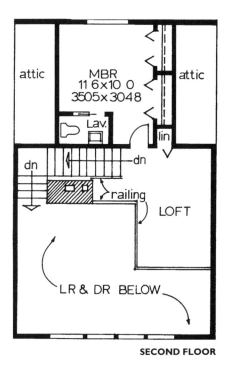

SECOND FLOOR

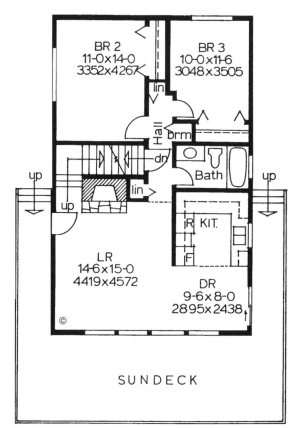

FIRST FLOOR

Design 99719

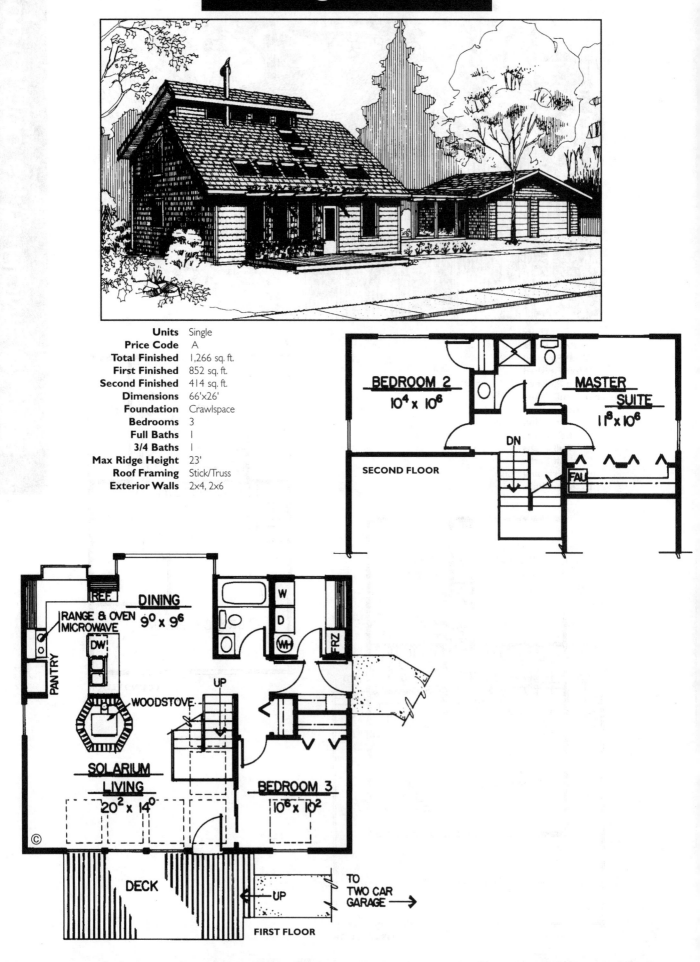

Units	Single
Price Code	A
Total Finished	1,266 sq. ft.
First Finished	852 sq. ft.
Second Finished	414 sq. ft.
Dimensions	66'x26'
Foundation	Crawlspace
Bedrooms	3
Full Baths	1
3/4 Baths	1
Max Ridge Height	23'
Roof Framing	Stick/Truss
Exterior Walls	2x4, 2x6

BEDROOM 2
10^4 x 10^6

MASTER SUITE
11^8 x 10^6

DN

FAU

SECOND FLOOR

REF.

DINING
9^0 x 9^6

RANGE & OVEN
MICROWAVE

W

D

FRZ

PANTRY

DW

WH

UP

WOODSTOVE

SOLARIUM

LIVING
20^2 x 14^0

BEDROOM 3
10^6 x 10^2

DECK

UP

TO TWO CAR GARAGE

FIRST FLOOR

Design 32505

PHOTOGRAPHY: COURTESY OF THE DESIGNER

Units	Single
Price Code	A
Total Finished	1,272 sq. ft.
First Finished	860 sq. ft.
Second Finished	412 sq. ft.
Dimensions	32'x36'
Foundation	Combo Crawlspace/Slab
Bedrooms	2
Full Baths	2
First Ceiling	8'
Second Ceiling	8'
Vaulted Ceiling	18'-22'
Max Ridge Height	25'
Roof Framing	Stick
Exterior Walls	2x4

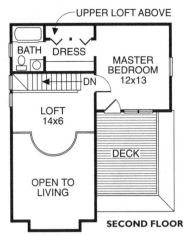

SECOND FLOOR

Please note: The photographed home may have been modified to suit homeowner preferences. If you order plans, have a builder or design professional check them against the photograph to confirm actual construction details.

FIRST FLOOR

Design 90048

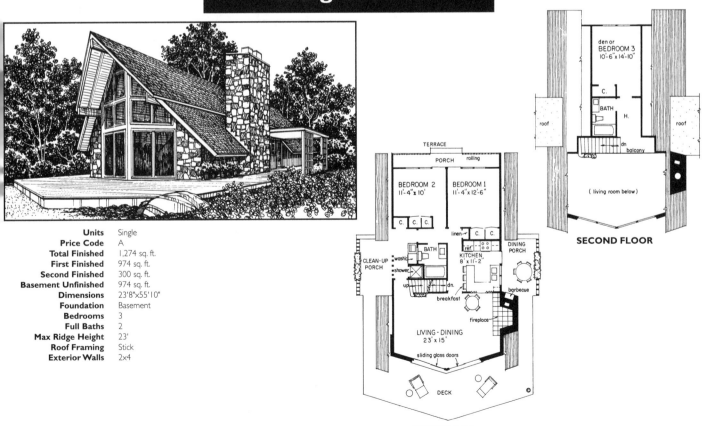

Units	Single
Price Code	A
Total Finished	1,274 sq. ft.
First Finished	974 sq. ft.
Second Finished	300 sq. ft.
Basement Unfinished	974 sq. ft.
Dimensions	23'8"x55'10"
Foundation	Basement
Bedrooms	3
Full Baths	2
Max Ridge Height	23'
Roof Framing	Stick
Exterior Walls	2x4

SECOND FLOOR

FIRST FLOOR

Units	Single
Price Code	A
Total Finished	1,278 sq. ft.
Main Finished	1,278 sq. ft.
Basement Unfinished	1,278 sq. ft.
Dimensions	40'x61'
Foundation	Basement
	Crawlspace
	Slab
Bedrooms	3
Full Baths	2
Main Ceiling	9'
Max Ridge Height	19'6"
Roof Framing	Stick
Exterior Walls	2x4

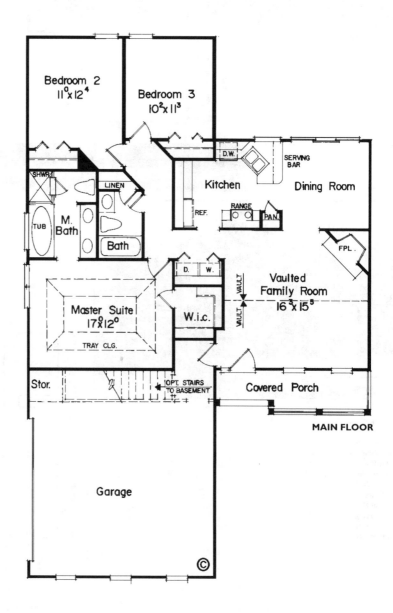

MAIN FLOOR

Design 98747

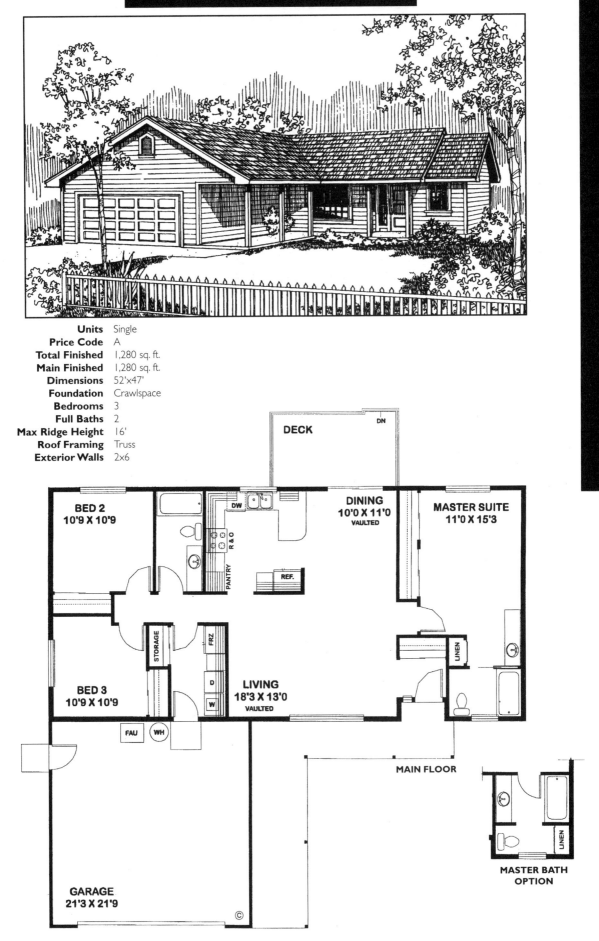

Units	Single
Price Code	A
Total Finished	1,280 sq. ft.
Main Finished	1,280 sq. ft.
Dimensions	52'x47'
Foundation	Crawlspace
Bedrooms	3
Full Baths	2
Max Ridge Height	16'
Roof Framing	Truss
Exterior Walls	2x6

DECK

DN

BED 2
10'9 X 10'9

DW

DINING
10'0 X 11'0
VAULTED

MASTER SUITE
11'0 X 15'3

PANTRY

R & O

REF.

LINEN

STORAGE

FRZ

BED 3
10'9 X 10'9

D

LIVING
18'3 X 13'0
VAULTED

W

FAU

WH

MAIN FLOOR

GARAGE
21'3 X 21'9

MASTER BATH
OPTION

LINEN

Design 65010

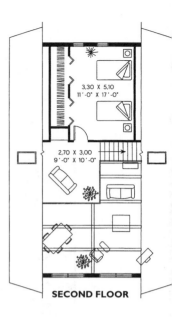

SECOND FLOOR

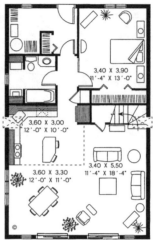

FIRST FLOOR

Units	Single
Price Code	A
Total Finished	1,280 sq. ft.
First Finished	945 sq. ft.
Second Finished	335 sq. ft.
Basement Unfinished	945 sq. ft.
Dimensions	24'8"x38'4"
Foundation	Basement
Bedrooms	2
Full Baths	1
First Ceiling	8'2"
Second Ceiling	8'2"
Max Ridge Height	25'
Roof Framing	Truss
Exterior Walls	2x6

Design 97237

CAD FILES AVAILABLE
For more information call
800-235-5700

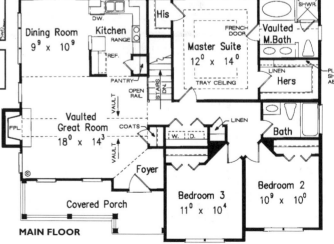

MAIN FLOOR

Units	Single
Price Code	A
Total Finished	1,283 sq. ft.
Main Finished	1,283 sq. ft.
Basement Unfinished	480 sq. ft.
Garage Unfinished	470 sq. ft.
Dimensions	45'4"x34'
Foundation	Basement
Bedrooms	3
Full Baths	2
Main Ceiling	9'
Max Ridge Height	25'
Roof Framing	Stick
Exterior Walls	2x4

Design 90004

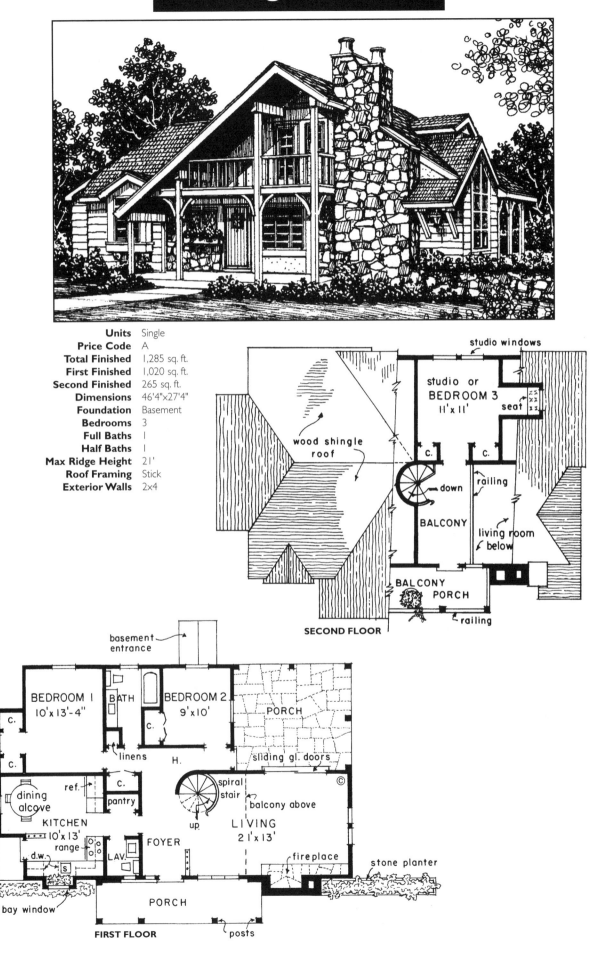

Units	Single
Price Code	A
Total Finished	1,285 sq. ft.
First Finished	1,020 sq. ft.
Second Finished	265 sq. ft.
Dimensions	46'4"x27'4"
Foundation	Basement
Bedrooms	3
Full Baths	1
Half Baths	1
Max Ridge Height	21'
Roof Framing	Stick
Exterior Walls	2x4

studio windows

studio or
BEDROOM 3
11'x11'

seat

wood shingle roof

c.

c.

down

railing

BALCONY

living room below

BALCONY PORCH

railing

SECOND FLOOR

basement entrance

BEDROOM 1
10'x13'-4"

BATH

BEDROOM 2
9'x10'

PORCH

c.

linens

H.

c.

sliding gl. doors

c.

ref.

c.

pantry

dining alcove

spiral stair

balcony above

©

KITCHEN
10'x13'

range

up

LIVING
21'x13'

d.w.

s

LAV.

FOYER

fireplace

stone planter

bay window

PORCH

posts

FIRST FLOOR

Units	Single
Price Code	A
Total Finished	1,287 sq. ft.
Main Finished	1,287 sq. ft.
Bonus Unfinished	312 sq. ft.
Basement Unfinished	1,287 sq. ft.
Garage Unfinished	516 sq. ft.
Dimensions	50'x55'10"
Foundation	Basement
	Crawlspace
Bedrooms	3
Full Baths	2
Max Ridge Height	24'
Roof Framing	Stick
Exterior Walls	2x4

CAD FILES AVAILABLE
For more information call
800-235-5700

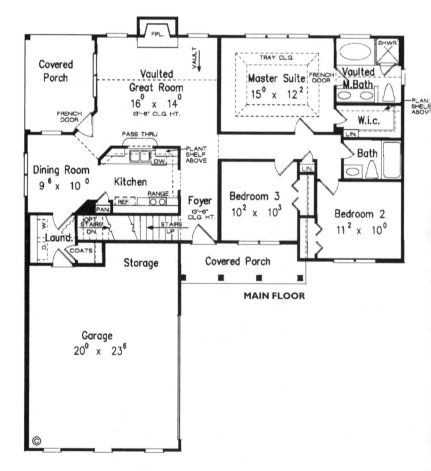

MAIN FLOOR

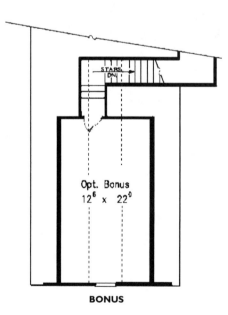

BONUS

Design 94263

Units	Single
Price Code	D
Total Finished	1,288 sq. ft.
Main Finished	1,288 sq. ft.
Dimensions	32'x60'
Foundation	Crawlspace
	Pier/Post
Bedrooms	2
Full Baths	2
Roof Framing	Truss
Exterior Walls	2x6

* Alternate foundation options available at an additional charge.
Please call 1-800-235-5700 for more information.

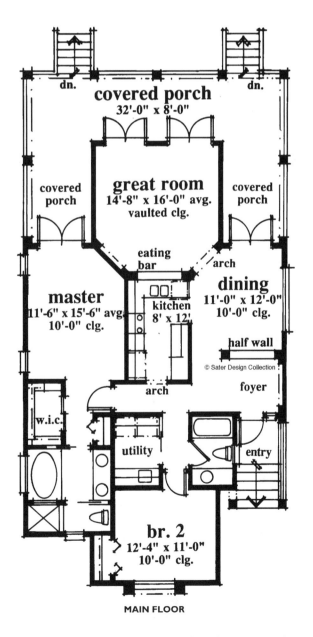

dn.

covered porch
32'-0" x 8'-0"

dn.

covered porch

great room
14'-8" x 16'-0" avg.
vaulted clg.

covered porch

eating bar

arch

master
11'-6" x 15'-6" avg.
10'-0" clg.

kitchen
8' x 12'

dining
11'-0" x 12'-0"
10'-0" clg.

half wall

© Sater Design Collection

arch

foyer

w.i.c.

utility

entry

br. 2
12'-4" x 11'-0"
10'-0" clg.

MAIN FLOOR

Units	Single
Price Code	A
Total Finished	1,289 sq. ft.
First Finished	768 sq. ft.
Second Finished	521 sq. ft.
Dimensions	24'x32'
Foundation	Slab
Bedrooms	2
Full Baths	1
Half Baths	1
Max Ridge Height	19'
Roof Framing	Stick
Exterior Walls	2x4

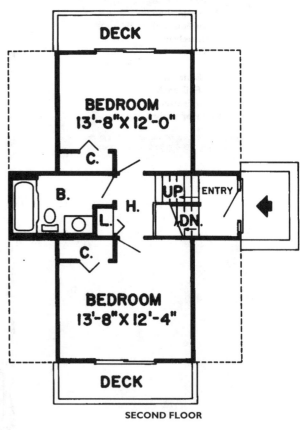

SECOND FLOOR

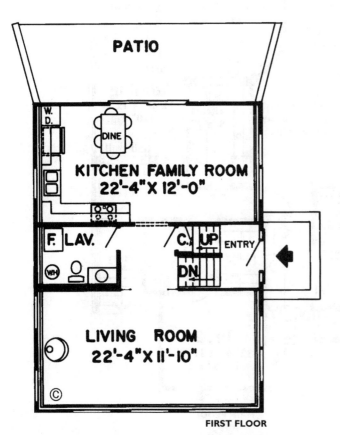

FIRST FLOOR

Design 97476

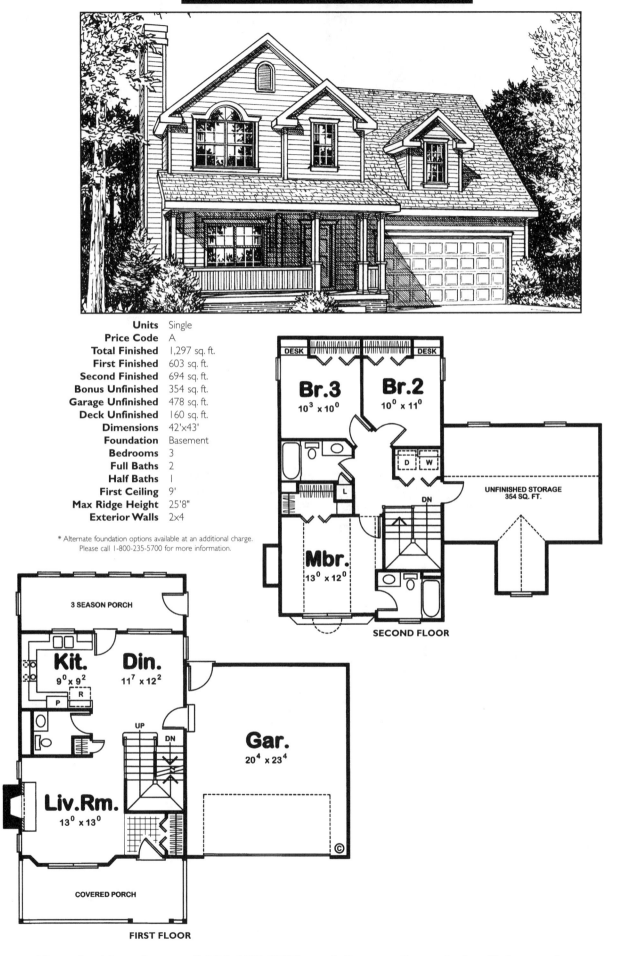

Units	Single
Price Code	A
Total Finished	1,297 sq. ft.
First Finished	603 sq. ft.
Second Finished	694 sq. ft.
Bonus Unfinished	354 sq. ft.
Garage Unfinished	478 sq. ft.
Deck Unfinished	160 sq. ft.
Dimensions	42'x43'
Foundation	Basement
Bedrooms	3
Full Baths	2
Half Baths	1
First Ceiling	9'
Max Ridge Height	25'8"
Exterior Walls	2x4

* Alternate foundation options available at an additional charge.
Please call 1-800-235-5700 for more information.

SECOND FLOOR

DESK DESK

Br.3
$10^3 \times 10^0$

Br.2
$10^0 \times 11^0$

D W

DN

UNFINISHED STORAGE
354 SQ. FT.

L

Mbr.
$13^0 \times 12^0$

FIRST FLOOR

3 SEASON PORCH

Kit.
$9^0 \times 9^2$

Din.
$11^7 \times 12^2$

P R

UP DN

Gar.
$20^4 \times 23^4$

Liv.Rm.
$13^0 \times 13^0$

COVERED PORCH

Design 84058

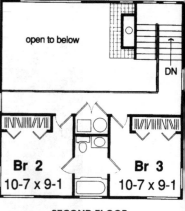

SECOND FLOOR

Br 2
10-7 x 9-1

Br 3
10-7 x 9-1

open to below

DN

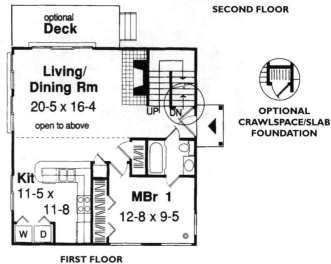

optional **Deck**

Living/
Dining Rm
20-5 x 16-4
open to above

UP DN

Kit
11-5 x
11-8

MBr 1
12-8 x 9-5

W D

FIRST FLOOR

**OPTIONAL
CRAWLSPACE/SLAB
FOUNDATION**

Units	Single
Price Code	A
Total Finished	1,298 sq. ft.
First Finished	779 sq. ft.
Second Finished	519 sq. ft.
Dimensions	27'6"x28'4"
Foundation	Basement
	Crawlspace
	Slab
Bedrooms	3
Full Baths	2
Max Ridge Height	23'
Roof Framing	Stick
Exterior Walls	2x4, 2x6

Design 24312

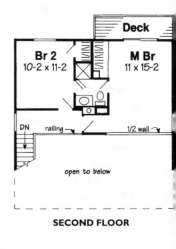

Deck

Br 2
10-2 x 11-2

M Br
11 x 15-2

DN railing   1/2 wall

open to below

SECOND FLOOR

Deck

storage

Br 1
10-2 x 11-2

D W
w.h.
furn.

Kit.
10-5 x
11-7

fireplace

line of floor above

Dining
10-5 x 16

Living
17-1 x 16

UP

Deck

bench

FIRST FLOOR

Units	Single
Price Code	A
Total Finished	1,298 sq. ft.
First Finished	813 sq. ft.
Second Finished	485 sq. ft.
Dimensions	28'x32'
Foundation	Crawlspace
Bedrooms	3
3/4 Baths	2
Max Ridge Height	25'
Roof Framing	Stick
Exterior Walls	2x4

Design 65134

Units	Single
Price Code	A
Total Finished	1,304 sq. ft.
First Finished	681 sq. ft.
Second Finished	623 sq. ft.
Garage Unfinished	260 sq. ft.
Dimensions	28'x40'
Foundation	Basement
Bedrooms	2
Full Baths	I
Half Baths	I
First Ceiling	8'
Second Ceiling	8'
Roof Framing	Truss
Exterior Walls	2x6

SECOND FLOOR

3,30 X 4,70
11'-0" X 15'-8"

3,00 X 3,30
10'-0" X 11'-0"

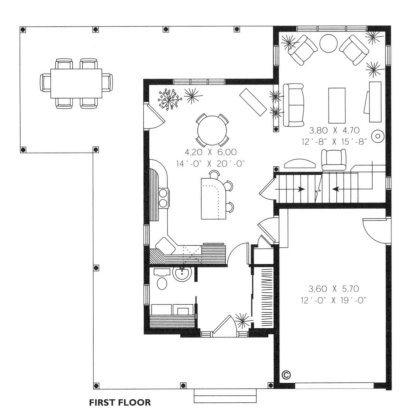

FIRST FLOOR

4,20 X 6,00
14'-0" X 20'-0"

3,80 X 4,70
12'-8" X 15'-8"

3,60 X 5,70
12'-0" X 19'-0"

PHOTOGRAPHY: JOHN EHRENCLOU

Units	Single
Price Code	A
Total Finished	1,307 sq. ft.
Main Finished	1,307 sq. ft.
Basement Unfinished	1,298 sq. ft.
Garage Unfinished	462 sq. ft.
Dimensions	50'x40'
Foundation	Basement
	Crawlspace
	Slab
Bedrooms	3
Full Baths	2
Main Ceiling	8'
Max Ridge Height	19'
Roof Framing	Stick
Exterior Walls	2x6

Crawl Space Access — W — F — Pantry

OPTIONAL CRAWLSPACE/SLAB FOUNDATION

Please note: The photographed home may have been modified to suit homeowner preferences. If you order plans, have a builder or design professional check them against the photograph to confirm actual construction details.

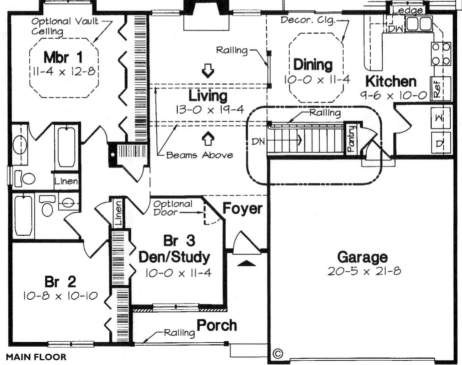

MAIN FLOOR

Design 65173

Units	Single
Price Code	A
Total Finished	1,311 sq. ft.
First Finished	713 sq. ft.
Second Finished	598 sq. ft.
Basement Unfinished	713 sq. ft.
Porch Unfinished	158 sq. ft.
Dimensions	30'8"x26'
Foundation	Basement
Bedrooms	2
Full Baths	1
3/4 Baths	1
First Ceiling	8'
Second Ceiling	8'
Max Ridge Height	28'4"
Roof Framing	Truss
Exterior Walls	2x6

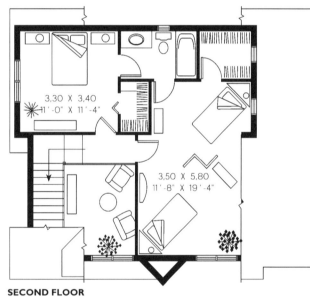

SECOND FLOOR

FIRST FLOOR

Units	Single
Price Code	A
Total Finished	1,311 sq. ft.
Main Finished	1,311 sq. ft.
Garage Unfinished	439 sq. ft.
Deck Unfinished	112 sq. ft.
Dimensions	34'8"x58'4"
Foundation	Crawlspace
	Slab
Bedrooms	3
Full Baths	2
Main Ceiling	9'
Max Ridge Height	22'6"
Exterior Walls	2x4

* Alternate foundation options available at an additional charge.
Please call 1-800-235-5700 for more information.

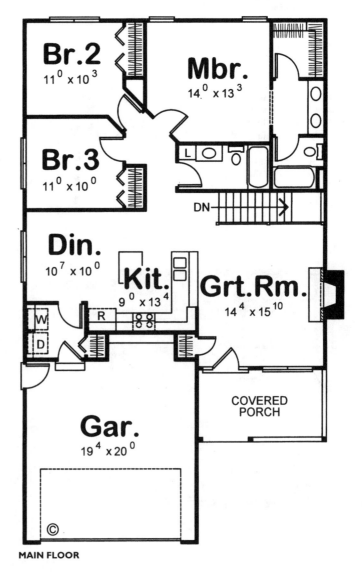

Br. 2 11^0 x 10^3

Mbr. 14^0 x 13^3

Br. 3 11^0 x 10^0

DN

Din. 10^7 x 10^0

Kit. 9^0 x 13^4

Grt.Rm. 14^4 x 15^{10}

W D R

Gar. 19^4 x 20^0

COVERED PORCH

MAIN FLOOR

Design 24700

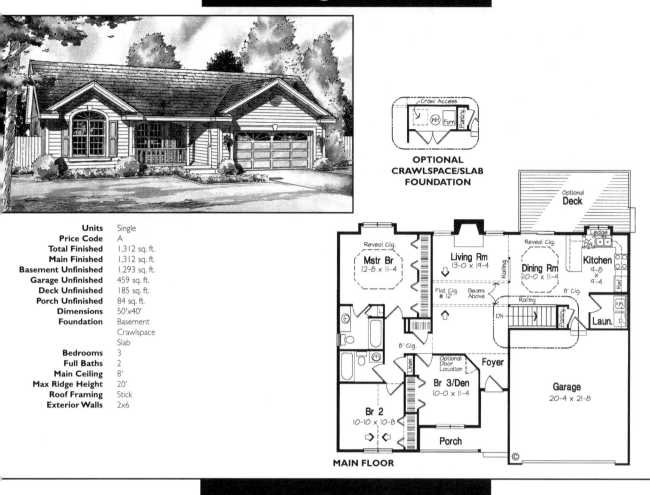

OPTIONAL
CRAWLSPACE/SLAB
FOUNDATION

Units	Single
Price Code	A
Total Finished	1,312 sq. ft.
Main Finished	1,312 sq. ft.
Basement Unfinished	1,293 sq. ft.
Garage Unfinished	459 sq. ft.
Deck Unfinished	185 sq. ft.
Porch Unfinished	84 sq. ft.
Dimensions	50'x40'
Foundation	Basement
	Crawlspace
	Slab
Bedrooms	3
Full Baths	2
Main Ceiling	8'
Max Ridge Height	20'
Roof Framing	Stick
Exterior Walls	2x6

MAIN FLOOR

Design 97731

Units	Single
Price Code	A
Total Finished	1,315 sq. ft.
Main Finished	1,315 sq. ft.
Basement Unfinished	1,315 sq. ft.
Garage Unfinished	488 sq. ft.
Porch Unfinished	75 sq. ft.
Dimensions	50'x54'8"
Foundation	Basement
Bedrooms	3
Full Baths	2
Main Ceiling	8'
Max Ridge Height	18'
Roof Framing	Truss
Exterior Walls	2x4

MAIN FLOOR

Design 65284

Units	Single
Price Code	A
Total Finished	1,324 sq. ft.
First Finished	737 sq. ft.
Second Finished	587 sq. ft.
Dimensions	26'x33'
Foundation	Basement
Bedrooms	1 or 2
Full Baths	1
Half Baths	1
First Ceiling	8'
Second Ceiling	8'
Max Ridge Height	34'9"
Roof Framing	Truss
Exterior Walls	2x6

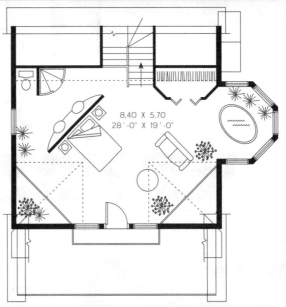

OPTIONAL SECOND FLOOR W/ ONE BEDROOM

FIRST FLOOR

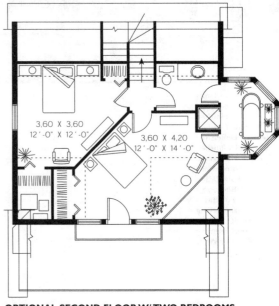

OPTIONAL SECOND FLOOR W/ TWO BEDROOMS

Design 34600

PHOTOGRAPHY: MICHELE EVANS CHRISTY

Units	Single
Price Code	A
Total Finished	1,328 sq. ft.
First Finished	1,013 sq. ft.
Second Finished	315 sq. ft.
Basement Unfinished	1,013 sq. ft.
Dimensions	36'x36'
Foundation	Basement
	Crawlspace
	Slab
Bedrooms	3
Full Baths	2
First Ceiling	8'
Second Ceiling	7'6"
Max Ridge Height	23'6"
Roof Framing	Stick
Exterior Walls	2x4, 2x6

FURN   WH

Crawl Space Access

OPTIONAL CRAWLSPACE/SLAB FOUNDATION

DN

Flat Clg @ 7'-6"
Master Br
12-0 x 13-4

SECOND FLOOR

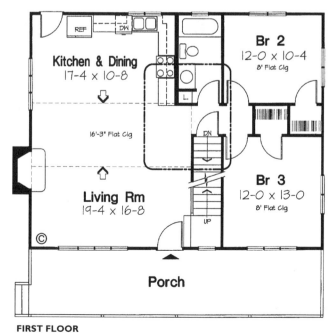

REF   DW

Kitchen & Dining
17-4 x 10-8

16'-3" Flat Clg

L.

DN

Br 2
12-0 x 10-4
8' Flat Clg

Br 3
12-0 x 13-0
8' Flat Clg

Living Rm
19-4 x 16-8

UP

©

Porch

FIRST FLOOR

Please note: The photographed home may have been modified to suit homeowner preferences. If you order plans, have a builder or design professional check them against the photograph to confirm actual construction details.

Design 24306

Units	Single
Price Code	A
Total Finished	1,330 sq. ft.
First Finished	841 sq. ft.
Second Finished	489 sq. ft.
Dimensions	37'x30'
Foundation	Crawlspace
Bedrooms	3
Full Baths	2
Max Ridge Height	26'
Roof Framing	Stick
Exterior Walls	2x6

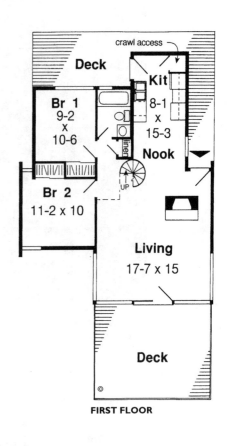

FIRST FLOOR

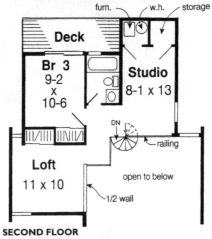

SECOND FLOOR

Design 90669

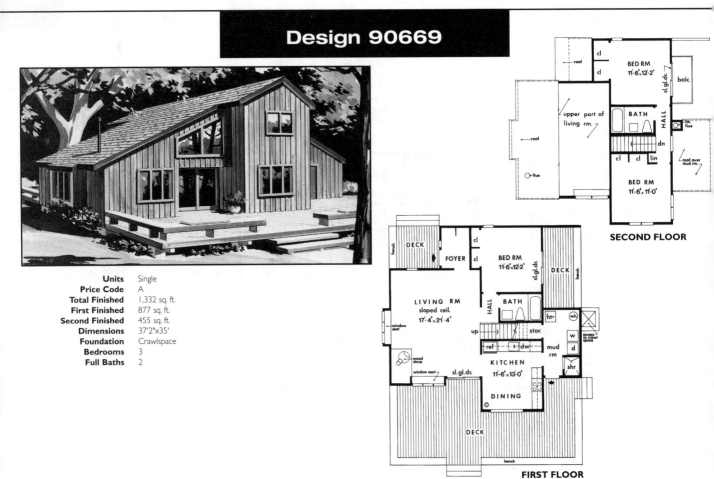

Units	Single
Price Code	A
Total Finished	1,332 sq. ft.
First Finished	877 sq. ft.
Second Finished	455 sq. ft.
Dimensions	37'2"x35'
Foundation	Crawlspace
Bedrooms	3
Full Baths	2

SECOND FLOOR

FIRST FLOOR

Design 93453

Units	Single
Price Code	A
Total Finished	1,333 sq. ft.
Main Finished	1,333 sq. ft.
Garage Unfinished	520 sq. ft.
Dimensions	55'6"x64'3"
Foundation	Crawlspace
	Slab
Bedrooms	3
Full Baths	2
Main Ceiling	8'
Max Ridge Height	19'5"
Roof Framing	Stick
Exterior Walls	2x4

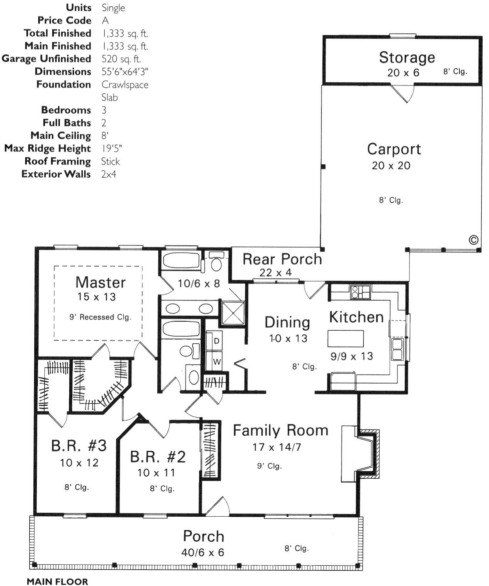

Storage
20 x 6   8' Clg.

Carport
20 x 20

8' Clg.

Rear Porch
22 x 4

Master
15 x 13

9' Recessed Clg.

10/6 x 8

Dining
10 x 13

8' Clg.

Kitchen
9/9 x 13

D
W

B.R. #3
10 x 12

8' Clg.

B.R. #2
10 x 11

8' Clg.

Family Room
17 x 14/7

9' Clg.

Porch
40/6 x 6   8' Clg.

MAIN FLOOR

Design 26113

Units	Single
Price Code	A
Total Finished	1,338 sq. ft.
First Finished	846 sq. ft.
Second Finished	492 sq. ft.
Basement Unfinished	846 sq. ft.
Garage Unfinished	540 sq. ft.
Deck Unfinished	423 sq. ft.
Dimensions	50'x40'
Foundation	Basement
Bedrooms	3
Full Baths	1
3/4 Baths	1
Max Ridge Height	30'
Roof Framing	Stick
Exterior Walls	2x6

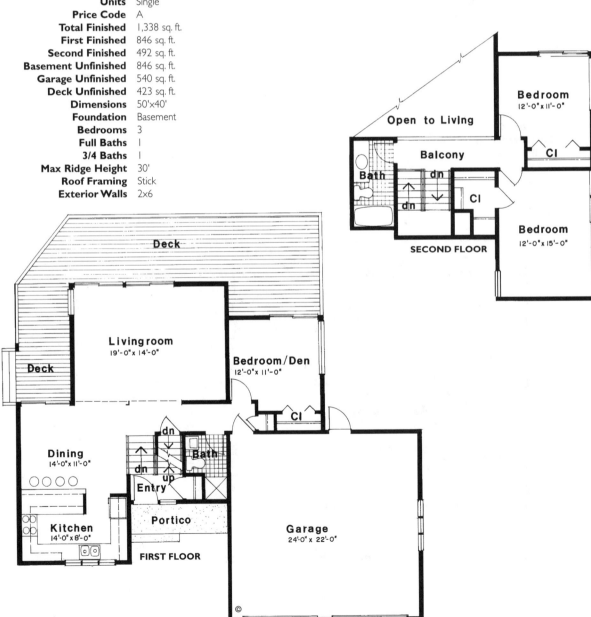

Design 26111

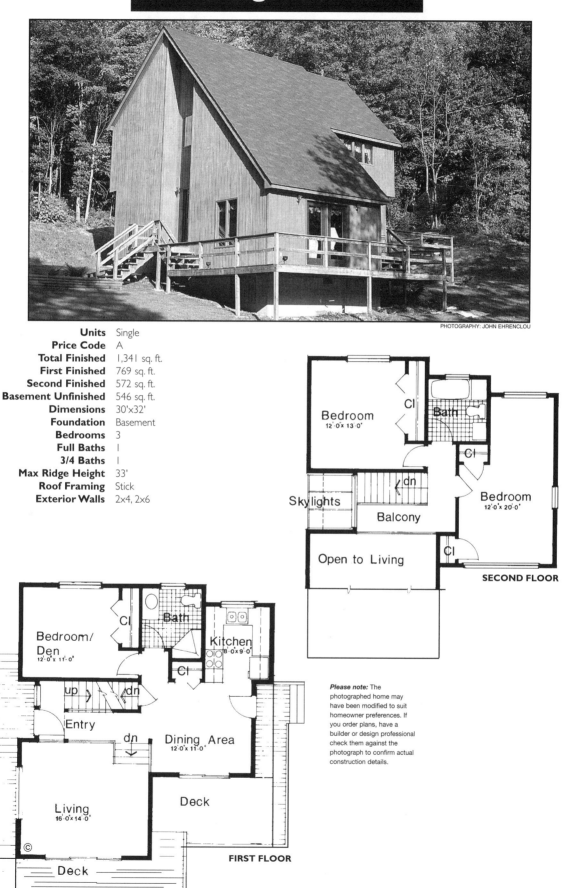

PHOTOGRAPHY: JOHN EHRENCLOU

Units	Single
Price Code	A
Total Finished	1,341 sq. ft.
First Finished	769 sq. ft.
Second Finished	572 sq. ft.
Basement Unfinished	546 sq. ft.
Dimensions	30'x32'
Foundation	Basement
Bedrooms	3
Full Baths	1
3/4 Baths	1
Max Ridge Height	33'
Roof Framing	Stick
Exterior Walls	2x4, 2x6

Bedroom
12'-0" x 13'-0"

Cl

Bath

Cl

Bedroom
12'-0" x 20'-0"

Skylights

dn

Balcony

Cl

Open to Living

SECOND FLOOR

Bedroom/
Den
12'-0" x 11'-0"

Cl

Bath

Kitchen
8'-0" x 9'-0"

Cl

up

dn

Entry

dn

Dining Area
12'-0" x 11'-0"

Living
16'-0" x 14'-0"

Deck

©

Deck

FIRST FLOOR

Please note: The photographed home may have been modified to suit homeowner preferences. If you order plans, have a builder or design professional check them against the photograph to confirm actual construction details.

Units	Single
Price Code	A
Total Finished	1,345 sq. ft.
Main Finished	1,325 sq. ft.
Lower Finished	20 sq. ft.
Basement Unfinished	556 sq. ft.
Garage Unfinished	724 sq. ft.
Deck Unfinished	157 sq. ft.
Porch Unfinished	216 sq. ft.
Dimensions	52'x42'
Foundation	Basement
Bedrooms	3
Full Baths	2
Main Ceiling	8'
Max Ridge Height	19'
Roof Framing	Stick
Exterior Walls	2x4

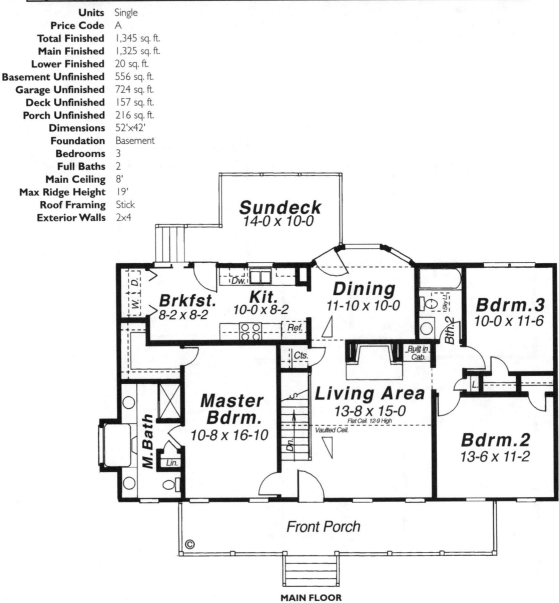

MAIN FLOOR

Design 91342

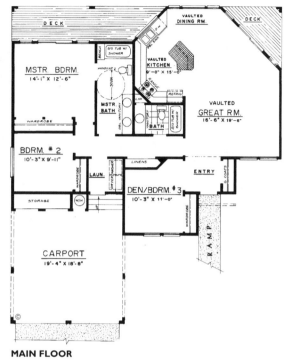

MAIN FLOOR

Units	Single
Price Code	A
Total Finished	1,345 sq. ft.
Main Finished	1,345 sq. ft.
Dimensions	47'8"x56'
Foundation	Crawlspace
	Slab
Bedrooms	3
Full Baths	2
Max Ridge Height	19"
Roof Framing	Stick/Truss
Exterior Walls	2x4

Design 24402

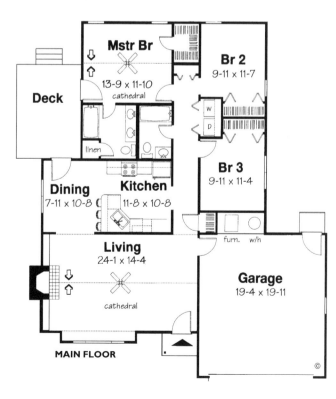

MAIN FLOOR

Units	Single
Price Code	A
Total Finished	1,346 sq. ft.
Main Finished	1,346 sq. ft.
Garage Unfinished	449 sq. ft.
Dimensions	46'1"x53'1"
Foundation	Crawlspace
	Slab
Bedrooms	3
Full Baths	2
Main Ceiling	9'
Max Ridge Height	21'
Roof Framing	Stick
Exterior Walls	2x4

Design 94821

Units	Single
Price Code	B
Total Finished	1,352 sq. ft.
First Finished	1,050 sq. ft.
Second Finished	302 sq. ft.
Basement Unfinished	1,050 sq. ft.
Dimensions	28'x37'6"
Foundation	Basement
	Crawlspace
Bedrooms	3
Full Baths	2
Max Ridge Height	22'
Roof Framing	Stick
Exterior Walls	2x4

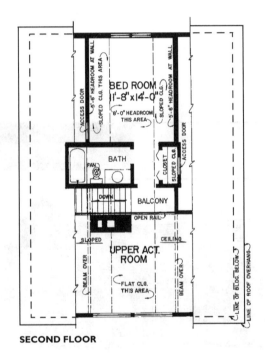

SECOND FLOOR

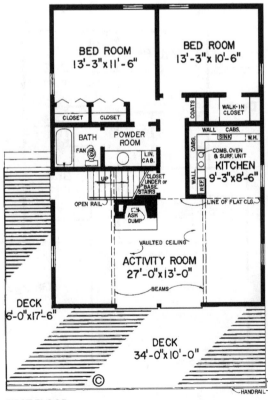

FIRST FLOOR

Design 91026

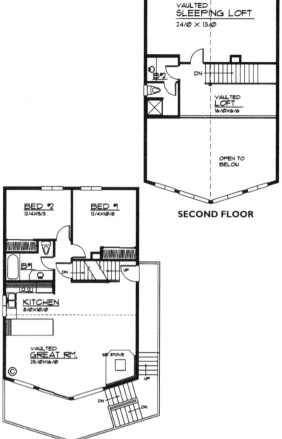

VAULTED
SLEEPING LOFT
24/0 X 13/0

DN

VAULTED
LOFT
16/0X8/6

OPEN TO
BELOW

SECOND FLOOR

Units	Single
Price Code	A
Total Finished	1,354 sq. ft.
First Finished	988 sq. ft.
Second Finished	366 sq. ft.
Basement Unfinished	742 sq. ft.
Garage Unfinished	283 sq. ft.
Dimensions	26'x48'
Foundation	Basement
Bedrooms	3
Full Baths	1
3/4 Baths	1
First Ceiling	8'
Vaulted Ceiling	13'6"
Max Ridge Height	32'
Roof Framing	Stick
Exterior Walls	2x6

BED #2
12/4X9/3

BED #1
12/4X10/8

DN

KITCHEN
8/0X10/0

VAULTED
GREAT RM.
25/0X16/0

UP STOVE

UP

DN   DN

FIRST FLOOR

Design 50035

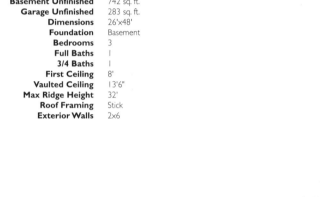

Bath

Bedroom
12'3" x 12'2"

Bedroom
12'6" x 12'2"

SECOND FLOOR

Units	Single
Price Code	A
Total Finished	1,354 sq. ft.
First Finished	873 sq. ft.
Second Finished	481 sq. ft.
Basement Unfinished	873 sq. ft.
Garage Unfinished	253 sq. ft.
Porch Unfinished	95 sq. ft.
Dimensions	51'6"x31'8"
Foundation	Basement
Bedrooms	3
Full Baths	2
First Ceiling	8'
Second Ceiling	8'
Max Ridge Height	23'
Roof Framing	Stick
Exterior Walls	2x4

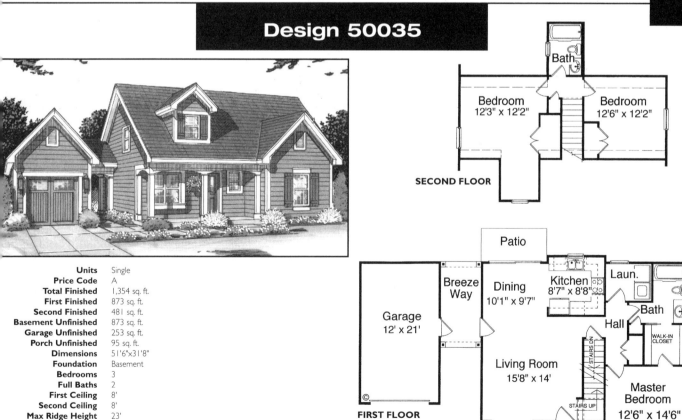

Patio

Breeze
Way

Dining
10'1" x 9'7"

Kitchen
8'7" x 8'8"

Laun.

Garage
12' x 21'

Bath

Hall

WALK-IN
CLOSET

Living Room
15'8" x 14'

STAIRS DN

STAIRS UP

Master
Bedroom
12'6" x 14'6"

FIRST FLOOR

Porch

Design 97272

Units	Single
Price Code	A
Total Finished	1,354 sq. ft.
Main Finished	1,354 sq. ft.
Basement Unfinished	1,390 sq. ft.
Garage Unfinished	434 sq. ft.
Dimensions	47'x46'
Foundation	Basement
	Crawlspace
Bedrooms	3
Full Baths	2
Main Ceiling	9'
Max Ridge Height	24'9"
Roof Framing	Stick
Exterior Walls	2x4

CAD FILES AVAILABLE
For more information call
800-235-5700

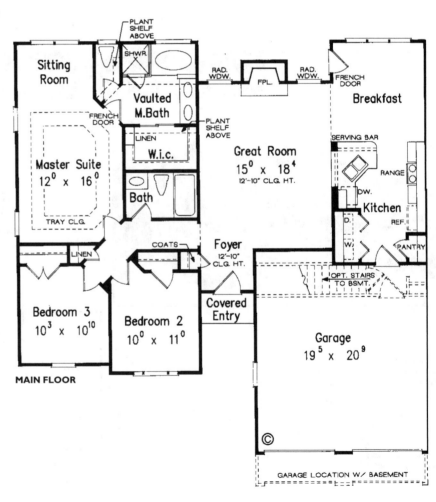

MAIN FLOOR

Design 10519

Units	Single
Price Code	A
Total Finished	1,355 sq. ft.
First Finished	872 sq. ft.
Second Finished	483 sq. ft.
Dimensions	34'x26'
Foundation	Basement
Bedrooms	3
Full Baths	2
Half Baths	1
Max Ridge Height	23'
Roof Framing	Stick
Exterior Walls	2x6

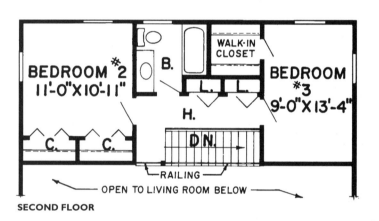

SECOND FLOOR

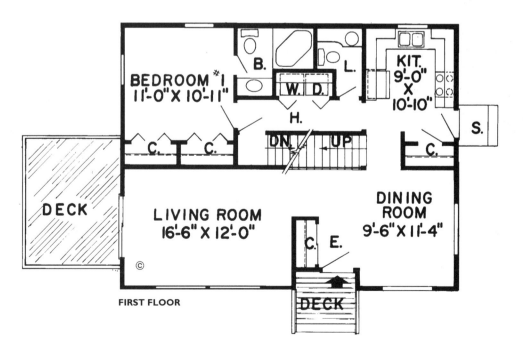

FIRST FLOOR

Design 65015

SECOND FLOOR

Units	Single
Price Code	A
Total Finished	1,360 sq. ft.
First Finished	858 sq. ft.
Second Finished	502 sq. ft.
Basement Unfinished	858 sq. ft.
Dimensions	35'x29'8"
Foundation	Basement
Bedrooms	3
Full Baths	2
First Ceiling	8'
Second Ceiling	8'
Max Ridge Height	26'6"
Roof Framing	Truss
Exterior Walls	2x6

FIRST FLOOR

Design 90847

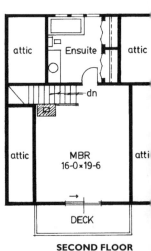

SECOND FLOOR

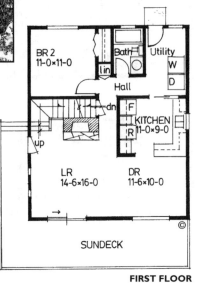

Units	Single
Price Code	A
Total Finished	1,362 sq. ft.
First Finished	864 sq. ft.
Second Finished	498 sq. ft.
Basement Unfinished	864 sq. ft.
Deck Unfinished	340 sq. ft.
Dimensions	35'x40'
Foundation	Basement
Bedrooms	2
Full Baths	2
Roof Framing	Stick
Exterior Walls	2x6

FIRST FLOOR

Design 99241

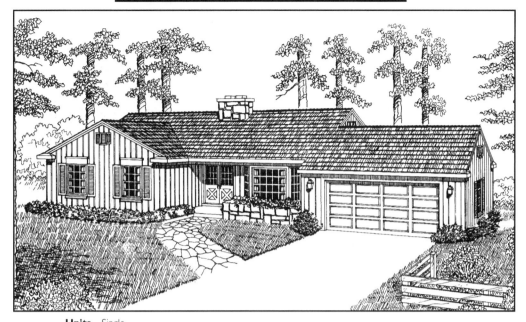

Units	Single
Price Code	A
Total Finished	1,366 sq. ft.
Main Finished	1,366 sq. ft.
Basement Unfinished	1,241 sq. ft.
Garage Unfinished	484 sq. ft.
Dimensions	65'x37'4"
Foundation	Basement
Bedrooms	3
Full Baths	2
Max Ridge Height	18'
Roof Framing	Truss
Exterior Walls	2x4

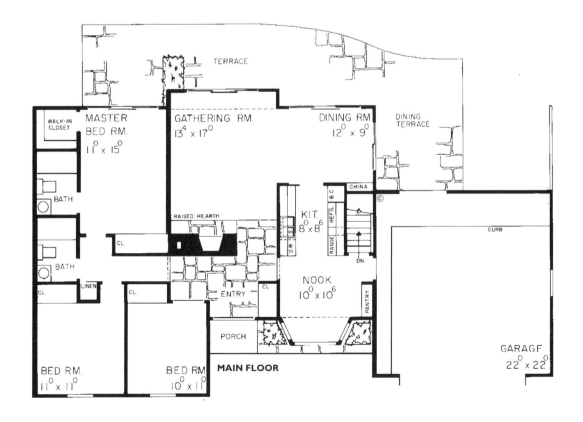

Units	Single
Price Code	A
Total Finished	1,368 sq. ft.
Main Finished	1,368 sq. ft.
Basement Unfinished	1,368 sq. ft.
Garage Unfinished	412 sq. ft.
Dimensions	48'4"x48'4"
Foundation	Basement
Bedrooms	3
Full Baths	2
Max Ridge Height	18'
Roof Framing	Truss
Exterior Walls	2x4

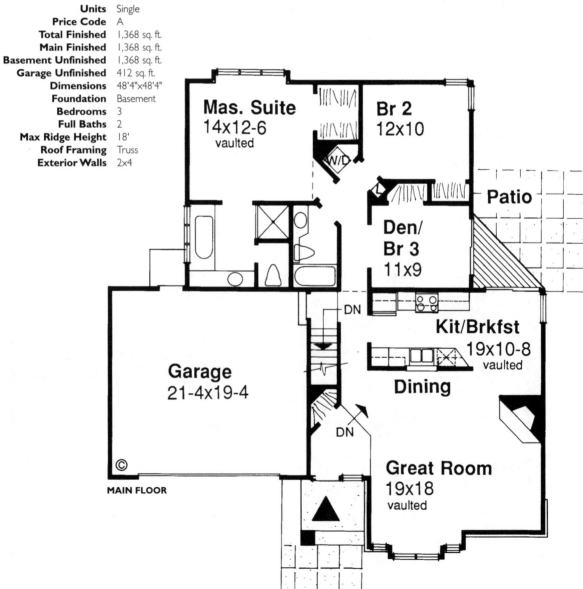

Mas. Suite
14x12-6
vaulted

Br 2
12x10

W/D

Patio

Den/
Br 3
11x9

DN

Garage
21-4x19-4

Kit/Brkfst
19x10-8
vaulted

Dining

DN

Great Room
19x18
vaulted

MAIN FLOOR

Design 94311

Units	Single
Price Code	A
Total Finished	1,370 sq. ft.
First Finished	810 sq. ft.
Second Finished	560 sq. ft.
Dimensions	30'x52'
Foundation	Crawlspace
Bedrooms	3
Full Baths	1
3/4 Baths	1
First Ceiling	8'
Second Ceiling	8'
Roof Framing	Truss
Exterior Walls	2x6

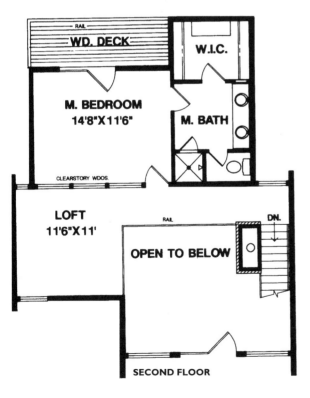

WD. DECK

RAIL

M. BEDROOM
14'8"X11'6"

W.I.C.

M. BATH

CLEARSTORY WDOS.

LOFT
11'6"X11'

RAIL

DN.

OPEN TO BELOW

SECOND FLOOR

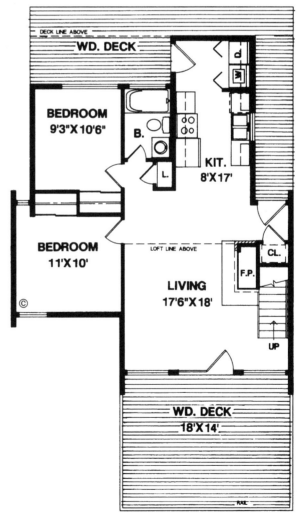

DECK LINE ABOVE

WD. DECK

BEDROOM
9'3"X10'6"

B.

KIT.
8'X17'

BEDROOM
11'X10'

LOFT LINE ABOVE

CL.

F.P.

LIVING
17'6"X18'

UP

WD. DECK
18'X14'

RAIL

FIRST FLOOR

Design 62115

Units	Single
Price Code	A
Total Finished	1,374 sq. ft.
First Finished	1,070 sq. ft.
Second Finished	304 sq. ft.
Dimensions	40'4"x41'6"
Foundation	Crawlspace
	Slab
Bedrooms	4
Full Baths	2
First Ceiling	8'
Second Ceiling	8'
Max Ridge Height	23'
Exterior Walls	2x6

Hot New Design

SECOND FLOOR

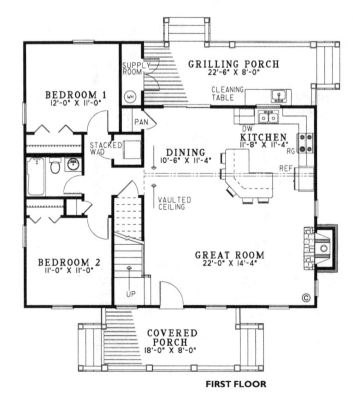

FIRST FLOOR

Design 94304

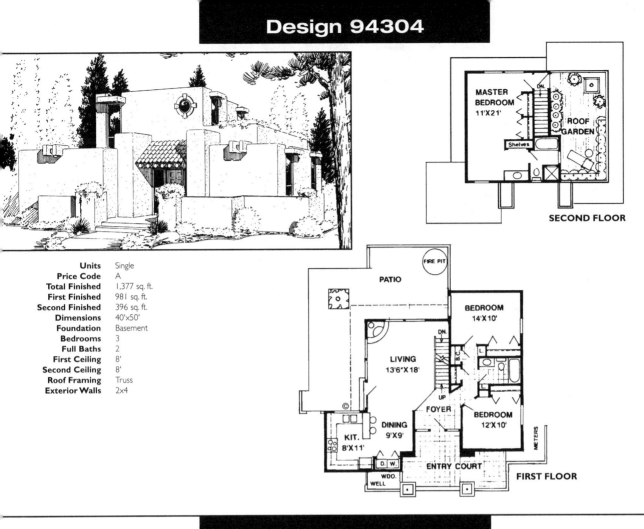

SECOND FLOOR

MASTER BEDROOM 11'X21'

ROOF GARDEN

Shelves

PATIO

FIRE PIT

BEDROOM 14'X10'

LIVING 13'6"X18'

DINING 9'X9'

KIT. 8'X11'

FOYER

UP

BEDROOM 12'X10'

ENTRY COURT

WDO. WELL

METERS

FIRST FLOOR

Units	Single
Price Code	A
Total Finished	1,377 sq. ft.
First Finished	981 sq. ft.
Second Finished	396 sq. ft.
Dimensions	40'x50'
Foundation	Basement
Bedrooms	3
Full Baths	2
First Ceiling	8'
Second Ceiling	8'
Roof Framing	Truss
Exterior Walls	2x4

Design 98709

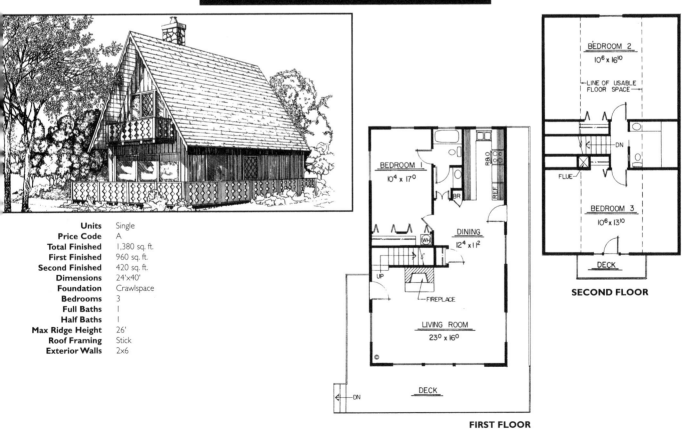

BEDROOM 2 10⁶ x 16¹⁰

LINE OF USABLE FLOOR SPACE

FLUE

BEDROOM 3 10⁶ x 13¹⁰

DN

DECK

SECOND FLOOR

BEDROOM 1 10⁴ x 17⁰

DINING 12⁴ x 11²

WH

REF

UP

FIREPLACE

LIVING ROOM 23⁰ x 16⁰

DECK

DN

FIRST FLOOR

Units	Single
Price Code	A
Total Finished	1,380 sq. ft.
First Finished	960 sq. ft.
Second Finished	420 sq. ft.
Dimensions	24'x40'
Foundation	Crawlspace
Bedrooms	3
Full Baths	1
Half Baths	1
Max Ridge Height	26'
Roof Framing	Stick
Exterior Walls	2x6

Units	Single
Price Code	A
Total Finished	1,393 sq. ft.
Main Finished	1,393 sq. ft.
Garage Unfinished	528 sq. ft.
Porch Unfinished	97 sq. ft.
Dimensions	42'x42'
Foundation	Crawlspace
	Slab
Bedrooms	3
Full Baths	2
Main Ceiling	9'
Max Ridge Height	26'6"
Roof Framing	Stick
Exterior Walls	2x4

GARAGE
22x24

Drive

Patio

Stoop

DINING
10x13

Desk

9' Clg.

KITCHEN
10x13

MASTER
16x13
9' Clg.

BR.#2
12x10
9' Clg.

FAMILY ROOM
16x15
10' Clg.

BR.#3
12x10

PORCH
5x16

MAIN FLOOR

Design 62116

Hot New Design

Units	Single
Price Code	A
Total Finished	1,397 sq. ft.
First Finished	890 sq. ft.
Second Finished	507 sq. ft.
Dimensions	31'8"x38'4"
Foundation	Crawlspace
	Slab
Bedrooms	3
Full Baths	2
First Ceiling	8'
Second Ceiling	8'
Max Ridge Height	21'6"
Exterior Walls	2x6

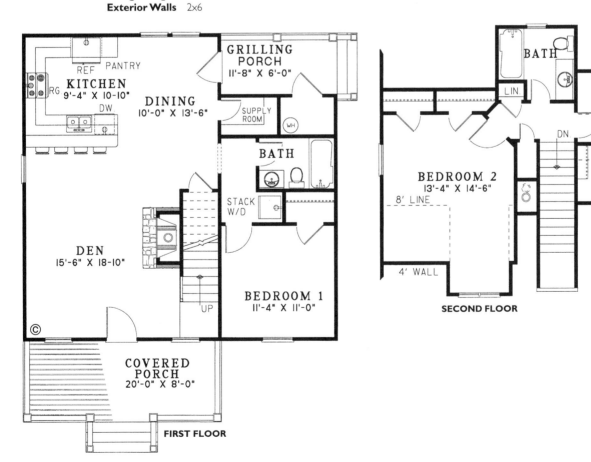

FIRST FLOOR

KITCHEN 9'-4" X 10'-10"
REF   PANTRY
RG
DW
DINING 10'-0" X 13'-6"
GRILLING PORCH 11'-8" X 6'-0"
SUPPLY ROOM
WH
BATH
STACK W/D
DEN 15'-6" X 18-10"
UP
BEDROOM 1 11'-4" X 11'-0"
COVERED PORCH 20'-0" X 8'-0"

SECOND FLOOR

BATH
LIN
5' WALL
8' LINE
DN
BEDROOM 3 11'-4" X 12'-8"
5' WALL
BEDROOM 2 13'-4" X 14'-6"
8' LINE
4' WALL

SECOND FLOOR

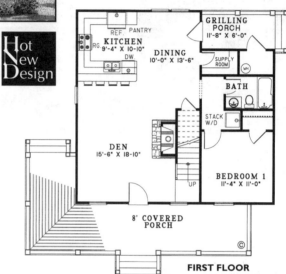

FIRST FLOOR

Hot New Design

Units	Single
Price Code	A
Total Finished	1,397 sq. ft.
First Finished	890 sq. ft.
Second Finished	507 sq. ft.
Dimensions	39'8"x38'4"
Foundation	Crawlspace
	Slab
Bedrooms	3
Full Baths	2
First Ceiling	8'
Second Ceiling	8'
Max Ridge Height	21'
Exterior Walls	2x6

FIRST FLOOR

SECOND FLOOR

Units	Single
Price Code	A
Total Finished	1,397 sq. ft.
First Finished	696 sq. ft.
Second Finished	701 sq. ft.
Basement Unfinished	696 sq. ft.
Porch Unfinished	210 sq. ft.
Dimensions	22'8"x36'
Foundation	Basement
Bedrooms	3
Full Baths	1
Half Baths	1
First Ceiling	9'
Second Ceiling	8'
Max Ridge Height	38'8"
Roof Framing	Truss
Exterior Walls	2x6

Design 62118

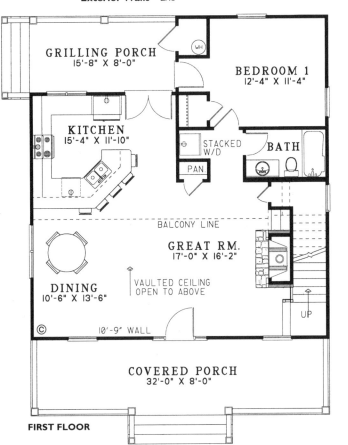

Units	Single
Price Code	A
Total Finished	1,400 sq. ft.
First Finished	948 sq. ft.
Second Finished	452 sq. ft.
Dimensions	32'x42'
Foundation	Crawlspace
	Slab
Bedrooms	2
Full Baths	2
First Ceiling	8'
Second Ceiling	8'
Max Ridge Height	23'6"
Exterior Walls	2x6

Hot New Design

FIRST FLOOR

GRILLING PORCH
15'-8" X 8'-0"

WH

BEDROOM 1
12'-4" X 11'-4"

KITCHEN
15'-4" X 11'-10"

STACKED W/D

BATH

PAN.

BALCONY LINE

GREAT RM.
17'-0" X 16'-2"

DINING
10'-6" X 13'-6"

VAULTED CEILING
OPEN TO ABOVE

UP

10'-9" WALL

COVERED PORCH
32'-0" X 8'-0"

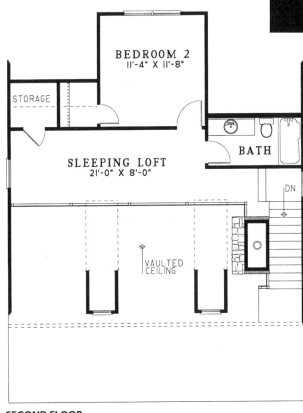

SECOND FLOOR

BEDROOM 2
11'-4" X 11'-8"

STORAGE

SLEEPING LOFT
21'-0" X 8'-0"

BATH

VAULTED CEILING

DN.

Units	Single
Price Code	A
Total Finished	1,415 sq. ft.
First Finished	1,007 sq. ft.
Second Finished	408 sq. ft.
Basement Unfinished	1,007 sq. ft.
Porch Unfinished	300 sq. ft.
Dimensions	38'4"x36'
Foundation	Basement
	Crawlspace
	Slab
Bedrooms	3
Full Baths	2
First Ceiling	8'
Second Ceiling	8'
Max Ridge Height	24'6"
Roof Framing	Stick
Exterior Walls	2x4, 2x6

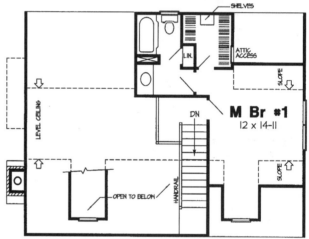

SECOND FLOOR

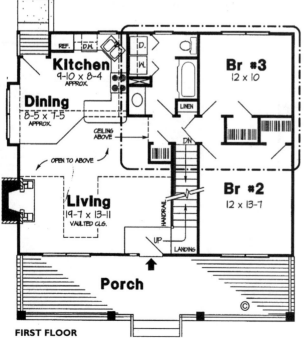

FIRST FLOOR

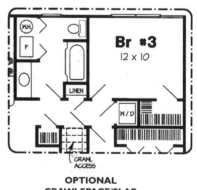

OPTIONAL CRAWLSPACE/SLAB FOUNDATION

Design 65150

Units	Single
Price Code	A
Total Finished	1,417 sq. ft.
First Finished	702 sq. ft.
Second Finished	715 sq. ft.
Garage Unfinished	279 sq. ft.
Porch Unfinished	32 sq. ft.
Dimensions	38'x28'
Foundation	Basement
Bedrooms	3
Full Baths	1
Half Baths	1
First Ceiling	8'
Second Ceiling	8'
Max Ridge Height	26'2"
Roof Framing	Truss
Exterior Walls	2x6

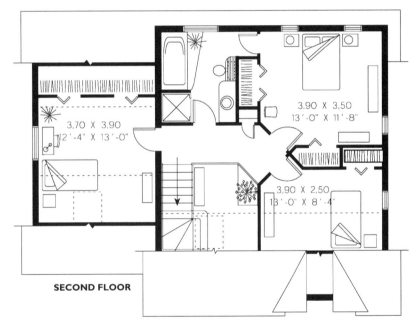

3.70 X 3.90
12'-4" X 13'-0"

3.90 X 3.50
13'-0" X 11'-8"

3.90 X 2.50
13'-0" X 8'-4"

SECOND FLOOR

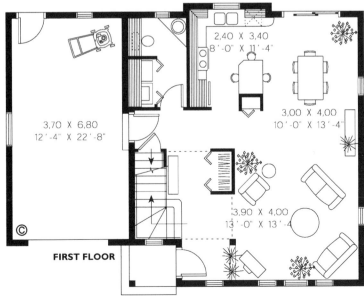

3.70 X 6,80
12'-4" X 22'-8"

2,40 X 3,40
8'-0" X 11'-4"

3,00 X 4,00
10'-0" X 13'-4"

3,90 X 4,00
13'-0" X 13'-4"

FIRST FLOOR

Design 10224

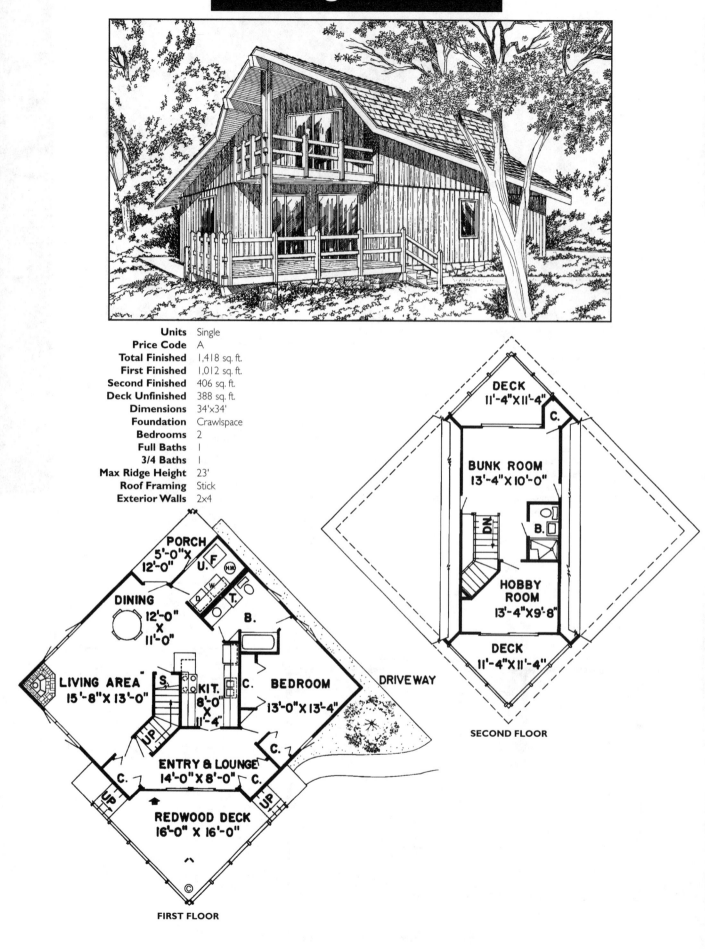

Units	Single
Price Code	A
Total Finished	1,418 sq. ft.
First Finished	1,012 sq. ft.
Second Finished	406 sq. ft.
Deck Unfinished	388 sq. ft.
Dimensions	34'x34'
Foundation	Crawlspace
Bedrooms	2
Full Baths	1
3/4 Baths	1
Max Ridge Height	23'
Roof Framing	Stick
Exterior Walls	2x4

DECK
11'-4" X 11'-4"

BUNK ROOM
13'-4" X 10'-0"

HOBBY ROOM
13'-4" X 9'-8"

DECK
11'-4" X 11'-4"

DN
B.

SECOND FLOOR

PORCH
5'-0" X 12'-0"

U. F
T.

DINING
12'-0" X 11'-0"

B.

LIVING AREA
15'-8" X 13'-0"

S.

KIT.
8'-0" X 11'-4"

C.

BEDROOM
13'-0" X 13'-4"

UP

ENTRY & LOUNGE
14'-0" X 8'-0"

C.

C.

DRIVEWAY

UP

UP

REDWOOD DECK
16'-0" X 16'-0"

FIRST FLOOR

Design 91545

Units	Single
Price Code	A
Total Finished	1,420 sq. ft.
Main Finished	1,420 sq. ft.
Dimensions	40'x58'
Foundation	Crawlspace
Bedrooms	2
Full Baths	2
Max Ridge Height	20'
Roof Framing	Truss
Exterior Walls	2x6

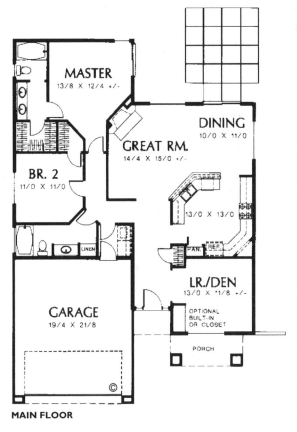

MASTER
13/8 X 12/4 +/-

GREAT RM.
14/4 X 15/0 +/-

DINING
10/0 X 11/0

BR. 2
11/0 X 11/0

13/0 X 13/0

LINEN

LR./DEN
13/0 X 11/8 +/-

GARAGE
19/4 X 21/8

PAN. REF.

OPTIONAL
BUILT-IN
OR CLOSET

PORCH

MAIN FLOOR

Design 99303

Units	Single
Price Code	A
Total Finished	1,421 sq. ft.
Main Finished	1,421 sq. ft.
Garage Unfinished	400 sq. ft.
Dimensions	42'8"x58'4"
Foundation	Basement
Bedrooms	2
Full Baths	2
Max Ridge Height	22'
Roof Framing	Stick/Truss
Exterior Walls	2x4

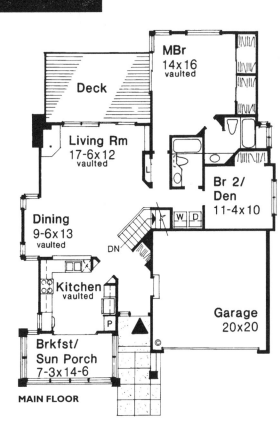

MBr
14x16
vaulted

Deck

Living Rm
17-6x12
vaulted

Br 2/
Den
11-4x10

Dining
9-6x13
vaulted

DN

W D

Kitchen
vaulted

P

Garage
20x20

Brkfst/
Sun Porch
7-3x14-6

MAIN FLOOR

Design 62119

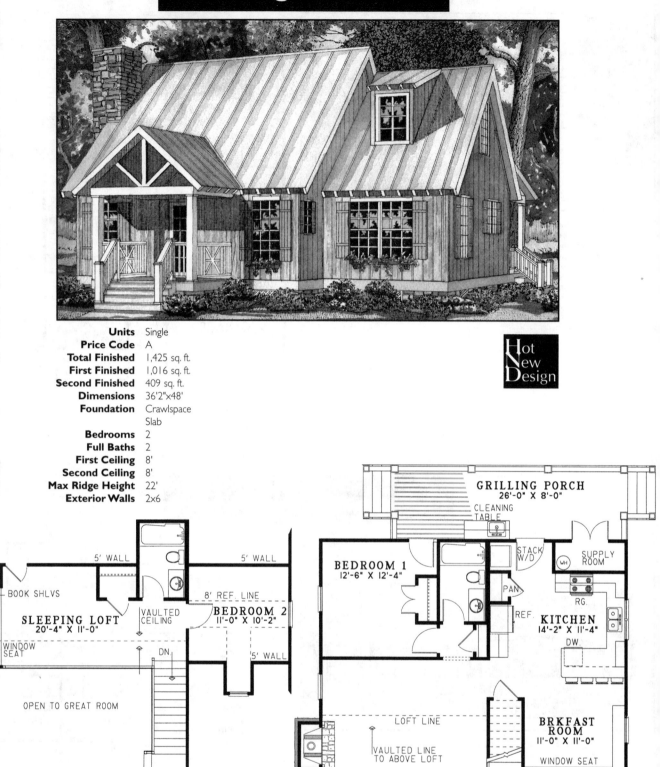

Units	Single
Price Code	A
Total Finished	1,425 sq. ft.
First Finished	1,016 sq. ft.
Second Finished	409 sq. ft.
Dimensions	36'2"×48'
Foundation	Crawlspace
	Slab
Bedrooms	2
Full Baths	2
First Ceiling	8'
Second Ceiling	8'
Max Ridge Height	22'
Exterior Walls	2x6

Hot New Design

SECOND FLOOR

5' WALL
5' WALL
BOOK SHLVS
VAULTED CEILING
8' REF. LINE
SLEEPING LOFT
20'-4" X 11'-0"
BEDROOM 2
11'-0" X 10'-2"
WINDOW SEAT
DN
5' WALL
OPEN TO GREAT ROOM

FIRST FLOOR

GRILLING PORCH
26'-0" X 8'-0"
CLEANING TABLE
STACK W/D
SUPPLY ROOM
WH
BEDROOM 1
12'-6" X 12'-4"
PAN
REF.
RG.
KITCHEN
14'-2" X 11'-4"
DW
LOFT LINE
VAULTED LINE TO ABOVE LOFT
BRKFAST ROOM
11'-0" X 11'-0"
WINDOW SEAT
GREAT ROOM
18'-0" X 18'-8"
UP
COVERED PORCH

Design 90844

Units	Single
Price Code	B
Total Finished	1,426 sq. ft.
First Finished	1,086 sq. ft.
Second Finished	340 sq. ft.
Basement Unfinished	1,086 sq. ft.
Deck Unfinished	510 sq. ft.
Porch Unfinished	25 sq. ft.
Dimensions	36'x50'
Foundation	Basement
Bedrooms	3
Full Baths	2
Half Baths	1
First Ceiling	8'
Max Ridge Height	29'
Roof Framing	Stick
Exterior Walls	2x6

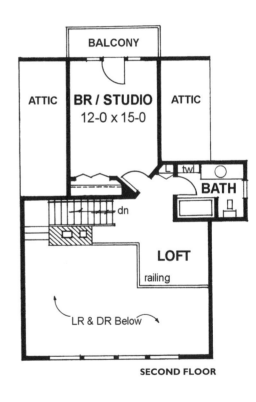

SECOND FLOOR

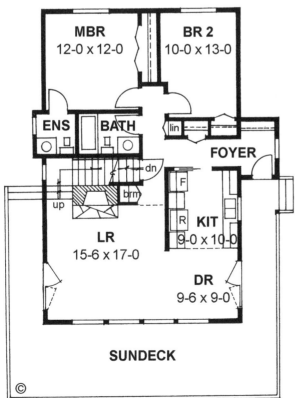

FIRST FLOOR

Design 19134

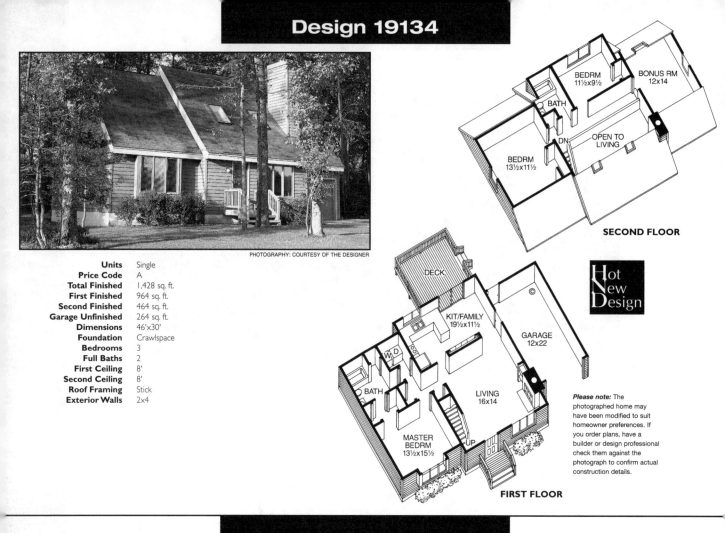

PHOTOGRAPHY: COURTESY OF THE DESIGNER

Units	Single
Price Code	A
Total Finished	1,428 sq. ft.
First Finished	964 sq. ft.
Second Finished	464 sq. ft.
Garage Unfinished	264 sq. ft.
Dimensions	46'x30'
Foundation	Crawlspace
Bedrooms	3
Full Baths	2
First Ceiling	8'
Second Ceiling	8'
Roof Framing	Stick
Exterior Walls	2x4

SECOND FLOOR

Hot New Design

FIRST FLOOR

Please note: The photographed home may have been modified to suit homeowner preferences. If you order plans, have a builder or design professional check them against the photograph to confirm actual construction details.

Design 90613

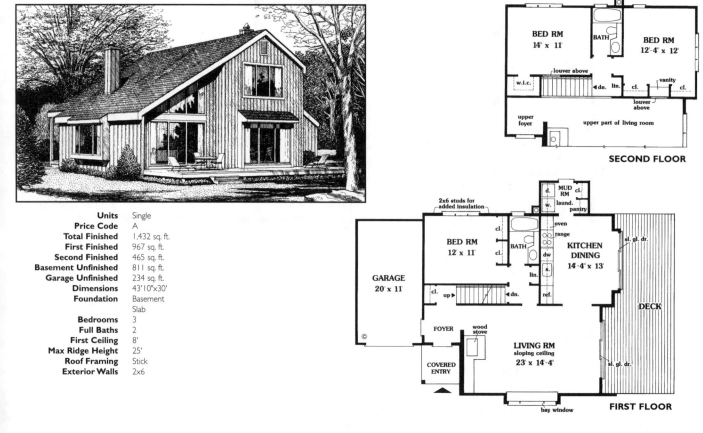

Units	Single
Price Code	A
Total Finished	1,432 sq. ft.
First Finished	967 sq. ft.
Second Finished	465 sq. ft.
Basement Unfinished	811 sq. ft.
Garage Unfinished	234 sq. ft.
Dimensions	43'10"x30'
Foundation	Basement
	Slab
Bedrooms	3
Full Baths	2
First Ceiling	8'
Max Ridge Height	25'
Roof Framing	Stick
Exterior Walls	2x6

SECOND FLOOR

FIRST FLOOR

Design 96509

Units	Single
Price Code	A
Total Finished	1,438 sq. ft.
Main Finished	1,438 sq. ft.
Garage Unfinished	486 sq. ft.
Deck Unfinished	282 sq. ft.
Porch Unfinished	126 sq. ft.
Dimensions	54'x57'
Foundation	Crawlspace
	Slab
Bedrooms	3
Full Baths	2
Max Ridge Height	19'
Roof Framing	Stick
Exterior Walls	2x4

MAIN FLOOR

Units	Single
Price Code	A
Total Finished	1,440 sq. ft.
First Finished	1,296 sq. ft.
Second Finished	144 sq. ft.
Dimensions	36'×36'
Foundation	Crawlspace
	Slab
	Pier/Post
Bedrooms	3
Full Baths	1
3/4 Baths	1
Max Ridge Height	22'
Roof Framing	Stick
Exterior Walls	2×6

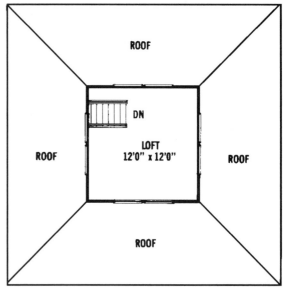

SECOND FLOOR

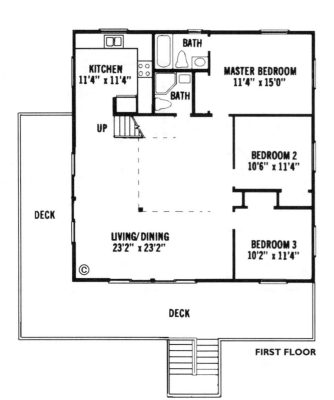

FIRST FLOOR

Design 97201

Units	Single
Price Code	A
Total Finished	1,448 sq. ft.
First Finished	1,049 sq. ft.
Second Finished	399 sq. ft.
Basement Unfinished	1,051 sq. ft.
Garage Unfinished	400 sq. ft.
Dimensions	41'x44'4"
Foundation	Basement
	Crawlspace
	Slab
Bedrooms	3
Full Baths	2
Half Baths	1
First Ceiling	8'
Second Ceiling	8'
Max Ridge Height	23'6"
Roof Framing	Stick
Exterior Walls	2x4

CAD **FILES AVAILABLE**
For more information call
800-235-5700

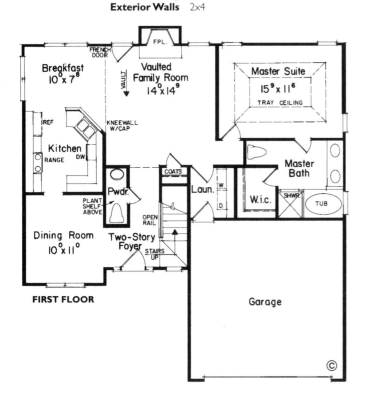

FIRST FLOOR

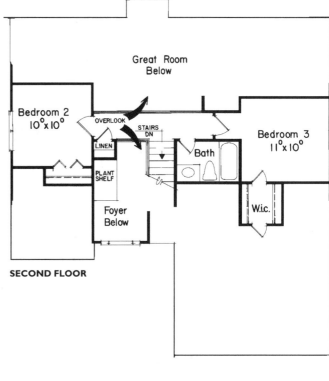

SECOND FLOOR

Units	Single
Price Code	A
Total Finished	1,452 sq. ft.
Main Finished	1,452 sq. ft.
Garage Unfinished	584 sq. ft.
Deck Unfinished	158 sq. ft.
Porch Unfinished	89 sq. ft.
Dimensions	67'x47'
Foundation	Crawlspace
	Slab
Bedrooms	3
Full Baths	2
Main Ceiling	8'
Max Ridge Height	21'
Roof Framing	Stick
Exterior Walls	2x4

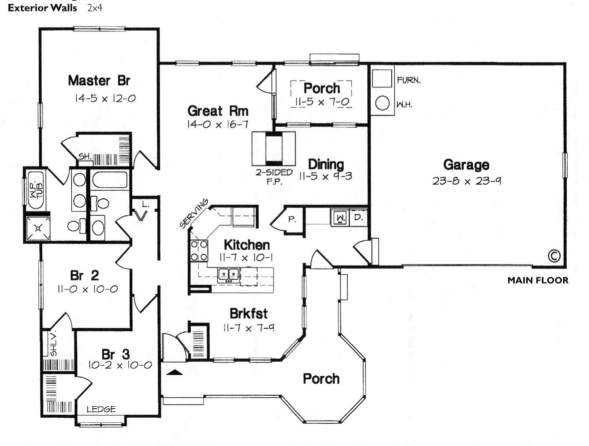

MAIN FLOOR

Design 90412

Units	Single
Price Code	A
Total Finished	1,454 sq. ft.
Main Finished	1,454 sq. ft.
Dimensions	67'x34'10"
Foundation	Basement
	Crawlspace
	Slab
Bedrooms	3
Full Baths	2
Max Ridge Height	16'2"
Roof Framing	Stick
Exterior Walls	2x4

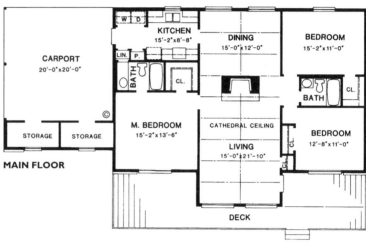

MAIN FLOOR

Design 65002

Units	Single
Price Code	B
Total Finished	1,460 sq. ft.
First Finished	895 sq. ft.
Second Finished	565 sq. ft.
Basement Unfinished	1,074 sq. ft.
Dimensions	38'x36'
Foundation	Basement
Bedrooms	2
Full Baths	1
Half Baths	1
First Ceiling	8'
Second Ceiling	8'
Max Ridge Height	32'8"
Roof Framing	Truss
Exterior Walls	2x6

SECOND FLOOR

FIRST FLOOR

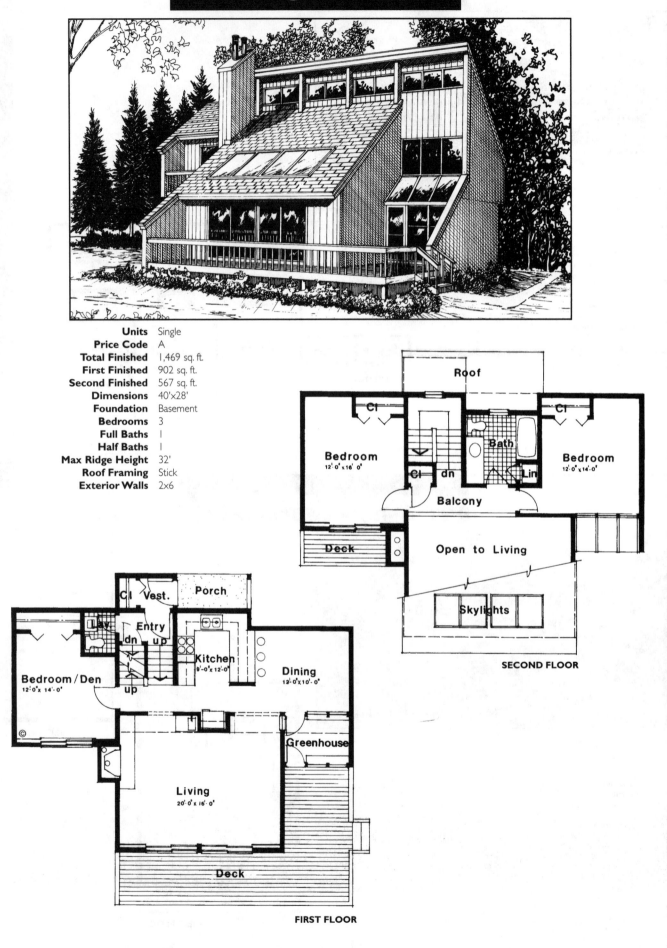

Units	Single
Price Code	A
Total Finished	1,469 sq. ft.
First Finished	902 sq. ft.
Second Finished	567 sq. ft.
Dimensions	40'x28'
Foundation	Basement
Bedrooms	3
Full Baths	I
Half Baths	I
Max Ridge Height	32'
Roof Framing	Stick
Exterior Walls	2x6

SECOND FLOOR

FIRST FLOOR

Design 24706

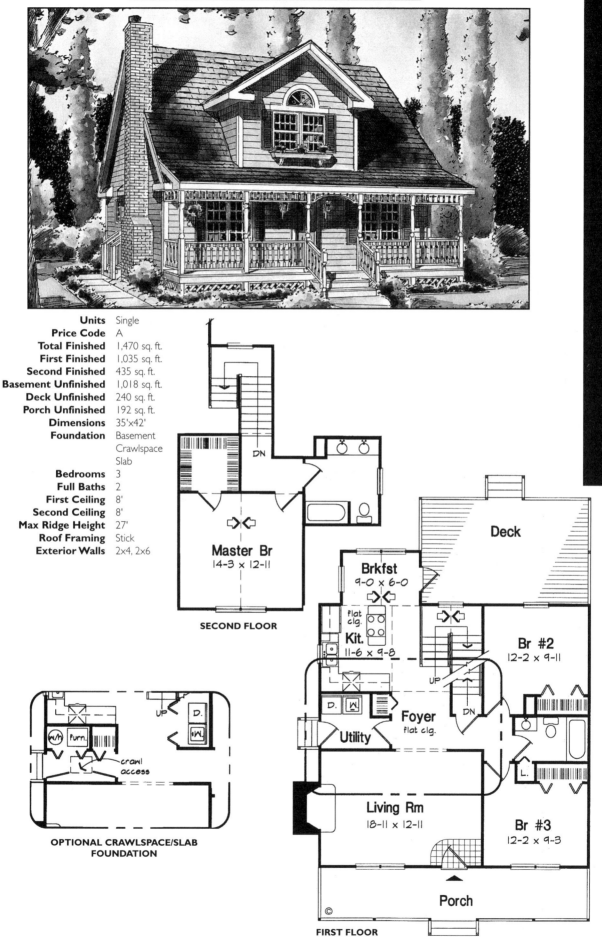

Units	Single
Price Code	A
Total Finished	1,470 sq. ft.
First Finished	1,035 sq. ft.
Second Finished	435 sq. ft.
Basement Unfinished	1,018 sq. ft.
Deck Unfinished	240 sq. ft.
Porch Unfinished	192 sq. ft.
Dimensions	35'x42'
Foundation	Basement
	Crawlspace
	Slab
Bedrooms	3
Full Baths	2
First Ceiling	8'
Second Ceiling	8'
Max Ridge Height	27'
Roof Framing	Stick
Exterior Walls	2x4, 2x6

SECOND FLOOR

DN

Master Br
14-3 x 12-11

Deck

Brkfst
9-0 x 6-0

flat clg.

Kit.
11-6 x 9-8

Br #2
12-2 x 9-11

UP

D. M.

Utility

Foyer
flat clg.

DN

Living Rm
18-11 x 12-11

Br #3
12-2 x 9-3

L.

Porch

FIRST FLOOR

UP

D.
M.

w/h   Furn.

crawl
access

**OPTIONAL CRAWLSPACE/SLAB
FOUNDATION**

Design 65000

Units	Single
Price Code	A
Total Finished	1,471 sq. ft.
First Finished	895 sq. ft.
Second Finished	576 sq. ft.
Basement Unfinished	895 sq. ft.
Dimensions	26'x36'
Foundation	Basement
Bedrooms	3
Full Baths	2
First Ceiling	8'2"
Second Ceiling	8'2"
Max Ridge Height	23'8"
Roof Framing	Truss
Exterior Walls	2x6

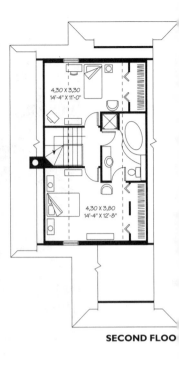

SECOND FLOO

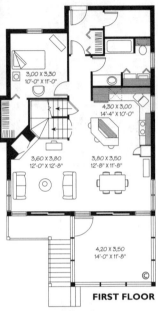

FIRST FLOOR

Design 65142

Units	Single
Price Code	A
Total Finished	1,471 sq. ft.
First Finished	895 sq. ft.
Second Finished	576 sq. ft.
Dimensions	26'x48'
Foundation	Basement
Bedrooms	3
Full Baths	2
First Ceiling	8'
Second Ceiling	8'
Max Ridge Height	32'8"
Roof Framing	Truss

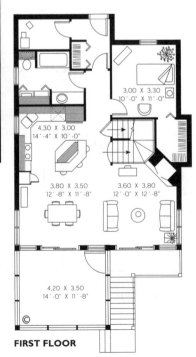

FIRST FLOOR

SECOND FLOOR

To order blueprints, call **800-235-5700** or visit us on the web, **familyhomeplans.com**

Design 62120

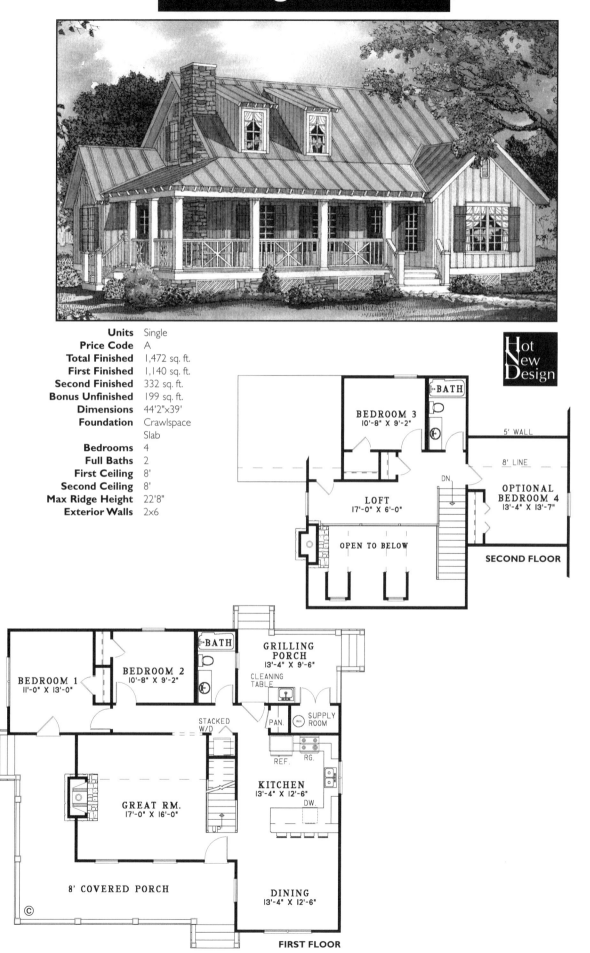

Units	Single
Price Code	A
Total Finished	1,472 sq. ft.
First Finished	1,140 sq. ft.
Second Finished	332 sq. ft.
Bonus Unfinished	199 sq. ft.
Dimensions	44'2"x39'
Foundation	Crawlspace Slab
Bedrooms	4
Full Baths	2
First Ceiling	8'
Second Ceiling	8'
Max Ridge Height	22'8"
Exterior Walls	2x6

Hot New Design

BATH

BEDROOM 3
10'-8" X 9'-2"

5' WALL

8' LINE

DN.

OPTIONAL BEDROOM 4
13'-4" X 13'-7"

LOFT
17'-0" X 6'-0"

OPEN TO BELOW

SECOND FLOOR

BATH

GRILLING PORCH
13'-4" X 9'-6"

BEDROOM 1
11'-0" X 13'-0"

BEDROOM 2
10'-8" X 9'-2"

CLEANING TABLE

PAN.

WH SUPPLY ROOM

STACKED W/D

REF.

RG.

DW.

GREAT RM.
17'-0" X 16'-0"

UP

KITCHEN
13'-4" X 12'-6"

8' COVERED PORCH

DINING
13'-4" X 12'-6"

©

FIRST FLOOR

Units	Single
Price Code	A
Total Finished	1,472 sq. ft.
Main Finished	1,472 sq. ft.
Deck Unfinished	128 sq. ft.
Porch Unfinished	320 sq. ft.
Dimensions	62'x36'
Foundation	Crawlspace
	Slab
Bedrooms	3
Full Baths	2
Main Ceiling	8'
Vaulted Ceiling	12'1"
Max Ridge Height	19'10"
Roof Framing	Truss
Exterior Walls	2x4

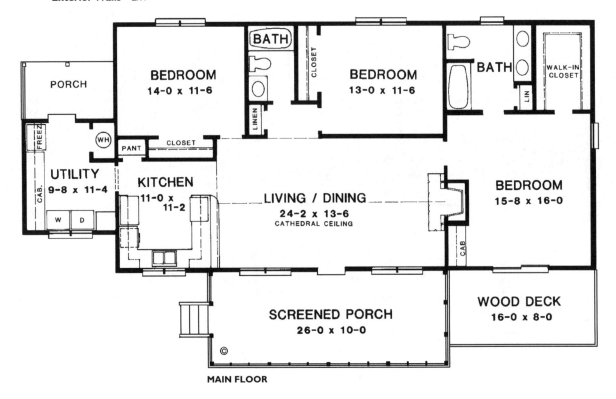

MAIN FLOOR

Design 97444

Units	Single
Price Code	A
Total Finished	1,472 sq. ft.
Main Finished	1,472 sq. ft.
Bonus Unfinished	1,169 sq. ft.
Garage Unfinished	494 sq. ft.
Dimensions	49'8"x45'
Foundation	Basement
Bedrooms	1
Full Baths	1
3/4 Baths	1
Main Ceiling	9'
Max Ridge Height	22'
Roof Framing	Stick
Exterior Walls	2x4

* Alternate foundation options available at an additional charge.
Please call 1-800-235-5700 for more information.

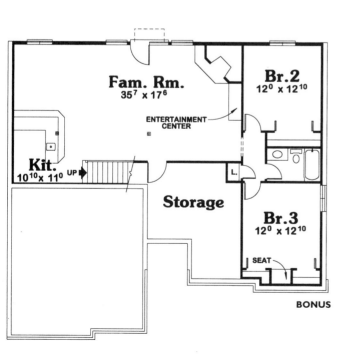

BONUS

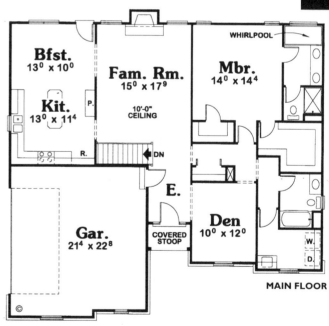

MAIN FLOOR

Units	Single
Price Code	A
Total Finished	1,474 sq. ft.
Main Finished	1,474 sq. ft.
Garage Unfinished	454 sq. ft.
Deck Unfinished	72 sq. ft.
Porch Unfinished	142 sq. ft.
Dimensions	43'x42'6"
Foundation	Crawlspace
	Slab
Bedrooms	3
Full Baths	2
Main Ceiling	9'
Max Ridge Height	22'
Roof Framing	Stick
Exterior Walls	2x4

OPTIONAL MASTER BATH

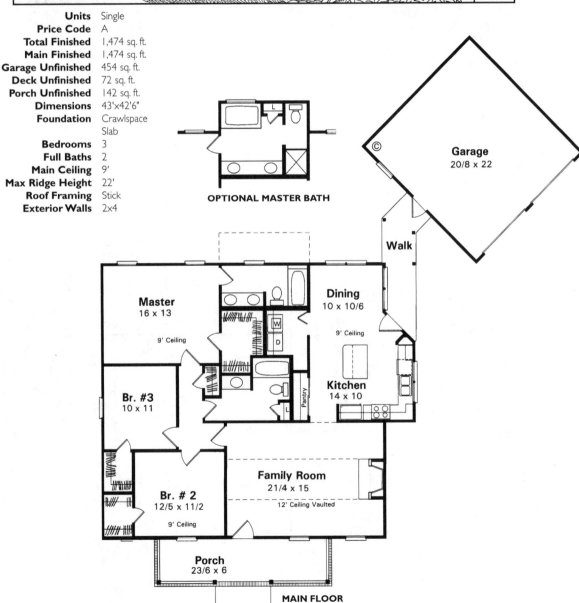

Garage
20/8 x 22

Walk

Master
16 x 13

9' Ceiling

Dining
10 x 10/6

9' Ceiling

Kitchen
14 x 10

Br. #3
10 x 11

Pantry

Br. # 2
12/5 x 11/2

9' Ceiling

Family Room
21/4 x 15

12' Ceiling Vaulted

Porch
23/6 x 6

MAIN FLOOR

Design 99707

1,001–1,500 sq. ft. HOME PLANS

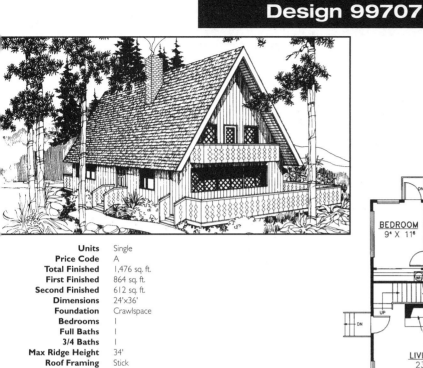

Units	Single
Price Code	A
Total Finished	1,476 sq. ft.
First Finished	864 sq. ft.
Second Finished	612 sq. ft.
Dimensions	24'x36'
Foundation	Crawlspace
Bedrooms	1
Full Baths	1
3/4 Baths	1
Max Ridge Height	34'
Roof Framing	Stick
Exterior Walls	2x6

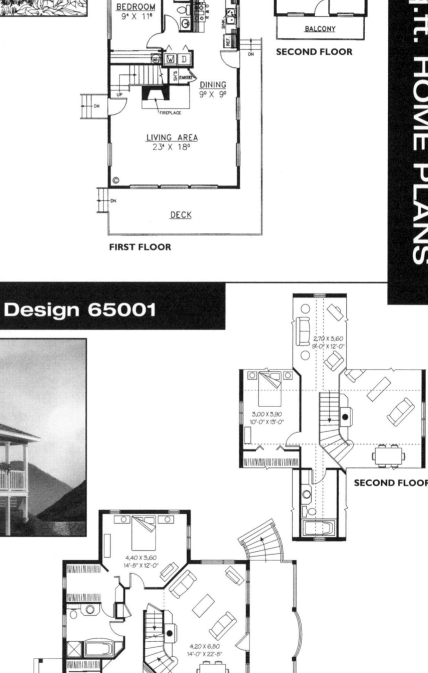

SECOND FLOOR

FIRST FLOOR

Design 65001

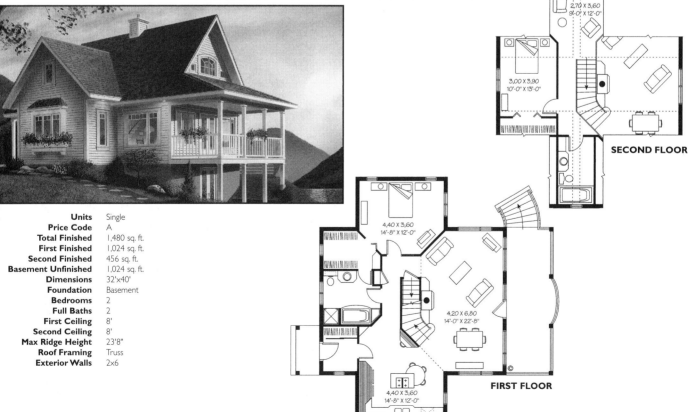

Units	Single
Price Code	A
Total Finished	1,480 sq. ft.
First Finished	1,024 sq. ft.
Second Finished	456 sq. ft.
Basement Unfinished	1,024 sq. ft.
Dimensions	32'x40'
Foundation	Basement
Bedrooms	2
Full Baths	2
First Ceiling	8'
Second Ceiling	8'
Max Ridge Height	23'8"
Roof Framing	Truss
Exterior Walls	2x6

SECOND FLOOR

FIRST FLOOR

Units	Single
Price Code	A
Total Finished	1,482 sq. ft.
Main Finished	1,482 sq. ft.
Garage Unfinished	564 sq. ft.
Dimensions	79'x50'
Foundation	Slab
Bedrooms	2
Full Baths	2
Max Ridge Height	19'
Roof Framing	Stick/Truss
Exterior Walls	2x4, 2x6

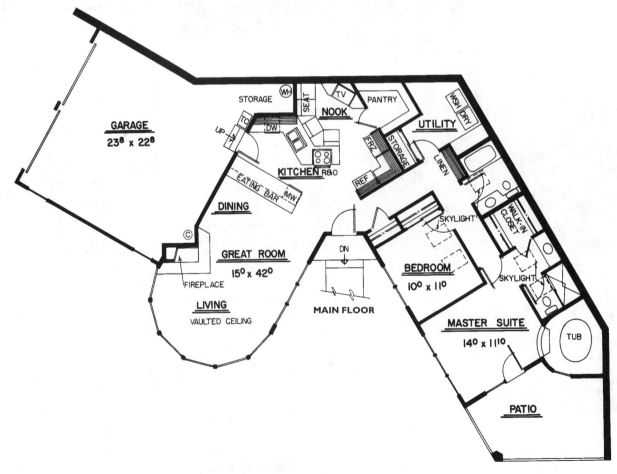

Design 91797

Units	Single
Price Code	A
Total Finished	1,485 sq. ft.
Main Finished	1,485 sq. ft.
Garage Unfinished	701 sq. ft.
Dimensions	51'6"x63'
Foundation	Crawlspace
Bedrooms	3
Full Baths	2
Max Ridge Height	22'
Roof Framing	Stick/Truss
Exterior Walls	2x6

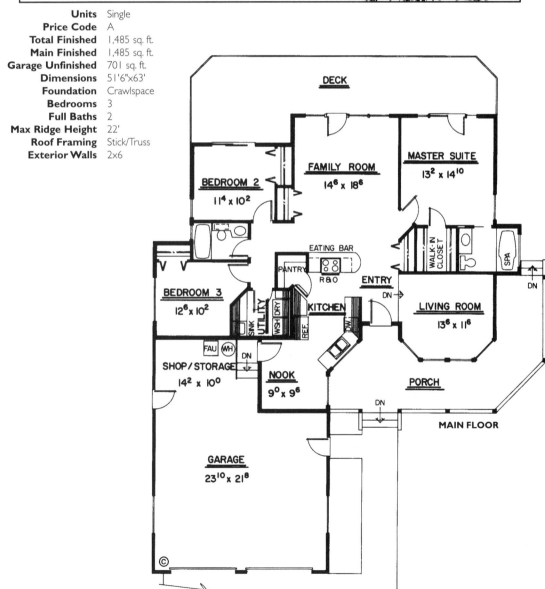

Design 26112

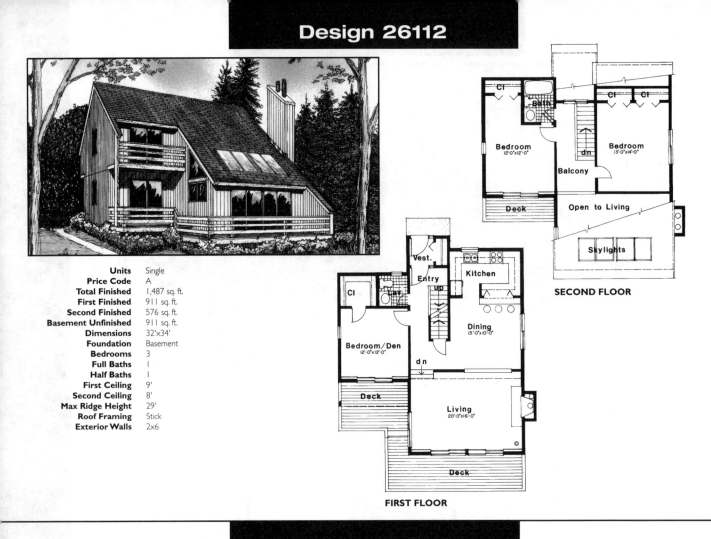

Units	Single
Price Code	A
Total Finished	1,487 sq. ft.
First Finished	911 sq. ft.
Second Finished	576 sq. ft.
Basement Unfinished	911 sq. ft.
Dimensions	32'x34'
Foundation	Basement
Bedrooms	3
Full Baths	1
Half Baths	1
First Ceiling	9'
Second Ceiling	8'
Max Ridge Height	29'
Roof Framing	Stick
Exterior Walls	2x6

SECOND FLOOR

FIRST FLOOR

Design 91753

Units	Single
Price Code	A
Total Finished	1,490 sq. ft.
Main Finished	1,490 sq. ft.
Basement Unfinished	1,490 sq. ft.
Garage Unfinished	579 sq. ft.
Porch Unfinished	120 sq. ft.
Dimensions	58'x61'
Foundation	Basement
Bedrooms	3
Full Baths	2
Main Ceiling	8'
Vaulted Ceiling	16'

MAIN FLOOR

To order blueprints, call **800-235-5700** or visit us on the web, **familyhomeplans.com**

Design 97203

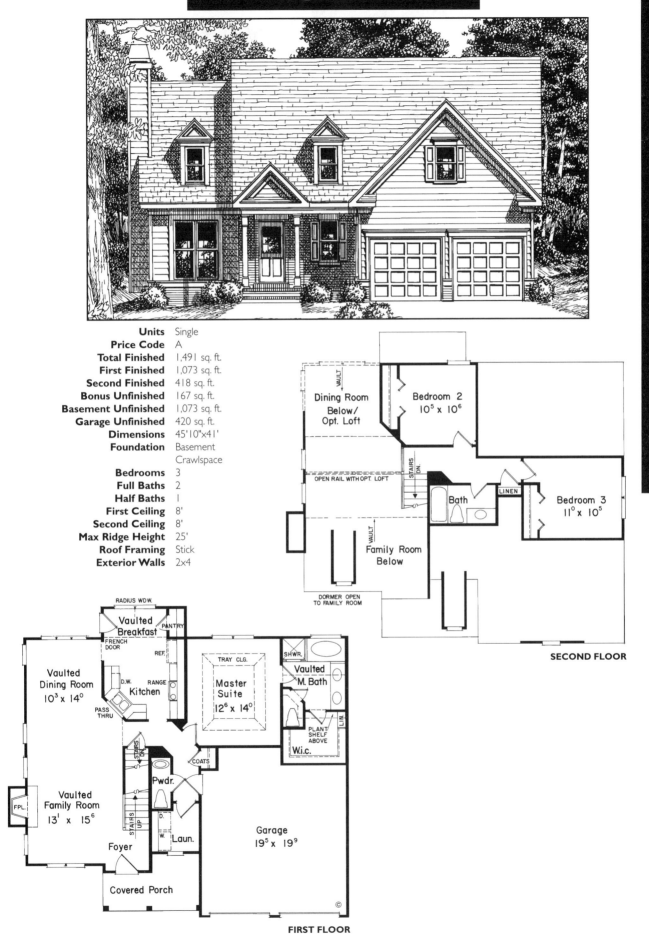

Units	Single
Price Code	A
Total Finished	1,491 sq. ft.
First Finished	1,073 sq. ft.
Second Finished	418 sq. ft.
Bonus Unfinished	167 sq. ft.
Basement Unfinished	1,073 sq. ft.
Garage Unfinished	420 sq. ft.
Dimensions	45'10"x41'
Foundation	Basement
	Crawlspace
Bedrooms	3
Full Baths	2
Half Baths	1
First Ceiling	8'
Second Ceiling	8'
Max Ridge Height	25'
Roof Framing	Stick
Exterior Walls	2x4

SECOND FLOOR

FIRST FLOOR

Design 94283

Units	Single
Price Code	F
Total Finished	1,492 sq. ft.
Main Finished	1,360 sq. ft.
Lower Finished	132 sq. ft.
Bonus Unfinished	397 sq. ft.
Basement Unfinished	149 sq. ft.
Garage Unfinished	572 sq. ft.
Deck Unfinished	293 sq. ft.
Porch Unfinished	70 sq. ft.
Dimensions	48'x43'8"
Foundation	Basement
Bedrooms	3
Full Baths	2
3/4 Baths	1
Main Ceiling	8'4"
Max Ridge Height	31'
Roof Framing	Stick
Exterior Walls	2x6

* Alternate foundation options available at an additional charge.
Please call 1-800-235-5700 for more information.

MAIN FLOOR

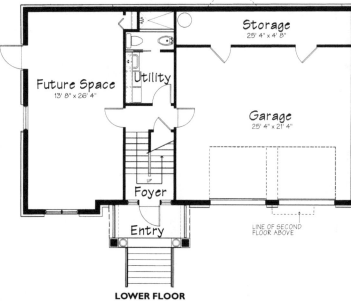

LOWER FLOOR

Design 65275

SECOND FLOOR

FIRST FLOOR

Units	Single
Price Code	A
Total Finished	1,492 sq. ft.
First Finished	856 sq. ft.
Second Finished	636 sq. ft.
Dimensions	44'x26'
Foundation	Basement
Bedrooms	3
Full Baths	1
Half Baths	1
Max Ridge Height	31'9"
Roof Framing	Stick
Exterior Walls	2x6

Design 32191

Hot New Design

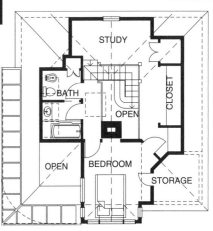

SECOND FLOOR

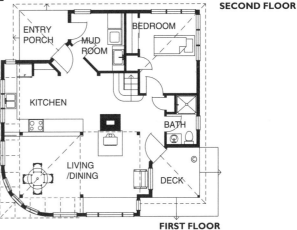

FIRST FLOOR

Units	Single
Price Code	A
Total Finished	1,495 sq. ft.
First Finished	903 sq. ft.
Second Finished	592 sq. ft.
Dimensions	33'x33'
Foundation	Crawlspace
Bedrooms	2
Full Baths	1
3/4 Baths	1
First Ceiling	8'8"
Second Ceiling	8'
Vaulted Ceiling	25'
Max Ridge Height	28'8"
Roof Framing	Stick
Exterior Walls	2x6

Design 92802

Units	Single
Price Code	B
Total Finished	1,505 sq. ft.
First Finished	1,320 sq. ft.
Second Finished	185 sq. ft.
Dimensions	44'x30'
Foundation	Crawlspace
	Slab
Bedrooms	3
Full Baths	2
Max Ridge Height	20'
Roof Framing	Stick
Exterior Walls	2x6

LOFT

DN

OPEN TO BELOW

SECOND FLOOR

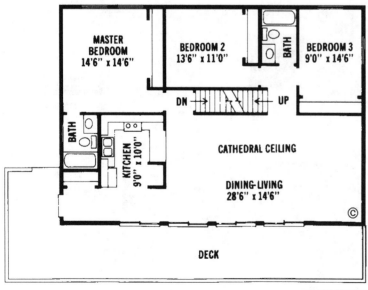

MASTER BEDROOM
14'6" x 14'6"

BEDROOM 2
13'6" x 11'0"

BATH

BEDROOM 3
9'0" x 14'6"

BATH

KITCHEN
9'0" x 10'0"

DN   UP

CATHEDRAL CEILING

DINING-LIVING
28'6" x 14'6"

DECK

FIRST FLOOR

Units	Single
Price Code	B
Total Finished	1,505 sq. ft.
First Finished	692 sq. ft.
Second Finished	813 sq. ft.
Basement Unfinished	699 sq. ft.
Garage Unfinished	484 sq. ft.
Dimensions	42'x34'4"
Foundation	Basement
	Crawlspace
	Slab
Bedrooms	4
Full Baths	1
3/4 Baths	1
Half Baths	1
First Ceiling	8'
Second Ceiling	8'
Max Ridge Height	26'
Roof Framing	Stick
Exterior Walls	2x6

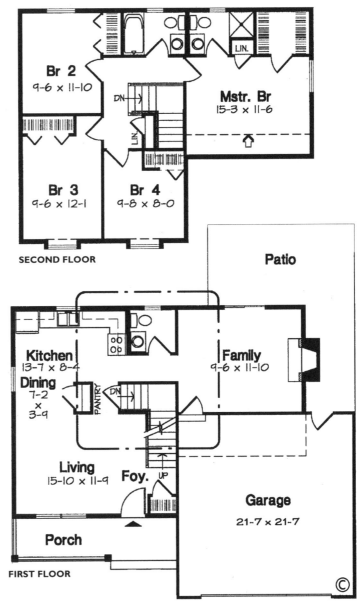

Br 2
9-6 × 11-10

Mstr. Br
15-3 × 11-6

Br 3
9-6 × 12-1

Br 4
9-8 × 8-0

LIN.

DN

LIN

SECOND FLOOR

Patio

Kitchen
13-7 × 8-4

Dining
7-2 × 3-9

Family
9-6 × 11-10

PANTRY

DN

Living
15-10 × 11-9

Foy.

UP

Garage
21-7 × 21-7

Porch

FIRST FLOOR

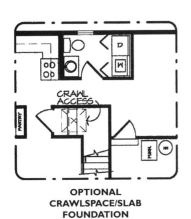

OPTIONAL CRAWLSPACE/SLAB FOUNDATION

CRAWL ACCESS

PANTRY

Units	Single
Price Code	B
Total Finished	1,508 sq. ft.
First Finished	1,050 sq. ft.
Second Finished	458 sq. ft.
Porch Unfinished	233 sq. ft.
Dimensions	35'6"x39'9"
Foundation	Pier/Post
Bedrooms	3
Full Baths	2
Half Baths	1
First Ceiling	9'
Second Ceiling	8'
Max Ridge Height	23'6"
Roof Framing	Stick
Exterior Walls	2x4

*This home is not to be built within a 20-mile radius of Madisonville, LA or in the city of Baton Rouge, LA.

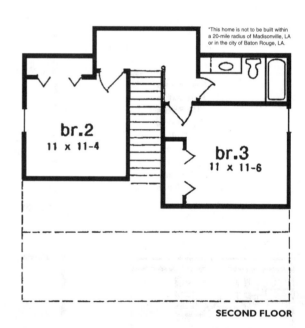

SECOND FLOOR

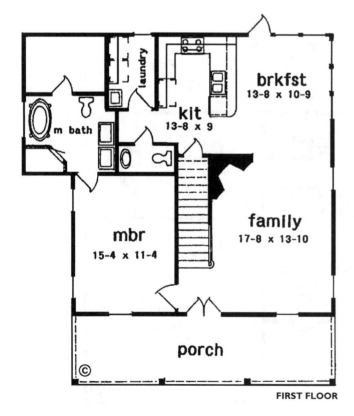

FIRST FLOOR

Design 94310

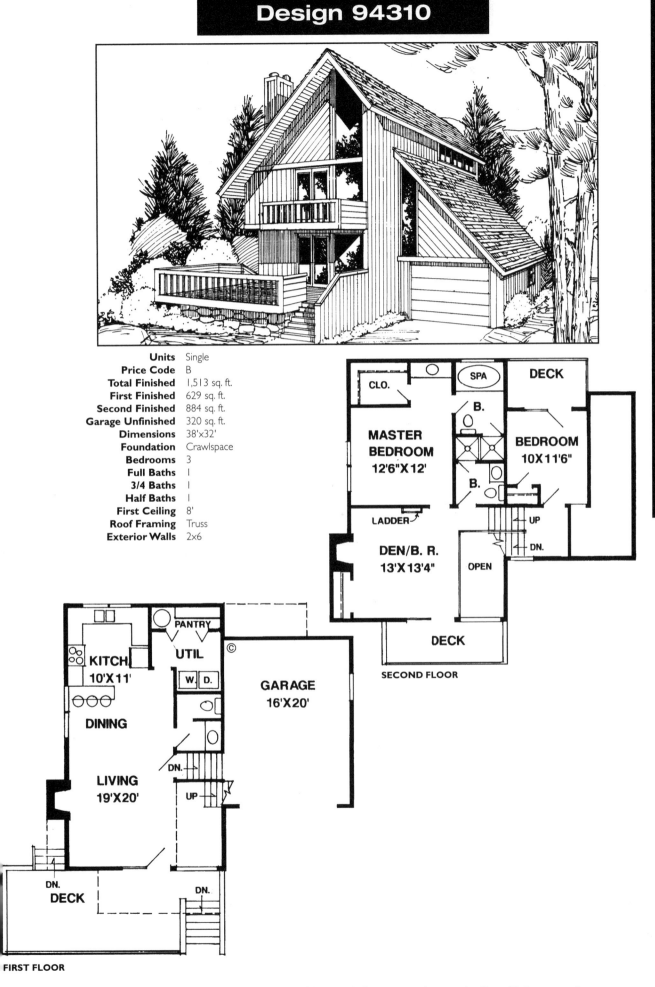

Units	Single
Price Code	B
Total Finished	1,513 sq. ft.
First Finished	629 sq. ft.
Second Finished	884 sq. ft.
Garage Unfinished	320 sq. ft.
Dimensions	38'x32'
Foundation	Crawlspace
Bedrooms	3
Full Baths	1
3/4 Baths	1
Half Baths	1
First Ceiling	8'
Roof Framing	Truss
Exterior Walls	2x6

CLO.

SPA

DECK

B.

MASTER BEDROOM
12'6"X12'

BEDROOM
10X11'6"

B.

LADDER

UP

DN.

DEN/B. R.
13'X13'4"

OPEN

DECK

SECOND FLOOR

PANTRY

UTIL

©

KITCH
10'X11'

W | D.

GARAGE
16'X20'

DINING

DN.

LIVING
19'X20'

UP

DN.

DN.

DECK

FIRST FLOOR

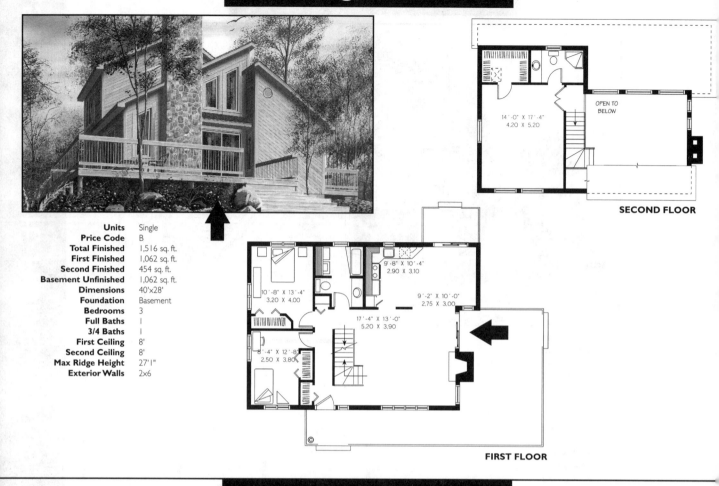

SECOND FLOOR

14'-0" X 17'-4"
4.20 X 5.20

OPEN TO BELOW

Units	Single
Price Code	B
Total Finished	1,516 sq. ft.
First Finished	1,062 sq. ft.
Second Finished	454 sq. ft.
Basement Unfinished	1,062 sq. ft.
Dimensions	40'x28'
Foundation	Basement
Bedrooms	3
Full Baths	1
3/4 Baths	1
First Ceiling	8'
Second Ceiling	8'
Max Ridge Height	27'1"
Exterior Walls	2x6

9'-8" X 10'-4"
2.90 X 3.10

9'-2" X 10'-0"
2.75 X 3.00

10'-8" X 13'-4"
3.20 X 4.00

17'-4" X 13'-0"
5.20 X 3.90

8'-4" X 12'-8"
2.50 X 3.80

FIRST FLOOR

3,00 X 3,30
10'-0" X 11'-0"

2,70 X 2,80
9'-0" X 9'-4"

3,80 X 3,90
12'-8" X 13'-0"

SECOND FLOOR

3,30 X 3,90
11'-0" X 13'-0"

3,1 X 2,70
10'-4" X 9'-0"

2,70 X 2,00
9'-0" X 6'-8"

4,20 X 5,10
14'-0" X 17'-0"

3,80 X 6,20
12'-8" X 20'-8"

Units	Single
Price Code	B
Total Finished	1,519 sq. ft.
First Finished	788 sq. ft.
Second Finished	731 sq. ft.
Garage Unfinished	266 sq. ft.
Dimensions	32'x36'
Foundation	Basement
Bedrooms	3
Full Baths	1
3/4 Baths	1

FIRST FLOOR

Design 94650

1,501-2,000 sq. ft. HOME PLANS

Units	Single
Price Code	B
Total Finished	1,520 sq. ft.
Main Finished	1,520 sq. ft.
Dimensions	40'x59'
Foundation	Pier/Post
Bedrooms	4
Full Baths	2
Main Ceiling	9'
Max Ridge Height	32'
Roof Framing	Stick
Exterior Walls	2x4

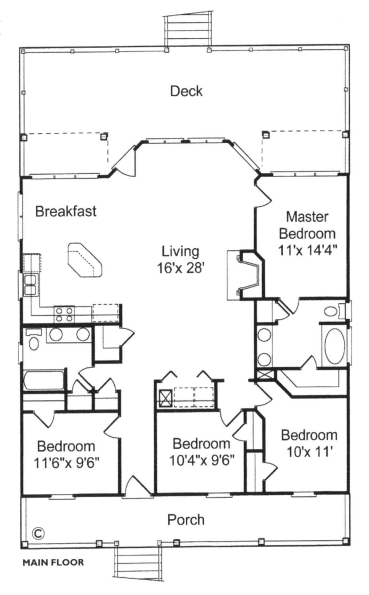

Deck

Breakfast

Living
16'x 28'

Master
Bedroom
11'x 14'4"

Bedroom
11'6"x 9'6"

Bedroom
10'4"x 9'6"

Bedroom
10'x 11'

Porch

MAIN FLOOR

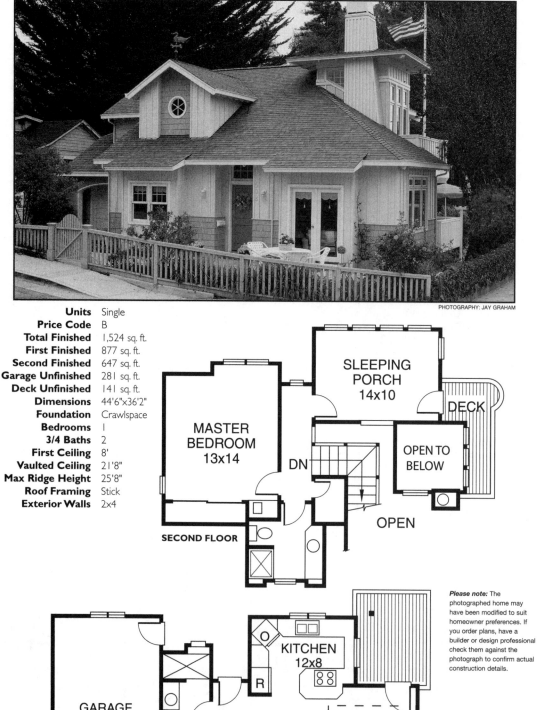

PHOTOGRAPHY: JAY GRAHAM

Units	Single
Price Code	B
Total Finished	1,524 sq. ft.
First Finished	877 sq. ft.
Second Finished	647 sq. ft.
Garage Unfinished	281 sq. ft.
Deck Unfinished	141 sq. ft.
Dimensions	44'6"x36'2"
Foundation	Crawlspace
Bedrooms	1
3/4 Baths	2
First Ceiling	8'
Vaulted Ceiling	21'8"
Max Ridge Height	25'8"
Roof Framing	Stick
Exterior Walls	2x4

SLEEPING PORCH 14x10

DECK

MASTER BEDROOM 13x14

DN

OPEN TO BELOW

OPEN

SECOND FLOOR

Please note: The photographed home may have been modified to suit homeowner preferences. If you order plans, have a builder or design professional check them against the photograph to confirm actual construction details.

KITCHEN 12x8

GARAGE 12x21

W D

DINING 12x9

LIGHT TOWER ABOVE

FIRST FLOOR

FAMILY 13x15

UP

ENTR

LIVING 13x13

Design 34055

Units	Single
Price Code	B
Total Finished	1,527 sq. ft.
Main Finished	1,527 sq. ft.
Basement Unfinished	1,344 sq. ft.
Garage Unfinished	425 sq. ft.
Dimensions	70'×28'
Foundation	Basement
	Crawlspace
	Slab
Bedrooms	4
Full Baths	2
Max Ridge Height	18'
Roof Framing	Stick
Exterior Walls	2x4, 2x6

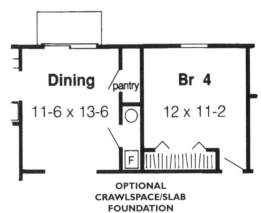

**OPTIONAL
CRAWLSPACE/SLAB
FOUNDATION**

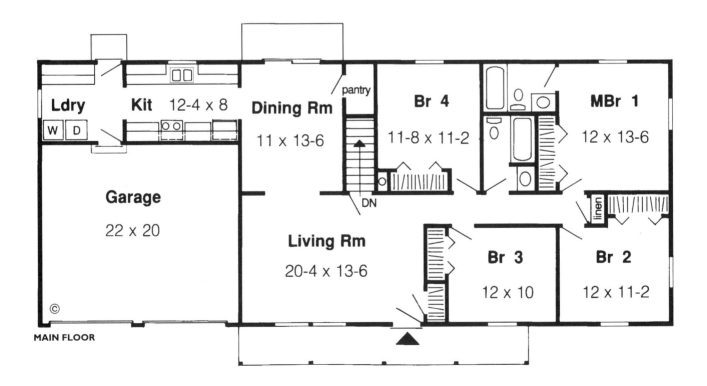

MAIN FLOOR

Units	Single
Price Code	B
Total Finished	1,531 sq. ft.
First Finished	1,067 sq. ft.
Second Finished	464 sq. ft.
Bonus Unfinished	207 sq. ft.
Basement Unfinished	1,067 sq. ft.
Garage Unfinished	398 sq. ft.
Dimensions	41'x44'4"
Foundation	Basement
	Crawlspace
Bedrooms	3
Full Baths	2
Half Baths	1
Max Ridge Height	25'
Roof Framing	Stick
Exterior Walls	2x4

FILES AVAILABLE
For more information call
800-235-5700

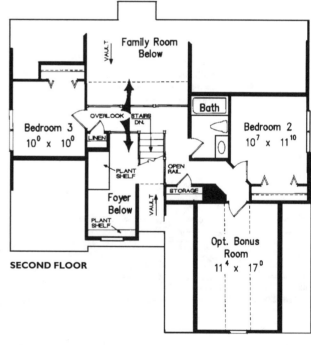

SECOND FLOOR

FIRST FLOOR

Design 19191

PHOTOGRAPHY: COURTESY OF THE DESIGNER

Units	Single
Price Code	B
Total Finished	1,533 sq. ft.
First Finished	1,079 sq. ft.
Second Finished	454 sq. ft.
Garage Unfinished	240 sq. ft.
Dimensions	35'x65'
Foundation	Crawlspace
Bedrooms	3
Full Baths	2
First Ceiling	8'
Second Ceiling	8'
Max Ridge Height	24'
Roof Framing	Stick
Exterior Walls	2x6

Hot New Design

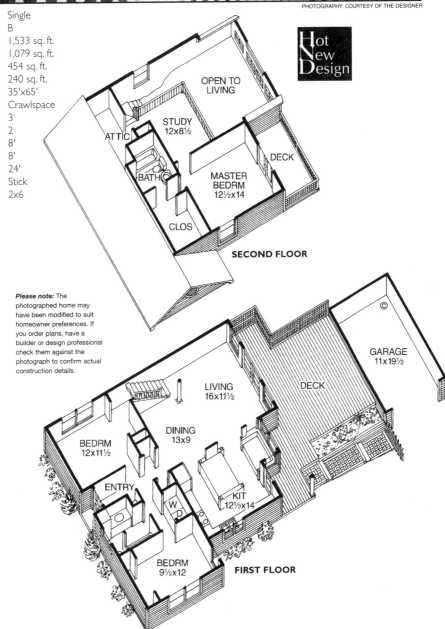

Please note: The photographed home may have been modified to suit homeowner preferences. If you order plans, have a builder or design professional check them against the photograph to confirm actual construction details.

SECOND FLOOR

OPEN TO LIVING

STUDY 12x8½

ATTIC

BATH

MASTER BEDRM 12½x14

DECK

CLOS

GARAGE 11x19½

LIVING 16x11½

DINING 13x9

DECK

BEDRM 12x11½

ENTRY

W D

KIT 12½x14

BEDRM 9½x12

FIRST FLOOR

Design 24721

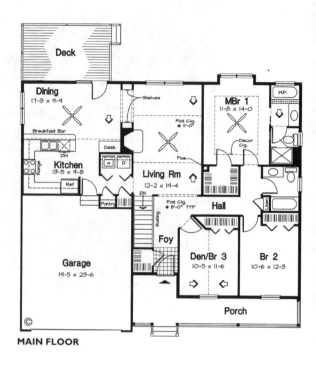

MAIN FLOOR

Units	Single
Price Code	B
Total Finished	1,539 sq. ft.
Main Finished	1,539 sq. ft.
Basement Unfinished	1,530 sq. ft.
Garage Unfinished	460 sq. ft.
Deck Unfinished	160 sq. ft.
Porch Unfinished	182 sq. ft.
Dimensions	50'x45'4"
Foundation	Basement
	Crawlspace
	Slab
Bedrooms	3
Full Baths	2
Main Ceiling	8'
Max Ridge Height	21'
Roof Framing	Stick
Exterior Walls	2x6

Design 10748

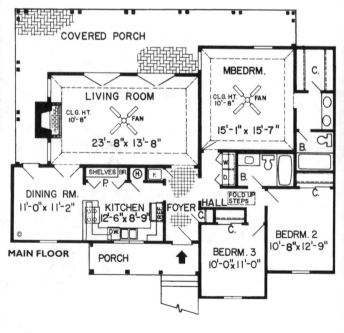

MAIN FLOOR

Units	Single
Price Code	B
Total Finished	1,540 sq. ft.
Main Finished	1,540 sq. ft.
Porch Unfinished	530 sq. ft.
Dimensions	52'x45'
Foundation	Slab
	Post/Pier
Bedrooms	3
Full Baths	2
Max Ridge Height	21'
Roof Framing	Stick
Exterior Walls	2x6

Design 91058

Units	Single
Price Code	B
Total Finished	1,538 sq. ft.
Main Finished	1,538 sq. ft.
Dimensions	45'6"x50'
Foundation	Crawlspace
Bedrooms	3
Full Baths	1
3/4 Baths	1
Roof Framing	Truss
Exterior Walls	2x6

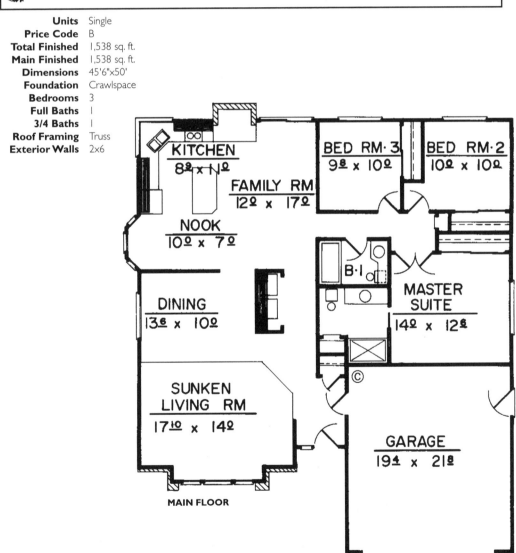

MAIN FLOOR

Design 62121

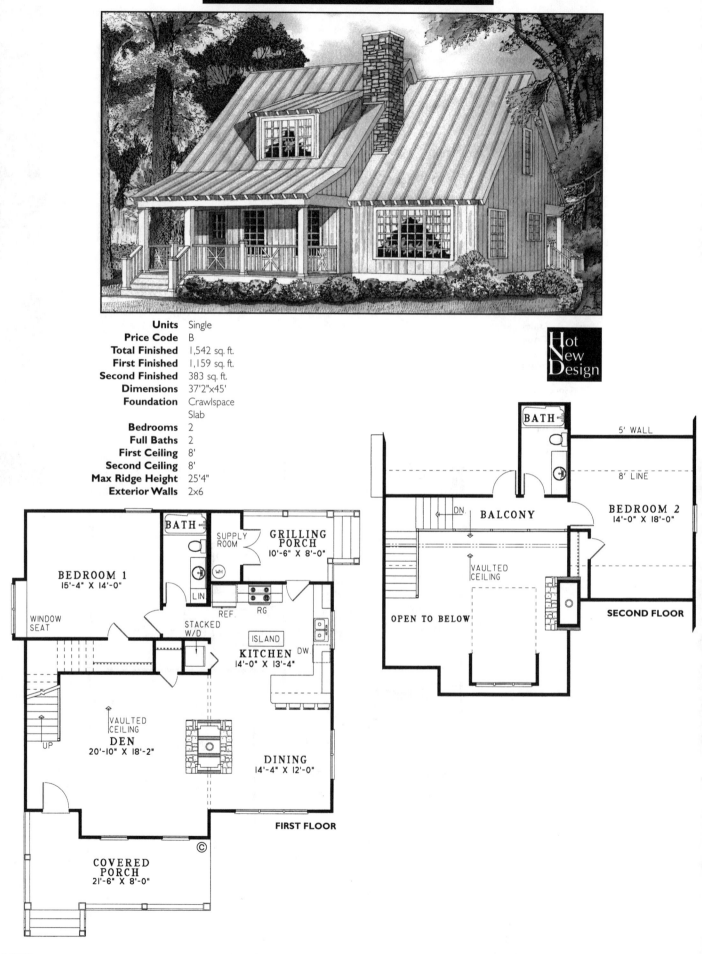

Units	Single
Price Code	B
Total Finished	1,542 sq. ft.
First Finished	1,159 sq. ft.
Second Finished	383 sq. ft.
Dimensions	37'2"x45'
Foundation	Crawlspace
	Slab
Bedrooms	2
Full Baths	2
First Ceiling	8'
Second Ceiling	8'
Max Ridge Height	25'4"
Exterior Walls	2x6

Hot New Design

BATH

SUPPLY ROOM

GRILLING PORCH
10'-6" X 8'-0"

BEDROOM 1
15'-4" X 14'-0"

WINDOW SEAT

LIN

REF. RG

STACKED W/D

ISLAND

KITCHEN
14'-0" X 13'-4"

DW

UP

VAULTED CEILING
DEN
20'-10" X 18'-2"

DINING
14'-4" X 12'-0"

FIRST FLOOR

COVERED PORCH
21'-6" X 8'-0"

BATH

5' WALL

8' LINE

DN.

BALCONY

BEDROOM 2
14'-0" X 18'-0"

VAULTED CEILING

OPEN TO BELOW

SECOND FLOOR

Design 62122

Units	Single
Price Code	B
Total Finished	1,544 sq. ft.
First Finished	1,031 sq. ft.
Second Finished	513 sq. ft.
Dimensions	34'4"×48'4"
Foundation	Crawlspace
	Slab
Bedrooms	3
Full Baths	2
First Ceiling	8'
Second Ceiling	8'
Max Ridge Height	24'4"
Exterior Walls	2x6

Hot New Design

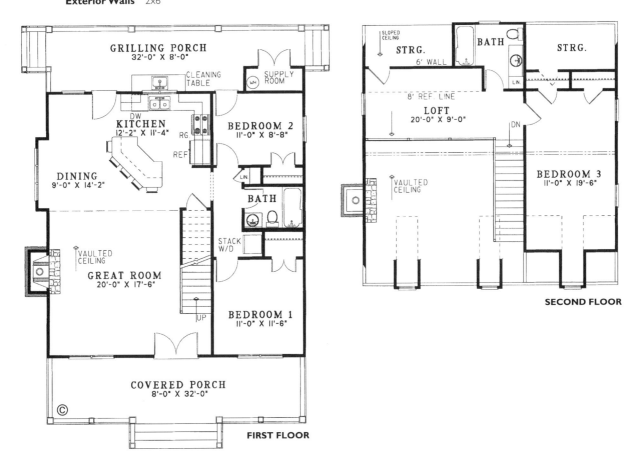

FIRST FLOOR

GRILLING PORCH
32'-0" X 8'-0"

CLEANING TABLE

SUPPLY ROOM

WH

KITCHEN
12'-2" X 11'-4"

DW

RG

REF

BEDROOM 2
11'-0" X 8'-8"

LIN

DINING
9'-0" X 14'-2"

BATH

LIN

STACK W/D

VAULTED CEILING

GREAT ROOM
20'-0" X 17'-6"

UP

BEDROOM 1
11'-0" X 11'-6"

©

COVERED PORCH
8'-0" X 32'-0"

SECOND FLOOR

SLOPED CEILING

STRG.
6' WALL

BATH

STRG.

8' REF. LINE

LIN.

LOFT
20'-0" X 9'-0"

DN

VAULTED CEILING

BEDROOM 3
11'-0" X 19'-6"

Design 65192

Units	Single
Price Code	B
Total Finished	1,544 sq. ft.
First Finished	984 sq. ft.
Second Finished	560 sq. ft.
Deck Unfinished	468 sq. ft.
Dimensions	34'x28'
Foundation	Basement
Bedrooms	3
Full Baths	1
3/4 Baths	1
First Ceiling	8'
Second Ceiling	8'
Max Ridge Height	25'2"
Roof Framing	Truss
Exterior Walls	2x6

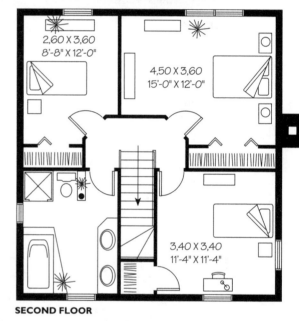

SECOND FLOOR

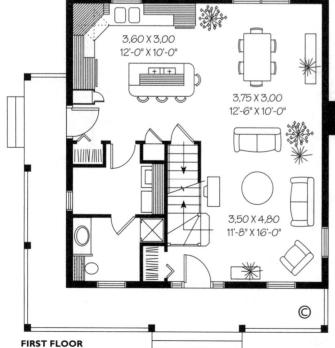

FIRST FLOOR

Design 94315

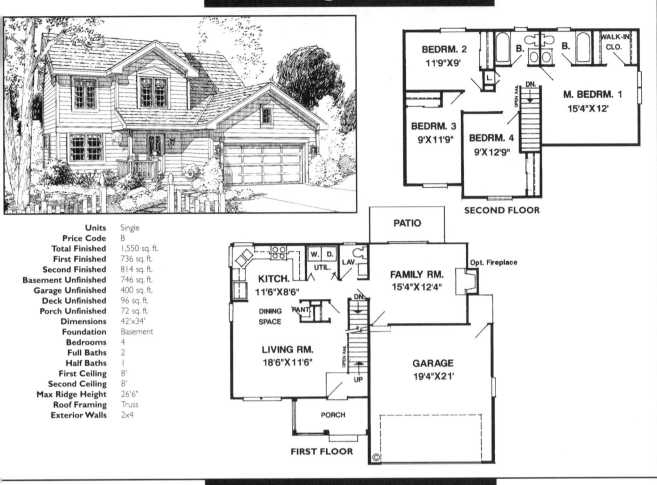

SECOND FLOOR

FIRST FLOOR

Units	Single
Price Code	B
Total Finished	1,550 sq. ft.
First Finished	736 sq. ft.
Second Finished	814 sq. ft.
Basement Unfinished	746 sq. ft.
Garage Unfinished	400 sq. ft.
Deck Unfinished	96 sq. ft.
Porch Unfinished	72 sq. ft.
Dimensions	42'x34'
Foundation	Basement
Bedrooms	4
Full Baths	2
Half Baths	1
First Ceiling	8'
Second Ceiling	8'
Max Ridge Height	26'6"
Roof Framing	Truss
Exterior Walls	2x4

Design 98801

MAIN FLOOR

LOWER FLOOR

Units	Single
Price Code	B
Total Finished	1,557 sq. ft.
Main Finished	1,388 sq. ft.
Lower Finished	169 sq. ft.
Basement Unfinished	930 sq. ft.
Garage Unfinished	453 sq. ft.
Deck Unfinished	260 sq. ft.
Dimensions	40'x43'6"
Foundation	Basement
	Slab
Bedrooms	3
Full Baths	1
3/4 Baths	1
Max Ridge Height	27'
Roof Framing	Truss
Exterior Walls	2x6

Design 32140

PHOTOGRAPHY: JENIFER JORDAN

Units	Single
Price Code	B
Total Finished	1,557 sq. ft.
Main Finished	1,557 sq. ft.
Garage Unfinished	392 sq. ft.
Dimensions	81'8"x51'4"
Foundation	Slab
Bedrooms	2
Full Baths	1
3/4 Baths	1
Main Ceiling	10'5"
Vaulted Ceiling	21'7"
Max Ridge Height	26'4
Roof Framing	Stick/Truss
Exterior Walls	2x6

Please note: The photographed home may have been modified to suit homeowner preferences. If you order plans, have a builder or design professional check them against the photograph to confirm actual construction details.

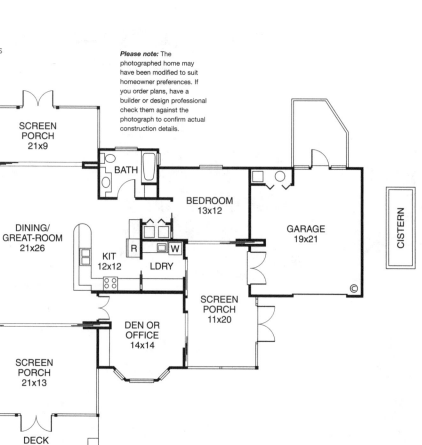

SCREEN PORCH 21x9

DECK

SHOWER   BATH

CLOS

CISTERN

MASTER BEDROOM 12x14

DINING/ GREAT-ROOM 21x26

KIT 12x12

BATH

R   W

LDRY

BEDROOM 13x12

GARAGE 19x21

CISTERN

SCREEN PORCH 11x20

DEN OR OFFICE 14x14

MAIN FLOOR

SCREEN PORCH 21x13

DECK

Design 65384

Units	Single
Price Code	B
Total Finished	1,559 sq. ft.
First Finished	945 sq. ft.
Second Finished	614 sq. ft.
Dimensions	34'x31'
Foundation	Basement
Bedrooms	3
Full Baths	1
3/4 Baths	1

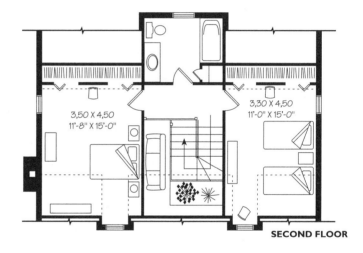

SECOND FLOOR

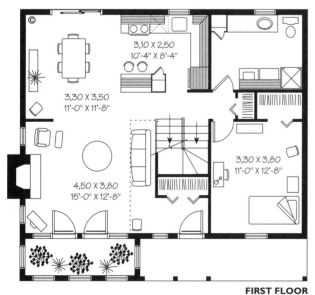

FIRST FLOOR

Design 34602

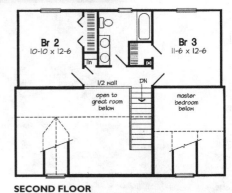

SECOND FLOOR

Units	Single
Price Code	B
Total Finished	1,560 sq. ft.
First Finished	1,061 sq. ft.
Second Finished	499 sq. ft.
Basement Unfinished	1,061 sq. ft.
Porch Unfinished	339 sq. ft.
Dimensions	44'x34'
Foundation	Basement
	Crawlspace
	Slab
Bedrooms	3
Full Baths	2
Half Baths	1
First Ceiling	8'
Second Ceiling	8'
Max Ridge Height	26'
Roof Framing	Stick
Exterior Walls	2x4, 2x6

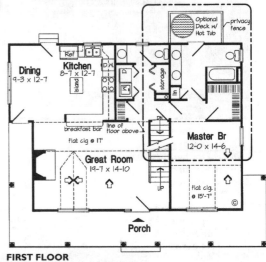

OPTIONAL CRAWLSPACE/SLAB FOUNDATION

FIRST FLOOR

Design 24705

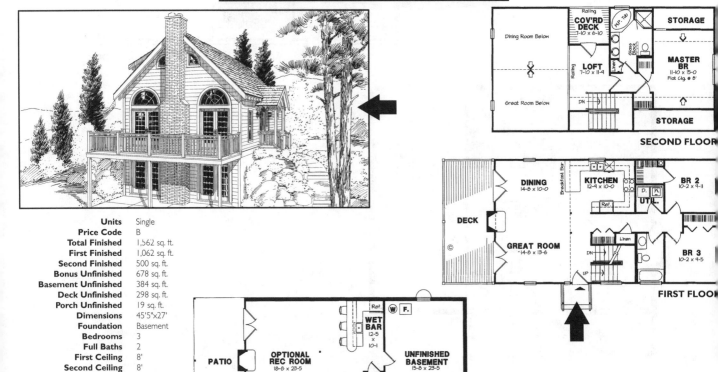

Units	Single
Price Code	B
Total Finished	1,562 sq. ft.
First Finished	1,062 sq. ft.
Second Finished	500 sq. ft.
Bonus Unfinished	678 sq. ft.
Basement Unfinished	384 sq. ft.
Deck Unfinished	298 sq. ft.
Porch Unfinished	19 sq. ft.
Dimensions	45'5"x27'
Foundation	Basement
Bedrooms	3
Full Baths	2
First Ceiling	8'
Second Ceiling	8'
Max Ridge Height	32'
Roof Framing	Stick
Exterior Walls	2x4

SECOND FLOOR

FIRST FLOOR

LOWER FLOOR

Design 10594

Units	Single
Price Code	B
Total Finished	1,565 sq. ft.
Main Finished	1,565 sq. ft.
Basement Unfinished	1,576 sq. ft.
Garage Unfinished	430 sq. ft.
Dimensions	56'8"x40'
Foundation	Basement
Bedrooms	3
Full Baths	2
Max Ridge Height	18'
Roof Framing	Stick
Exterior Walls	2x6

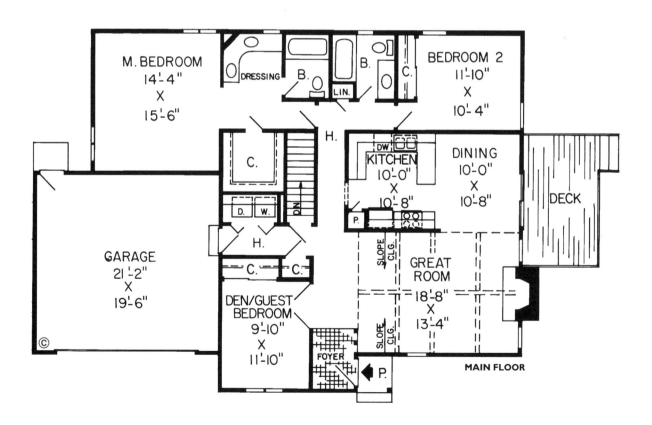

MAIN FLOOR

Design 19863

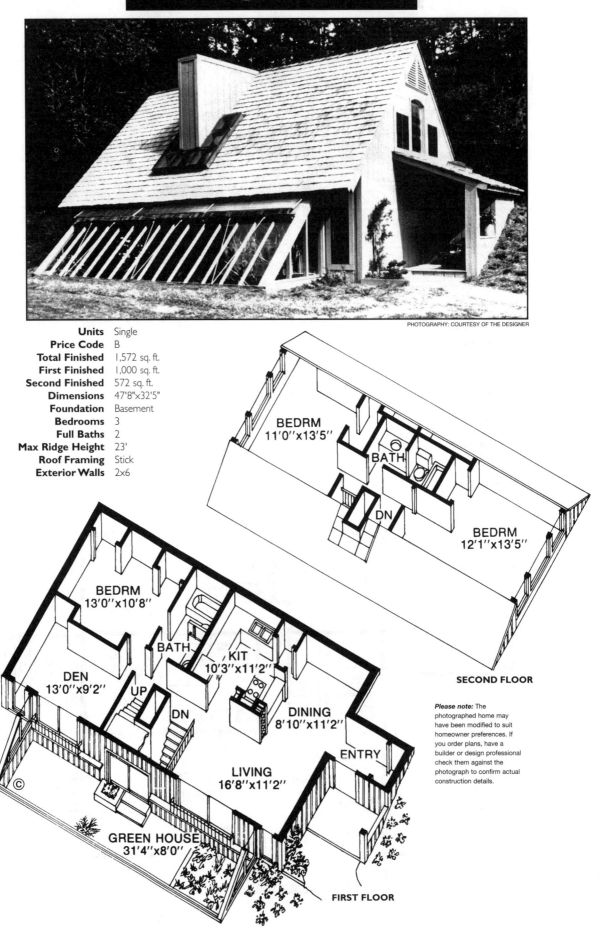

PHOTOGRAPHY: COURTESY OF THE DESIGNER

Units	Single
Price Code	B
Total Finished	1,572 sq. ft.
First Finished	1,000 sq. ft.
Second Finished	572 sq. ft.
Dimensions	47'8"x32'5"
Foundation	Basement
Bedrooms	3
Full Baths	2
Max Ridge Height	23'
Roof Framing	Stick
Exterior Walls	2x6

BEDRM 11'0''x13'5''

BATH

DN

BEDRM 12'1''x13'5''

SECOND FLOOR

BEDRM 13'0''x10'8''

BATH

KIT 10'3''x11'2''

DEN 13'0''x9'2''

UP

DN

DINING 8'10''x11'2''

ENTRY

LIVING 16'8''x11'2''

GREEN HOUSE 31'4''x8'0''

FIRST FLOOR

Please note: The photographed home may have been modified to suit homeowner preferences. If you order plans, have a builder or design professional check them against the photograph to confirm actual construction details.

Design 24708

Units	Single
Price Code	B
Total Finished	1,576 sq. ft.
Main Finished	1,576 sq. ft.
Basement Unfinished	1,454 sq. ft.
Garage Unfinished	576 sq. ft.
Porch Unfinished	391 sq. ft.
Dimensions	93'x36'
Foundation	Basement
	Crawlspace
	Slab
Bedrooms	3
Full Baths	2
Main Ceiling	8'
Max Ridge Height	19'
Roof Framing	Stick
Exterior Walls	2x4

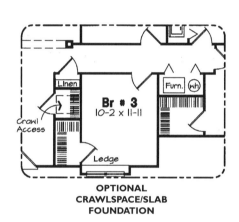

**OPTIONAL
CRAWLSPACE/SLAB
FOUNDATION**

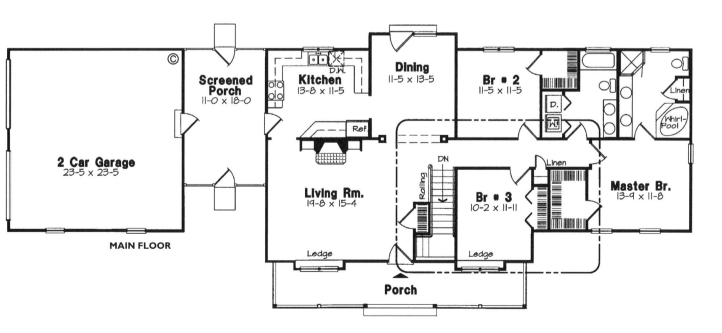

MAIN FLOOR

Design 32194

PHOTOGRAPHY: JAMES SALOMON

Units	Single
Price Code	B
Total Finished	1,579 sq. ft.
First Finished	892 sq. ft.
Second Finished	518 sq. ft.
Third Finished	169 sq. ft.
Deck Unfinished	141 sq. ft.
Porch Unfinished	82 sq. ft.
Dimensions	43'x32'6"
Foundation	Crawlspace
Bedrooms	1
3/4 Baths	1
Half Baths	1
First Ceiling	8'
Second Ceiling	8'
Vaulted Ceiling	26'8"
Max Ridge Height	42'
Roof Framing	Stick
Exterior Walls	2x6

Please note: The photographed home may have been modified to suit homeowner preferences. If you order plans, have a builder or design professional check them against the photograph to confirm actual construction details.

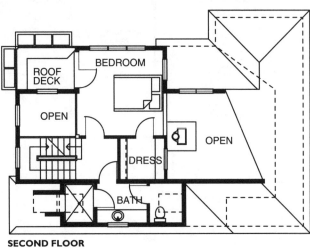

THIRD FLOOR

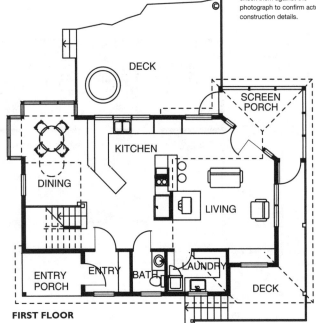

FIRST FLOOR

SECOND FLOOR

Design 81009

MAIN FLOOR

Units	Single
Price Code	B
Total Finished	1,580 sq. ft.
Main Finished	1,580 sq. ft.
Garage Unfinished	452 sq. ft.
Dimensions	48'x50'
Foundation	Crawlspace
Bedrooms	3
Full Baths	2
Half Baths	1

Design 90633

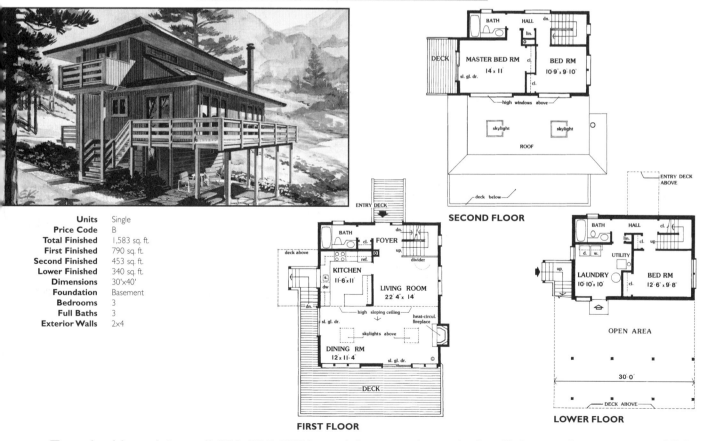

Units	Single
Price Code	B
Total Finished	1,583 sq. ft.
First Finished	790 sq. ft.
Second Finished	453 sq. ft.
Lower Finished	340 sq. ft.
Dimensions	30'x40'
Foundation	Basement
Bedrooms	3
Full Baths	3
Exterior Walls	2x4

SECOND FLOOR

FIRST FLOOR

LOWER FLOOR

Units	Single
Price Code	B
Total Finished	1,590 sq. ft.
Main Finished	1,590 sq. ft.
Basement Unfinished	900 sq. ft.
Dimensions	81'2"x27'8"
Foundation	Basement
	Slab
Bedrooms	3
Full Baths	2
Half Baths	1
Max Ridge Height	17'6"
Roof Framing	Stick
Exterior Walls	2x4

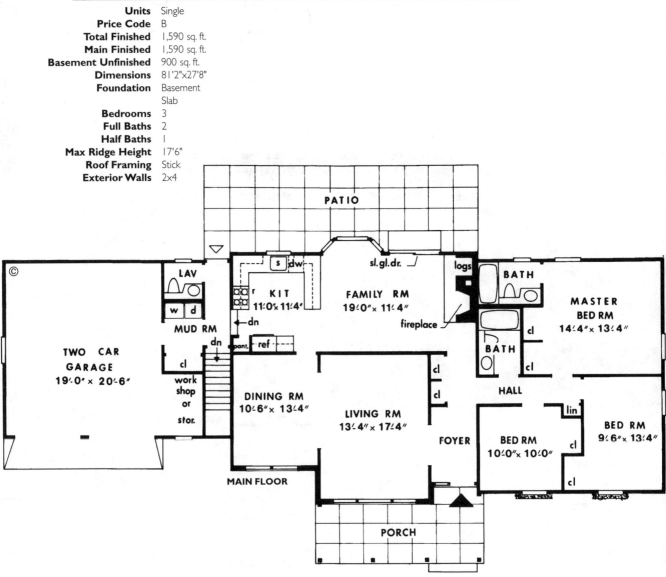

Design 97762

Units	Single
Price Code	B
Total Finished	1,594 sq. ft.
Main Finished	1,594 sq. ft.
Basement Unfinished	1,594 sq. ft.
Garage Unfinished	512 sq. ft.
Deck Unfinished	328 sq. ft.
Porch Unfinished	125 sq. ft.
Dimensions	52'8"x55'5"
Foundation	Basement
Bedrooms	3
Full Baths	2
Main Ceiling	8'
Vaulted Ceiling	10'
Max Ridge Height	23'6"
Roof Framing	Truss
Exterior Walls	2x4

Bedroom 11'8" x 10'5"

THIRD BEDROOM OPTION

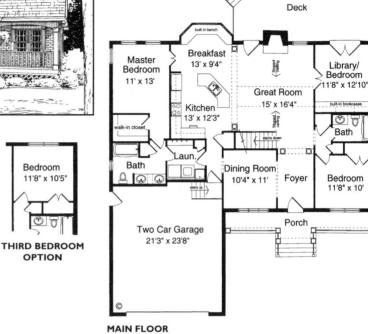

MAIN FLOOR

Design 97769

Units	Single
Price Code	B
Total Finished	1,594 sq. ft.
Main Finished	1,594 sq. ft.
Basement Unfinished	1,594 sq. ft.
Garage Unfinished	512 sq. ft.
Deck Unfinished	328 sq. ft.
Porch Unfinished	125 sq. ft.
Dimensions	52'8"x55'5"
Foundation	Basement
Bedrooms	3
Full Baths	2
Main Ceiling	8'
Vaulted Ceiling	10'
Max Ridge Height	23'6"
Roof Framing	Truss
Exterior Walls	2x4

MAIN FLOOR

Design 24242

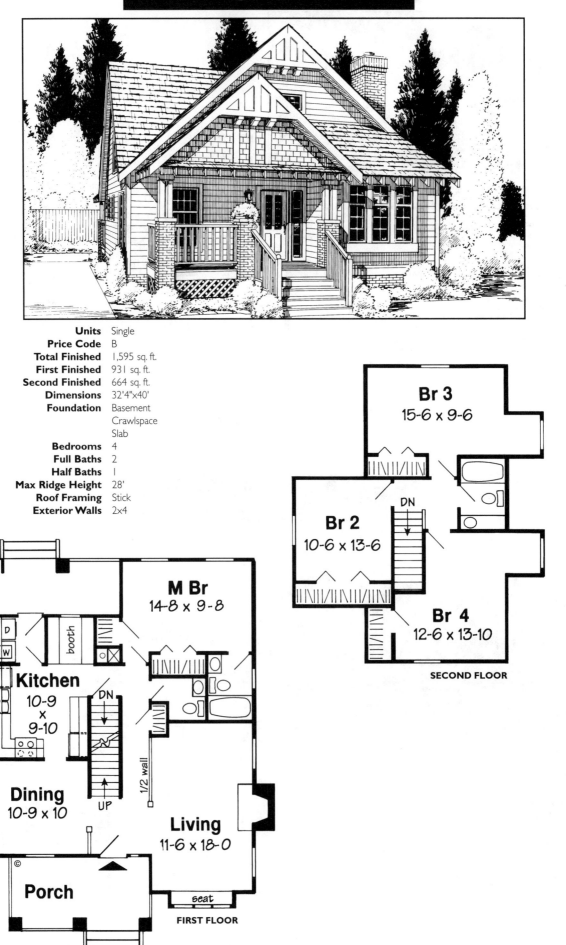

Units	Single
Price Code	B
Total Finished	1,595 sq. ft.
First Finished	931 sq. ft.
Second Finished	664 sq. ft.
Dimensions	32'4"x40'
Foundation	Basement
	Crawlspace
	Slab
Bedrooms	4
Full Baths	2
Half Baths	1
Max Ridge Height	28'
Roof Framing	Stick
Exterior Walls	2x4

Br 3
15-6 x 9-6

Br 2
10-6 x 13-6

DN

Br 4
12-6 x 13-10

SECOND FLOOR

Kitchen
10-9 x 9-10

D W
booth

M Br
14-8 x 9-8

DN

1/2 wall

Dining
10-9 x 10

UP

Living
11-6 x 18-0

seat

Porch

FIRST FLOOR

Design 10328

Units	Single
Price Code	B
Total Finished	1,600 sq. ft.
First Finished	1,024 sq. ft.
Second Finished	576 sq. ft.
Basement Unfinished	1,024 sq. ft.
Dimensions	32'x32'
Foundation	Basement
Bedrooms	3
Full Baths	1
3/4 Baths	1
Max Ridge Height	25'
Roof Framing	Stick
Exterior Walls	2x4

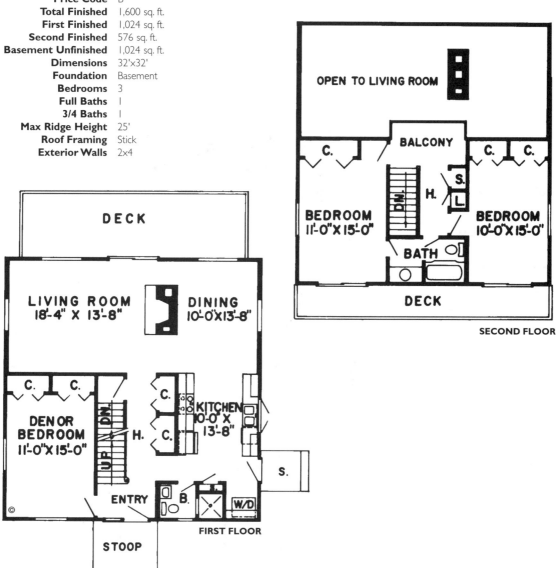

Design 92803

Units	Single
Price Code	B
Total Finished	1,600 sq. ft.
Main Finished	1,600 sq. ft.
Dimensions	48'x40'
Foundation	Crawlspace
	Slab
	Pier/Post
Bedrooms	4
Full Baths	2
Max Ridge Height	16'
Roof Framing	Stick/Truss
Exterior Walls	2x6

MAIN FLOOR

BEDROOM 4
11'0" x 9'6"

MASTER BEDROOM
13'6" x 13'4"

SCREENED PORCH
8'0" x 24'0"

GREAT ROOM/DINING
19'6" x 23'0"

KITCHEN
11'6" x 12'0"

BATH

WIC

BATH

LAUNDRY

DECK
14'0" x 4'0"

BEDROOM 3
11'0" x 9'6"

BEDROOM 2
11'0" x 9'6"

Design 65191

Units	Single
Price Code	B
Total Finished	1,606 sq. ft.
First Finished	902 sq. ft.
Second Finished	704 sq. ft.
Dimensions	34'8"x37'4"
Foundation	Basement
Bedrooms	3
Full Baths	1
Half Baths	1

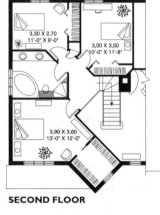

SECOND FLOOR

3,30 X 2,70
11'-0" X 9'-0"

3,00 X 3,50
10'-0" X 11'-8"

3,90 X 3,60
13'-0" X 12'-0"

3,70 X 3,80
12'-4" X 12'-8"

3,60 X 3,80
12'-0" X 12'-8"

3,60 X 5,40
12'-0" X 18'-0"

3,90 X 6,20
13'-0" X 20'-8"

FIRST FLOOR

Design 90418

Units	Single
Price Code	B
Total Finished	1,607 sq. ft.
First Finished	1,304 sq. ft.
Second Finished	303 sq. ft.
Dimensions	68'x33'
Foundation	Basement
	Crawlspace
	Slab
Bedrooms	3
Full Baths	2
Exterior Walls	2x4

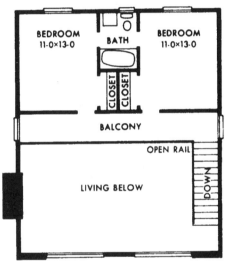

SECOND FLOOR

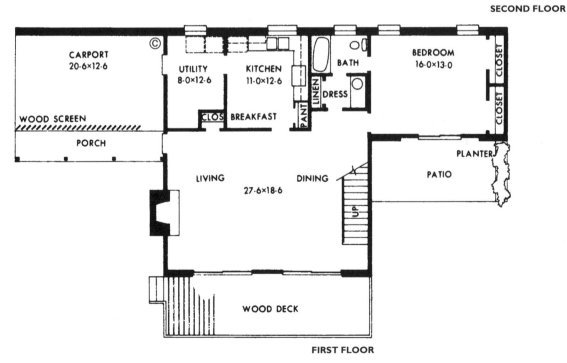

FIRST FLOOR

Design 90859

Units	Single
Price Code	B
Total Finished	1,611 sq. ft.
First Finished	843 sq. ft.
Second Finished	768 sq. ft.
Deck Finished	250 sq. ft.
Dimensions	28'x48'6"
Foundation	Crawlspace
Bedrooms	3
Full Baths	1
Half Baths	1
Max Ridge Height	24'
Roof Framing	Stick
Exterior Walls	2x6

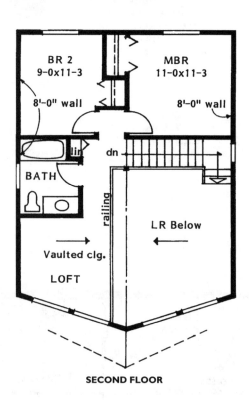

SECOND FLOOR

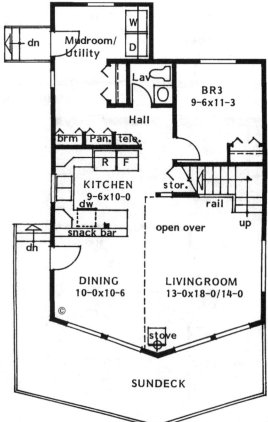

FIRST FLOOR

Design 90601

Units	Single
Price Code	B
Total Finished	1,613 sq. ft.
First Finished	1,613 sq. ft.
Basement Unfinished	1,060 sq. ft.
Garage Unfinished	461 sq. ft.
Dimensions	83'8"x27'4"
Foundation	Basement
	Slab
Bedrooms	3
Full Baths	2
Half Baths	1
Max Ridge Height	20'
Roof Framing	Stick
Exterior Walls	2x4

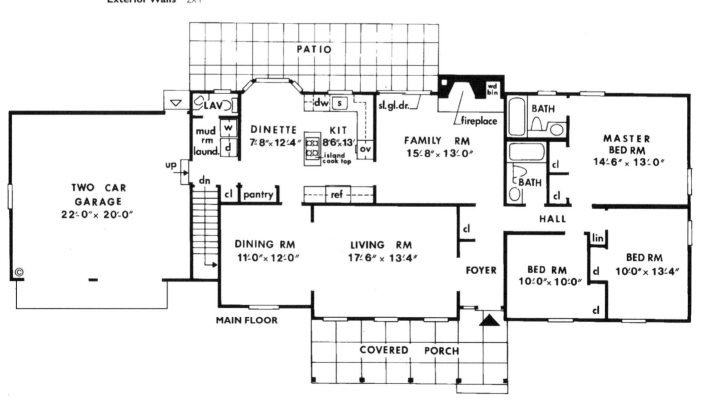

Design 97632

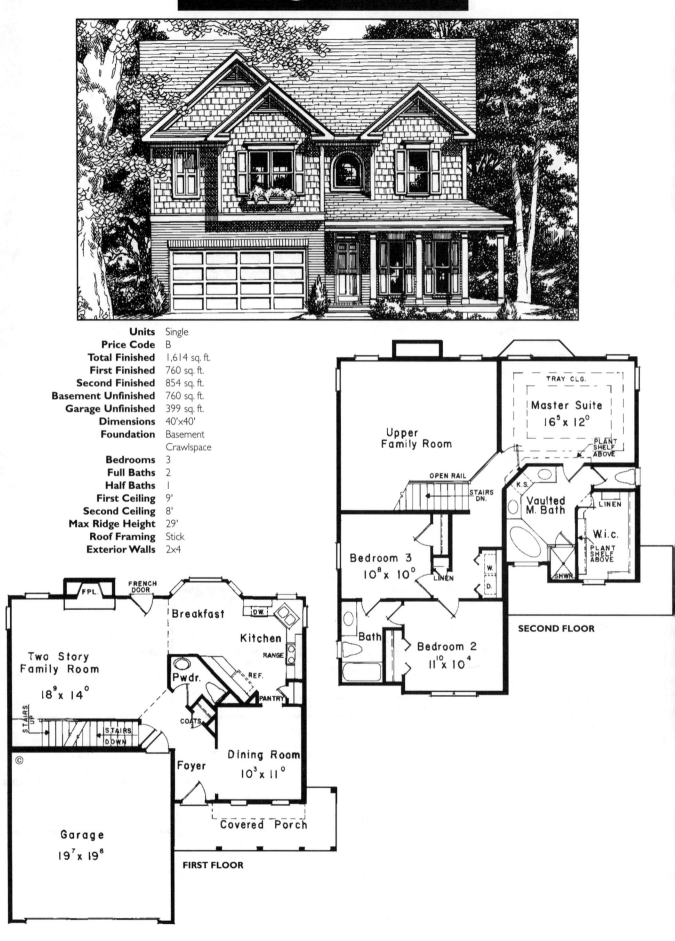

Units	Single
Price Code	B
Total Finished	1,614 sq. ft.
First Finished	760 sq. ft.
Second Finished	854 sq. ft.
Basement Unfinished	760 sq. ft.
Garage Unfinished	399 sq. ft.
Dimensions	40'x40'
Foundation	Basement
	Crawlspace
Bedrooms	3
Full Baths	2
Half Baths	1
First Ceiling	9'
Second Ceiling	8'
Max Ridge Height	29'
Roof Framing	Stick
Exterior Walls	2x4

SECOND FLOOR

TRAY CLG.

Master Suite
16⁵ x 12⁰

PLANT SHELF ABOVE

Upper Family Room

OPEN RAIL

STAIRS DN.

K.S.

Vaulted M. Bath

LINEN

W.i.c.

PLANT SHELF ABOVE

Bedroom 3
10⁸ x 10⁰

LINEN

W.

D.

SHWR.

Bath

Bedroom 2
11¹⁰ x 10⁴

FIRST FLOOR

FPL.

FRENCH DOOR

Breakfast

DW.

Kitchen

RANGE

Two Story Family Room
18⁹ x 14⁰

Pwdr.

REF.

PANTRY

STAIRS UP

STAIRS DOWN

COATS

Dining Room
10³ x 11⁰

Foyer

Garage
19⁷ x 19⁸

Covered Porch

Design 65194

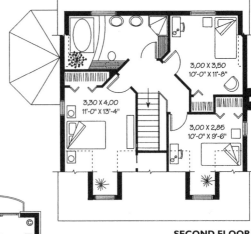

SECOND FLOOR

Units	Single
Price Code	B
Total Finished	1,635 sq. ft.
First Finished	907 sq. ft.
Second Finished	728 sq. ft.
Dimensions	35'6"x28'8"
Foundation	Basement
Bedrooms	3
Full Baths	1
Half Baths	1

3.00 X 3.50
10'-0" X 11'-8"

3.30 X 4.00
11'-0" X 13'-4"

3.00 X 2.85
10'-0" X 9'-6"

3.10 X 2.30
10'-4" X 7'-8"

3.60 X 3.60
12'-0" X 12'-0"

3.15 X 3.10
10'-6" X 10'-4"

3.60 X 4.40
12'-0" X 14'-8"

FIRST FLOOR

Design 24717

Units	Single
Price Code	B
Total Finished	1,642 sq. ft.
Main Finished	1,642 sq. ft.
Basement Unfinished	1,642 sq. ft.
Garage Unfinished	430 sq. ft.
Porch Unfinished	156 sq. ft.
Dimensions	59'x44'
Foundation	Basement
	Crawlspace
	Slab
Bedrooms	3
Full Baths	2
Main Ceiling	9'
Vaulted Ceiling	13'6"
Max Ridge Height	24'
Roof Framing	Stick
Exterior Walls	2x4

**OPTIONAL BASEMENT
STAIR LOCATION**

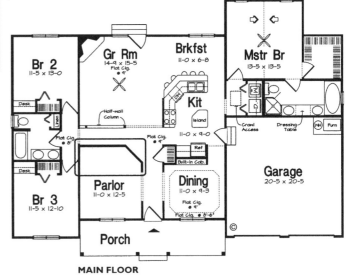

Br 2
11-5 x 13-0

Gr Rm
14-9 x 15-5
Flat Clg.
• 9'

Brkfst
11-0 x 6-8

Mstr Br
13-5 x 13-5

Kit

Half-Wall
Column

Crawl
Access

Dressing
Table

Flat Clg.
• 8'

Flat Clg.
• 9'

Built-in Cab.

11-0 x 9-0

Br 3
11-5 x 12-10

Parlor
11-0 x 12-5

Dining
11-0 x 9-3

Flat Clg.
• 9'

Flat Clg. • 9'-8"

Garage
20-5 x 20-5

Porch

MAIN FLOOR

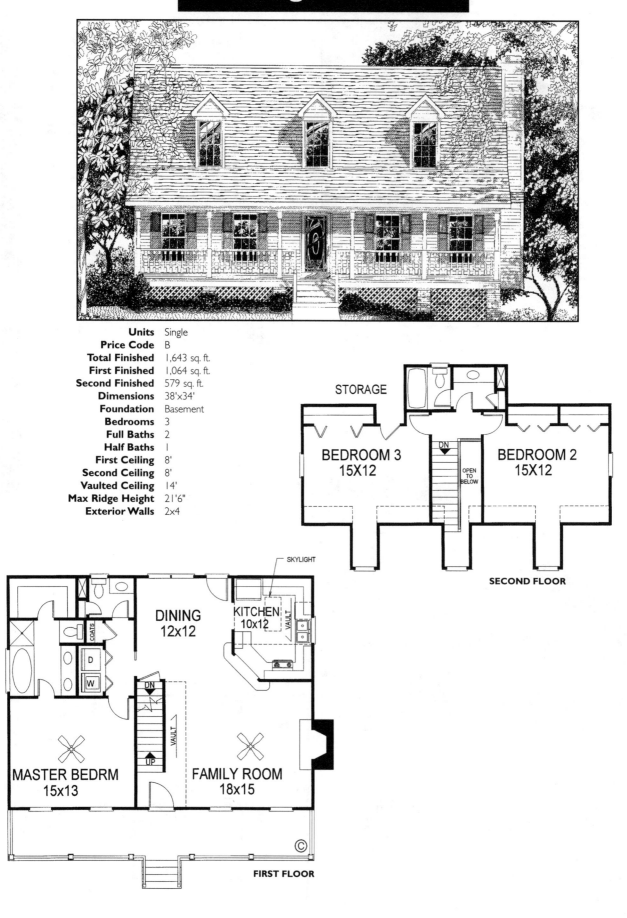

Units	Single
Price Code	B
Total Finished	1,643 sq. ft.
First Finished	1,064 sq. ft.
Second Finished	579 sq. ft.
Dimensions	38'x34'
Foundation	Basement
Bedrooms	3
Full Baths	2
Half Baths	1
First Ceiling	8'
Second Ceiling	8'
Vaulted Ceiling	14'
Max Ridge Height	21'6"
Exterior Walls	2x4

STORAGE

BEDROOM 3
15X12

DN

OPEN
TO
BELOW

BEDROOM 2
15X12

SECOND FLOOR

SKYLIGHT

DINING
12x12

KITCHEN
10x12

VAULT

COATS

D

W

DN

VAULT

UP

VAULT

MASTER BEDRM
15x13

FAMILY ROOM
18x15

FIRST FLOOR

Design 94240

Units	Single
Price Code	E
Total Finished	1,647 sq. ft.
Main Finished	1,647 sq. ft.
Garage Unfinished	427 sq. ft.
Porch Unfinished	341 sq. ft.
Dimensions	58'x58'
Foundation	Slab
Bedrooms	3
Full Baths	2
Main Ceiling	8'
Vaulted Ceiling	12'
Max Ridge Height	17'
Roof Framing	Truss

* Alternate foundation options available at an additional charge.
Please call 1-800-235-5700 for more information.

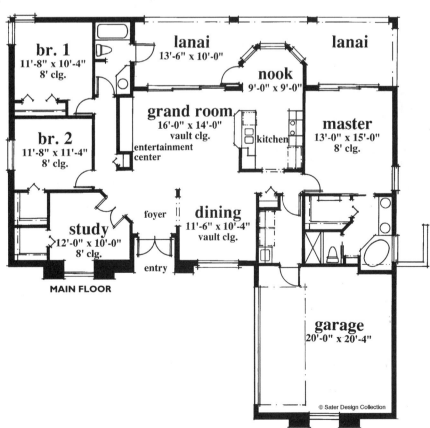

MAIN FLOOR

br. 1
11'-8" x 10'-4"
8' clg.

br. 2
11'-8" x 11'-4"
8' clg.

study
12'-0" x 10'-0"
8' clg.

lanai
13'-6" x 10'-0"

lanai

nook
9'-0" x 9'-0"

grand room
16'-0" x 14'-0"
vault clg.

entertainment
center

kitchen

master
13'-0" x 15'-0"
8' clg.

foyer

dining
11'-6" x 10'-4"
vault clg.

entry

garage
20'-0" x 20'-4"

© Sater Design Collection

Design 92422

SECOND FLOOR

LOFT
23'-1" x 15'-6"

40" KNEE WALL

OPEN BELOW
20' HIGH CEILING

VAULT   VAULT

VAULT   VAULT

Units	Single
Price Code	B
Total Finished	1,647 sq. ft.
First Finished	1,288 sq. ft.
Second Finished	359 sq. ft.
Dimensions	28'x46'
Foundation	Slab
Bedrooms	2
Full Baths	1
First Ceiling	8'
Second Ceiling	11'
Vaulted Ceiling	20'
Max Ridge Height	25'3"
Roof Framing	Stick
Exterior Walls	2x4

BEDROOM 1
11'-10" x 10'-0"

COATS

BEDROOM 2
11'-4" x 10'-0"

W/D

LINEN

PANTRY

GREAT ROOM
27'-4" x 29'-5"
20' HIGH CEILING

VAULT   VAULT

DECK/PATIO
11'-6" x 18'-8"

DECK
7'-6" x 36'-0"

PORCH
24'-4" x 7'-6"

FIRST FLOOR

Design 96513

Units	Single
Price Code	B
Total Finished	1,648 sq. ft.
Main Finished	1,648 sq. ft.
Garage Unfinished	479 sq. ft.
Dimensions	68'x50'
Foundation	Crawlspace
	Slab
Bedrooms	3
Full Baths	2
Half Baths	1
Main Ceiling	9'
Max Ridge Height	20'
Roof Framing	Stick
Exterior Walls	2x4

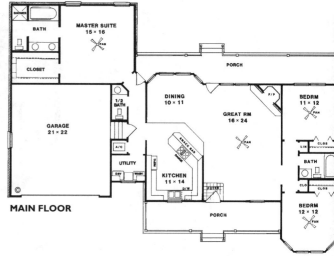

BATH

MASTER SUITE
15 x 16
FAN

CLOSET

GARAGE
21 x 22

1/2 BATH

A/C

UTILITY

DRY   WASH

DINING
10 x 11

PORCH

F/P

GREAT RM
16 x 24
FAN

BEDRM
11 x 12
FAN

KITCHEN
11 x 14
D/W

FAN

LIN   CLOS

BATH

CLOS   CLOS

BEDRM
12 x 12
FAN

PORCH

MAIN FLOOR

Design 99635

Units	Single
Price Code	B
Total Finished	1,650 sq. ft.
Main Finished	1,650 sq. ft.
Garage Unfinished	491 sq. ft.
Dimensions	83'2"×42'4"
Foundation	Basement
	Slab
Bedrooms	3
Full Baths	2
Half Baths	1
Max Ridge Height	24'
Roof Framing	Stick
Exterior Walls	2x6

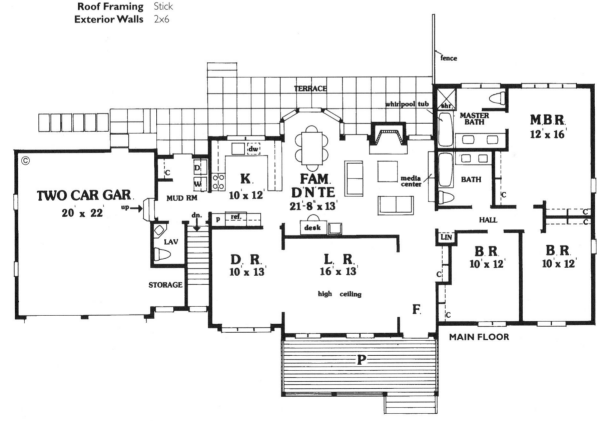

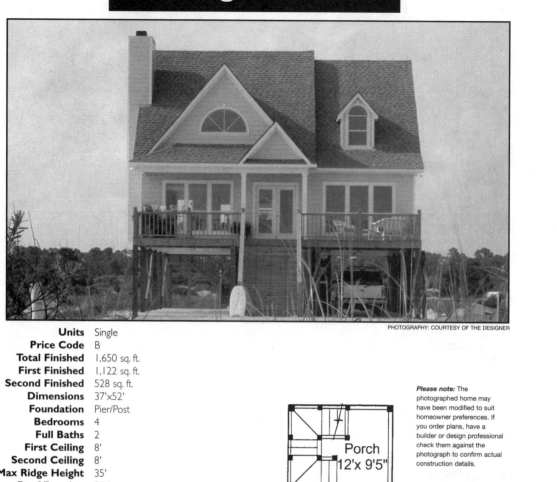

PHOTOGRAPHY: COURTESY OF THE DESIGNER

Units	Single
Price Code	B
Total Finished	1,650 sq. ft.
First Finished	1,122 sq. ft.
Second Finished	528 sq. ft.
Dimensions	37'x52'
Foundation	Pier/Post
Bedrooms	4
Full Baths	2
First Ceiling	8'
Second Ceiling	8'
Max Ridge Height	35'
Roof Framing	Stick
Exterior Walls	2x4

Please note: The photographed home may have been modified to suit homeowner preferences. If you order plans, have a builder or design professional check them against the photograph to confirm actual construction details.

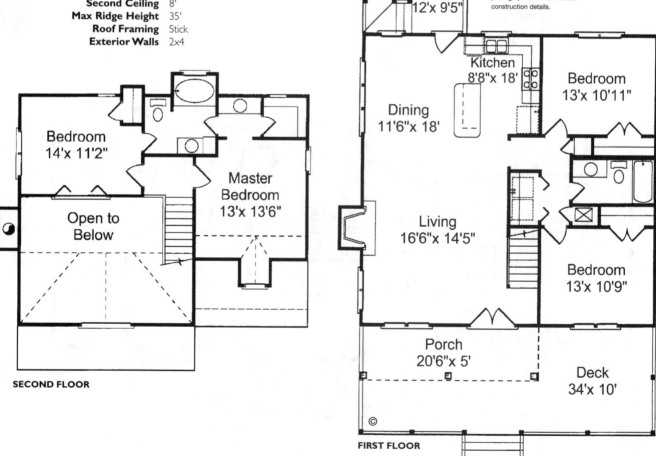

SECOND FLOOR

Bedroom 14'x 11'2"

Open to Below

Master Bedroom 13'x 13'6"

FIRST FLOOR

Porch 12'x 9'5"

Kitchen 8'8"x 18'

Dining 11'6"x 18'

Bedroom 13'x 10'11"

Living 16'6"x 14'5"

Bedroom 13'x 10'9"

Porch 20'6"x 5'

Deck 34'x 10'

Design 94938

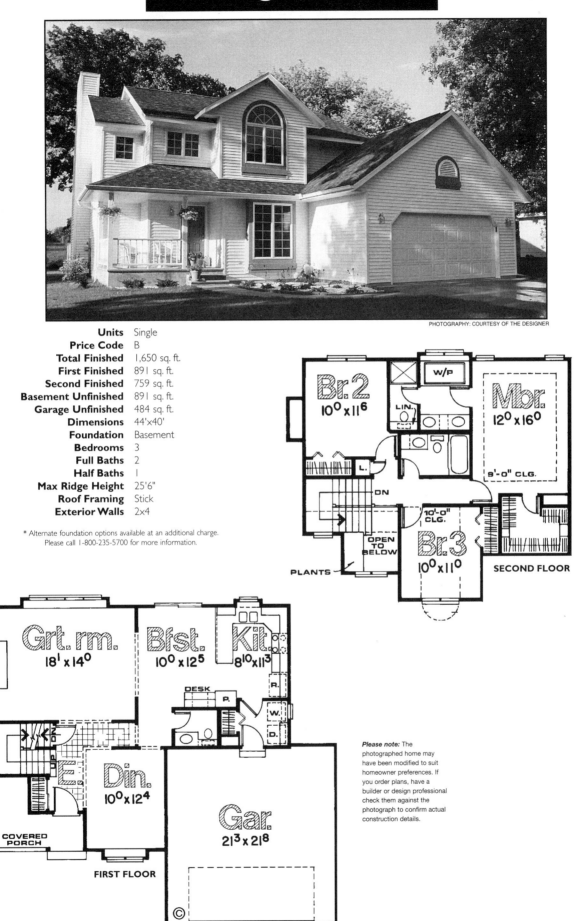

PHOTOGRAPHY: COURTESY OF THE DESIGNER

Units	Single
Price Code	B
Total Finished	1,650 sq. ft.
First Finished	891 sq. ft.
Second Finished	759 sq. ft.
Basement Unfinished	891 sq. ft.
Garage Unfinished	484 sq. ft.
Dimensions	44'x40'
Foundation	Basement
Bedrooms	3
Full Baths	2
Half Baths	1
Max Ridge Height	25'6"
Roof Framing	Stick
Exterior Walls	2x4

* Alternate foundation options available at an additional charge. Please call 1-800-235-5700 for more information.

Please note: The photographed home may have been modified to suit homeowner preferences. If you order plans, have a builder or design professional check them against the photograph to confirm actual construction details.

SECOND FLOOR

FIRST FLOOR

Units	Single
Price Code	B
Total Finished	1,654 sq. ft.
Main Finished	1,654 sq. ft.
Garage Unfinished	480 sq. ft.
Porch Unfinished	401 sq. ft.
Dimensions	68'x46'
Foundation	Crawlspace
	Slab
Bedrooms	3
Full Baths	2
Half Baths	1
Main Ceiling	9'
Max Ridge Height	21'
Roof Framing	Stick
Exterior Walls	2x4

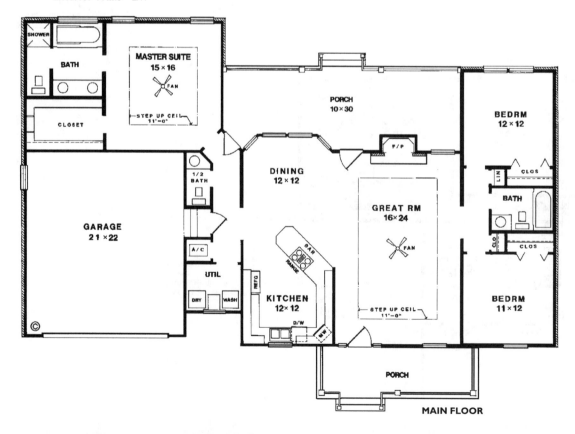

MAIN FLOOR

Design 32088

PHOTOGRAPHY: COURTESY OF THE DESIGNER

Units	Single
Price Code	B
Total Finished	1,654 sq. ft.
First Finished	1,096 sq. ft.
Second Finished	558 sq. ft.
Garage Unfinished	520 sq. ft.
Porch Unfinished	144 sq. ft.
Dimensions	62'x44'
Foundation	Crawlspace
Bedrooms	3
Full Baths	1
3/4 Baths	1
Half Baths	1
First Ceiling	9'
Second Ceiling	8'
Max Ridge Height	24'
Roof Framing	Stick/Truss
Exterior Walls	2x6

SECOND FLOOR

Hot New Design

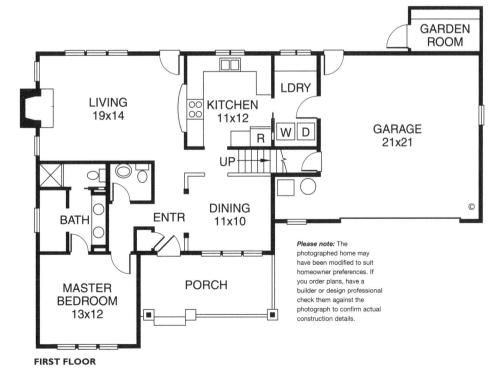

FIRST FLOOR

Please note: The photographed home may have been modified to suit homeowner preferences. If you order plans, have a builder or design professional check them against the photograph to confirm actual construction details.

Design 65246

SECOND FLOOR

Units	Single
Price Code	B
Total Finished	1,659 sq. ft.
First Finished	1,109 sq. ft.
Second Finished	550 sq. ft.
Basement Unfinished	1,659 sq. ft.
Porch Unfinished	211 sq. ft.
Dimensions	36'x36'
Foundation	Basement
Bedrooms	3
Full Baths	2
First Ceiling	8'
Second Ceiling	8'
Max Ridge Height	26'4"
Roof Framing	Truss
Exterior Walls	2x6

FIRST FLOOR

Design 94655

PHOTOGRAPHY: COURTESY OF THE DESIGNER

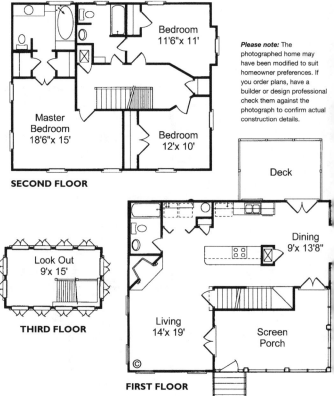

SECOND FLOOR

Please note: The photographed home may have been modified to suit homeowner preferences. If you order plans, have a builder or design professional check them against the photograph to confirm actual construction details.

Units	Single
Price Code	C
Total Finished	1,666 sq. ft.
First Finished	731 sq. ft.
Second Finished	935 sq. ft.
Third Finished	138 sq. ft.
Dimensions	35'x38'
Foundation	Pier/Post
Bedrooms	3
Full Baths	3
First Ceiling	9'
Second Ceiling	8'
Max Ridge Height	39'
Roof Framing	Stick
Exterior Walls	2x4

THIRD FLOOR

FIRST FLOOR

Design 93219

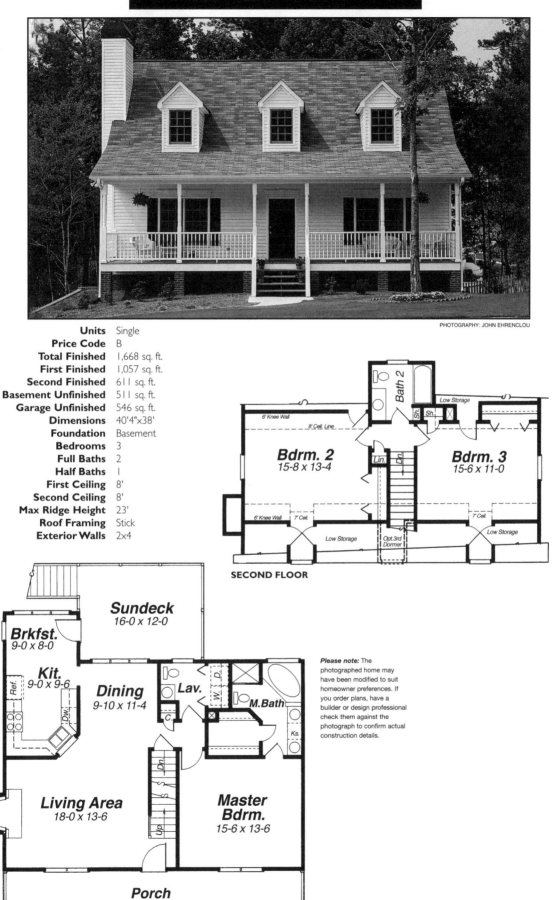

PHOTOGRAPHY: JOHN EHRENCLOU

Units	Single
Price Code	B
Total Finished	1,668 sq. ft.
First Finished	1,057 sq. ft.
Second Finished	611 sq. ft.
Basement Unfinished	511 sq. ft.
Garage Unfinished	546 sq. ft.
Dimensions	40'4"x38'
Foundation	Basement
Bedrooms	3
Full Baths	2
Half Baths	1
First Ceiling	8'
Second Ceiling	8'
Max Ridge Height	23'
Roof Framing	Stick
Exterior Walls	2x4

SECOND FLOOR

Bath 2

Low Storage

6' Knee Wall

8' Ceil. Line

Bdrm. 2
15-8 x 13-4

Lin.

Dn

Bdrm. 3
15-6 x 11-0

6' Knee Wall

7' Ceil.

7' Ceil.

Low Storage

Opt. 3rd Dormer

Low Storage

FIRST FLOOR

Sundeck
16-0 x 12-0

Brkfst.
9-0 x 8-0

Kit.
9-0 x 9-6

Ref.

Dw.

Dining
9-10 x 11-4

Lav.

W. D.

C.

M.Bath

Ks.

Dn

Living Area
18-0 x 13-6

Up

Master Bdrm.
15-6 x 13-6

Porch

Please note: The photographed home may have been modified to suit homeowner preferences. If you order plans, have a builder or design professional check them against the photograph to confirm actual construction details.

Design 32513

PHOTOGRAPHY: COURTESY OF THE DESIGNER

Units	Single
Price Code	B
Total Finished	1,669 sq. ft.
First Finished	1,113 sq. ft.
Second Finished	556 sq. ft.
Garage Unfinished	272 sq. ft.
Dimensions	34'6"x42'
Foundation	Crawlspace
Bedrooms	3
Full Baths	1
3/4 Baths	1
Max Ridge Height	26'
Roof Framing	Stick
Exterior Walls	2x6

Hot New Design

SECOND FLOOR

CLOSET

STOR

MASTER BEDROOM
12x18

PORCH

DN

STUDY
11x6

MECH

OPEN TO LIVING

FIRST FLOOR

BEDROOM
12x10

BEDROOM
11x11

DECK

KITCHEN
10x18

DINING
11x9

UP

ENTRY

LIVING
12x15

PORCH

Please note: The photographed home may have been modified to suit homeowner preferences. If you order plans, have a builder or design professional check them against the photograph to confirm actual construction details.

Win free blueprints!

2 Easy Ways to Enter

1. Log on to www.garlinghouse.com and fill out our questionnaire on-line

—OR—

2. Fill out the questionnaire below and mail to:

   Free Home Plans Contest
   Garlinghouse, LLC
   4125 Lafayette Rd. Ste. 100
   Chantilly, VA 20151

1. To Enter
No purchase necessary. Limit one entry per person per calendar month.

2. Contest Period
May 15, 2004 to May 15, 2005.

3. Selection of Winners
One drawing will be held on or near the last day of each month during the drawing period. One winner will be selected each month by a random drawing from all entries received during the previous month. Odds of winning depend on the number of entries received.

4. Prize
A four-copy set (our "Minimum 4-Set Construction Package") of the home plan of the winner's choice will be awarded to one winner per month during the contest period. Home plans not offered for sale by the Garlinghouse Company are not eligible.

5. Eligibility
This drawing is open to U.S. residents who are 18 years of age or older at the time of entry. Employees and consultants of Garlinghouse and its parent, affiliates, subsidiaries, advertising and promotion agencies and members of the immediate families of any Garlinghouse employee or consultant are not eligible to enter. Void where prohibited by law.

6. Terms & Conditions
The Garlinghouse Company is not responsible for taxes or shipping charges. *For complete rules, terms and conditions, additional fine print, and information regarding notification of winners, log on to* www.garlinghouse.com.

Name: _____

Address: _____

City: _____ **State:** _____ **Zip:** _____

Daytime telephone number: ( ) _____ **Email:** _____

the **Garlinghouse** company

Where did you buy this publication?
- ❏ Newsstand
- ❏ Grocery store
- ❏ Pharmacy/Conv. store
- ❏ Lumberyard/Home Center
- ❏ Bookstore
- ❏ Other _____
- Please specify store: _____

Why did you buy this publication?
- ❏ Value
- ❏ Number of plans
- ❏ Appealing cover photo
- ❏ Impulse
- ❏ Other _____

What style are you most interested in?
- ❏ Farmhouse or Country
- ❏ Colonial
- ❏ Rustic Cottage or Cabin
- ❏ Victorian
- ❏ European
- ❏ Traditional
- ❏ Other _____

When are you planning to build?
- ❏ Within 6 months
- ❏ 6-12 months
- ❏ 1-2 years
- ❏ More than 2 years
- ❏ Undecided

What is the approximate size of the home?
- ❏ Under 1,000 square feet
- ❏ 1,000 to 2,000
- ❏ 2,000 to 3,000
- ❏ 3,000 to 4,000
- ❏ Over 4,000

What type of home?
- ❏ One level
- ❏ Two story with all bedrooms on second floor
- ❏ Two story with one or two bedrooms on first floor
- ❏ Other _____

Have you bought land? ❏ Yes ❏ No

Please provide any other comments.
Let us know if you have special requirements (e.g. you want a great-room but no living room) or specific property features (e.g. you have a sloped or narrow lot).

_____

_____

Design 90409

Units	Single
Price Code	B
Total Finished	1,670 sq. ft.
Main Finished	1,670 sq. ft.
Basement Unfinished	1,670 sq. ft.
Garage Unfinished	427 sq. ft.
Dimensions	73'8"x30'
Foundation	Basement
	Crawlspace
	Slab
Bedrooms	3
Full Baths	2
Max Ridge Height	18'6"
Roof Framing	Stick
Exterior Walls	2x4

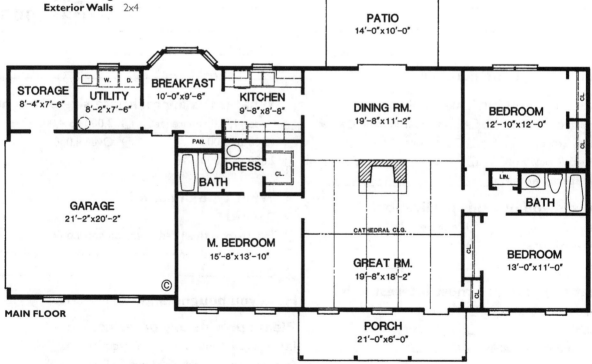

MAIN FLOOR

Design 91071

SECOND FLOOR

Units	Single
Price Code	B
Total Finished	1,671 sq. ft.
First Finished	1,329 sq. ft.
Second Finished	342 sq. ft.
Garage Unfinished	885 sq. ft.
Deck Unfinished	461 sq. ft.
Dimensions	32'x45'7"
Foundation	Crawlspace
	Slab
Bedrooms	3
Full Baths	2
Max Ridge Height	31'
Roof Framing	Stick
Exterior Walls	2x6

LOWER FLOOR

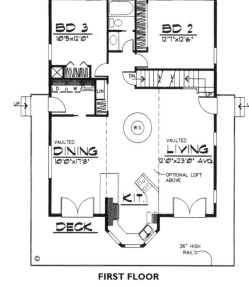

FIRST FLOOR

Design 99914

Units	Single
Price Code	B
Total Finished	1,677 sq. ft.
First Finished	1,064 sq. ft.
Second Finished	613 sq. ft.
Porch Unfinished	32 sq. ft.
Dimensions	28'x40'
Foundation	Basement
	Crawlspace
Bedrooms	2
Full Baths	2
First Ceiling	8'
Second Ceiling	8'
Vaulted Ceiling	22'
Roof Framing	Stick
Exterior Walls	2x6

SECOND FLOOR

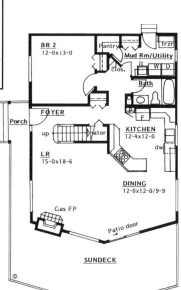

FIRST FLOOR

Design 68213

Units	Single
Price Code	B
Total Finished	1,678 sq. ft.
Main Finished	1,678 sq. ft.
Basement Unfinished	1,678 sq. ft.
Garage Unfinished	509 sq. ft.
Dimensions	46'x55'
Foundation	Basement
Bedrooms	3
Full Baths	2
Main Ceiling	9'
Max Ridge Height	24'11"
Roof Framing	Stick
Exterior Walls	2x4

* Alternate foundation options available at an additional charge.
Please call 1-800-235-5700 for more information.

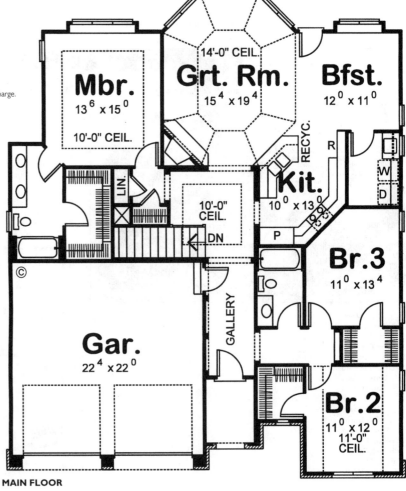

MAIN FLOOR

Design 91785

Units	Single
Price Code	B
Total Finished	1,680 sq. ft.
First Finished	960 sq. ft.
Second Finished	720 sq. ft.
Dimensions	40'x24'
Foundation	Crawlspace
Bedrooms	3
Full Baths	1
3/4 Baths	1
Max Ridge Height	25'
Roof Framing	Stick
Exterior Walls	2x6

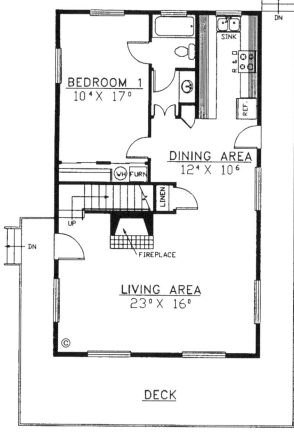

BEDROOM 1
10⁴ X 17⁰

DINING AREA
12⁴ X 10⁶

LIVING AREA
23⁰ X 16⁰

FIREPLACE

DECK

FIRST FLOOR

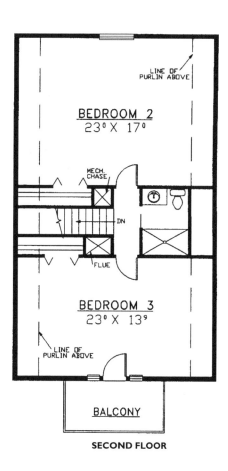

LINE OF
PURLIN ABOVE

BEDROOM 2
23⁰ X 17⁰

MECH.
CHASE

FLUE

BEDROOM 3
23⁰ X 13⁹

LINE OF
PURLIN ABOVE

BALCONY

SECOND FLOOR

Design 94256

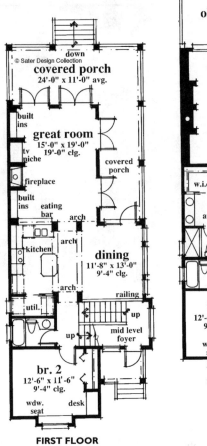

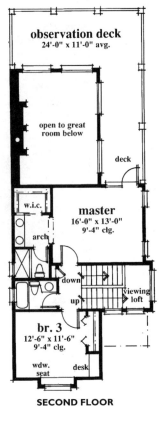

© Sater Design Collection

FIRST FLOOR

covered porch
24'-0" x 11'-0" avg.

down

built ins

great room
15'-0" x 19'-0"
19'-0" clg.

tv niche

fireplace

covered porch

built ins

eating bar

arch

kitchen

arch

dining
11'-8" x 13'-0"
9'-4" clg.

arch

util.

arch

railing

up

br. 2
12'-6" x 11'-6"
9'-4" clg.

up

mid level foyer

wdw. seat

desk

SECOND FLOOR

observation deck
24'-0" x 11'-0" avg.

open to great room below

deck

w.i.c.

arch

master
16'-0" x 13'-0"
9'-4" clg.

down

up

viewing loft

br. 3
12'-6" x 11'-6"
9'-4" clg.

wdw. seat

desk

Units	Single
Price Code	F
Total Finished	1,684 sq. ft.
First Finished	1,046 sq. ft.
Second Finished	638 sq. ft.
Dimensions	25'x65'6"
Foundation	Crawlspace
	Post/Pier
Bedrooms	3
Full Baths	2
3/4 Baths	1
Max Ridge Height	38'
Roof Framing	Stick/Truss
Exterior Walls	2x6

* Alternate foundation options available at an additional charge.
Please call 1-800-235-5700 for more information.

Design 92804

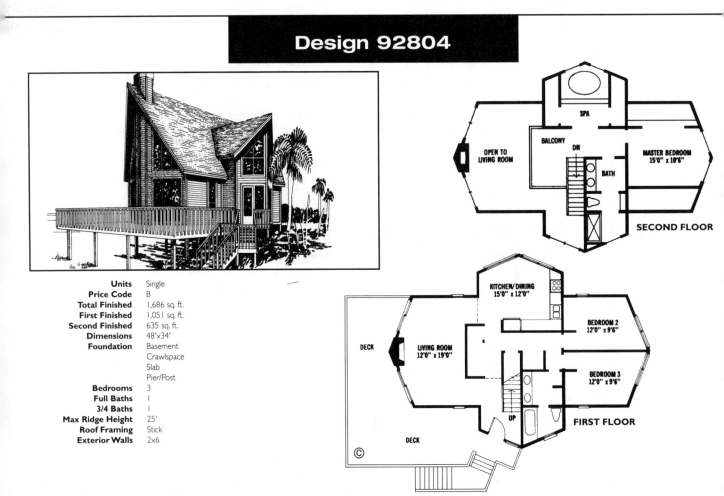

SECOND FLOOR

SPA

BALCONY

DN

OPEN TO LIVING ROOM

BATH

MASTER BEDROOM
15'0" x 10'6"

FIRST FLOOR

KITCHEN/DINING
15'0" x 12'0"

DECK

LIVING ROOM
12'0" x 19'0"

BEDROOM 2
12'0" x 9'6"

BEDROOM 3
12'0" x 9'6"

UP

DECK

Units	Single
Price Code	B
Total Finished	1,686 sq. ft.
First Finished	1,051 sq. ft.
Second Finished	635 sq. ft.
Dimensions	48'x34'
Foundation	Basement
	Crawlspace
	Slab
	Pier/Post
Bedrooms	3
Full Baths	1
3/4 Baths	1
Max Ridge Height	25'
Roof Framing	Stick
Exterior Walls	2x6

Design 10548

Units	Single
Price Code	B
Total Finished	1,688 sq. ft.
Main Finished	1,688 sq. ft.
Basement Unfinished	1,688 sq. ft.
Garage Unfinished	489 sq. ft.
Porch Unfinished	120 sq. ft.
Dimensions	68'x41'
Foundation	Basement
Bedrooms	3
Full Baths	1
3/4 Baths	1
Half Baths	1
Max Ridge Height	20'
Roof Framing	Stick
Exterior Walls	2x6

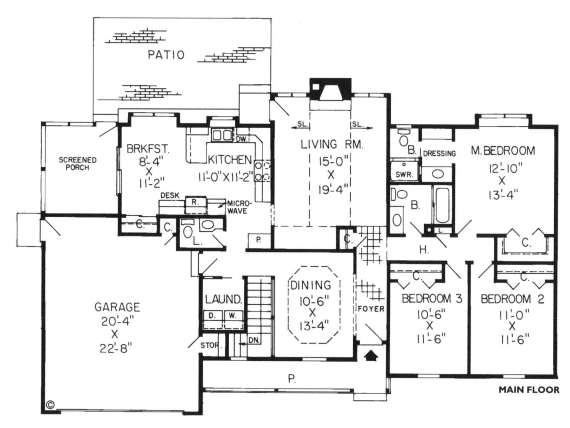

PATIO

SCREENED PORCH

BRKFST.
8'-4"
X
11'-2"

KITCHEN
11'-0"X11'-2"

DESK

MICROWAVE

R.

C.

C.

L.

LIVING RM.
15'-0"
X
19'-4"

SL.   SL.

B.   DRESSING

SWR.

B.

H.

M. BEDROOM
12'-10"
X
13'-4"

C.

GARAGE
20'-4"
X
22'-8"

LAUND.

D.   W.

STOR.

DN.

DINING
10'-6"
X
13'-4"

FOYER

P.

P.

C.

BEDROOM 3
10'-6"
X
11'-6"

BEDROOM 2
11'-0"
X
11'-6"

C.

MAIN FLOOR

Design 97254

Units	Single
Price Code	B
Total Finished	1,692 sq. ft.
Main Finished	1,692 sq. ft.
Bonus Unfinished	358 sq. ft.
Basement Unfinished	1,705 sq. ft.
Garage Unfinished	472 sq. ft.
Dimensions	54'x56'6"
Foundation	Basement
	Crawlspace
Bedrooms	3
Full Baths	2
Max Ridge Height	27'
Roof Framing	Stick
Exterior Walls	2x4

CAD FILES AVAILABLE
For more information call
800-235-5700

Vaulted M.Bath
SHWR.
LINEN
W.i.c.

RADIUS WINDOW
FPL.
RADIUS WINDOW

Breakfast

Bedroom 3
11³ x 11⁰

PLANT SHELF ABOVE

Vaulted Great Room
15⁰ x 20⁰
14'-6" CLG. HT.

SERVING BAR
Kitchen
REF
PANTRY
DW.
RANGE

LINEN
Bath

FRENCH DOOR

Master Suite
15⁰ x 13²
TRAY CLG.

DECORATIVE COLUMN
COATS
Bedroom 2
11⁰ x 11⁰

ARCHED OPG.
VAULT
Sitting Room
STAIRS UP

ARCHED OPG.
Foyer
14'-6" CLG. HT.

Dining Room
11⁰ x 12⁴
12'-0" CLG. HT.

RADIUS WINDOW
VAULT
W. D.
Laund.

STAIRS TO OPT. BSMT.

MAIN FLOOR

Garage
20⁵ x 22²

Covered Porch

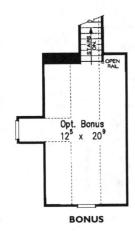

STAIRS DN
OPEN RAIL
Opt. Bonus
12⁵ x 20⁹

BONUS

Design 50013

Units	Single
Price Code	B
Total Finished	1,697 sq. ft.
First Finished	1,263 sq. ft.
Second Finished	434 sq. ft.
Basement Unfinished	1,263 sq. ft.
Garage Unfinished	393 sq. ft.
Porch Unfinished	111 sq. ft.
Dimensions	55'2"x57'3"
Foundation	Basement
Bedrooms	3
Full Baths	2
Half Baths	1
First Ceiling	8'
Second Ceiling	8'
Max Ridge Height	24'6"
Roof Framing	Truss
Exterior Walls	2x4

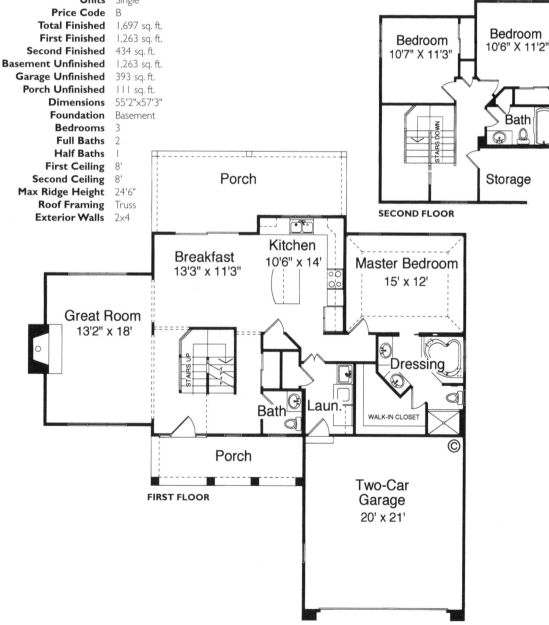

SECOND FLOOR

Bedroom 10'7" X 11'3"

Bedroom 10'6" X 11'2"

Bath

Storage

FIRST FLOOR

Porch

Breakfast 13'3" x 11'3"

Kitchen 10'6" x 14'

Master Bedroom 15' x 12'

Great Room 13'2" x 18'

STAIRS UP

Bath

Laun.

Dressing

WALK-IN CLOSET

Porch

Two-Car Garage 20' x 21'

Units	Single
Price Code	B
Total Finished	1,702 sq. ft.
First Finished	1,238 sq. ft.
Second Finished	464 sq. ft.
Basement Unfinished	1,175 sq. ft.
Garage Unfinished	484 sq. ft.
Deck Unfinished	509 sq. ft.
Dimensions	34'x56'
Foundation	Basement
Bedrooms	3
Full Baths	1
3/4 Baths	1
First Ceiling	8'
Max Ridge Height	26'6"
Roof Framing	Stick
Exterior Walls	2x6

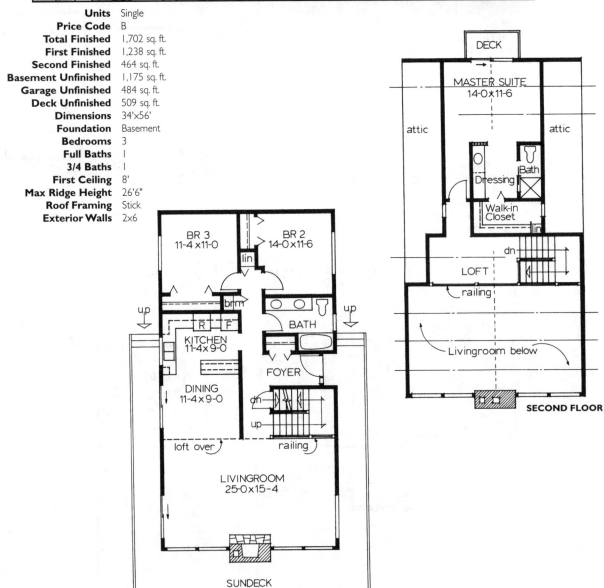

FIRST FLOOR

SECOND FLOOR

Rear Elevation

SECOND FLOOR

3,60 X 3,60	12'-0" X 12'-0"
3,90 X 6,10	13'-0" X 20'-4"
2,70 X 3,60	9'-0" X 12'-0"

FIRST FLOOR

3,60 X 3,00	12'-0" X 10'-0"
4,50 X 4,20	15'-0" X 14'-0"
2,70 X 2,60	9'-0" X 8'-8"
3,90 X 3,60	13'-0" X 12'-0"

Units	Single
Price Code	B
Total Finished	1,704 sq. ft.
First Finished	1,008 sq. ft.
Second Finished	696 sq. ft.
Garage Unfinished	320 sq. ft.
Dimensions	34'x34'
Foundation	Basement
Bedrooms	3
Full Baths	2
First Ceiling	8'
Second Ceiling	8'
Max Ridge Height	33'
Roof Framing	Truss

Design 32343

PHOTOGRAPHY: JAMES YOCHUM PHOTOGRAPHY

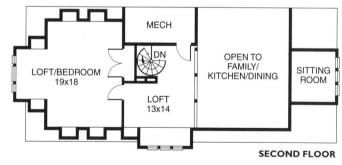

SECOND FLOOR

LOFT/BEDROOM 19x18

MECH

DN

LOFT 13x14

OPEN TO FAMILY/ KITCHEN/DINING

SITTING ROOM

FIRST FLOOR

PORCH

W/D

UP ENTRY

FAMILY 17x12

SCREEN PORCH 10x27

MASTER BEDROOM 11x13

GUEST 10x13

KIT/DINING 17x11

R

PORCH

Units	Single
Price Code	B
Total Finished	1,705 sq. ft.
First Finished	1,124 sq. ft.
Second Finished	581 sq. ft.
Porch Unfinished	513 sq. ft.
Dimensions	60'x29'2"
Foundation	Crawlspace Pier/Post
Bedrooms	3
Full Baths	1
3/4 Baths	1
Half Baths	1
First Ceiling	8'
Second Ceiling	7'6"
Vaulted Ceiling	16'2"
Max Ridge Height	24'4"
Roof Framing	Stick
Exterior Walls	2x6

Please note: The photographed home may have been modified to suit homeowner preferences. If you order plans, have a builder or design professional check them against the photograph to confirm actual construction details.

Design 94250

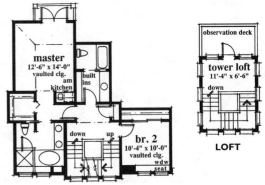

master 12'-6" x 14'-0" vaulted clg. am kitchen built ins

br. 2 10'-4" x 10'-0" vaulted clg. w d w seat

down up

SECOND FLOOR

observation deck

tower loft 11'-4" x 6'-6"

down

LOFT

Units	Single
Price Code	F
Total Finished	1,706 sq. ft.
First Finished	906 sq. ft.
Second Finished	714 sq. ft.
Lower Finished	86 sq. ft.
Basement Unfinished	155 sq. ft.
Garage Unfinished	950 sq. ft.
Deck Unfinished	116 sq. ft.
Porch Unfinished	471 sq. ft.
Dimensions	40'x37'
Foundation	Pier/Post
Bedrooms	2
Full Baths	2
Half Baths	1
First Ceiling	8'
Second Ceiling	8'
Max Ridge Height	47'6"
Roof Framing	Stick/Truss
Exterior Walls	2x6

* Alternate foundation options available at an additional charge.
Please call 1-800-235-5700 for more information.

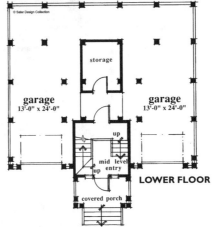

© Sater Design Collection

storage

garage 13'-0" x 24'-0"

garage 13'-0" x 24'-0"

up

up mid level entry up

covered porch

LOWER FLOOR

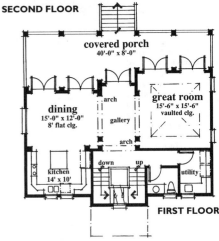

covered porch 40'-0" x 8'-0"

dining 15'-0" x 12'-0" 8' flat clg.

arch gallery arch

great room 15'-6" x 15'-6" vaulted clg.

kitchen 14' x 10'

down up

utility

FIRST FLOOR

Design 24319

PHOTOGRAPHY: JOHN EHRENCLOU

Please note: The photographed home may have been modified to suit homeowner preferences. If you order plans, have a builder or design professional check them against the photograph to confirm actual construction details.

Units	Single
Price Code	B
Total Finished	1,710 sq. ft.
First Finished	728 sq. ft.
Second Finished	573 sq. ft.
Lower Finished	409 sq. ft.
Garage Unfinished	244 sq. ft.
Dimensions	28'x32'
Foundation	Basement
Bedrooms	3
Full Baths	2
First Ceiling	8'
Second Ceiling	8'
Max Ridge Height	33'
Roof Framing	Stick
Exterior Walls	2x4, 2x6

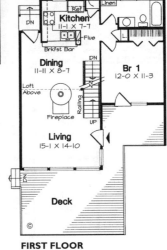

DN Ref Broom Linen

Kitchen 11-1 X 7-7

Brkfst Bar Flue

Dining 11-11 X 8-7

DN

Loft Above Railing

Br 1 12-0 X 11-3

Fireplace UP

Living 15-1 X 14-10

DN

Deck

©

FIRST FLOOR

Loft/ Br 3 11-7 X 16-6 Clg @ 9'-6"

Railing DN

Open to Below

Clerestory Windows Above

Roof

Mbr 11-8 X 14-0

Balcony

SECOND FLOOR

Util Rm 10-11 X 5-9

Wet Bar

Garage 11-8 X 19-0

Rec Rm 11-1 X 20-2

Optional Hot Tub

storage Step

LOWER FLOOR

Design 93909

Units	Single
Price Code	B
Total Finished	1,716 sq. ft.
Main Finished	1,716 sq. ft.
Basement Unfinished	1,716 sq. ft.
Dimensions	72'x46'
Foundation	Basement
Bedrooms	3
Full Baths	2
Max Ridge Height	22'6"
Exterior Walls	2x6

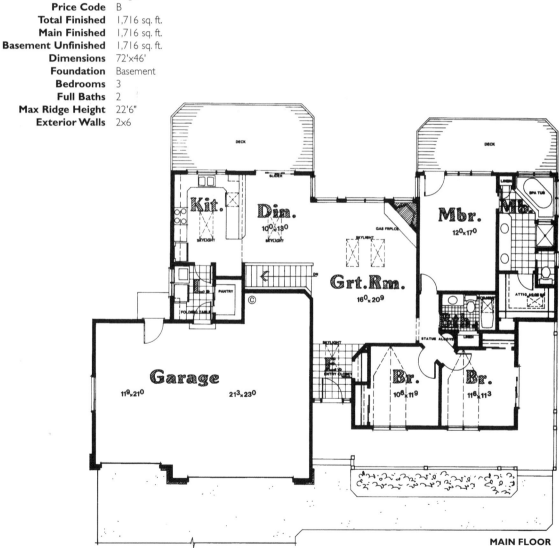

MAIN FLOOR

Design 97773

Units	Single
Price Code	B
Total Finished	1,727 sq. ft.
First Finished	939 sq. ft.
Second Finished	788 sq. ft.
Bonus Unfinished	210 sq. ft.
Basement Unfinished	939 sq. ft.
Garage Unfinished	401 sq. ft.
Porch Unfinished	65 sq. ft.
Dimensions	34'x52'2"
Foundation	Basement
Bedrooms	3
Full Baths	1
3/4 Baths	1
Half Baths	1
First Ceiling	8'
Second Ceiling	8'
Max Ridge Height	27'10"
Roof Framing	Truss
Exterior Walls	2x4

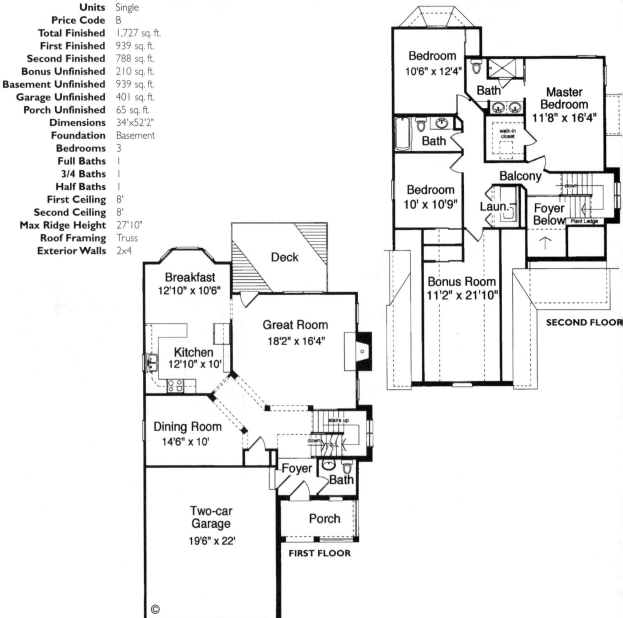

Bedroom 10'6" x 12'4"

Bath

Master Bedroom 11'8" x 16'4"

walk-in closet

Bath

Balcony

Bedroom 10' x 10'9"

Laun.

Foyer Below

Plant Ledge

Bonus Room 11'2" x 21'10"

SECOND FLOOR

Deck

Breakfast 12'10" x 10'6"

Great Room 18'2" x 16'4"

Kitchen 12'10" x 10'

Dining Room 14'6" x 10'

stairs up

down

Foyer

Bath

Two-car Garage 19'6" x 22'

Porch

FIRST FLOOR

Design 68211

Units	Single
Price Code	B
Total Finished	1,728 sq. ft.
First Finished	1,071 sq. ft.
Second Finished	657 sq. ft.
Bonus Unfinished	368 sq. ft.
Garage Unfinished	525 sq. ft.
Dimensions	41'8"x48'4"
Foundation	Basement
Bedrooms	3
Full Baths	3
First Ceiling	9'
Second Ceiling	8'
Max Ridge Height	30'
Roof Framing	Stick
Exterior Walls	2x4

* Alternate foundation options available at an additional charge.
Please call 1-800-235-5700 for more information.

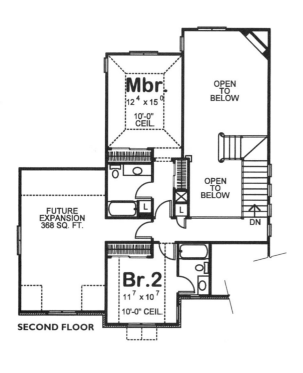

SECOND FLOOR

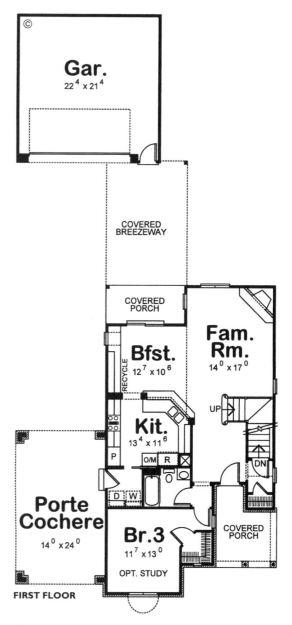

FIRST FLOOR

Design 90611

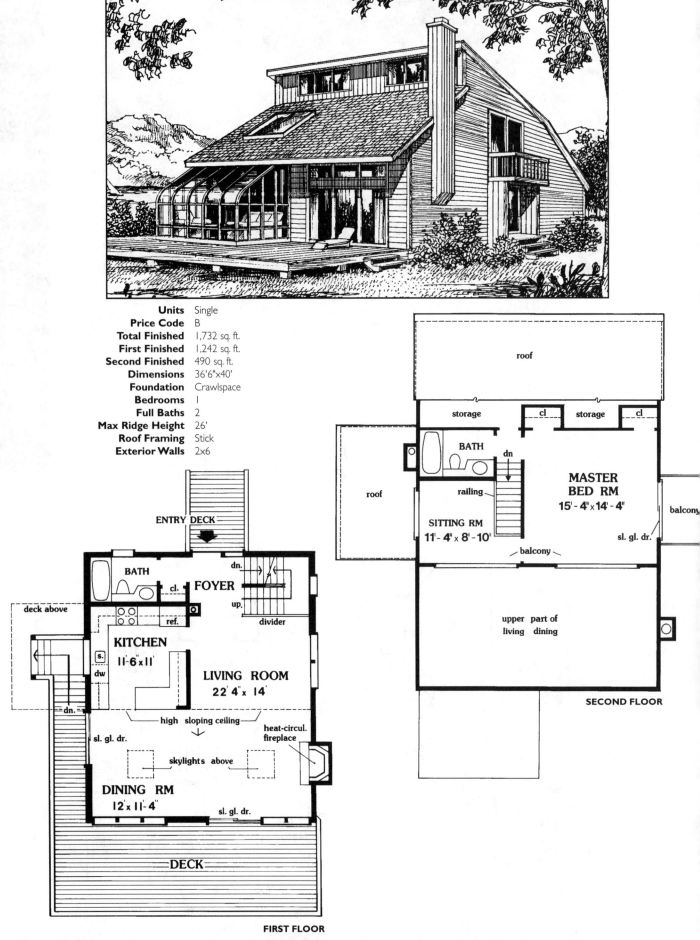

Units	Single
Price Code	B
Total Finished	1,732 sq. ft.
First Finished	1,242 sq. ft.
Second Finished	490 sq. ft.
Dimensions	36'6"x40'
Foundation	Crawlspace
Bedrooms	1
Full Baths	2
Max Ridge Height	26'
Roof Framing	Stick
Exterior Walls	2x6

SECOND FLOOR

roof

storage   cl   storage   cl

BATH

dn

MASTER
BED RM
15'-4" x 14'-4"

balcony

roof

railing

SITTING RM
11'-4" x 8'-10"

sl. gl. dr.

balcony

upper   part of
living   dining

FIRST FLOOR

ENTRY DECK

dn.

BATH   cl.   FOYER

up.

deck above

divider

KITCHEN
11'-6" x 11'

ref.

s.

dw

LIVING ROOM
22'-4" x 14'

dn.

high   sloping ceiling

heat-circul.
fireplace

sl. gl. dr.

skylights   above

DINING RM
12' x 11'-4"

sl. gl. dr.

DECK

Design 94646

PHOTOGRAPHY: COURTESY OF THE DESIGNER

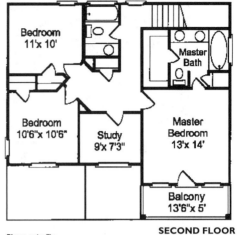

SECOND FLOOR

Please note: The photographed home may have been modified to suit homeowner preferences. If you order plans, have a builder or design professional check them against the photograph to confirm actual construction details.

Units	Single
Price Code	B
Total Finished	1,743 sq. ft.
First Finished	912 sq. ft.
Second Finished	831 sq. ft.
Dimensions	34'x32'
Foundation	Post
Bedrooms	3
Full Baths	3
First Ceiling	9'
Second Ceiling	8'
Max Ridge Height	36'
Roof Framing	Stick
Exterior Walls	2x4

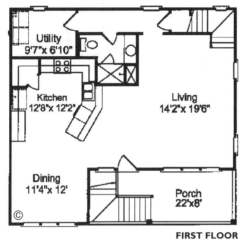

FIRST FLOOR

Design 97456

Units	Single
Price Code	C
Total Finished	1,758 sq. ft.
Main Finished	1,758 sq. ft.
Garage Unfinished	494 sq. ft.
Dimensions	55'4"x49'8"
Foundation	Basement
Bedrooms	3
Full Baths	2
Main Ceiling	9'
Max Ridge Height	26'
Roof Framing	Stick
Exterior Walls	2x4

Alternate foundation options available at an additional charge. Please call 1-800-235-5700 for more information.

MAIN FLOOR

© William E. Poole Designs, Inc.

Units	Single
Price Code	Please call for pricing
Total Finished	1,762 sq. ft.
First Finished	1,211 sq. ft.
Second Finished	551 sq. ft.
Bonus Unfinished	378 sq. ft.
Dimensions	64'4"x39'4"
Foundation	Combo Basement/ Crawlspace
Bedrooms	3
Full Baths	2
Half Baths	1
Max Ridge Height	27'
Roof Framing	Stick
Exterior Walls	2x4

Hot New Design

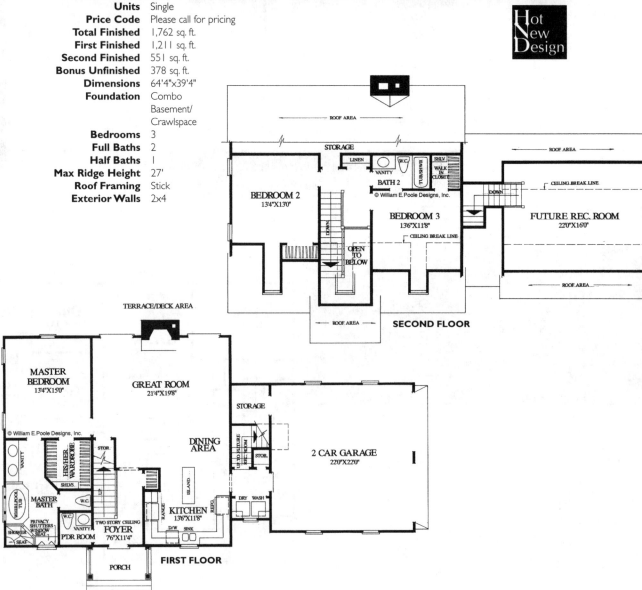

Design 34901

Units	Single
Price Code	C
Total Finished	1,763 sq. ft.
First Finished	909 sq. ft.
Second Finished	854 sq. ft.
Basement Unfinished	899 sq. ft.
Garage Unfinished	491 sq. ft.
Dimensions	48'x44'
Foundation	Basement
	Crawlspace
	Slab
Bedrooms	3
Full Baths	1
3/4 Baths	1
Half Baths	1
First Ceiling	8'
Second Ceiling	8'
Tray Ceiling	9'
Max Ridge Height	29'
Roof Framing	Stick
Exterior Walls	2x4, 2x6

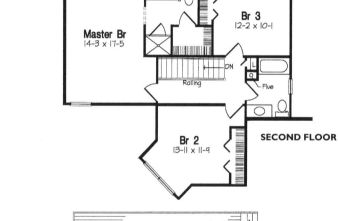

SECOND FLOOR

Master Br
14-3 x 17-5

Br 3
12-2 x 10-1

Br 2
13-11 x 11-9

**OPTIONAL
CRAWLSPACE/SLAB
FOUNDATION**

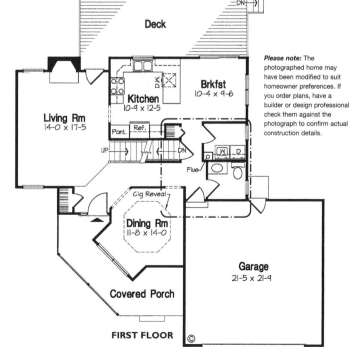

Deck

Living Rm
14-0 x 17-5

Kitchen
10-9 x 12-5

Brkfst
10-4 x 9-6

Dining Rm
11-8 x 14-0

Garage
21-5 x 21-9

Covered Porch

FIRST FLOOR

Please note: The photographed home may have been modified to suit homeowner preferences. If you order plans, have a builder or design professional check them against the photograph to confirm actual construction details.

Design 94204

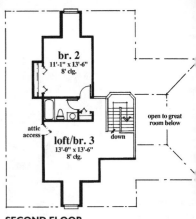

SECOND FLOOR

br. 2
11'-1" x 13'-6"
8' clg.

loft/br. 3
13'-0" x 13'-6"
8' clg.

attic access

down

open to great room below

Please note: The photographed home may have been modified to suit homeowner preferences. If you order plans, have a builder or design professional check them against the photograph to confirm actual construction details.

PHOTOGRAPHY: COURTESY OF THE DESIGNER

Units	Single
Price Code	C
Total Finished	1,764 sq. ft.
First Finished	1,189 sq. ft.
Second Finished	575 sq. ft.
Bonus Unfinished	581 sq. ft.
Garage Unfinished	658 sq. ft.
Dimensions	46'x44'6"
Foundation	Pier/Post
Bedrooms	3
Full Baths	2
Half Baths	1
Max Ridge Height	36'
Roof Framing	Stick/Truss
Exterior Walls	2x6

* Alternate foundation options available at an additional charge. Please call 1-800-235-5700 for more information.

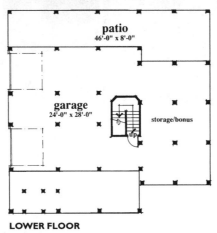

patio
46'-0" x 8'-0"

garage
24'-0" x 28'-0"

storage/bonus

up

LOWER FLOOR

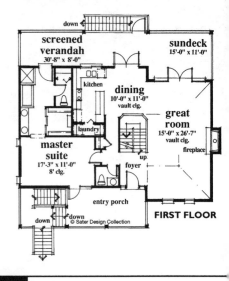

screened verandah
30'-8" x 8'-0"

sundeck
15'-0" x 11'-0"

kitchen

dining
10'-0" x 11'-0"
vault clg.

great room
15'-0" x 26'-7"
vault clg.

laundry

master suite
17'-3" x 11'-0"
8' clg.

foyer

fireplace

up

down

entry porch

down

© Sater Design Collection

FIRST FLOOR

Design 32603

PHOTOGRAPHY: BRYAN WHITNEY

Units	Single
Price Code	C
Total Finished	1,765 sq. ft.
First Finished	1,110 sq. ft.
Second Finished	655 sq. ft.
Dimensions	28'x47'6"
Foundation	Basement
Bedrooms	2
Full Baths	1
Max Ridge Height	32'
Roof Framing	Stick
Exterior Walls	2x6

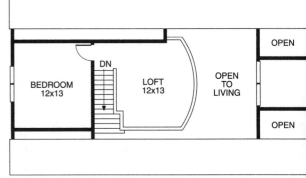

DN

BEDROOM
12x13

LOFT
12x13

OPEN TO LIVING

OPEN

OPEN

SECOND FLOOR

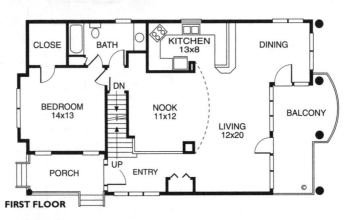

CLOSE

BATH

KITCHEN
13x8

DINING

DN

BEDROOM
14x13

NOOK
11x12

LIVING
12x20

BALCONY

PORCH

UP

ENTRY

FIRST FLOOR

Please note: The photographed home may have been modified to suit homeowner preferences. If you order plans, have a builder or design professional check them against the photograph to confirm actual construction details.

Design 90869

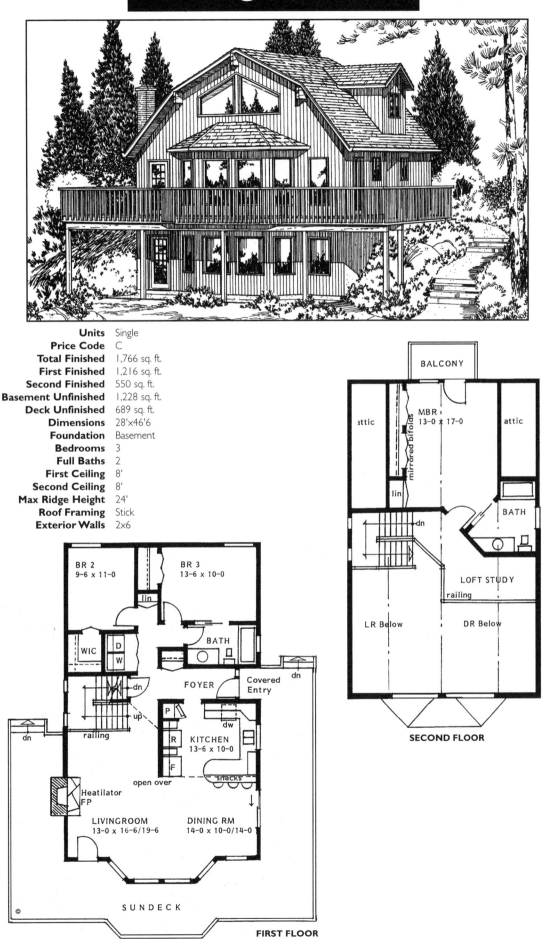

Units	Single
Price Code	C
Total Finished	1,766 sq. ft.
First Finished	1,216 sq. ft.
Second Finished	550 sq. ft.
Basement Unfinished	1,228 sq. ft.
Deck Unfinished	689 sq. ft.
Dimensions	28'x46'6
Foundation	Basement
Bedrooms	3
Full Baths	2
First Ceiling	8'
Second Ceiling	8'
Max Ridge Height	24'
Roof Framing	Stick
Exterior Walls	2x6

BALCONY

attic

MBR
13-0 x 17-0

attic

mirrored bifolds

lin

dn

BATH

LOFT STUDY

railing

LR Below

DR Below

SECOND FLOOR

BR 2
9-6 x 11-0

BR 3
13-6 x 10-0

lin

WIC

D W

BATH

FOYER

Covered Entry

dn

dn

railing

up

dn

P

dw

R

KITCHEN
13-6 x 10-0

F

snacks

open over

Heatilator FP

LIVINGROOM
13-0 x 16-6/19-6

DINING RM
14-0 x 10-0/14-0

S U N D E C K

FIRST FLOOR

Units	Single
Price Code	C
Total Finished	1,768 sq. ft.
Main Finished	1,768 sq. ft.
Dimensions	58'x36'
Foundation	Basement
	Crawlspace
	Slab
Bedrooms	3
Full Baths	2
Max Ridge Height	17'
Roof Framing	Stick/Truss
Exterior Walls	2x6

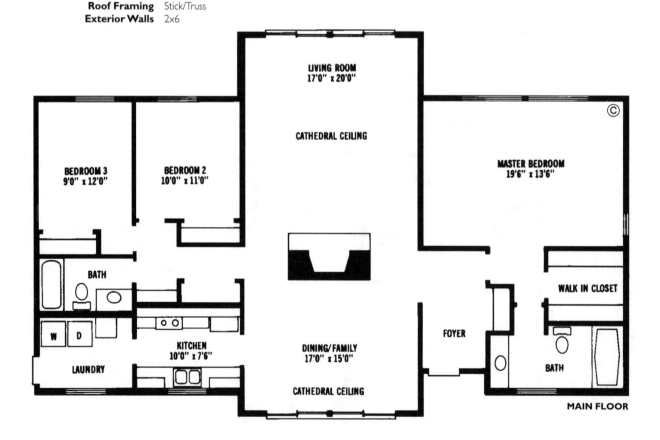

LIVING ROOM
17'0" x 20'0"

CATHEDRAL CEILING

MASTER BEDROOM
19'6" x 13'6"

BEDROOM 3
9'0" x 12'0"

BEDROOM 2
10'0" x 11'0"

WALK IN CLOSET

BATH

W D

FOYER

BATH

KITCHEN
10'0" x 7'6"

DINING/FAMILY
17'0" x 15'0"

LAUNDRY

CATHEDRAL CEILING

MAIN FLOOR

Design 90423

Units	Single
Price Code	C
Total Finished	1,773 sq. ft.
Main Finished	1,773 sq. ft.
Porch Unfinished	240 sq. ft.
Dimensions	88'8"x43'8"
Foundation	Basement
	Crawlspace
	Slab
Bedrooms	3
Full Baths	2
Max Ridge Height	16'4"
Roof Framing	Stick
Exterior Walls	2x4

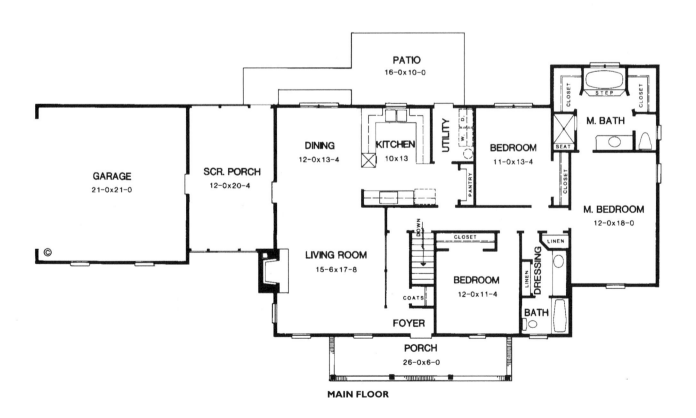

MAIN FLOOR

Units	Single
Price Code	C
Total Finished	1,778 sq. ft.
Main Finished	1,778 sq. ft.
Basement Unfinished	1,008 sq. ft.
Garage Unfinished	728 sq. ft.
Dimensions	62'x28'
Foundation	Basement
Bedrooms	3
Full Baths	2
Main Ceiling	8'
Vaulted Ceiling	10'4"
Max Ridge Height	26'
Roof Framing	Stick/Truss
Exterior Walls	2x4

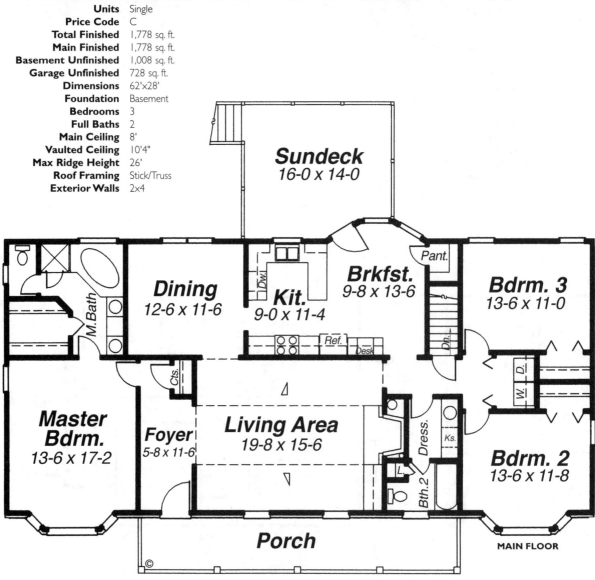

Sundeck
16-0 x 14-0

Pant.

Dining
12-6 x 11-6

Kit.
9-0 x 11-4

Dwl

Brkfst.
9-8 x 13-6

Bdrm. 3
13-6 x 11-0

Ref.

Desk

Dn.

W. D.

Master
Bdrm.
13-6 x 17-2

M. Bath

Cts.

Foyer
5-8 x 11-6

Living Area
19-8 x 15-6

Dress.

Ks.

Bth.2

Bdrm. 2
13-6 x 11-8

Porch

MAIN FLOOR

Design 68212

OPEN TO BELOW CATH. CEIL.

DN

Br.3
11¹⁰ x 11¹⁰
10'-0" CEIL.

Br.2
11⁴ x 13⁰
10'-0" CEIL.

SECOND FLOOR

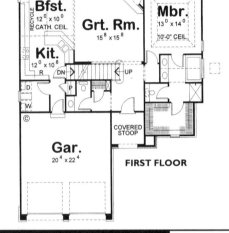

Bfst.
12⁰ x 10⁰
CATH. CEIL.

RECYCLE

Grt. Rm.
15⁸ x 15⁸

Mbr.
13⁰ x 14⁰
10'-0" CEIL.

Kit.
12⁰ x 10⁸

DN

UP

Gar.
20⁴ x 22⁴

COVERED STOOP

FIRST FLOOR

Units	Single
Price Code	C
Total Finished	1,780 sq. ft.
First Finished	1,233 sq. ft.
Second Finished	547 sq. ft.
Basement Unfinished	1,233 sq. ft.
Garage Unfinished	476 sq. ft.
Dimensions	42'x52'
Foundation	Basement
Bedrooms	3
Full Baths	2
Half Baths	1
First Ceiling	9'
Second Ceiling	8'
Max Ridge Height	30'
Roof Framing	Stick
Exterior Walls	2x4

* Alternate foundation options available at an additional charge.
Please call 1-800-235-5700 for more information.

Design 10274

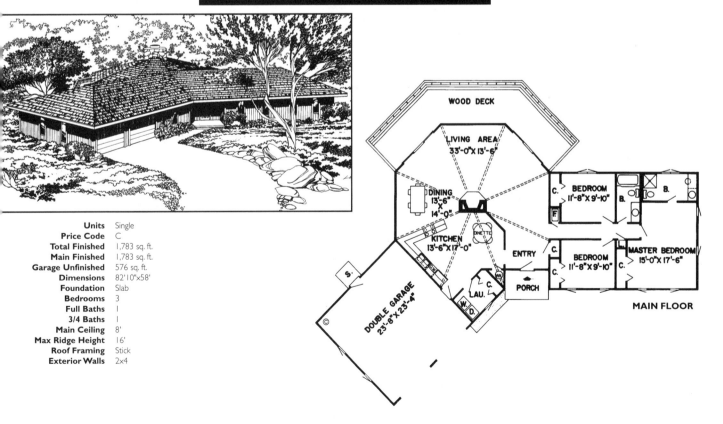

WOOD DECK

LIVING AREA
33'-0" X 13'-6"

DINING
13'-6" X 14'-0"

KITCHEN
13'-6" X 17'-0"

DINETTE

ENTRY

DOUBLE GARAGE
23'-8" X 23'-4"

LAU.

PORCH

BEDROOM
11'-8" X 9'-10"

BEDROOM
11'-8" X 9'-10"

MASTER BEDROOM
15'-0" X 17'-6"

MAIN FLOOR

Units	Single
Price Code	C
Total Finished	1,783 sq. ft.
Main Finished	1,783 sq. ft.
Garage Unfinished	576 sq. ft.
Dimensions	82'10"x58'
Foundation	Slab
Bedrooms	3
Full Baths	1
3/4 Baths	1
Main Ceiling	8'
Max Ridge Height	16'
Roof Framing	Stick
Exterior Walls	2x4

Units	Single
Price Code	B
Total Finished	1,787 sq. ft.
Main Finished	1,787 sq. ft.
Bonus Unfinished	263 sq. ft.
Basement Unfinished	1,787 sq. ft.
Dimensions	55'8"x56'6"
Foundation	Basement
	Crawlspace
Bedrooms	3
Full Baths	2
Main Ceiling	9'
Vaulted Ceiling	11'
Tray Ceiling	11'
Max Ridge Height	21'
Roof Framing	Stick
Exterior Walls	2x4

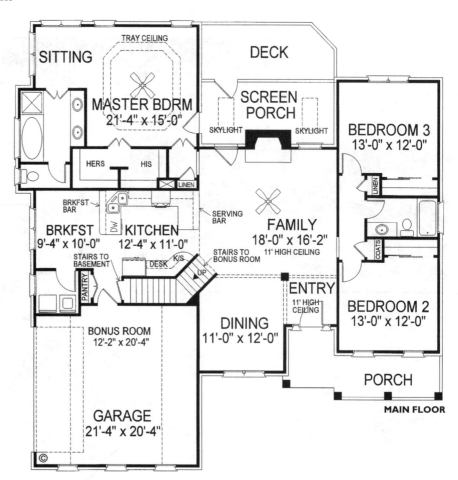

Design 20198

Units	Single
Price Code	C
Total Finished	1,792 sq. ft.
Main Finished	1,792 sq. ft.
Basement Unfinished	818 sq. ft.
Garage Unfinished	857 sq. ft.
Porch Unfinished	336 sq. ft.
Dimensions	56'x32'
Foundation	Basement
Bedrooms	3
Full Baths	1
3/4 Baths	1
Main Ceiling	8'
Max Ridge Height	25'
Roof Framing	Stick
Exterior Walls	2x4, 2x6

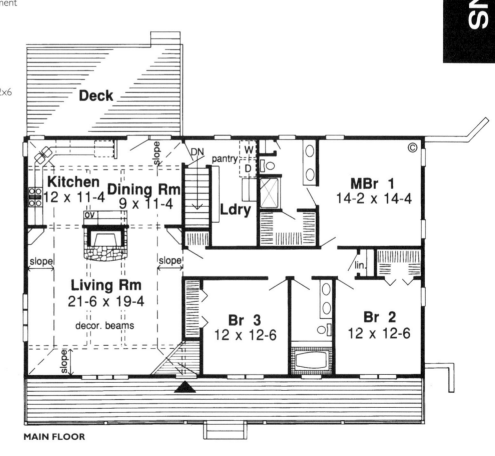

MAIN FLOOR

Units	Single
Price Code	F
Total Finished	1,792 sq. ft.
Main Finished	1,792 sq. ft.
Deck Unfinished	113 sq. ft.
Porch Unfinished	583 sq. ft.
Dimensions	36'x82'
Foundation	Crawlspace
Bedrooms	2
Full Baths	2
Roof Framing	Stick/Truss
Exterior Walls	2x6

*Alternate foundation options available at an additional charge.
Please call 1-800-235-5700 for more information.*

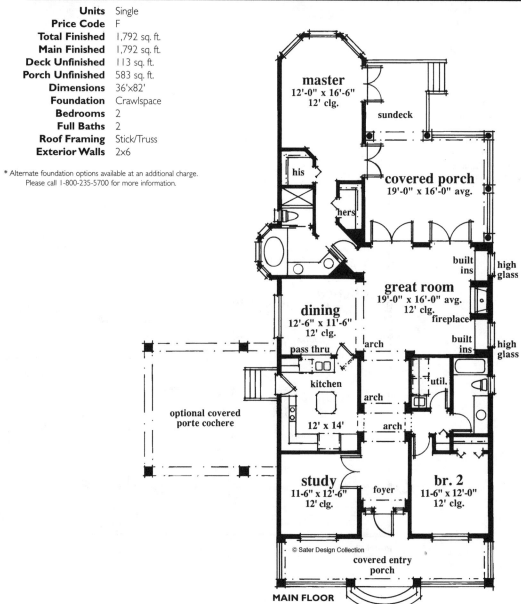

Design 63051

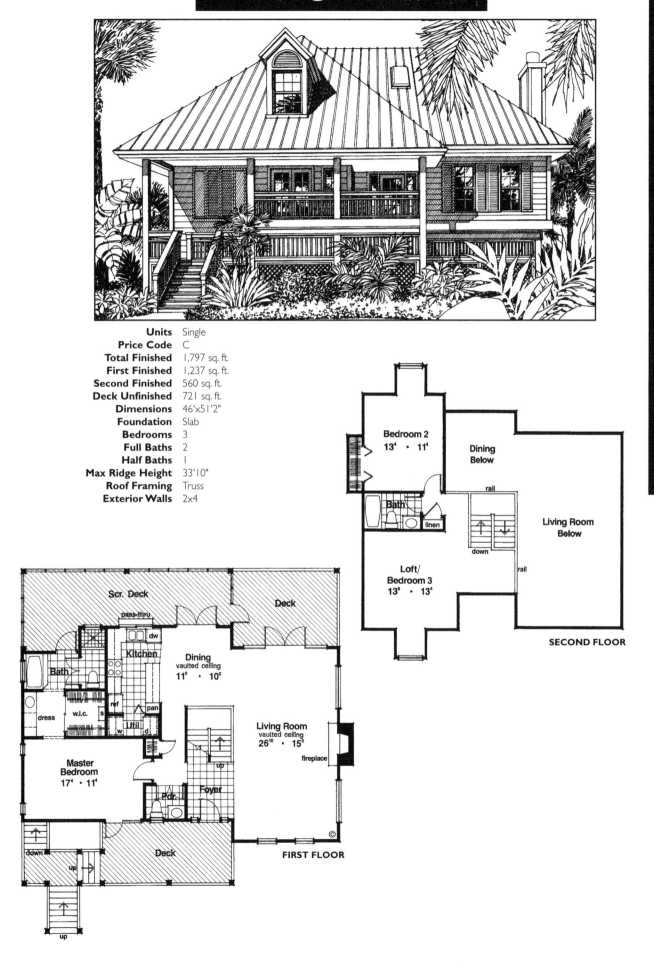

Units	Single
Price Code	C
Total Finished	1,797 sq. ft.
First Finished	1,237 sq. ft.
Second Finished	560 sq. ft.
Deck Unfinished	721 sq. ft.
Dimensions	46'x51'2"
Foundation	Slab
Bedrooms	3
Full Baths	2
Half Baths	1
Max Ridge Height	33'10"
Roof Framing	Truss
Exterior Walls	2x4

SECOND FLOOR

Bedroom 2
13⁴ • 11⁴

Dining
Below

Living Room
Below

Loft/
Bedroom 3
13⁶ • 13⁴

Bath
linen
down
rail
rail

FIRST FLOOR

Scr. Deck
pass-thru
Deck
Kitchen
dw
Dining
vaulted ceiling
11⁰ • 10⁰
Bath
dress
w.i.c.
ref
pan
Util
Living Room
vaulted ceiling
26¹⁰ • 15⁰
fireplace
Master
Bedroom
17⁴ • 11⁴
Pdr.
Foyer
Deck
down
up
up
up

MAIN FLOOR

Units	Single
Price Code	C
Total Finished	1,804 sq. ft.
Main Finished	1,804 sq. ft.
Basement Unfinished	1,804 sq. ft.
Garage Unfinished	506 sq. ft.
Deck Unfinished	220 sq. ft.
Porch Unfinished	156 sq. ft.
Dimensions	62'x55'8"
Foundation	Basement
	Crawlspace
	Slab
Bedrooms	3
Full Baths	2
Main Ceiling	8'
Max Ridge Height	22'1"
Roof Framing	Stick
Exterior Walls	2x4

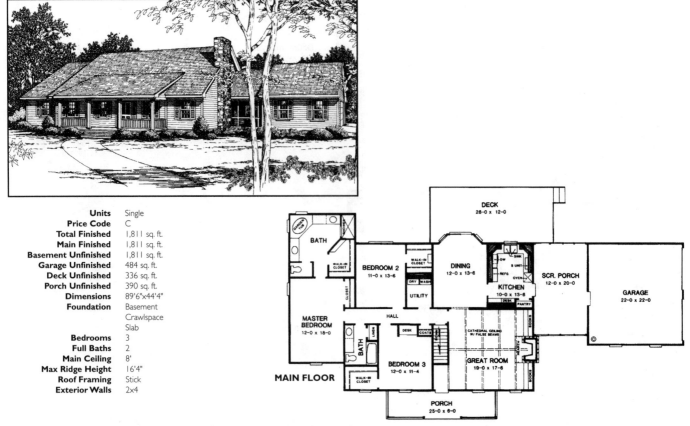

MAIN FLOOR

Units	Single
Price Code	C
Total Finished	1,811 sq. ft.
Main Finished	1,811 sq. ft.
Basement Unfinished	1,811 sq. ft.
Garage Unfinished	484 sq. ft.
Deck Unfinished	336 sq. ft.
Porch Unfinished	390 sq. ft.
Dimensions	89'6"x44'4"
Foundation	Basement
	Crawlspace
	Slab
Bedrooms	3
Full Baths	2
Main Ceiling	8'
Max Ridge Height	16'4"
Roof Framing	Stick
Exterior Walls	2x4

Design 67000

Units	Single
Price Code	C
Total Finished	1,815 sq. ft.
Main Finished	1,815 sq. ft.
Dimensions	58'3"x66'1"
Foundation	Slab
Bedrooms	3
Full Baths	2
Main Ceiling	8'
Max Ridge Height	24'
Roof Framing	Stick
Exterior Walls	2x4

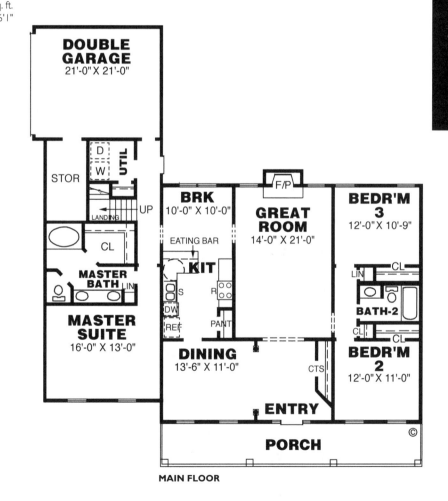

MAIN FLOOR

PHOTOGRAPHY: JOHN EHRENCLOU

Units	Single
Price Code	C
Total Finished	1,821 sq. ft.
Main Finished	1,821 sq. ft.
Basement Unfinished	742 sq. ft.
Garage Unfinished	1,075 sq. ft.
Dimensions	56'x42'
Foundation	Basement
Bedrooms	3
Full Baths	2
Main Ceiling	8'
Max Ridge Height	25'
Roof Framing	Stick
Exterior Walls	2x4

Please note: The photographed home may have been modified to suit homeowner preferences. If you order plans, have a builder or design professional check them against the photograph to confirm actual construction details.

MAIN FLOOR

Design 64131

Units	Single
Price Code	G
Total Finished	1,822 sq. ft.
Main Finished	1,822 sq. ft.
Garage Unfinished	537 sq. ft.
Deck Unfinished	264 sq. ft.
Porch Unfinished	287 sq. ft.
Dimensions	58'x66'8"
Foundation	Basement
Bedrooms	3
Full Baths	2
Max Ridge Height	26'10"
Exterior Walls	2x6

* Alternate foundation options available at an additional charge.
Please call 1-800-235-5700 for more information.

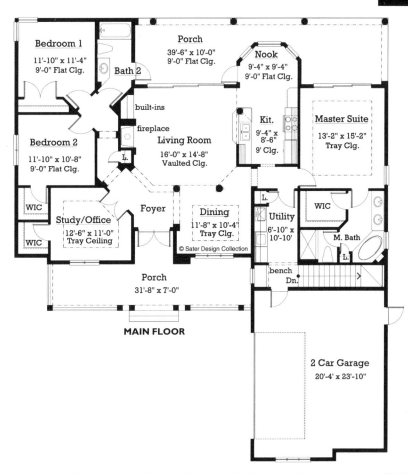

MAIN FLOOR

Units	Single
Price Code	G
Total Finished	1,822 sq. ft.
Main Finished	1,822 sq. ft.
Garage Unfinished	537 sq. ft.
Dimensions	58'x67'2"
Foundation	Basement
Bedrooms	3
Full Baths	2
Max Ridge Height	26'10"
Roof Framing	Stick
Exterior Walls	2x6

* Alternate foundation options available at an additional charge.
Please call 1-800-235-5700 for more information.

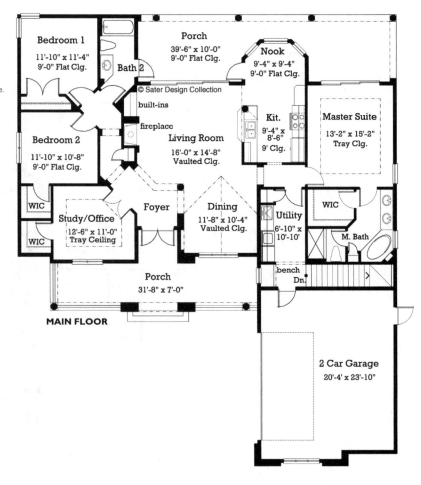

MAIN FLOOR

Design 94258

1,501-2,000 sq. ft. HOME PLANS

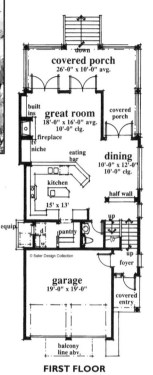

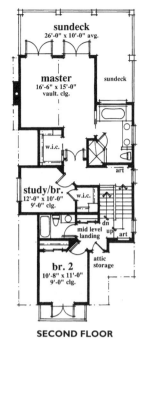

Units	Single
Price Code	F
Total Finished	1,824 sq. ft.
First Finished	876 sq. ft.
Second Finished	948 sq. ft.
Garage Unfinished	361 sq. ft.
Deck Unfinished	360 sq. ft.
Porch Unfinished	360 sq. ft.
Dimensions	27'6"x64'
Foundation	Crawlspace
	Slab
Bedrooms	3
Full Baths	2
Half Baths	1
Max Ridge Height	32'8"
Roof Framing	Stick/Truss
Exterior Walls	2x6

* Alternate foundation options available at an additional charge.
Please call 1-800-235-5700 for more information.

SECOND FLOOR

FIRST FLOOR

Design 93423

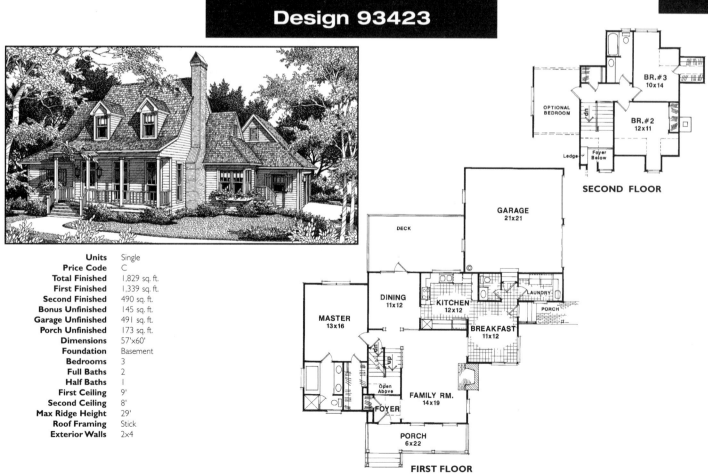

Units	Single
Price Code	C
Total Finished	1,829 sq. ft.
First Finished	1,339 sq. ft.
Second Finished	490 sq. ft.
Bonus Unfinished	145 sq. ft.
Garage Unfinished	491 sq. ft.
Porch Unfinished	173 sq. ft.
Dimensions	57'x60'
Foundation	Basement
Bedrooms	3
Full Baths	2
Half Baths	1
First Ceiling	9'
Second Ceiling	8'
Max Ridge Height	29'
Roof Framing	Stick
Exterior Walls	2x4

SECOND FLOOR

FIRST FLOOR

Units	Single
Price Code	C
Total Finished	1,830 sq. ft.
Main Finished	1,830 sq. ft.
Garage Unfinished	759 sq. ft.
Deck Unfinished	315 sq. ft.
Porch Unfinished	390 sq. ft.
Dimensions	75'×52'3"
Foundation	Basement
	Crawlspace
	Slab
Bedrooms	3
Full Baths	2
Max Ridge Height	27'3"
Roof Framing	Stick
Exterior Walls	2x4

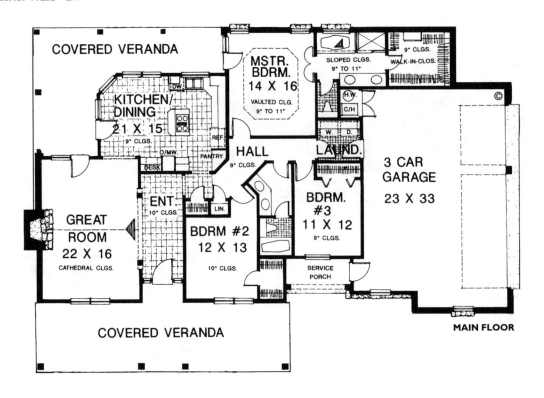

Design 82107

Units	Single
Price Code	C
Total Finished	1,914 sq. ft.
Main Finished	1,914 sq. ft.
Garage Unfinished	473 sq. ft.
Porch Unfinished	345 sq. ft.
Dimensions	59'8"×69'
Foundation	Basement
	Crawlspace
	Slab
Bedrooms	3
Full Baths	2
Main Ceiling	9'
Max Ridge Height	21'4"
Roof Framing	Stick
Exterior Walls	2x4, 2x6

Design 65380

SECOND FLOOR

Units	Single
Price Code	C
Total Finished	1,832 sq. ft.
First Finished	1,212 sq. ft.
Second Finished	620 sq. ft.
Basement Unfinished	1,212 sq. ft.
Dimensions	38'x40'
Foundation	Basement
Bedrooms	3
Full Baths	2
First Ceiling	8'
Max Ridge Height	26'4"

FIRST FLOOR

Design 94313

Units	Single
Price Code	C
Total Finished	1,836 sq. ft.
First Finished	967 sq. ft.
Second Finished	869 sq. ft.
Basement Unfinished	967 sq. ft.
Garage Unfinished	462 sq. ft.
Dimensions	45'x50'
Foundation	Basement
Bedrooms	3
Full Baths	2
Half Baths	1
First Ceiling	8'
Second Ceiling	8'
Max Ridge Height	29'
Roof Framing	Truss
Exterior Walls	2x6

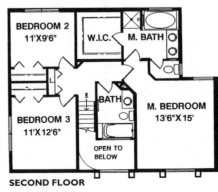

SECOND FLOOR

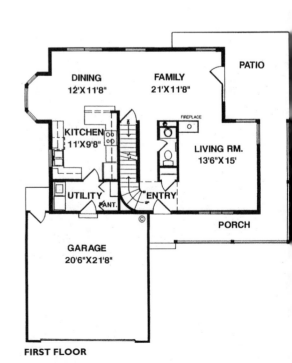

FIRST FLOOR

Design 91704

Units	Single
Price Code	C
Total Finished	1,837 sq. ft.
First Finished	1,448 sq. ft.
Second Finished	389 sq. ft.
Garage Unfinished	312 sq. ft.
Dimensions	54'x44'
Foundation	Crawlspace
Bedrooms	2
Full Baths	1
3/4 Baths	2
Max Ridge Height	28'
Roof Framing	Stick
Exterior Walls	2x6

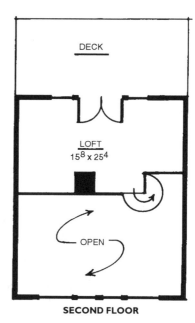

SECOND FLOOR

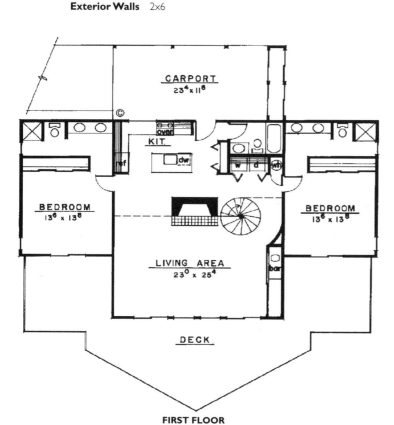

FIRST FLOOR

Units	Single
Price Code	F
Total Finished	1,838 sq. ft.
First Finished	1,290 sq. ft.
Second Finished	548 sq. ft.
Deck Unfinished	230 sq. ft.
Porch Unfinished	301 sq. ft.
Dimensions	38'x50'
Foundation	Basement
	Crawlspace
	Slab
	Pier/Post
Bedrooms	3
Full Baths	2
Half Baths	1
Max Ridge Height	32'8"
Roof Framing	Stick
Exterior Walls	2x6

* Alternate foundation options available at an additional charge.
Please call 1-800-235-5700 for more information.

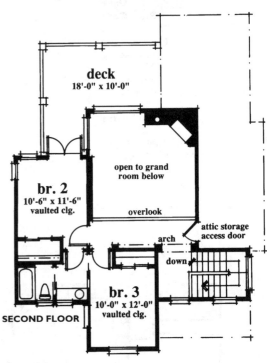

SECOND FLOOR

deck 18'-0" x 10'-0"

open to grand room below

overlook

br. 2 10'-6" x 11'-6" vaulted clg.

br. 3 10'-0" x 12'-0" vaulted clg.

attic storage access door

arch

down

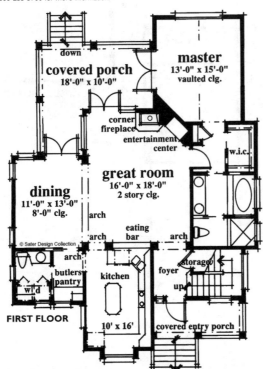

FIRST FLOOR

covered porch 18'-0" x 10'-0"

down

master 13'-0" x 15'-0" vaulted clg.

corner fireplace

entertainment center

great room 16'-0" x 18'-0" 2 story clg.

dining 11'-0" x 13'-0" 8'-0" clg.

w.i.c.

arch

eating bar

arch

arch

© Sater Design Collection

butlers pantry

w/d

kitchen

10' x 16'

foyer

storage

up

covered entry porch

Design 92806

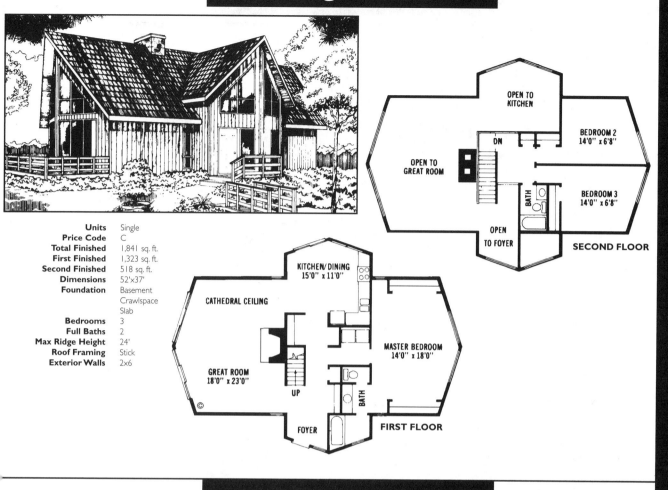

OPEN TO KITCHEN

OPEN TO GREAT ROOM

DN

BEDROOM 2
14'0" x 6'8"

BATH

BEDROOM 3
14'0" x 6'8"

OPEN TO FOYER

SECOND FLOOR

KITCHEN/ DINING
15'0" x 11'0"

CATHEDRAL CEILING

MASTER BEDROOM
14'0" x 18'0"

GREAT ROOM
18'0" x 23'0"

UP

BATH

FOYER

FIRST FLOOR

Units	Single
Price Code	C
Total Finished	1,841 sq. ft.
First Finished	1,323 sq. ft.
Second Finished	518 sq. ft.
Dimensions	52'x37'
Foundation	Basement
	Crawlspace
	Slab
Bedrooms	3
Full Baths	2
Max Ridge Height	24'
Roof Framing	Stick
Exterior Walls	2x6

Design 64122

Units	Single
Price Code	G
Total Finished	1,848 sq. ft.
Main Finished	1,848 sq. ft.
Garage Unfinished	571 sq. ft.
Deck Unfinished	254 sq. ft.
Porch Unfinished	217 sq. ft.
Dimensions	58'x58'6"
Foundation	Slab
Bedrooms	3
Full Baths	1
3/4 Baths	1
Max Ridge Height	30'6"
Roof Framing	Stick/Truss
Exterior Walls	2x6

Bedroom 1
10'-4" x 12'-0"
8'-0"Flat Clg.

Bath 2

Nook
8'-8" x 8'-8"
Vaulted Clg.

Porch
25'-4" x 10'-0"

ent. center

Family Room
12'-4" x 17'-4"
Vaulted Clg.

desk

Bedroom 2
10'-4" x 12'-0"
8'-0"Flat Clg.

Kitchen
8'-8" x 14'-6"
Vaulted Clg.

Living Room
13'-0" x 15'-0"
Stepped Clg.

Master Suite
11'-8" x 15'-0"
Tray Clg.

P.

A/C

L.T.

D W

wet bar

Utility
6'-8" x 6'-8"

Dining Room
11'-8" x 11'-0"
Tray Clg.

Foyer
Vaulted Clg.

WIC

M. Bath

Garage
22'-8" x 23'-4"

© Sater Design Collection

Porch
26'-8" x 8'-0"

MAIN FLOOR

* Alternate foundation options available at an additional charge.
Please call 1-800-235-5700 for more information.

Units	Single
Price Code	G
Total Finished	1,848 sq. ft.
Main Finished	1,848 sq. ft.
Garage Unfinished	571 sq. ft.
Deck Unfinished	254 sq. ft.
Porch Unfinished	217 sq. ft.
Dimensions	58'×60'
Foundation	Crawlspace
Bedrooms	3
Full Baths	1
3/4 Baths	1
Max Ridge Height	30'6"
Exterior Walls	2x6
Roof Framing	Stick/Truss

* Alternate foundation options available at an additional charge.
Please call 1-800-235-5700 for more information.

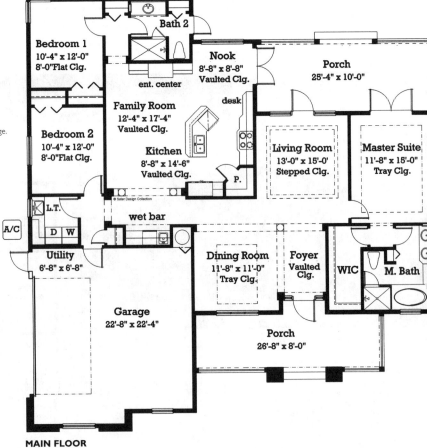

MAIN FLOOR

Design 20066

Units	Single
Price Code	C
Total Finished	1,850 sq. ft.
Main Finished	1,850 sq. ft.
Basement Unfinished	1,850 sq. ft.
Garage Unfinished	503 sq. ft.
Dimensions	63'8"x52'
Foundation	Basement
Bedrooms	3
Full Baths	2
Max Ridge Height	21'
Roof Framing	Stick
Exterior Walls	2x6

DECK

BRKFST.
9'-0" X 10'-0"

LIVING ROOM
16'-10" X 19'-6"

MASTER
BEDROOM
16'-0 X13'-4"

B. 1

PANT. DESK

DW

KITCHEN
13'-0"X 11'-0"

RAIL

DOWN 13 RS.

HALL

CLO.

FOYER

C.

DINING ROOM
11'-8" X 11'-10"

COURT

S.

B.2

BEDROOM 2
11'-4" X 13'-10"

BEDROOM 3
11'-4" X 13'-10"

W. D.

LAUN.

S.

MAIN FLOOR

2-CAR GARAGE
21'-4" X 21'-8"

W.

©

DRIVE

Design 94248

Units	Single
Price Code	D
Total Finished	1,853 sq. ft.
First Finished	1,342 sq. ft.
Second Finished	511 sq. ft.
Garage Unfinished	1,740 sq. ft.
Dimensions	44'x40'
Foundation	Pier/Post
Bedrooms	3
Full Baths	2
First Ceiling	8'
Second Ceiling	8'
Max Ridge Height	37'
Roof Framing	Stick
Exterior Walls	2x6

* Alternate foundation options available at an additional charge.
Please call 1-800-235-5700 for more information.

SECOND FLOOR

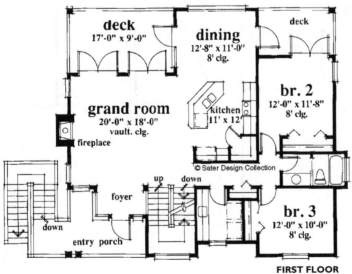

FIRST FLOOR

Design 66118

Units	Single
Price Code	C
Total Finished	1,855 sq. ft.
Main Finished	1,855 sq. ft.
Garage Unfinished	567 sq. ft.
Dimensions	40'x70'
Foundation	Slab
Bedrooms	3
Full Baths	2
Max Ridge Height	26'
Roof Framing	Stick
Exterior Walls	2x4

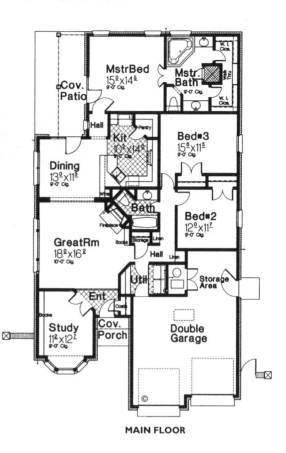

MAIN FLOOR

Design 24704

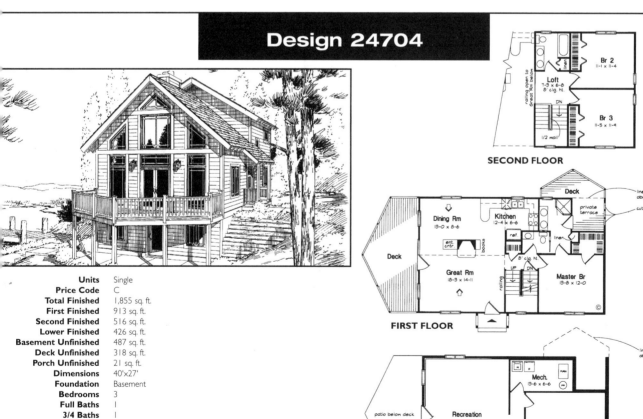

SECOND FLOOR

FIRST FLOOR

LOWER FLOOR

Units	Single
Price Code	C
Total Finished	1,855 sq. ft.
First Finished	913 sq. ft.
Second Finished	516 sq. ft.
Lower Finished	426 sq. ft.
Basement Unfinished	487 sq. ft.
Deck Unfinished	318 sq. ft.
Porch Unfinished	21 sq. ft.
Dimensions	40'x27'
Foundation	Basement
Bedrooms	3
Full Baths	1
3/4 Baths	1
Half Baths	1
First Ceiling	8'
Second Ceiling	8'
Max Ridge Height	32'
Roof Framing	Stick
Exterior Walls	2x4

Design 91731

Units	Single
Price Code	C
Total Finished	1,857 sq. ft.
Main Finished	1,857 sq. ft.
Garage Unfinished	681 sq. ft.
Dimensions	51'6"x65'
Foundation	Crawlspace
Bedrooms	3
Full Baths	2
Max Ridge Height	21'
Roof Framing	Stick/Truss
Exterior Walls	2x6

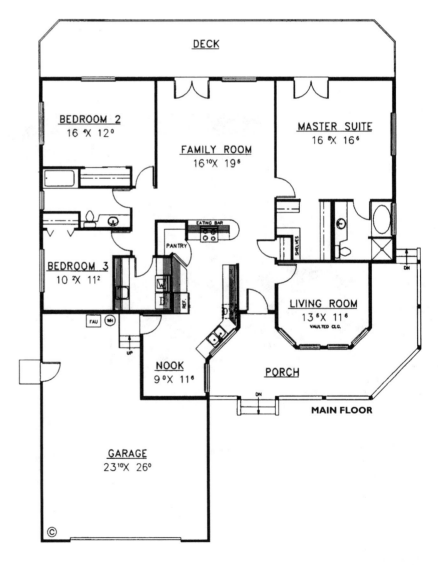

Design 98316

Units	Single
Price Code	C
Total Finished	1,859 sq. ft.
Main Finished	1,859 sq. ft.
Garage Unfinished	393 sq. ft.
Dimensions	54'x57'
Foundation	Slab
Bedrooms	3
Full Baths	2
Max Ridge Height	20'
Roof Framing	Truss
Exterior Walls	2x6

Design 65207

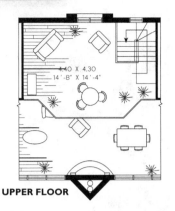

UPPER FLOOR

Units	Single
Price Code	C
Total Finished	1,864 sq. ft.
Main Finished	790 sq. ft.
Upper Finished	287 sq. ft.
Lower Finished	787 sq. ft.
Dimensions	32'4"x24'4"
Foundation	Basement
Bedrooms	3
Full Baths	1
3/4 Baths	1
Max Ridge Height	29'6"
Roof Framing	Truss

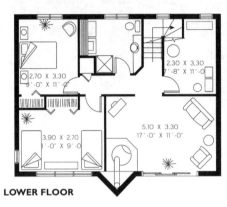

LOWER FLOOR

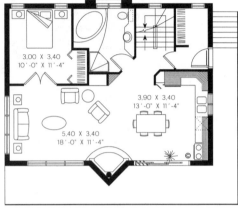

MAIN FLOOR

Design 94301

Units	Single
Price Code	C
Total Finished	1,871 sq. ft.
First Finished	1,145 sq. ft.
Second Finished	726 sq. ft.
Garage Unfinished	433 sq. ft.
Dimensions	49'6"x45'
Foundation	Crawlspace
Bedrooms	3
Full Baths	2
First Ceiling	8'
Second Ceiling	8'
Max Ridge Height	33'
Roof Framing	Truss
Exterior Walls	2x4

SECOND FLOOR

FIRST FLOOR

Units	Single
Price Code	F
Total Finished	1,876 sq. ft.
First Finished	1,007 sq. ft.
Second Finished	869 sq. ft.
Deck Unfinished	60 sq. ft.
Porch Unfinished	418 sq. ft.
Dimensions	44'x53'
Foundation	Crawlspace
	Post
Bedrooms	3
Full Baths	3
First Ceiling	8'
Second Ceiling	8'
Max Ridge Height	36'6"
Exterior Walls	2x6

* Alternate foundation options available at an additional charge.
Please call 1-800-235-5700 for more information.

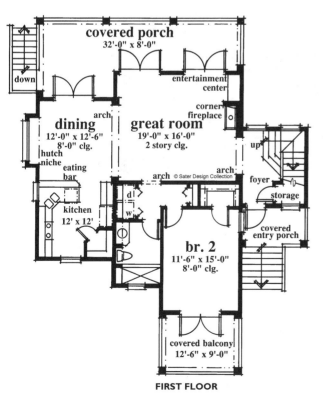

FIRST FLOOR

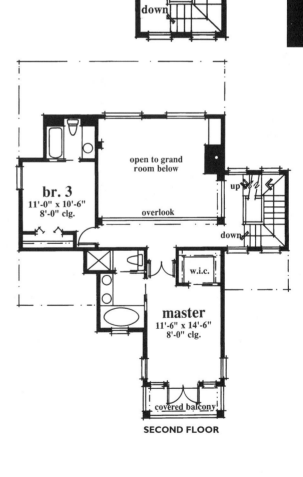

SECOND FLOOR

Units	Single
Price Code	C
Total Finished	1,898 sq. ft.
Main Finished	1,898 sq. ft.
Dimensions	55'x59'4"
Foundation	Slab
Bedrooms	4
Full Baths	2
Roof Framing	Stick
Exterior Walls	2x4

Hot New Design

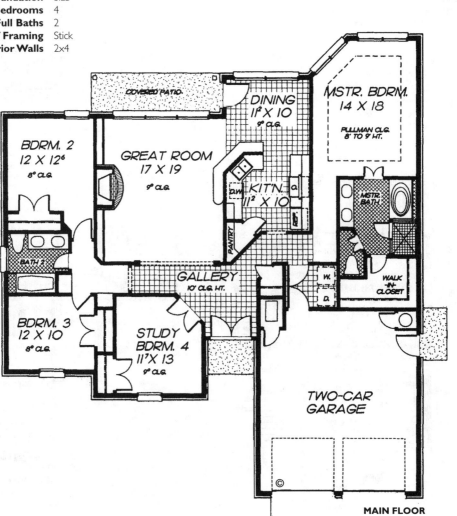

MAIN FLOOR

Design 10785

Units	Single
Price Code	C
Total Finished	1,907 sq. ft.
First Finished	1,269 sq. ft.
Second Finished	638 sq. ft.
Basement Unfinished	1,269 sq. ft.
Dimensions	47'x39'
Foundation	Basement
	Crawlspace
	Slab
Bedrooms	3
Full Baths	2
Half Baths	1
First Ceiling	8'
Second Ceiling	8'
Max Ridge Height	24'
Roof Framing	Stick
Exterior Walls	2x6

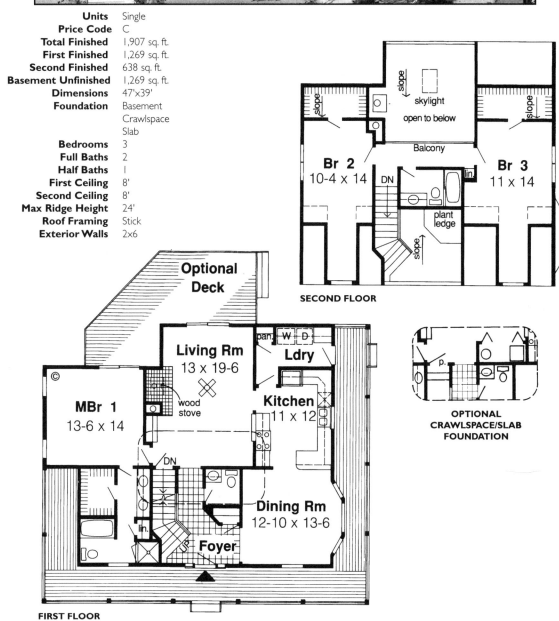

SECOND FLOOR

slope
skylight
open to below
Balcony

Br 2
10-4 x 14

DN

Br 3
11 x 14

lin.

plant ledge

slope

OPTIONAL CRAWLSPACE/SLAB FOUNDATION

p.

Optional Deck

Living Rm
13 x 19-6

pan. W D

Ldry

wood stove

Kitchen
11 x 12

MBr 1
13-6 x 14

DN

Dining Rm
12-10 x 13-6

lin.

Foyer

FIRST FLOOR

PHOTOGRAPHY: GLENN WOODELL

Units	Single
Price Code	C
Total Finished	1,908 sq. ft.
First Finished	1,316 sq. ft.
Second Finished	592 sq. ft.
Dimensions	39'x48'
Foundation	Basement
	Crawlspace
Bedrooms	3
Full Baths	2
Max Ridge Height	34'
Roof Framing	Stick
Exterior Walls	2x6

attic access   knee space

shelf

linen   step   shelf

36" wall

DN   UP

books   slope

Mstr. Suite 17-8 x 16-4   slope   8'-0" ceiling

Balcony

SECOND FLOOR

Please note: The photographed home may have been modified to suit homeowner preferences. If you order plans, have a builder or design professional check them against the photograph to confirm actual construction details.

Br #2 12-8 x 11-8   **Br #3** 12-8 x 11-8

W   **Util.**

UP

railing   UP   DN

Kitchen

Util. W D   furn.   UP

w.h.   UP

OPTIONAL CRAWLSPACE FOUNDATION

slope

42" counter

Living 19-8 x 15-8   14 x 9-6

slope

Dining 17-8 x 11-8

balcony above

Deck

FIRST FLOOR

Design 82019

Units	Single
Price Code	C
Total Finished	1,915 sq. ft.
Main Finished	1,915 sq. ft.
Garage Unfinished	401 sq. ft.
Porch Unfinished	279 sq. ft.
Dimensions	39'x72'
Foundation	Crawlspace
	Slab
Bedrooms	3
Full Baths	2
Main Ceiling	10'
Roof Framing	Stick
Exterior Walls	2x4

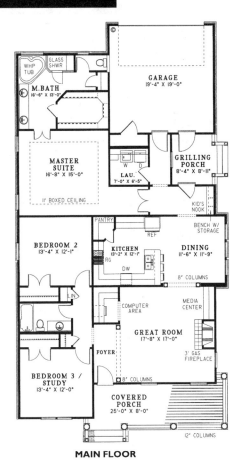

MAIN FLOOR

Design 65012

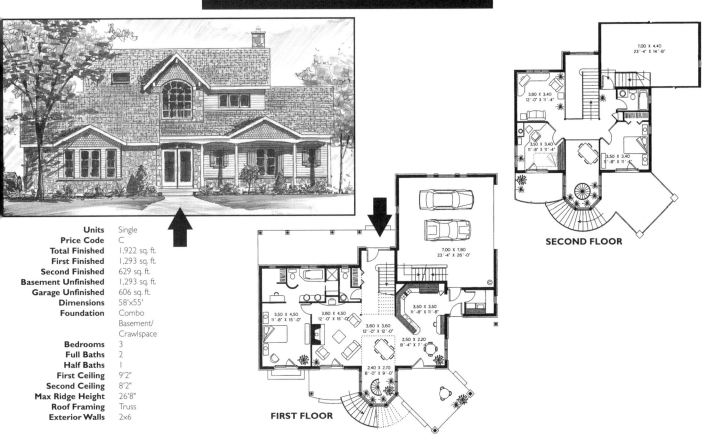

Units	Single
Price Code	C
Total Finished	1,922 sq. ft.
First Finished	1,293 sq. ft.
Second Finished	629 sq. ft.
Basement Unfinished	1,293 sq. ft.
Garage Unfinished	606 sq. ft.
Dimensions	58'x55'
Foundation	Combo
	Basement/
	Crawlspace
Bedrooms	3
Full Baths	2
Half Baths	1
First Ceiling	9'2"
Second Ceiling	8'2"
Max Ridge Height	26'8"
Roof Framing	Truss
Exterior Walls	2x6

SECOND FLOOR

FIRST FLOOR

Design 96544

Units	Single
Price Code	C
Total Finished	1,925 sq. ft.
First Finished	1,329 sq. ft.
Second Finished	596 sq. ft.
Garage Unfinished	316 sq. ft.
Porch Unfinished	533 sq. ft.
Dimensions	64'x46'
Foundation	Crawlspace
	Slab
Bedrooms	3
Full Baths	2
Half Baths	1
First Ceiling	9'
Tray Ceiling	12'
Max Ridge Height	27'
Roof Framing	Stick
Exterior Walls	2x4

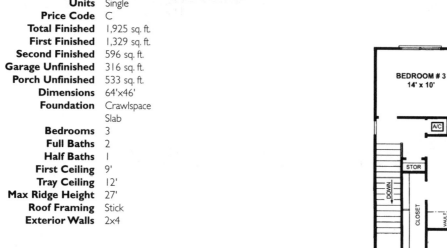

SECOND FLOOR

FIRST FLOOR

Design 57020

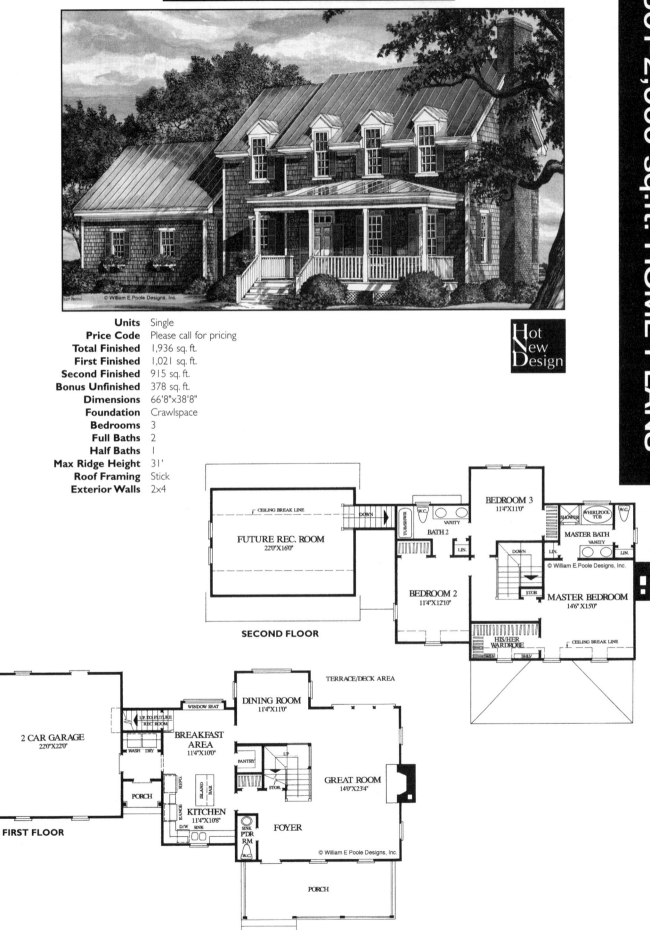

Hot New Design

Units	Single
Price Code	Please call for pricing
Total Finished	1,936 sq. ft.
First Finished	1,021 sq. ft.
Second Finished	915 sq. ft.
Bonus Unfinished	378 sq. ft.
Dimensions	66'8"x38'8"
Foundation	Crawlspace
Bedrooms	3
Full Baths	2
Half Baths	1
Max Ridge Height	31'
Roof Framing	Stick
Exterior Walls	2x4

© William E Poole Designs, Inc.

SECOND FLOOR

CEILING BREAK LINE

FUTURE REC. ROOM
22'0"X16'0"

DOWN

TUB/SHWR
W.C.
BATH 2
VANITY
LIN.

BEDROOM 3
11'4"X11'0"

SHOWER
WHIRLPOOL TUB
W.C.
MASTER BATH
VANITY
LIN.

DOWN
STOR

BEDROOM 2
11'4"X12'10"

MASTER BEDROOM
14'6" X15'0"

HIS/HER WARDROBE
SHLV.
SHLV.

CEILING BREAK LINE

FIRST FLOOR

2 CAR GARAGE
22'0"X22'0"

UP TO FUTURE REC ROOM

WINDOW SEAT

DINING ROOM
11'4"X11'0"

TERRACE/DECK AREA

WASH DRY

BREAKFAST AREA
11'4"X10'0"

PORCH

REF.

ISLAND BAR

PANTRY

UP
STOR.

GREAT ROOM
14'0"X23'4"

RANGE

KITCHEN
11'4"X10'8"

D/W
SINK

SINK
PDR RM.
W.C.

FOYER

© William E Poole Designs, Inc.

PORCH

Design 94314

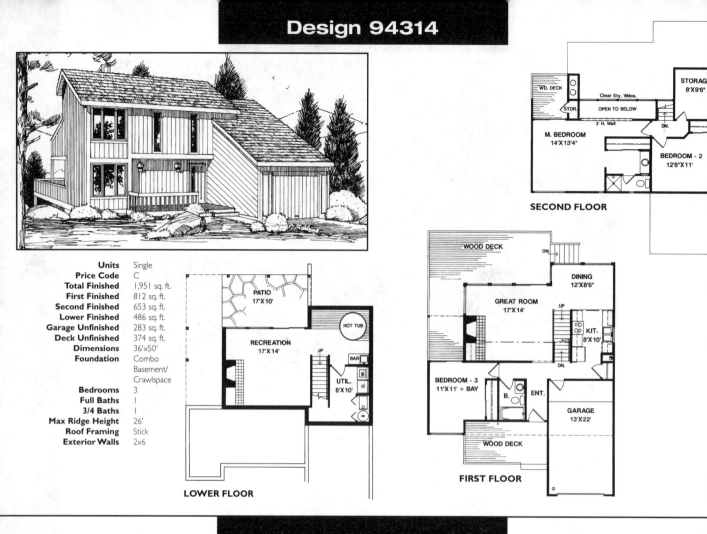

SECOND FLOOR

- STORAGE 8'X9'6"
- WD. DECK
- STOR.
- Clear Sty. Wdos.
- OPEN TO BELOW
- DN.
- 3' H. Wall
- M. BEDROOM 14'X13'4"
- BEDROOM - 2 12'6"X11'

Units	Single
Price Code	C
Total Finished	1,951 sq. ft.
First Finished	812 sq. ft.
Second Finished	653 sq. ft.
Lower Finished	486 sq. ft.
Garage Unfinished	283 sq. ft.
Deck Unfinished	374 sq. ft.
Dimensions	36'x50'
Foundation	Combo Basement/ Crawlspace
Bedrooms	3
Full Baths	1
3/4 Baths	1
Max Ridge Height	26'
Roof Framing	Stick
Exterior Walls	2x6

LOWER FLOOR

- PATIO 17'X10'
- HOT TUB
- RECREATION 17'X14'
- BAR
- UP
- UTIL. 8'X10'
- W. D.

FIRST FLOOR

- WOOD DECK
- DN.
- DINING 12'X8'6"
- GREAT ROOM 17'X14'
- UP
- KIT. 8'X10'
- DN.
- BEDROOM - 3 11'X11' + BAY
- B.
- ENT.
- GARAGE 13'X22'
- WOOD DECK

Design 24301

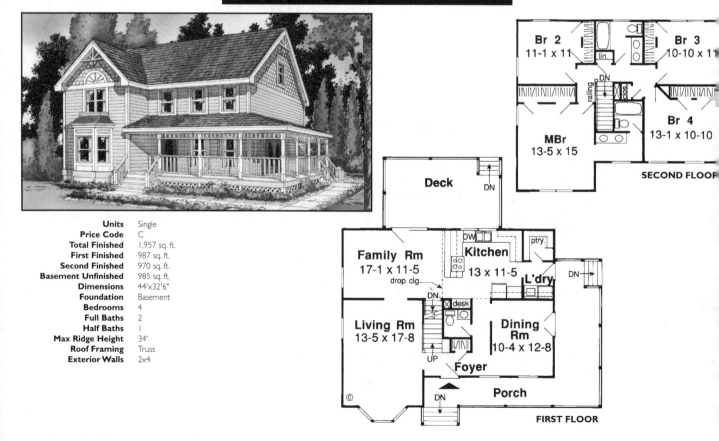

SECOND FLOOR

- Br 2 11-1 x 11
- Br 3 10-10 x 11
- lin.
- DN
- railing
- clos.
- MBr 13-5 x 15
- Br 4 13-1 x 10-10

Units	Single
Price Code	C
Total Finished	1,957 sq. ft.
First Finished	987 sq. ft.
Second Finished	970 sq. ft.
Basement Unfinished	985 sq. ft.
Dimensions	44'x32'6"
Foundation	Basement
Bedrooms	4
Full Baths	2
Half Baths	1
Max Ridge Height	34'
Roof Framing	Truss
Exterior Walls	2x4

FIRST FLOOR

- Deck
- DN
- DW
- Family Rm 17-1 x 11-5
- drop clg
- Kitchen 13 x 11-5
- ptry.
- L'dry
- DN
- DN
- desk
- Living Rm 13-5 x 17-8
- UP
- Dining Rm 10-4 x 12-8
- Foyer
- Porch
- DN

Design 82023

Units	Single
Price Code	C
Total Finished	1,966 sq. ft.
Main Finished	1,966 sq. ft.
Garage Unfinished	452 sq. ft.
Porch Unfinished	291 sq. ft.
Dimensions	38'x79'6"
Foundation	Crawlspace
	Slab
Bedrooms	3
Full Baths	2
Roof Framing	Stick
Exterior Walls	2x4

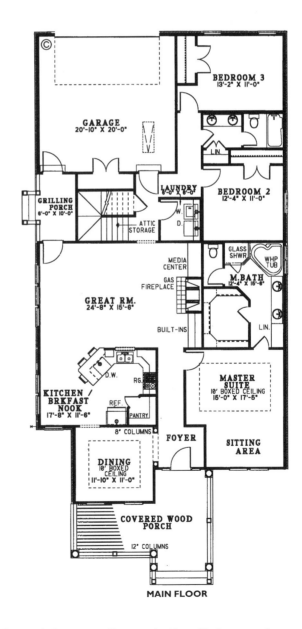

MAIN FLOOR

Design 62123

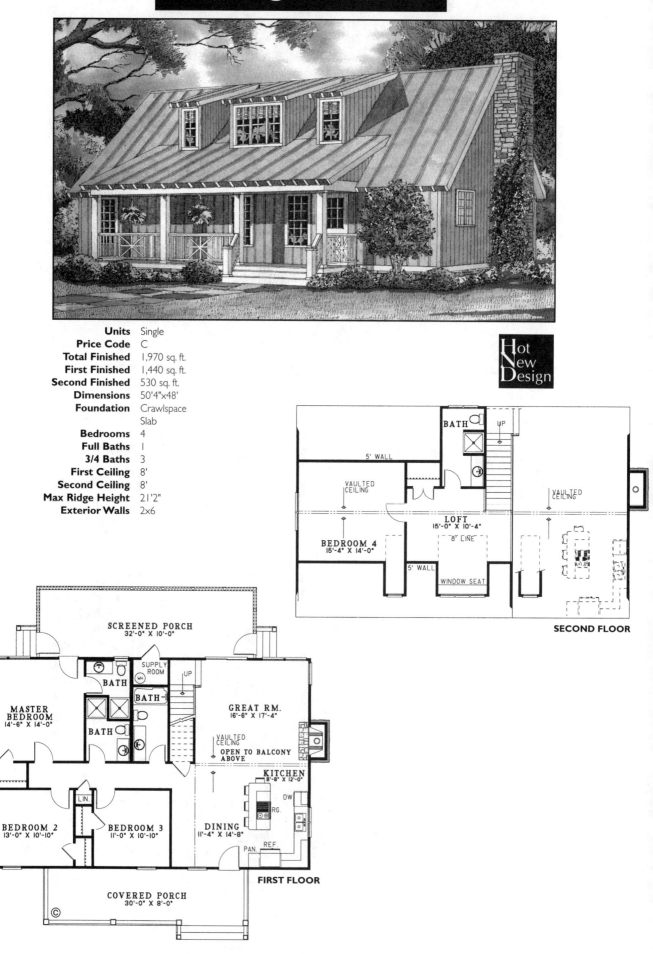

Units	Single
Price Code	C
Total Finished	1,970 sq. ft.
First Finished	1,440 sq. ft.
Second Finished	530 sq. ft.
Dimensions	50'4"x48'
Foundation	Crawlspace
	Slab
Bedrooms	4
Full Baths	1
3/4 Baths	3
First Ceiling	8'
Second Ceiling	8'
Max Ridge Height	21'2"
Exterior Walls	2x6

Hot New Design

SECOND FLOOR

BATH
UP
5' WALL
VAULTED CEILING
VAULTED CEILING
BEDROOM 4
15'-4" X 14'-0"
LOFT
15'-0" X 10'-4"
8" LINE
5' WALL
WINDOW SEAT

FIRST FLOOR

SCREENED PORCH
32'-0" X 10'-0"
SUPPLY ROOM
WH
UP
BATH
BATH
MASTER BEDROOM
14'-6" X 14'-0"
BATH
GREAT RM.
16'-6" X 17'-4"
VAULTED CEILING
OPEN TO BALCONY ABOVE
KITCHEN
8'-8" X 12'-0"
DW
RG.
LIN.
BEDROOM 2
13'-0" X 10'-10"
BEDROOM 3
11'-0" X 10'-10"
DINING
11'-4" X 14'-8"
PAN.
REF.

COVERED PORCH
30'-0" X 8'-0"

To order blueprints, call **800-235-5700** or visit us on the web, **familyhomeplans.com**

Design 32195

Units	Single
Price Code	C
Total Finished	1,976 sq. ft.
First Finished	1,547 sq. ft.
Second Finished	429 sq. ft.
Garage Unfinished	384 sq. ft.
Porch Unfinished	208 sq. ft.
Dimensions	60'x56'
Foundation	Slab
Bedrooms	2
Full Baths	1
3/4 Baths	1
First Ceiling	8'
Vaulted Ceiling	12'6"
Max Ridge Height	23'10"
Roof Framing	Stick
Exterior Walls	2x6

Hot New Design

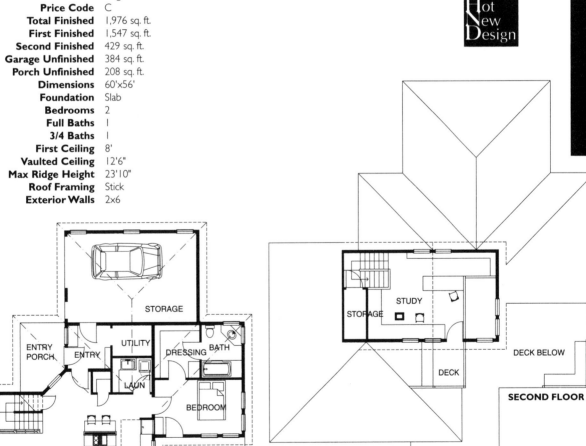

FIRST FLOOR

SECOND FLOOR

Design 65210

Units	Single
Price Code	C
Total Finished	1,976 sq. ft.
First Finished	924 sq. ft.
Second Finished	1,052 sq. ft.
Basement Unfinished	1,067 sq. ft.
Garage Unfinished	388 sq. ft.
Porch Unfinished	596 sq. ft.
Dimensions	44'8"x36'
Foundation	Basement
Bedrooms	4
Full Baths	2
Half Baths	1
First Ceiling	9'
Second Ceiling	8'
Max Ridge Height	33'5"
Roof Framing	Truss
Exterior Walls	2x6

SECOND FLOOR

FIRST FLOOR

Design 94291

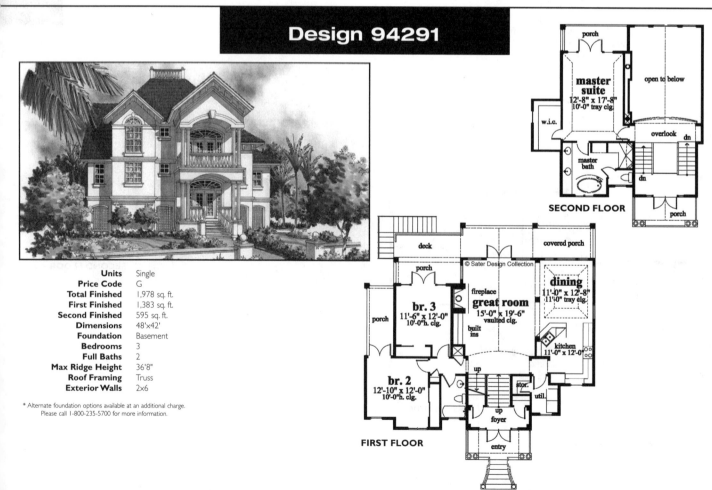

Units	Single
Price Code	G
Total Finished	1,978 sq. ft.
First Finished	1,383 sq. ft.
Second Finished	595 sq. ft.
Dimensions	48'x42'
Foundation	Basement
Bedrooms	3
Full Baths	2
Max Ridge Height	36'8"
Roof Framing	Truss
Exterior Walls	2x6

*Alternate foundation options available at an additional charge. Please call 1-800-235-5700 for more information.

SECOND FLOOR

FIRST FLOOR

Design 94293

Units	Single
Price Code	G
Total Finished	1,978 sq. ft.
First Finished	1,383 sq. ft.
Second Finished	595 sq. ft.
Basement Unfinished	617 sq. ft.
Deck Unfinished	157 sq. ft.
Porch Unfinished	429 sq. ft.
Dimensions	48'x42'
Foundation	Basement
Bedrooms	3
Full Baths	2
Max Ridge Height	40'
Roof Framing	Truss
Exterior Walls	2x6

* Alternate foundation options available at an additional charge.
Please call 1-800-235-5700 for more information.

SECOND FLOOR

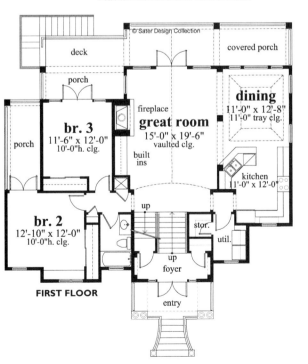

FIRST FLOOR

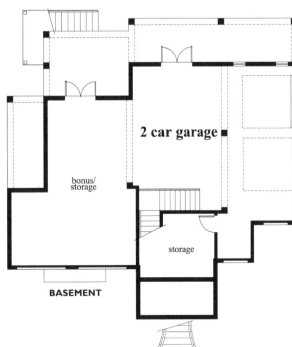

BASEMENT

PHOTOGRAPHY: VICTORIA PALAGI

Units	Single
Price Code	C
Total Finished	1,978 sq. ft.
First Finished	1,034 sq. ft.
Second Finished	944 sq. ft.
Basement Unfinished	984 sq. ft.
Garage Unfinished	675 sq. ft.
Dimensions	67'6"x39'6"
Foundation	Basement
	Crawlspace
	Slab
Bedrooms	4
Full Baths	2
Half Baths	1
First Ceiling	9'
Second Ceiling	8'
Max Ridge Height	29'
Roof Framing	Stick
Exterior Walls	2x4, 2x6

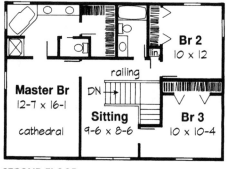

SECOND FLOOR

OPTIONAL MASTER BATH

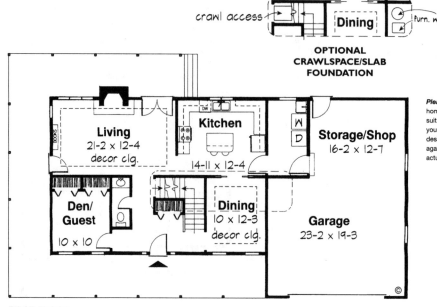

OPTIONAL CRAWLSPACE/SLAB FOUNDATION

FIRST FLOOR

Please note: The photographed home may have been modified to suit homeowner preferences. If you order plans, have a builder or design professional check them against the photograph to confirm actual construction details.

Design 20230

1,501-2,000 sq.ft. HOME PLANS

Units	Single
Price Code	C
Total Finished	1,995 sq. ft.
First Finished	1,365 sq. ft.
Second Finished	630 sq. ft.
Basement Unfinished	1,419 sq. ft.
Garage Unfinished	426 sq. ft.
Porch Unfinished	89 sq. ft.
Dimensions	44'x54'
Foundation	Basement
	Crawlspace
	Slab
Bedrooms	4
Full Baths	2
Half Baths	1
First Ceiling	9'
Second Ceiling	8'
Max Ridge Height	25'6"
Roof Framing	Truss
Exterior Walls	2x4

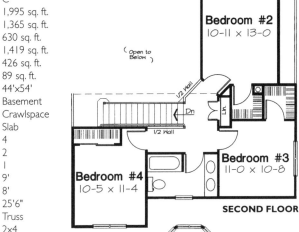

Bedroom #2
10-11 x 13-0

Open to Below

Bedroom #3
11-0 x 10-8

Bedroom #4
10-5 x 11-4

SECOND FLOOR

**OPTIONAL
CRAWLSPACE/SLAB
FOUNDATION**

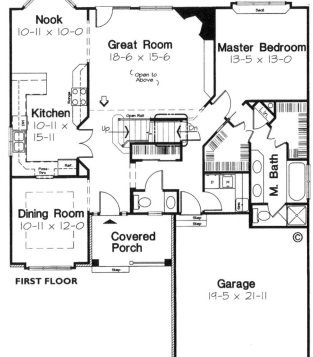

Nook
10-11 x 10-0

Great Room
18-6 x 15-6

Master Bedroom
13-5 x 13-0

Open to Above

Kitchen
10-11 x 15-11

M. Bath

Dining Room
10-11 x 12-0

Covered Porch

FIRST FLOOR

Garage
19-5 x 21-11

Units	Single
Price Code	C
Total Finished	1,995 sq. ft.
First Finished	1,525 sq. ft.
Second Finished	470 sq. ft.
Basement Unfinished	1,525 sq. ft.
Garage Unfinished	623 sq. ft.
Deck Unfinished	81 sq. ft.
Porch Unfinished	113 sq. ft.
Dimensions	56'x53'
Foundation	Basement
Bedrooms	2
Full Baths	2
Half Baths	1
First Ceiling	8'
Second Ceiling	8'
Max Ridge Height	29'9"
Roof Framing	Truss
Exterior Walls	2x6

SECOND FLOOR

FIRST FLOOR

Design 65252

SECOND FLOOR

3,40 X 3,60
11'-4" X 12'-0"

3,40 X 3,60
11'-4" X 12'-0"

3,70 X 4,80
12'-4" X 16'-0"

6.00 X 3,50
20'-0" X 11'-8"

4,20 X 2,80
14'-0" X 9'-4"

5,90 X 6,60
19'-8" X 22'-0"

3,70 X 6,80
12'-4" X 22'-8"

FIRST FLOOR

Units	Single
Price Code	C
Total Finished	1,996 sq. ft.
First Finished	916 sq. ft.
Second Finished	1,080 sq. ft.
Basement Unfinished	916 sq. ft.
Garage Unfinished	436 sq. ft.
Porch Unfinished	50 sq. ft.
Dimensions	44'8"x36'
Foundation	Basement
Bedrooms	3
Full Baths	1
3/4 Baths	1
Half Baths	1
First Ceiling	9'
Second Ceiling	8'
Max Ridge Height	33'5"
Roof Framing	Truss
Exterior Walls	2x6

Design 63049

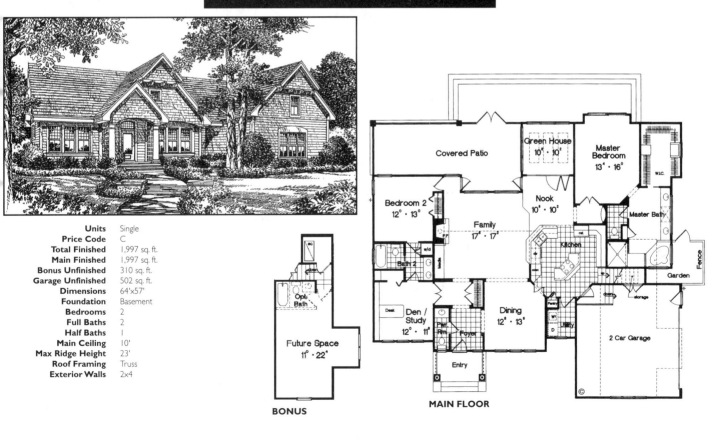

Units	Single
Price Code	C
Total Finished	1,997 sq. ft.
Main Finished	1,997 sq. ft.
Bonus Unfinished	310 sq. ft.
Garage Unfinished	502 sq. ft.
Dimensions	64'x57'
Foundation	Basement
Bedrooms	2
Full Baths	2
Half Baths	1
Main Ceiling	10'
Max Ridge Height	23'
Roof Framing	Truss
Exterior Walls	2x4

Covered Patio

Green House
10' · 10'

Master Bedroom
13' · 16'

W.I.C.

Bedroom 2
12' · 13'

Nook
10' · 10'

Master Bath

Family
17' · 17'

Kitchen

Garden

Fence

Bath 2

w/d

storage

Den / Study
12' · 11'

Dining
12' · 13'

Utility

2 Car Garage

Pwdr Rm

Foyer

Entry

MAIN FLOOR

Opt. Bath

Future Space
11' · 22'

BONUS

Design 20093

PHOTOGRAPHY: JOHN EHRENCLOU

Units	Single
Price Code	D
Total Finished	2,001 sq. ft.
First Finished	1,027 sq. ft.
Second Finished	974 sq. ft.
Basement Unfinished	978 sq. ft.
Garage Unfinished	476 sq. ft.
Dimensions	43'x56'
Foundation	Basement
Bedrooms	3
Full Baths	2
Half Baths	1
Max Ridge Height	34'
Roof Framing	Stick
Exterior Walls	2x6

Please note: The photographed home may have been modified to suit homeowner preferences. If you order plans, have a builder or design professional check them against the photograph to confirm actual construction details.

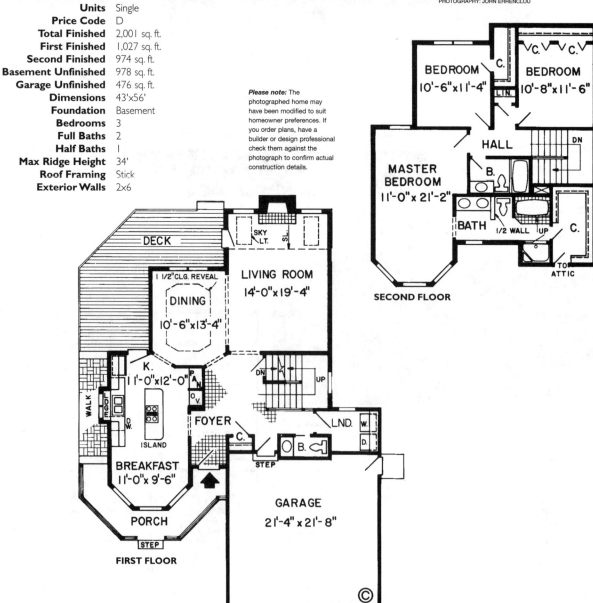

Design 65228

Units	Single
Price Code	D
Total Finished	2,005 sq. ft.
First Finished	880 sq. ft.
Second Finished	1,125 sq. ft.
Basement Unfinished	880 sq. ft.
Deck Unfinished	237 sq. ft.
Dimensions	30'x54'
Foundation	Basement
Bedrooms	3
Full Baths	2
Half Baths	1
First Ceiling	8'
Second Ceiling	8'
Max Ridge Height	29'3"

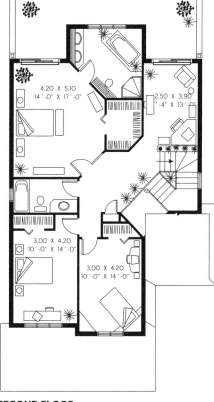

SECOND FLOOR

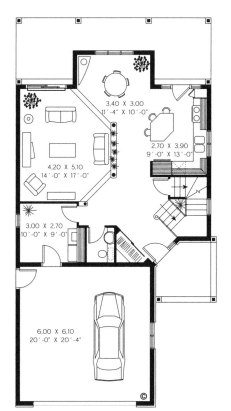

FIRST FLOOR

Design 65125

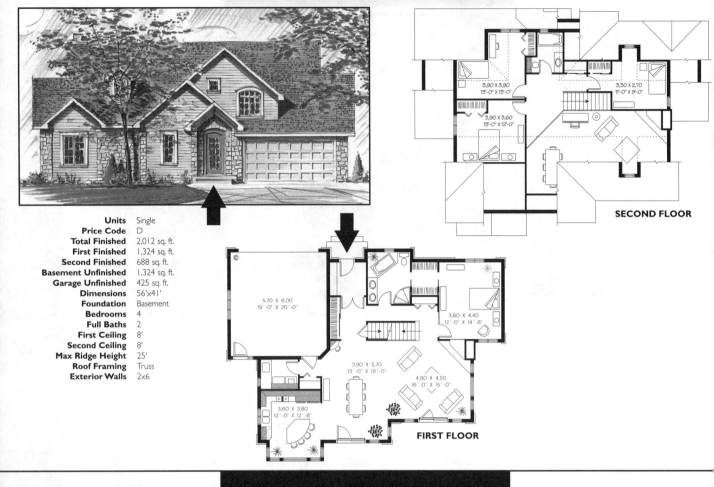

SECOND FLOOR

Units	Single
Price Code	D
Total Finished	2,012 sq. ft.
First Finished	1,324 sq. ft.
Second Finished	688 sq. ft.
Basement Unfinished	1,324 sq. ft.
Garage Unfinished	425 sq. ft.
Dimensions	56'x41'
Foundation	Basement
Bedrooms	4
Full Baths	2
First Ceiling	8'
Second Ceiling	8'
Max Ridge Height	25'
Roof Framing	Truss
Exterior Walls	2x6

FIRST FLOOR

Design 10515

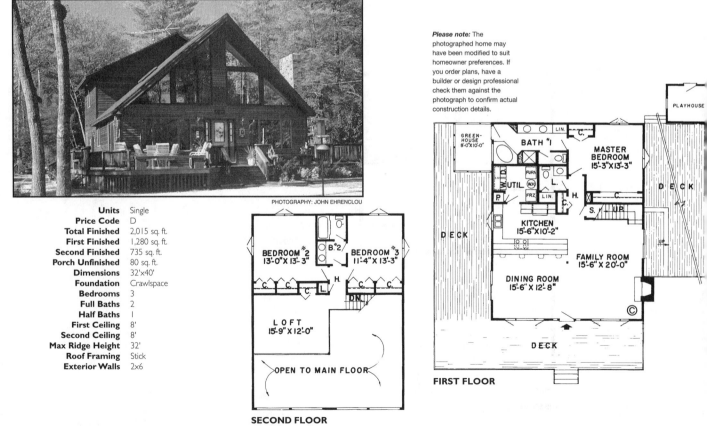

PHOTOGRAPHY: JOHN EHRENCLOU

Please note: The photographed home may have been modified to suit homeowner preferences. If you order plans, have a builder or design professional check them against the photograph to confirm actual construction details.

Units	Single
Price Code	D
Total Finished	2,015 sq. ft.
First Finished	1,280 sq. ft.
Second Finished	735 sq. ft.
Porch Unfinished	80 sq. ft.
Dimensions	32'x40'
Foundation	Crawlspace
Bedrooms	3
Full Baths	2
Half Baths	1
First Ceiling	8'
Second Ceiling	8'
Max Ridge Height	32'
Roof Framing	Stick
Exterior Walls	2x6

SECOND FLOOR

FIRST FLOOR

Design 98714

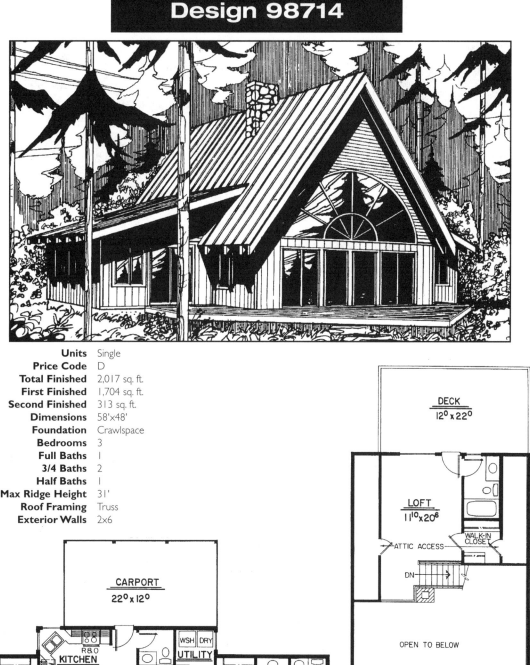

Units	Single
Price Code	D
Total Finished	2,017 sq. ft.
First Finished	1,704 sq. ft.
Second Finished	313 sq. ft.
Dimensions	58'x48'
Foundation	Crawlspace
Bedrooms	3
Full Baths	1
3/4 Baths	2
Half Baths	1
Max Ridge Height	31'
Roof Framing	Truss
Exterior Walls	2x6

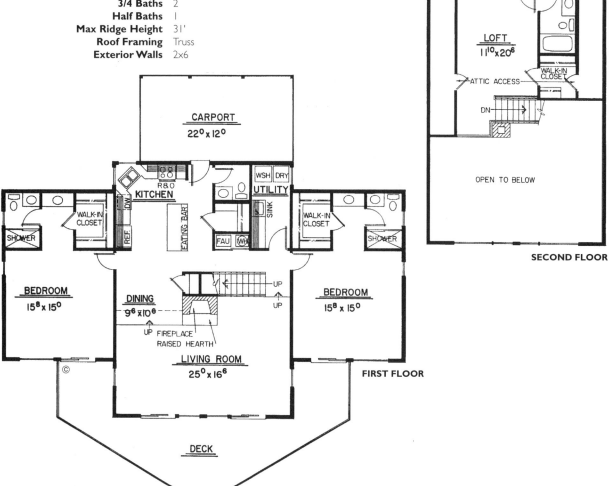

DECK
12⁰ x 22⁰

LOFT
11¹⁰ x 20⁶

WALK-IN CLOSET

ATTIC ACCESS

DN

OPEN TO BELOW

SECOND FLOOR

CARPORT
22⁰ x 12⁰

KITCHEN
R&O

UTILITY
WSH DRY
SINK

WALK-IN CLOSET

WALK-IN CLOSET

SHOWER

SHOWER

FAU WH

EATING BAR

REF. DW

BEDROOM
15⁸ x 15⁰

DINING
9⁶ x 10⁶

UP

UP

UP FIREPLACE RAISED HEARTH

BEDROOM
15⁸ x 15⁰

LIVING ROOM
25⁰ x 16⁶

FIRST FLOOR

DECK

Design 57019

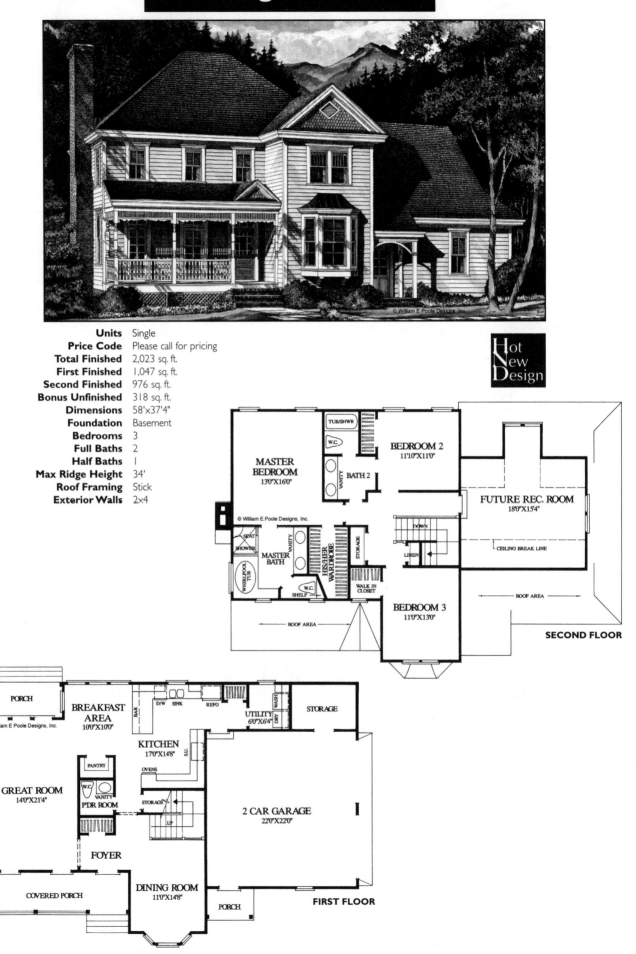

Units	Single
Price Code	Please call for pricing
Total Finished	2,023 sq. ft.
First Finished	1,047 sq. ft.
Second Finished	976 sq. ft.
Bonus Unfinished	318 sq. ft.
Dimensions	58'x37'4"
Foundation	Basement
Bedrooms	3
Full Baths	2
Half Baths	1
Max Ridge Height	34'
Roof Framing	Stick
Exterior Walls	2x4

Hot New Design

© William E. Poole Designs, Inc.

SECOND FLOOR

TUB/SHWR
W.C.
BEDROOM 2
11'10"X11'0"
MASTER BEDROOM
13'0"X16'0"
BATH 2
VANITY
FUTURE REC. ROOM
18'0"X15'4"
SEAT
SHOWER
MASTER BATH
VANITY
HIS/HER WARDROBE
STORAGE
DOWN
CEILING BREAK LINE
WHIRLPOOL TUB
W.C.
SHELF
WALK IN CLOSET
LINEN
BEDROOM 3
11'0"X13'0"
ROOF AREA
ROOF AREA

FIRST FLOOR

© William E Poole Designs, Inc.

PORCH
BREAKFAST AREA
10'0"X10'0"
BAR
D/W SINK REFG
UTILITY
6'0"X6'4"
WASH
DRY
STORAGE
KITCHEN
17'0"X14'8"
OVENS
PANTRY
W.C.
VANITY
PDR ROOM
GREAT ROOM
14'0"X21'4"
STORAGE
UP
2 CAR GARAGE
22'0"X22'0"
FOYER
COVERED PORCH
DINING ROOM
11'0"X14'8"
PORCH

Design 26760

Units	Single
Price Code	D
Total Finished	2,023 sq. ft.
Main Finished	2,023 sq. ft.
Deck Unfinished	589 sq. ft.
Dimensions	64'x45'
Foundation	Slab
Bedrooms	3
Full Baths	2
Half Baths	1

MAIN FLOOR

Units	Single
Price Code	D
Total Finished	2,026 sq. ft.
Main Finished	2,026 sq. ft.
Garage Unfinished	421 sq. ft.
Porch Unfinished	479 sq. ft.
Dimensions	58'x79'6"
Foundation	Crawlspace
	Slab
Bedrooms	3
Full Baths	2
Max Ridge Height	28'6'
Roof Framing	Stick
Exterior Walls	2x6

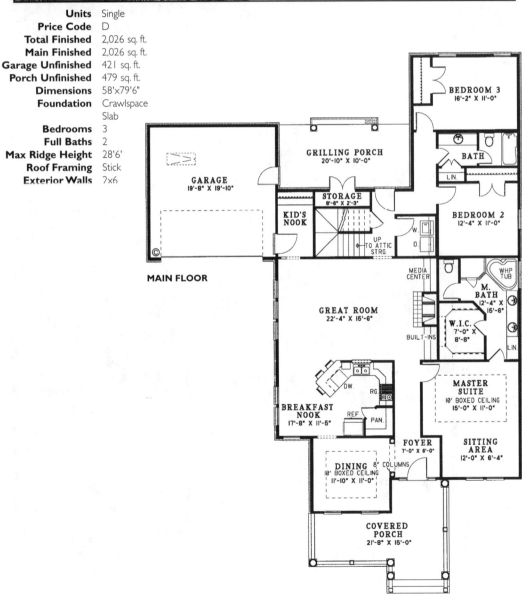

MAIN FLOOR

BEDROOM 3
16'-2" X 11'-0"

BATH

LIN.

BEDROOM 2
12'-4" X 11'-0"

GRILLING PORCH
20'-10" X 10'-0"

STORAGE
8'-6" X 2'-3"

KID'S NOOK

UP TO ATTIC STRG.

GARAGE
19'-8" X 19'-10"

MEDIA CENTER

WHP TUB

M. BATH
12'-4" X 15'-8"

GREAT ROOM
22'-4" X 15'-6"

W.I.C.
7'-0" X 8'-8"

LIN.

BUILT-INS

MASTER SUITE
10' BOXED CEILING
15'-0" X 11'-0"

BREAKFAST NOOK
17'-8" X 11'-5"

DW.

RG.

REF.

PAN.

FOYER
7'-0" X 6'-0"

SITTING AREA
12'-0" X 6'-4"

DINING
10' BOXED CEILING
11'-10" X 11'-0"

8' COLUMNS

COVERED PORCH
21'-8" X 15'-0"

Design 67001

Units	Single
Price Code	D
Total Finished	2,028 sq. ft.
Main Finished	2,028 sq. ft.
Garage Unfinished	442 sq. ft.
Porch Unfinished	232 sq. ft.
Dimensions	60'x58'
Foundation	Slab
Bedrooms	3
Full Baths	2
Main Ceiling	10'
Max Ridge Height	23'3"
Roof Framing	Stick
Exterior Walls	2x4

MAIN FLOOR

PORCH

BRK
12'-6"
X 12'-0"
(10' CLG.)

COMPUTER NOOK

BEDR'M 2
12'-0"
X 11'-0"
(10' CLG.)

GREAT ROOM
17'-0"
X 18'-0"
(10' CLG.)

12'-0"
X 13'-3"

SEAT

MASTER SUITE
14'-0"
X 18'-6"
(CLG. RAISED FROM 9' TO 10')

KIT
(10' CLG.)

BEDR'M 3
12'-0"
X 11'-0"
(10' CLG.)

GALLERY

HALL

BATH-2

DINING
11'-0"
X 13'-0"
(CLG. RAISED FROM 9' TO 10')

UTIL

DOUBLE GARAGE
20'-0" X 20'-0"

MASTER BATH

ENTRY
(10' CLG.)

W.I.C.

PORCH

STORAGE

Design 67003

Units	Single
Price Code	D
Total Finished	2,044 sq. ft.
First Finished	1,203 sq. ft.
Second Finished	841 sq. ft.
Garage Unfinished	462 sq. ft.
Porch Unfinished	323 sq. ft.
Dimensions	56'x44'5"
Foundation	Slab
Bedrooms	3
Full Baths	2
Half Bath	1
First Ceiling	8'
Second Ceiling	8'
Vaulted Ceiling	16'
Max Ridge Height	28'9"
Roof Framing	Stick
Exterior Walls	2x4

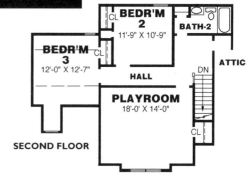

BEDR'M 2
11'-9" X 10'-9"

BATH-2

BEDR'M 3
12'-0" X 12'-7"

ATTIC

HALL

DN

PLAYROOM
18'-0' X 14'-0"

CL

SECOND FLOOR

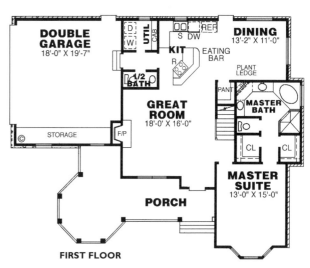

DOUBLE GARAGE
18'-0" X 19'-7"

UTIL

DINING
13'-2" X 11'-0"

KIT

EATING BAR

1/2 BATH

PLANT LEDGE

STORAGE

F/P

GREAT ROOM
18'-0" X 16'-0"

MASTER BATH

PANT

MASTER SUITE
13'-0" X 15'-0"

PORCH

FIRST FLOOR

Design 24736

Units	Single
Price Code	D
Total Finished	2,044 sq. ft.
First Finished	1,403 sq. ft.
Second Finished	641 sq. ft.
Basement Unfinished	1,394 sq. ft.
Garage Unfinished	680 sq. ft.
Deck Unfinished	156 sq. ft.
Porch Unfinished	231 sq. ft.
Dimensions	68'x47'
Foundation	Basement
	Crawlspace
	Slab
Bedrooms	3
Full Baths	2
Half Baths	1
First Ceiling	9'
Second Ceiling	8'
Vaulted Ceiling	12'9"
Roof Framing	Truss
Exterior Walls	2x4

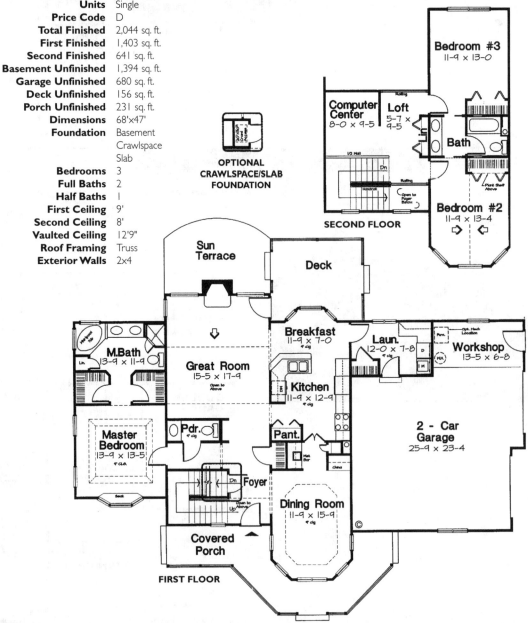

OPTIONAL CRAWLSPACE/SLAB FOUNDATION

SECOND FLOOR

Bedroom #3 11-9 x 13-0

Computer Center 8-0 x 9-5

Loft 5-7 x 9-5

Bath

Bedroom #2 11-9 x 13-4

FIRST FLOOR

Sun Terrace

Deck

M.Bath 13-9 x 11-9

Great Room 15-5 x 17-9 Open to Above

Breakfast 11-9 x 7-0

Laun. 12-0 x 7-8

Workshop 13-5 x 6-8

Master Bedroom 13-9 x 13-5

Pdr.

Kitchen 11-9 x 12-9

Pant.

2 - Car Garage 25-9 x 23-4

Foyer

Dining Room 11-9 x 15-9

Covered Porch

Design 94260

Units	Single
Price Code	F
Total Finished	2,068 sq. ft.
Main Finished	2,068 sq. ft.
Lower Unfinished	1,402 sq. ft.
Garage Unfinished	560 sq. ft.
Deck Unfinished	594 sq. ft.
Porch Unfinished	696 sq. ft.
Dimensions	54'x58'
Foundation	Pier/Post
Bedrooms	3
Full Baths	2
Max Ridge Height	37'
Roof Framing	Truss
Exterior Walls	2x6

* Alternate foundation options available at an additional charge.
Please call 1-800-235-5700 for more information.

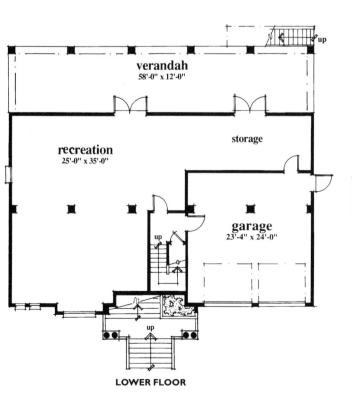

LOWER FLOOR

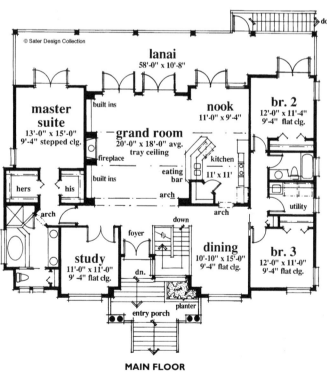

© Sater Design Collection

MAIN FLOOR

Design 96505

Units	Single
Price Code	D
Total Finished	2,069 sq. ft.
Main Finished	2,069 sq. ft.
Garage Unfinished	481 sq. ft.
Porch Unfinished	374 sq. ft.
Dimensions	70'x58'
Foundation	Crawlspace
	Slab
Bedrooms	3
Full Baths	2
Half Baths	I
Main Ceiling	9'
Max Ridge Height	23'
Exterior Walls	2x4

MAIN FLOOR

Design 57013

PHOTOGRAPHY: COURTESY OF WILLIAM E. POOLE DESIGNS, INC.

Hot New Design

Units	Single
Price Code	Please call for pricing
Total Finished	2,069 sq. ft.
First Finished	1,075 sq. ft.
Second Finished	994 sq. ft.
Bonus Unfinished	382 sq. ft.
Basement Unfinished	1,075 sq. ft.
Dimensions	56'4"x35'4"
Foundation	Basement
Bedrooms	3
Full Baths	2
Half Baths	I
Max Ridge Height	35'
Roof Framing	Stick
Exterior Walls	2x4

Please note: The photographed home may have been modified to suit homeowner preferences. If you order plans, have a builder or design professional check them against the photograph to confirm actual construction details.

SECOND FLOOR

FIRST FLOOR

Design 32336

PHOTOGRAPHY: JAMES YOCHUM PHOTOGRAPHY

Units	Single
Price Code	D
Total Finished	2,071 sq. ft.
First Finished	1,109 sq. ft.
Second Finished	962 sq. ft.
Basement Unfinished	1,015 sq. ft.
Garage Unfinished	462 sq. ft.
Deck Unfinished	140 sq. ft.
Porch Unfinished	264 sq. ft.
Dimensions	38'6"x56'
Foundation	Basement
Bedrooms	4
Full Baths	3
3/4 Baths	1
First Ceiling	9'
Second Ceiling	8'
Max Ridge Height	28'6"
Roof Framing	Truss
Exterior Walls	2x4

Please note: The photographed home may have been modified to suit homeowner preferences. If you order plans, have a builder or design professional check them against the photograph to confirm actual construction details.

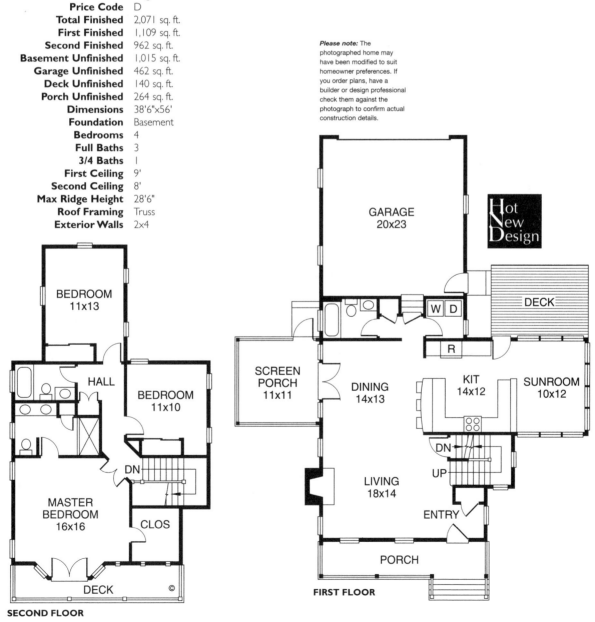

SECOND FLOOR

FIRST FLOOR

Units	Single
Price Code	D
Total Finished	2,089 sq. ft.
Main Finished	2,089 sq. ft.
Bonus Unfinished	497 sq. ft.
Garage Unfinished	541 sq. ft.
Dimensions	79'x52'
Foundation	Crawlspace
	Slab
Bedrooms	3
Full Baths	2
Half Baths	1
Main Ceiling	9'
Max Ridge Height	22'
Roof Framing	Stick
Exterior Walls	2x4

BONUS

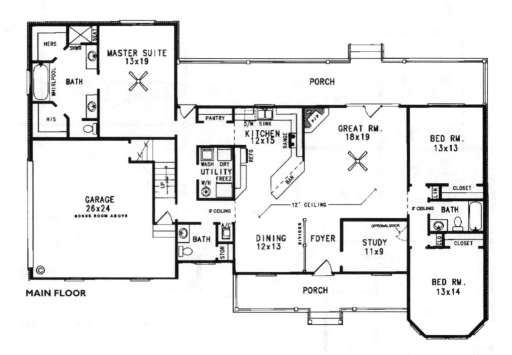

MAIN FLOOR

Design 65135

Units	Single
Price Code	D
Total Finished	2,089 sq. ft.
First Finished	1,146 sq. ft.
Second Finished	943 sq. ft.
Bonus Unfinished	313 sq. ft.
Basement Unfinished	483 sq. ft.
Porch Unfinished	168 sq. ft.
Dimensions	56'x38'
Foundation	Basement
Bedrooms	3
Full Baths	2
Half Baths	1
First Ceiling	9'
Second Ceiling	8'
Max Ridge Height	31'3"
Roof Framing	Truss
Exterior Walls	2x6

SECOND FLOOR

FIRST FLOOR

Units	Single
Price Code	D
Total Finished	2,089 sq. ft.
First Finished	1,146 sq. ft.
Second Finished	943 sq. ft.
Garage Unfinished	403 sq. ft.
Dimensions	56'x38'
Foundation	Basement
Bedrooms	3
Full Baths	1
Half Baths	1
First Ceiling	9'
Second Ceiling	8'
Max Ridge Height	31'8"
Roof Framing	Truss
Exterior Walls	2x6

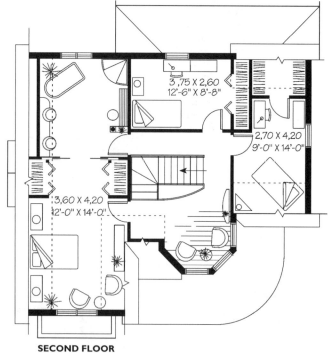

3,75 X 2,60
12'-6" X 8'-8"

2,70 X 4,20
9'-0" X 14'-0"

3,60 X 4,20
12'-0" X 14'-0"

SECOND FLOOR

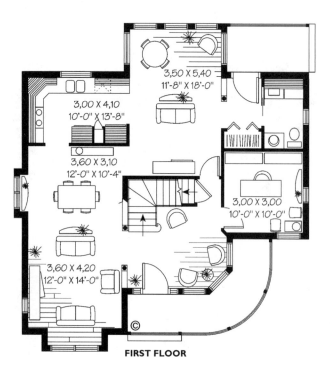

3,50 X 5,40
11'-8" X 18'-0"

3,00 X 4,10
10'-0" X 13'-8"

3,60 X 3,10
12'-0" X 10'-4"

3,00 X 3,00
10'-0" X 10'-0"

3,60 X 4,20
12'-0" X 14'-0"

FIRST FLOOR

Design 99705

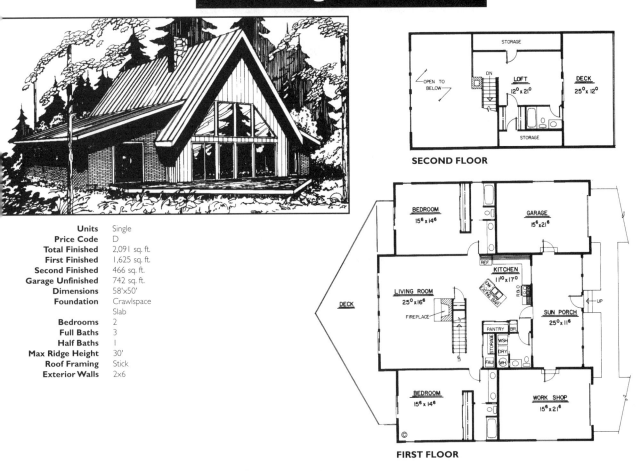

SECOND FLOOR

FIRST FLOOR

Units	Single
Price Code	D
Total Finished	2,091 sq. ft.
First Finished	1,625 sq. ft.
Second Finished	466 sq. ft.
Garage Unfinished	742 sq. ft.
Dimensions	58'x50'
Foundation	Crawlspace
	Slab
Bedrooms	2
Full Baths	3
Half Baths	1
Max Ridge Height	30'
Roof Framing	Stick
Exterior Walls	2x6

Design 65124

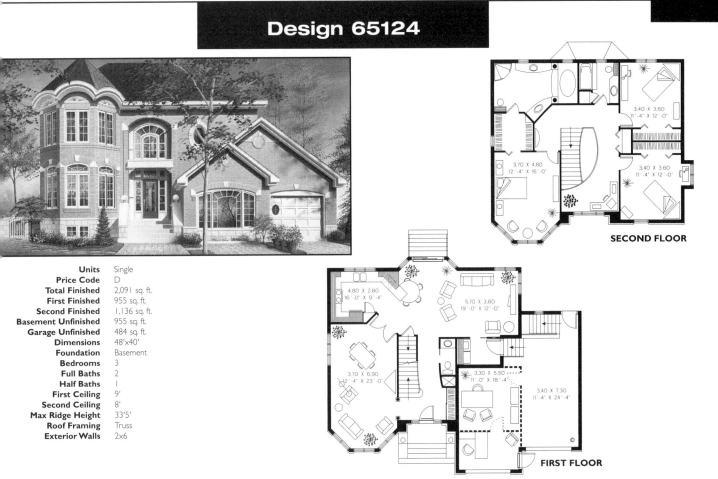

SECOND FLOOR

FIRST FLOOR

Units	Single
Price Code	D
Total Finished	2,091 sq. ft.
First Finished	955 sq. ft.
Second Finished	1,136 sq. ft.
Basement Unfinished	955 sq. ft.
Garage Unfinished	484 sq. ft.
Dimensions	48'x40'
Foundation	Basement
Bedrooms	3
Full Baths	2
Half Baths	1
First Ceiling	9'
Second Ceiling	8'
Max Ridge Height	33'5"
Roof Framing	Truss
Exterior Walls	2x6

Design 10012

Units	Single
Price Code	D
Total Finished	2,108 sq. ft.
Main Finished	1,198 sq. ft.
Lower Finished	910 sq. ft.
Garage Unfinished	288 sq. ft
Dimensions	32'x36'
Foundation	Basement
Bedrooms	3
Full Baths	2
Half Baths	I
Exterior Walls	2x4

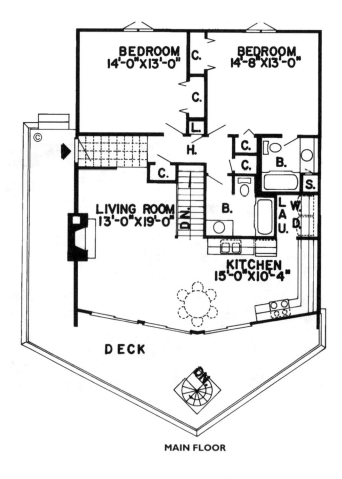

MAIN FLOOR

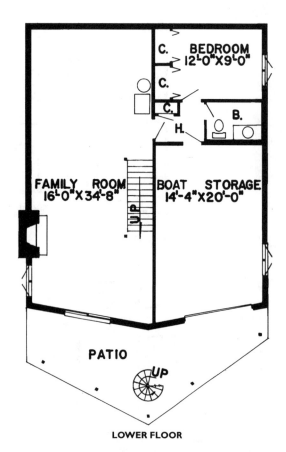

LOWER FLOOR

Design 65214

Units	Single
Price Code	D
Total Finished	2,129 sq. ft.
First Finished	1,162 sq. ft.
Second Finished	967 sq. ft.
Garage Unfinished	317 sq. ft.
Dimensions	40'x42'
Foundation	Basement
Bedrooms	3
Full Baths	1
Half Baths	1
First Ceiling	8'
Second Ceiling	8'
Max Ridge Height	30'4"
Roof Framing	Truss

SECOND FLOOR

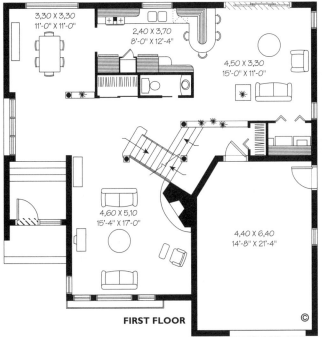

FIRST FLOOR

Units	Single
Price Code	D
Total Finished	2,135 sq. ft.
First Finished	1,085 sq. ft.
Second Finished	1,050 sq. ft.
Basement Unfinished	1,050 sq. ft.
Garage Unfinished	440 sq. ft.
Dimensions	50'8"x38'4"
Foundation	Basement
Bedrooms	4
Full Baths	2
Half Baths	1
First Ceiling	9'
Second Ceiling	8'
Max Ridge Height	31'2"
Roof Framing	Stick
Exterior Walls	2x6

SECOND FLOOR

FIRST FLOOR

Hot New Design

Units	Single
Price Code	Please call for pricing
Total Finished	2,151 sq. ft.
Main Finished	2,151 sq. ft.
Bonus Unfinished	786 sq. ft.
Dimensions	61'x55'8"
Foundation	Combo Basement/ Crawlspace
Bedrooms	3
Full Baths	2
Max Ridge Height	61'
Roof Framing	Stick
Exterior Walls	2x4

BONUS

MAIN FLOOR

Design 91343

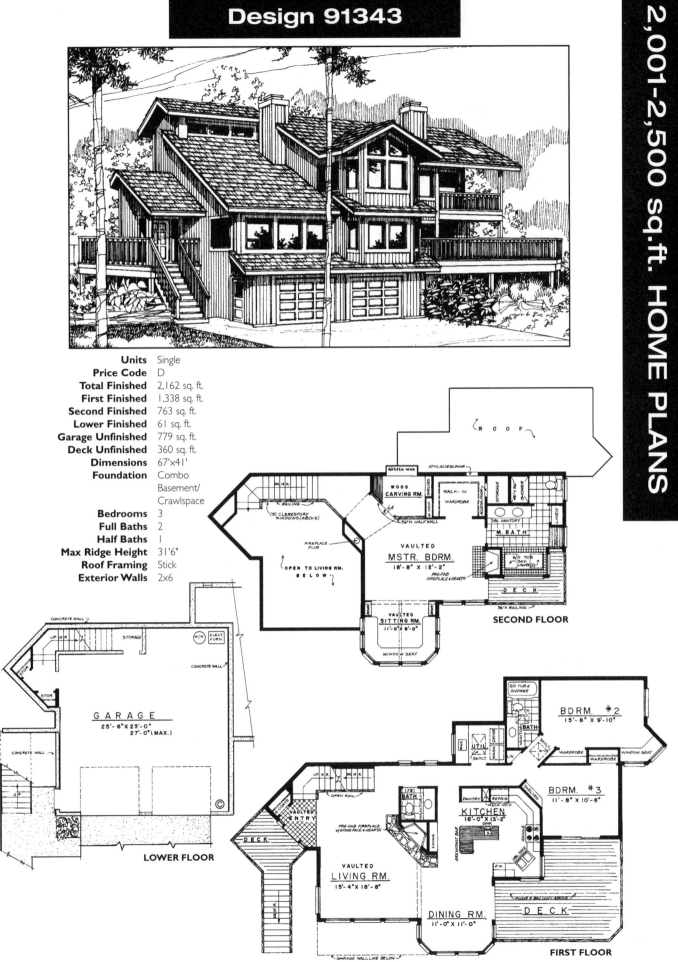

Units	Single
Price Code	D
Total Finished	2,162 sq. ft.
First Finished	1,338 sq. ft.
Second Finished	763 sq. ft.
Lower Finished	61 sq. ft.
Garage Unfinished	779 sq. ft.
Deck Unfinished	360 sq. ft.
Dimensions	67'x41'
Foundation	Combo Basement/ Crawlspace
Bedrooms	3
Full Baths	2
Half Baths	1
Max Ridge Height	31'6"
Roof Framing	Stick
Exterior Walls	2x6

Units	Single
Price Code	D
Total Finished	2,175 sq. ft.
First Finished	874 sq. ft.
Second Finished	1,301 sq. ft.
Bonus Unfinished	425 sq. ft.
Garage Unfinished	528 sq. ft.
Dimensions	48'x40'
Foundation	Basement
Bedrooms	3
Full Baths	1
3/4 Baths	1
Half Baths	1
First Ceiling	9'
Second Ceiling	8'
Max Ridge Height	29'10"
Exterior Walls	2x6

SECOND FLOOR

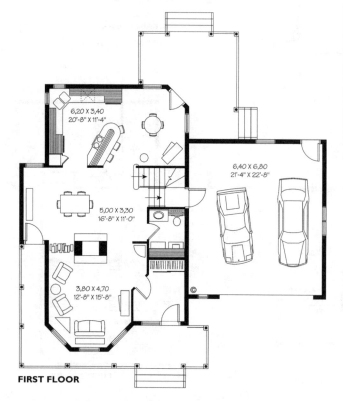

FIRST FLOOR

Design 57017

© William E Poole Designs, Inc.

Units	Single
Price Code	Please call for pricing
Total Finished	2,179 sq. ft.
First Finished	1,556 sq. ft.
Second Finished	623 sq. ft.
Bonus Unfinished	368 sq. ft.
Dimensions	73'4"x41'4"
Foundation	Crawlspace
Bedrooms	3
Full Baths	2
Half Baths	1
Max Ridge Height	29'
Roof Framing	Stick
Exterior Walls	2x4

Hot New Design

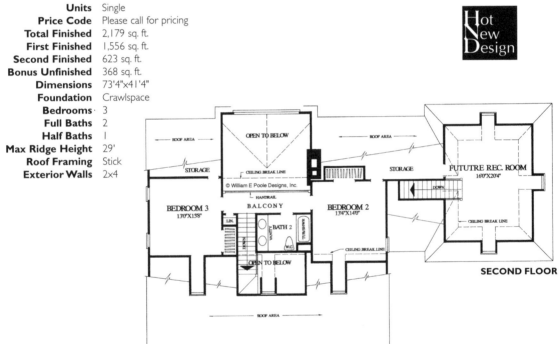

SECOND FLOOR

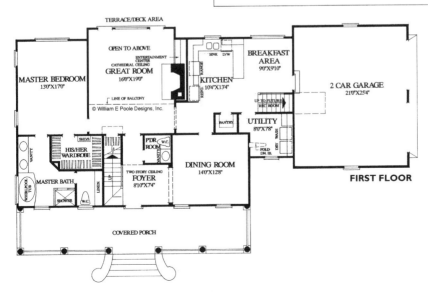

FIRST FLOOR

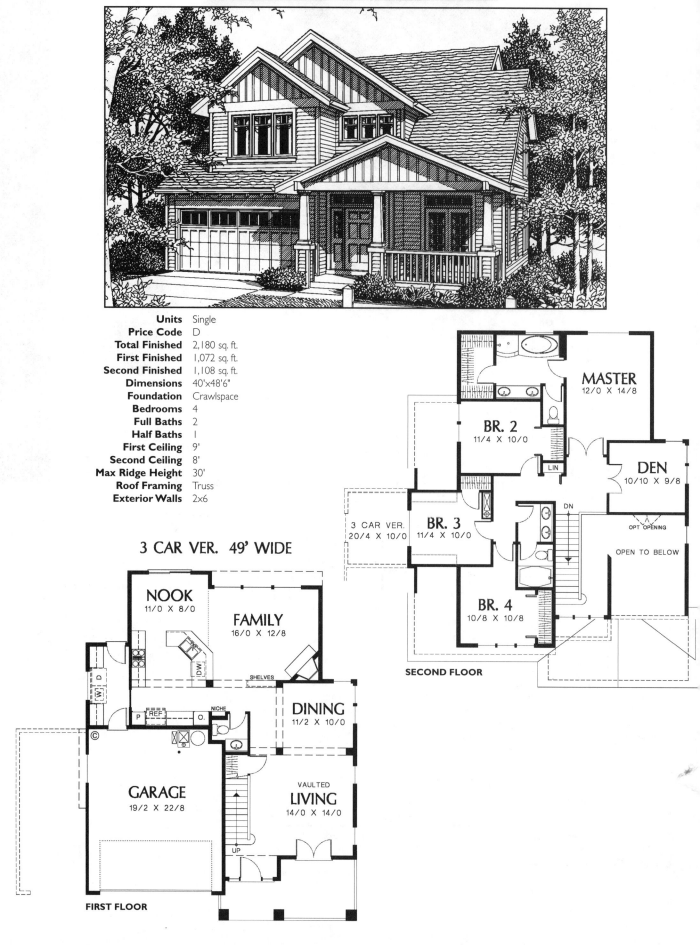

Units	Single
Price Code	D
Total Finished	2,180 sq. ft.
First Finished	1,072 sq. ft.
Second Finished	1,108 sq. ft.
Dimensions	40'x48'6"
Foundation	Crawlspace
Bedrooms	4
Full Baths	2
Half Baths	1
First Ceiling	9'
Second Ceiling	8'
Max Ridge Height	30'
Roof Framing	Truss
Exterior Walls	2x6

3 CAR VER. 49' WIDE

NOOK
11/0 X 8/0

FAMILY
16/0 X 12/8

SHELVES

DINING
11/2 X 10/0

W D

P REF O.

NICHE

GARAGE
19/2 X 22/8

VAULTED
LIVING
14/0 X 14/0

UP

FIRST FLOOR

MASTER
12/0 X 14/8

BR. 2
11/4 X 10/0

LIN

DEN
10/10 X 9/8

3 CAR VER.
20/4 X 10/0

BR. 3
11/4 X 10/0

OPT OPENING

OPEN TO BELOW

DN

BR. 4
10/8 X 10/8

SECOND FLOOR

Design 62065

Units	Single
Price Code	D
Total Finished	2,188 sq. ft.
Main Finished	2,188 sq. ft.
Bonus Unfinished	375 sq. ft.
Garage Unfinished	524 sq. ft.
Porch Unfinished	555 sq. ft.
Dimensions	66'x64'7"
Foundation	Crawlspace
	Slab
Bedrooms	4
Full Baths	2
Half Baths	1
First Ceiling	9'
Second Ceiling	8'
Max Ridge Height	27'4"
Roof Framing	Stick
Exterior Walls	2x4, 2x6

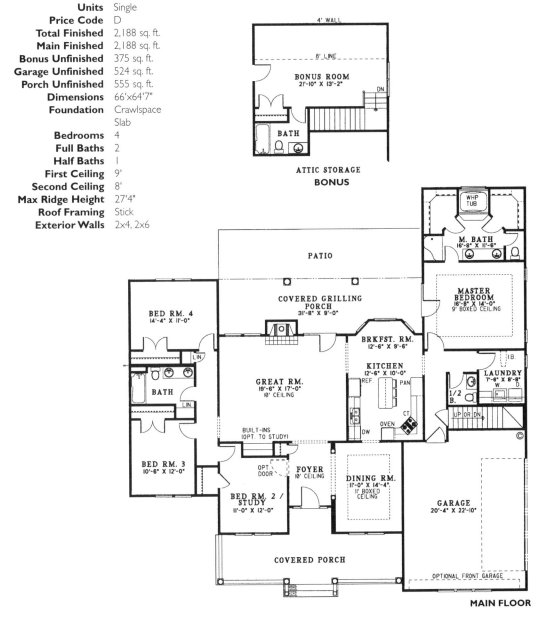

Units	Single
Price Code	D
Total Finished	2,196 sq. ft.
First Finished	1,658 sq. ft.
Second Finished	538 sq. ft.
Bonus Unfinished	496 sq. ft.
Garage Unfinished	608 sq. ft.
Dimensions	50'x56'
Foundation	Crawlspace
Bedrooms	4
Full Baths	2
Half Baths	1
First Ceiling	9'
Second Ceiling	8'
Max Ridge Height	28'
Roof Framing	Stick
Exterior Walls	2x6

Design 97710

Units	Single
Price Code	D
Total Finished	2,198 sq. ft.
First Finished	1,706 sq. ft.
Second Finished	492 sq. ft.
Basement Unfinished	1,706 sq. ft.
Deck Unfinished	175 sq. ft.
Porch Unfinished	38 sq. ft.
Dimensions	59'4"x65'
Foundation	Basement
Bedrooms	3
Full Baths	2
Half Baths	1
Max Ridge Height	31'
Roof Framing	Truss
Exterior Walls	2x4

SECOND FLOOR

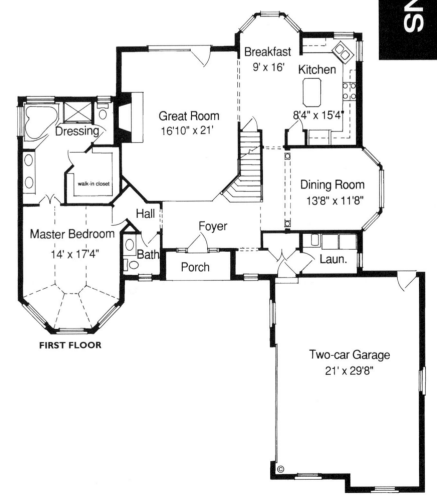

FIRST FLOOR

Design 57012

© William E Poole Designs, Inc.

Units	Single
Price Code	Please call for pricing
Total Finished	2,215 sq. ft.
Main Finished	2,215 sq. ft.
Bonus Unfinished	636 sq. ft.
Dimensions	69'10"x62'6"
Foundation	Combo Basement/ Crawlspace
Bedrooms	3
Full Baths	3
Max Ridge Height	30'
Roof Framing	Stick
Exterior Walls	2x4

Hot New Design

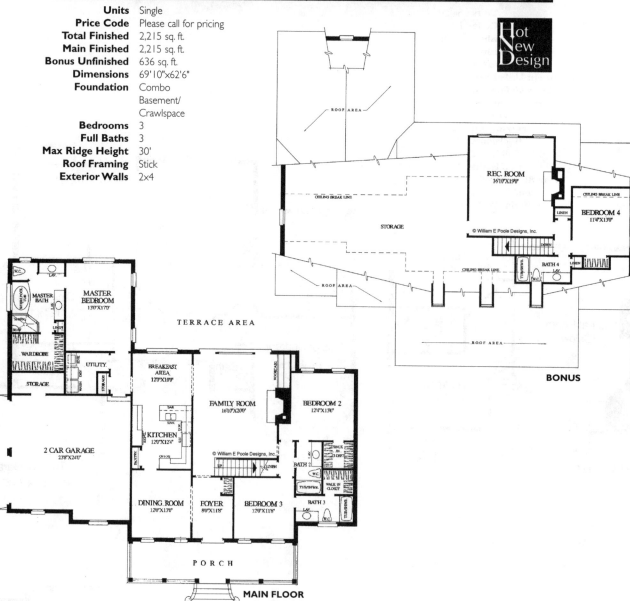

MAIN FLOOR

BONUS

Design 66115

Units	Single
Price Code	E
Total Finished	2,224 sq. ft.
Main Finished	2,224 sq. ft.
Garage Unfinished	621 sq. ft.
Dimensions	53'x71'4"
Foundation	Slab
Bedrooms	3
Full Baths	2
Half Baths	1
Main Ceiling	8'-10'
Max Ridge Height	27'
Roof Framing	Stick
Exterior Walls	2x4

Hot New Design

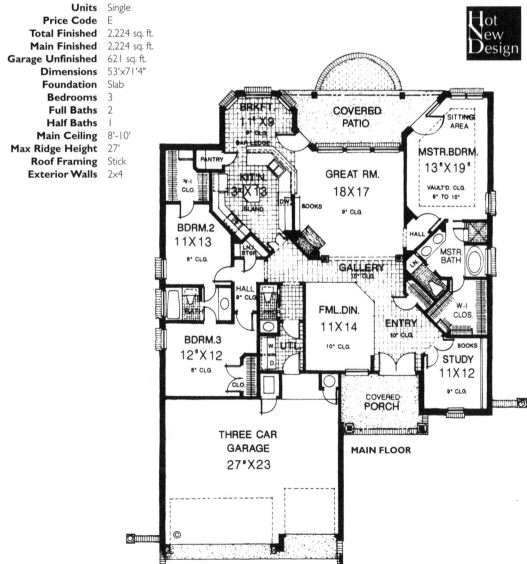

Design 32534

PHOTOGRAPHY: COURTESY OF THE DESIGNER

Units	Single
Price Code	D
Total Finished	2,245 sq. ft.
First Finished	1,103 sq. ft.
Second Finished	697 sq. ft.
Lower Finished	445 sq. ft.
Dimensions	40'3"x38'
Foundation	Basement
Bedrooms	3
Full Baths	3
Max Ridge Height	34'
Roof Framing	Stick
Exterior Walls	2x6

Hot New Design

Please note: The photographed home may have been modified to suit homeowner preferences. If you order plans, have a builder or design professional check them against the photograph to confirm actual construction details.

SECOND FLOOR

- CLOSET
- BATHE
- STUDY 5x7
- DN
- MASTER BEDROOM 14x13
- LOFT 17x9
- DECK
- OPEN TO LIVING

LOWER FLOOR

- STUDY 10x13
- FAMILY 15x11
- UP
- LAUN/MECH 15x10 — W / D
- GARAGE 19x20

FIRST FLOOR

- BEDROOM 10x11
- BEDROOM 12x11
- DN
- DESK
- KIT 11x11 — R
- BREAKFAST NOOK 10x10
- UP
- DINING/ LIVING 11x20
- PORCH
- ENTRY

To order blueprints, call **800-235-5700** or visit us on the web, **familyhomeplans.com**

Design 65143

Units	Single
Price Code	E
Total Finished	2,252 sq. ft.
First Finished	1,358 sq. ft.
Second Finished	894 sq. ft.
Bonus Unfinished	312 sq. ft.
Basement Unfinished	525 sq. ft.
Deck Unfinished	211 sq. ft.
Porch Unfinished	219 sq. ft.
Dimensions	58'x58'
Foundation	Basement
Bedrooms	4
Full Baths	1
3/4 Baths	2
Half Baths	1
First Ceiling	9'
Second Ceiling	8'
Max Ridge Height	29'8"
Roof Framing	Truss
Exterior Walls	2x6

FIRST FLOOR

SECOND FLOOR

Units	Single
Price Code	F
Total Finished	2,255 sq. ft.
Main Finished	2,255 sq. ft.
Bonus Unfinished	324 sq. ft.
Garage Unfinished	610 sq. ft.
Dimensions	55'x70'
Foundation	Slab
Bedrooms	4
Full Baths	2
3/4 Baths	1
Main Ceiling	9'-10'
Max Ridge Height	31'
Roof Framing	Stick
Exterior Walls	2x4

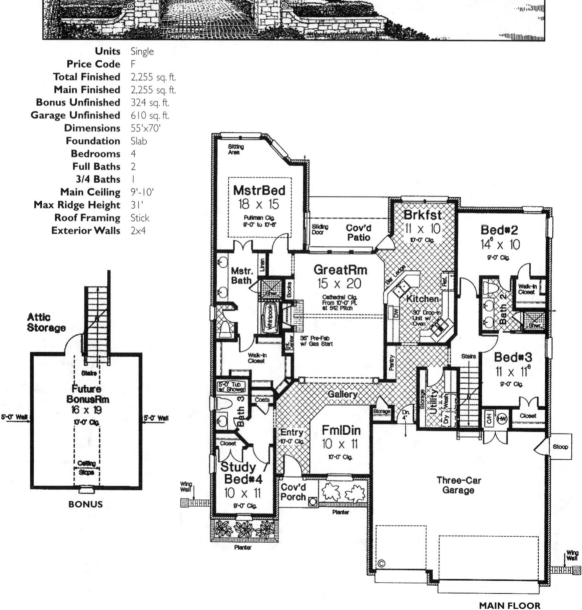

BONUS

MAIN FLOOR

Design 57018

© William E Poole Designs, Inc.

Units	Single
Price Code	Please call for pricing
Total Finished	2,268 sq. ft.
First Finished	1,601 sq. ft.
Second Finished	667 sq. ft.
Bonus Unfinished	378 sq. ft.
Dimensions	83'4"x39'8"
Foundation	Basement
Bedrooms	3
Full Baths	2
Half Baths	1
Max Ridge Height	29'
Roof Framing	Stick
Exterior Walls	2x4

Hot New Design

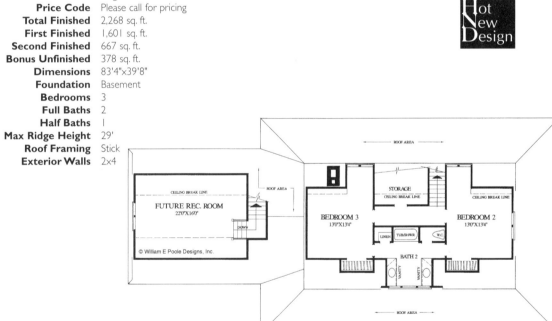

SECOND FLOOR

FIRST FLOOR

Design 10690

PHOTOGRAPHY: JOHN EHRENCLOU

Units	Single
Price Code	E
Total Finished	2,281 sq. ft.
First Finished	1,260 sq. ft.
Second Finished	1,021 sq. ft.
Basement Unfinished	1,186 sq. ft.
Garage Unfinished	851 sq. ft.
Dimensions	76'4"x45'10"
Foundation	Basement
	Crawlspace
	Slab
Bedrooms	3
Full Baths	2
Half Baths	1
First Ceiling	9'
Second Ceiling	8'
Vaulted Ceiling	10'
Max Ridge Height	29'6"
Roof Framing	Stick
Exterior Walls	2x4, 2x6

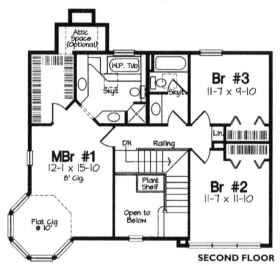

SECOND FLOOR

Please note: The photographed home may have been modified to suit homeowner preferences. If you order plans, have a builder or design professional check them against the photograph to confirm actual construction details.

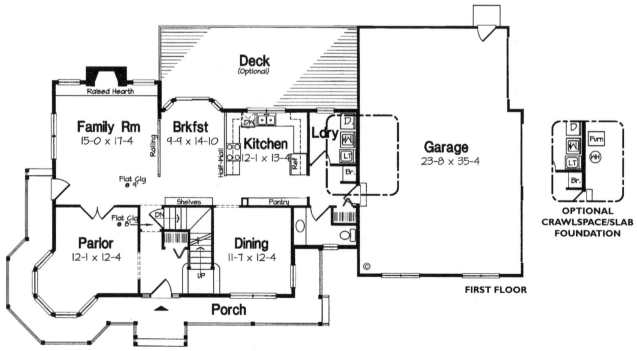

FIRST FLOOR

OPTIONAL CRAWLSPACE/SLAB FOUNDATION

Design 57009

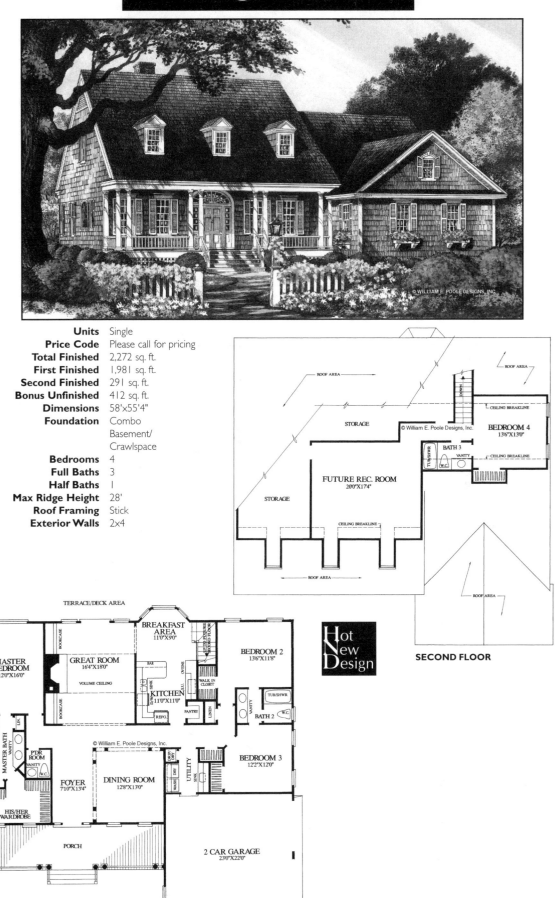

Units	Single
Price Code	Please call for pricing
Total Finished	2,272 sq. ft.
First Finished	1,981 sq. ft.
Second Finished	291 sq. ft.
Bonus Unfinished	412 sq. ft.
Dimensions	58'x55'4"
Foundation	Combo Basement/ Crawlspace
Bedrooms	4
Full Baths	3
Half Baths	1
Max Ridge Height	28'
Roof Framing	Stick
Exterior Walls	2x4

© WILLIAM E. POOLE DESIGNS, INC.

ROOF AREA

ROOF AREA

STORAGE

CEILING BREAKLINE

BEDROOM 4
13'6"X13'0"

© William E. Poole Designs, Inc.

BATH 3

TUB/SHWR   W.C.   VANITY

CEILING BREAKLINE

FUTURE REC. ROOM
20'0"X17'4"

STORAGE

CEILING BREAKLINE

ROOF AREA

ROOF AREA

SECOND FLOOR

TERRACE/DECK AREA

BREAKFAST AREA
11'0"X9'0"

UP TO FIXTURE SECOND FLOOR

Hot New Design

MASTER BEDROOM
12'0"X16'0"

GREAT ROOM
16'4"X18'0"

VOLUME CEILING

BAR

SINK

OVENS

BEDROOM 2
13'6"X11'8"

WALK IN CLOSET

BOOKCASE

BOOKCASE

KITCHEN
11'0"X11'0"

D.W.   SINK

PANTRY

LINEN

VANITY

TUB/SHWR

BATH 2

W.C.

SEAT
SHOWER

WHIRLPOOL TUB

VANITY

LIN.

© William E. Poole Designs, Inc.

P'DR ROOM

VANITY   W.C.

FOYER
7'10"X13'4"

DINING ROOM
12'8"X13'0"

DRIP DRY

UTILITY

SINK

WASH   DRY

BEDROOM 3
12'2"X12'0"

W.C.

HIS/HER WARDROBE

PORCH

2 CAR GARAGE
23'0"X22'0"

FIRST FLOOR

Design 65145

Units	Single
Price Code	E
Total Finished	2,292 sq. ft.
First Finished	1,246 sq. ft.
Second Finished	1,046 sq. ft.
Basement Unfinished	1,246 sq. ft.
Garage Unfinished	392 sq. ft.
Porch Unfinished	323 sq. ft.
Dimensions	58'x42'2"
Foundation	Basement
Bedrooms	3
Full Baths	1
3/4 Baths	1
Half Baths	1
First Ceiling	9'
Second Ceiling	8'
Max Ridge Height	33'1"
Roof Framing	Truss
Exterior Walls	2x6

SECOND FLOOR

FIRST FLOOR

Design 90474

Units	Single
Price Code	E
Total Finished	2,297 sq. ft.
First Finished	1,580 sq. ft.
Second Finished	717 sq. ft.
Bonus Unfinished	410 sq. ft.
Basement Unfinished	1,342 sq. ft.
Garage Unfinished	484 sq. ft.
Deck Unfinished	288 sq. ft.
Porch Unfinished	144 sq. ft.
Dimensions	72'x40'
Foundation	Basement Crawlspace
Bedrooms	3
Full Baths	2
Half Baths	1
First Ceiling	8'
Second Ceiling	8'
Vaulted Ceiling	11'4"
Max Ridge Height	25'6"
Roof Framing	Stick
Exterior Walls	2x4

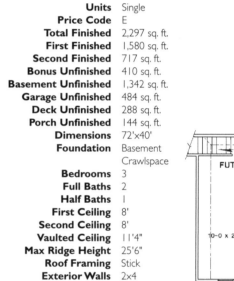

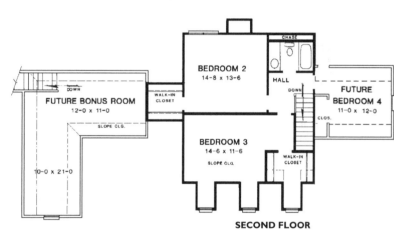

SECOND FLOOR

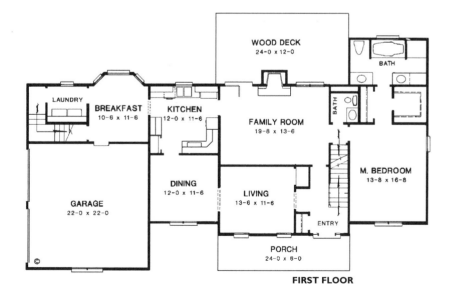

FIRST FLOOR

Design 65004

Units	Single
Price Code	E
Total Finished	2,300 sq. ft.
First Finished	1,067 sq. ft.
Second Finished	1,233 sq. ft.
Basement Unfinished	1,067 sq. ft.
Dimensions	58'x33'
Foundation	Basement
Bedrooms	3
Full Baths	2
Half Baths	1
First Ceiling	9'2"
Second Ceiling	8'2"
Max Ridge Height	24'6"
Roof Framing	Truss
Exterior Walls	2x6

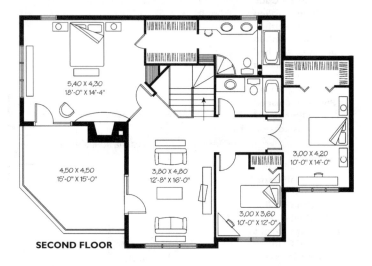

SECOND FLOOR

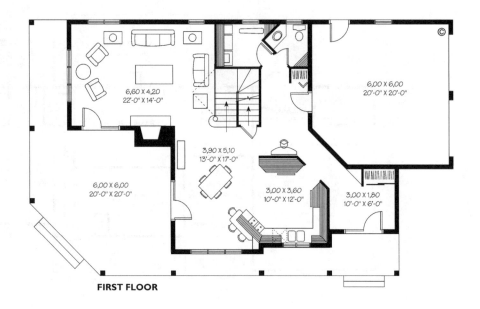

FIRST FLOOR

Design 57014

© WILLIAM E. POOLE DESIGNS, INC.

Hot New Design

Units	Single
Price Code	Please call for pricing
Total Finished	2,309 sq. ft.
First Finished	1,554 sq. ft.
Second Finished	755 sq. ft.
Basement Unfinished	869 sq. ft.
Dimensions	58'x39'6"
Foundation	Basement
Bedrooms	3
Full Baths	2
Half Baths	1
Max Ridge Height	35'
Roof Framing	Stick
Exterior Walls	2x4

© William E. Poole Designs, Inc.

ROOF AREA

STORAGE

STORAGE

W.C.

TUB/SHWR

DOWN

LINEN

BEDROOM 2
15'0"X14'0"

BATH 2

BEDROOM 3
13'0"X14'0"

CEILING BREAK LINE

ROOF AREA

SECOND FLOOR

DECK

© William E. Poole Designs, Inc.

BREAKFAST AREA
12'0"X10'0"

GREAT ROOM
20'6"X18'0"

WHIRLPOOL TUB

SEAT

SHOWER

WARDROBE

MASTER BATH

BAR

OVENS

DESK

P'DR ROOM

W.C.

LINEN CABINET

W.C.

KITCHEN
11'0"X13'6"

SINK

STU.

D.W.

REFRG.

PANTRY

ENTERTAINMENT CENTER

DRIP DRY

FOLD DN LB.

SINK

DRY

WASH

DINING ROOM
12'6"X12'6"

FOYER

DOWN

UP

MASTER BEDROOM
13'0"X16'8"

P O R C H

FIRST FLOOR

Design 98578

Units	Single
Price Code	E
Total Finished	2,314 sq. ft.
First Finished	1,595 sq. ft.
Second Finished	719 sq. ft.
Garage Unfinished	440 sq. ft.
Deck Unfinished	96 sq. ft.
Porch Unfinished	32 sq. ft.
Dimensions	52'4"x63'4"
Foundation	Slab
Bedrooms	4
Full Baths	2
3/4 Baths	1
Half Baths	1
Max Ridge Height	27'
Roof Framing	Stick
Exterior Walls	2x4

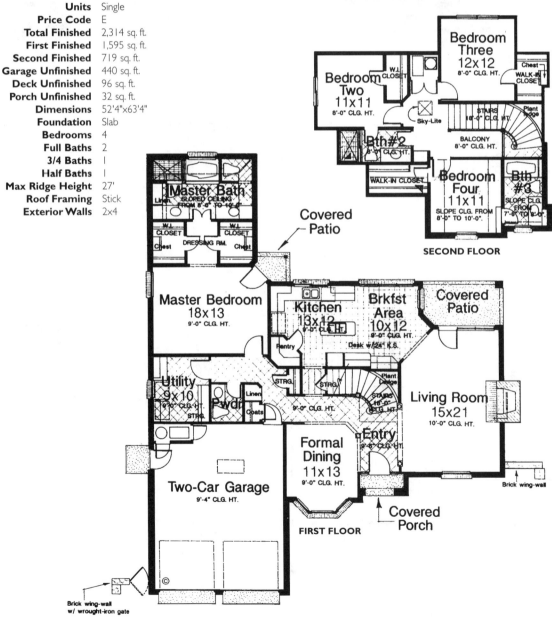

Design 64163

Price Code	H
Total Finished	2,329 sq. ft.
Main Finished	2,329 sq. ft.
Garage Unfinished	528 sq. ft.
Porch Unfinished	215 sq. ft.
Dimensions	72'6"x73'4"
Foundation	Crawlspace
Bedrooms	3
Full Baths	2
Half Baths	1
Max Ridge Height	25'6"
Exterior Walls	2x6

* Alternate foundation options available at an additional charge.
Please call 1-800-235-5700 for more information.

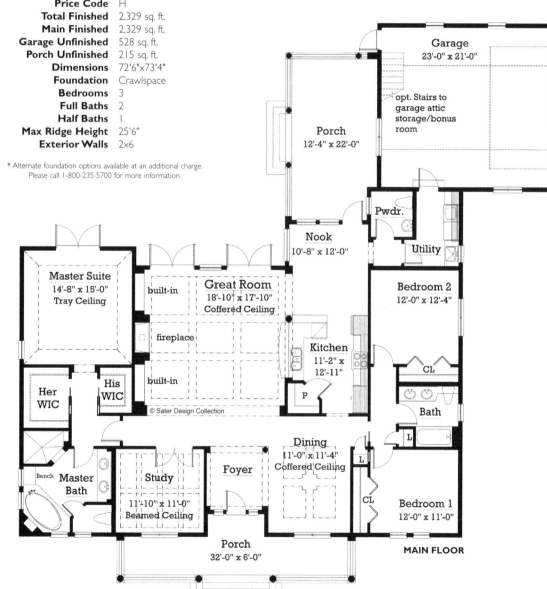

Units	Single
Price Code	E
Total Finished	2,331 sq. ft.
Main Finished	2,331 sq. ft.
Garage Unfinished	806 sq. ft.
Deck Unfinished	132 sq. ft.
Dimensions	74'11"x68'9½"
Foundation	Slab
Bedrooms	3
Full Baths	2
Half Baths	1
Main Ceiling	9'
Max Ridge Height	24'6½"
Roof Framing	Stick
Exterior Walls	2×4

* Alternate foundation options available at an additional charge.
  Please call 1-800-235-5700 for more information.

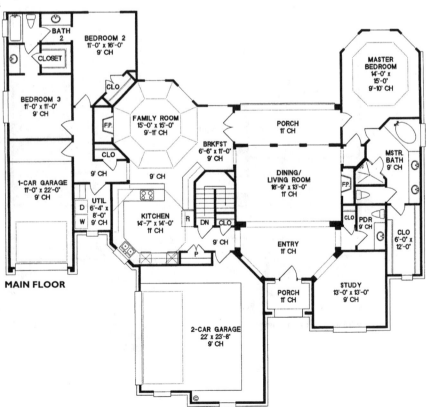

MAIN FLOOR

Design 97857

Units	Single
Price Code	E
Total Finished	2,332 sq. ft.
Main Finished	2,332 sq. ft.
Garage Unfinished	620 sq. ft.
Deck Unfinished	80 sq. ft.
Porch Unfinished	48 sq. ft.
Dimensions	82'3"x86'6"
Foundation	Slab
Bedrooms	3
Full Baths	2
Half Baths	1
Main Ceiling	9'-10'
Max Ridge Height	29'
Roof Framing	Stick
Exterior Walls	2x4

Design 64128

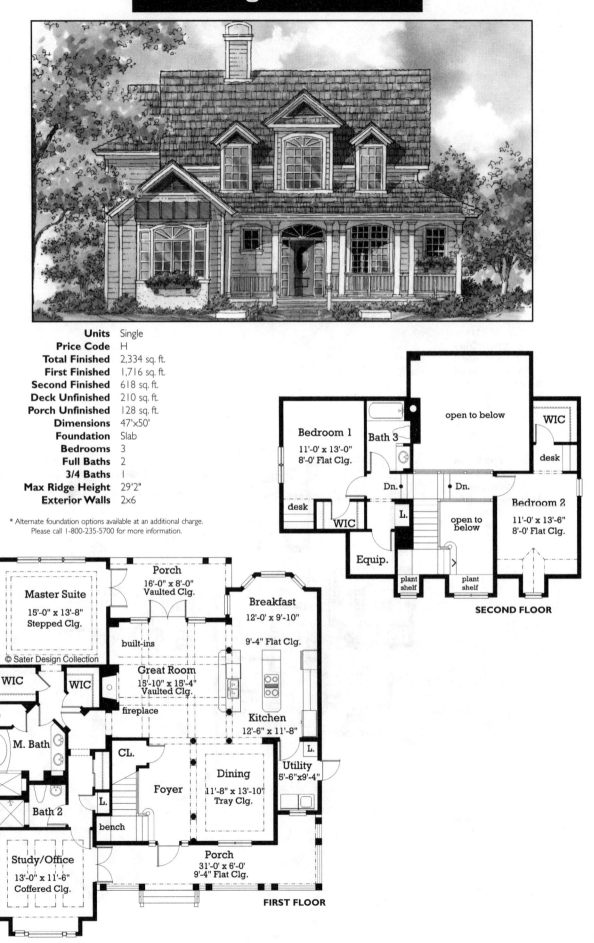

Units	Single
Price Code	H
Total Finished	2,334 sq. ft.
First Finished	1,716 sq. ft.
Second Finished	618 sq. ft.
Deck Unfinished	210 sq. ft.
Porch Unfinished	128 sq. ft.
Dimensions	47'x50'
Foundation	Slab
Bedrooms	3
Full Baths	2
3/4 Baths	1
Max Ridge Height	29'2"
Exterior Walls	2x6

* Alternate foundation options available at an additional charge.
Please call 1-800-235-5700 for more information.

SECOND FLOOR

Bedroom 1
11'-0" x 13'-0"
8'-0" Flat Clg.

Bath 3

open to below

WIC

desk

desk

Dn.

Dn.

L.

open to below

Bedroom 2
11'-0" x 13'-6"
8'-0" Flat Clg.

WIC

Equip.

plant shelf

plant shelf

FIRST FLOOR

© Sater Design Collection

Master Suite
15'-0" x 13'-8"
Stepped Clg.

Porch
16'-0" x 8'-0"
Vaulted Clg.

Breakfast
12'-0" x 9'-10"
9'-4" Flat Clg.

built-ins

WIC

WIC

Great Room
15'-10" x 15'-4"
Vaulted Clg.

fireplace

Kitchen
12'-6" x 11'-8"

M. Bath

CL.

Dining
11'-8" x 13'-10"
Tray Clg.

Utility
5'-6"x9'-4"

L.

L.

Foyer

Bath 2

bench

Study/Office
13'-0" x 11'-6"
Coffered Clg.

Porch
31'-0" x 6'-0"
9'-4" Flat Clg.

Design 62069

Units	Single
Price Code	E
Total Finished	2,338 sq. ft.
Main Finished	2,338 sq. ft.
Bonus Unfinished	553 sq. ft.
Garage Unfinished	510 sq. ft.
Porch Unfinished	628 sq. ft.
Dimensions	61'x71'8"
Foundation	Crawlspace
	Slab
Bedrooms	4
Full Baths	2
Main Ceiling	9'
Second Ceiling	8'
Max Ridge Height	24'8"
Roof Framing	Stick
Exterior Walls	2x4

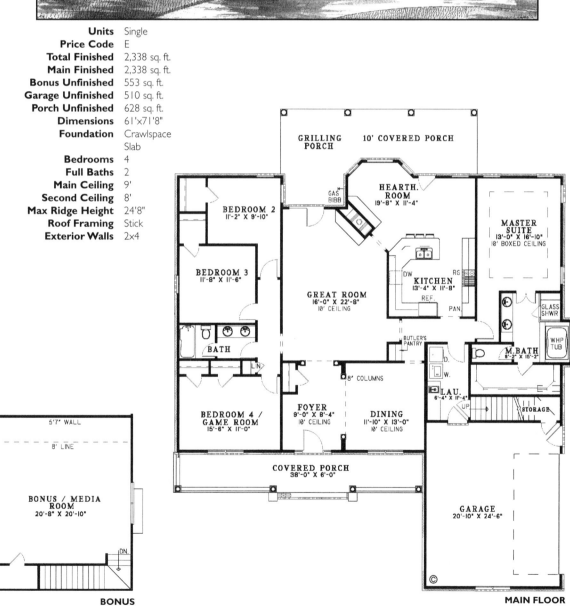

BONUS

MAIN FLOOR

Design 81003

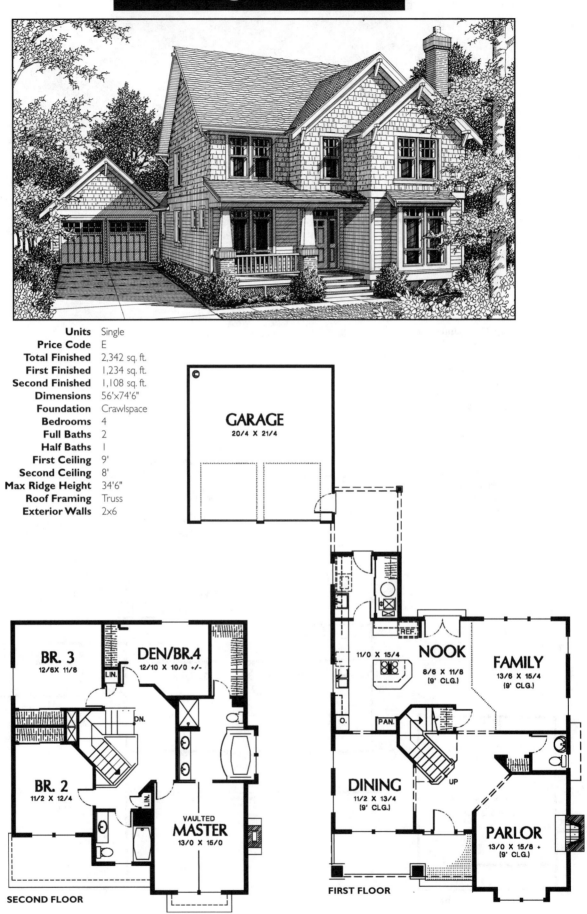

Units	Single
Price Code	E
Total Finished	2,342 sq. ft.
First Finished	1,234 sq. ft.
Second Finished	1,108 sq. ft.
Dimensions	56'x74'6"
Foundation	Crawlspace
Bedrooms	4
Full Baths	2
Half Baths	1
First Ceiling	9'
Second Ceiling	8'
Max Ridge Height	34'6"
Roof Framing	Truss
Exterior Walls	2x6

GARAGE
20/4 X 21/4

BR. 3
12/6X 11/8

DEN/BR.4
12/10 X 10/0 +/-

BR. 2
11/2 X 12/4

VAULTED
MASTER
13/0 X 15/0

SECOND FLOOR

NOOK
8/6 X 11/8
(9' CLG.)

FAMILY
13/6 X 15/4
(9' CLG.)

11/0 X 15/4

REF.

PAN.

UP

DINING
11/2 X 13/4
(9' CLG.)

PARLOR
13/0 X 15/8 +
(9' CLG.)

FIRST FLOOR

To order blueprints, call **800-235-5700** or visit us on the web, **familyhomeplans.com**

Design 20228

2,001-2,500 sq. ft. HOME PLANS

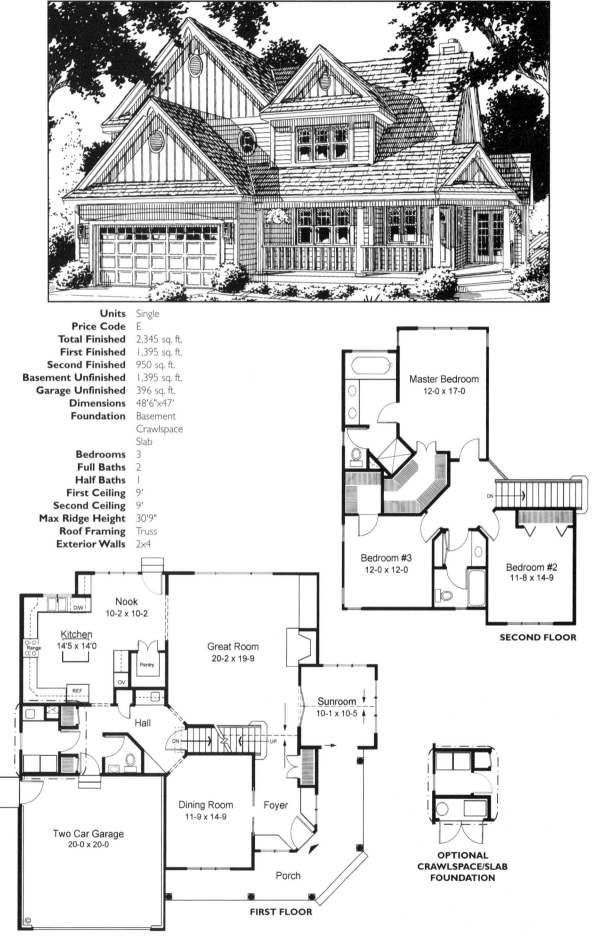

Units	Single
Price Code	E
Total Finished	2,345 sq. ft.
First Finished	1,395 sq. ft.
Second Finished	950 sq. ft.
Basement Unfinished	1,395 sq. ft.
Garage Unfinished	396 sq. ft.
Dimensions	48'6"x47'
Foundation	Basement
	Crawlspace
	Slab
Bedrooms	3
Full Baths	2
Half Baths	I
First Ceiling	9'
Second Ceiling	9'
Max Ridge Height	30'9"
Roof Framing	Truss
Exterior Walls	2x4

Master Bedroom
12-0 x 17-0

Bedroom #3
12-0 x 12-0

Bedroom #2
11-8 x 14-9

SECOND FLOOR

Nook
10-2 x 10-2

Kitchen
14'5 x 14'0

Pantry

Great Room
20-2 x 19-9

Hall

Sunroom
10-1 x 10-5

Dining Room
11-9 x 14-9

Foyer

Two Car Garage
20-0 x 20-0

Porch

FIRST FLOOR

OPTIONAL CRAWLSPACE/SLAB FOUNDATION

Units	Single
Price Code	E
Total Finished	2,350 sq. ft.
Main Finished	2,650 sq. ft.
Garage Unfinished	660 sq. ft.
Deck Unfinished	240 sq. ft.
Dimensions	60'×77'3"
Foundation	Slab
Bedrooms	4
Full Baths	3
Main Ceiling	9'-11'
Max Ridge Height	32'
Roof Framing	Stick
Exterior Walls	2x4

Hot New Design

MAIN FLOOR

Design 10619

Units	Single
Price Code	E
Total Finished	2,352 sq. ft.
Main Finished	2,352 sq. ft.
Basement Unfinished	2,352 sq. ft.
Garage Unfinished	696 sq. ft.
Dimensions	93'6"x48'
Foundation	Basement
Bedrooms	3
Full Baths	2
3/4 Baths	1
Max Ridge Height	20'
Roof Framing	Stick
Exterior Walls	2x6

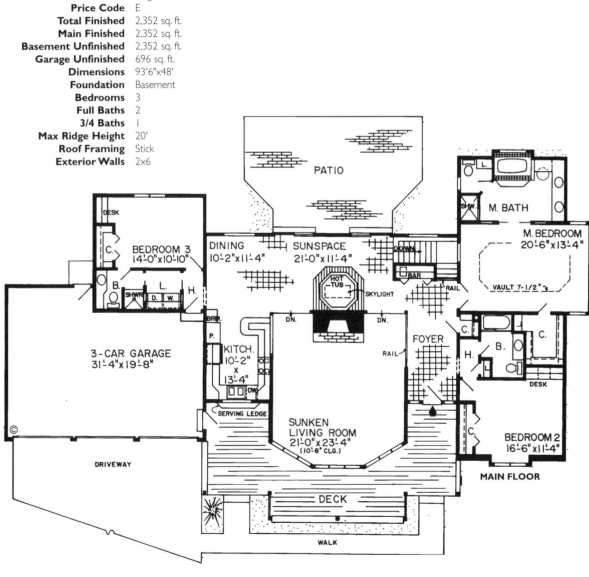

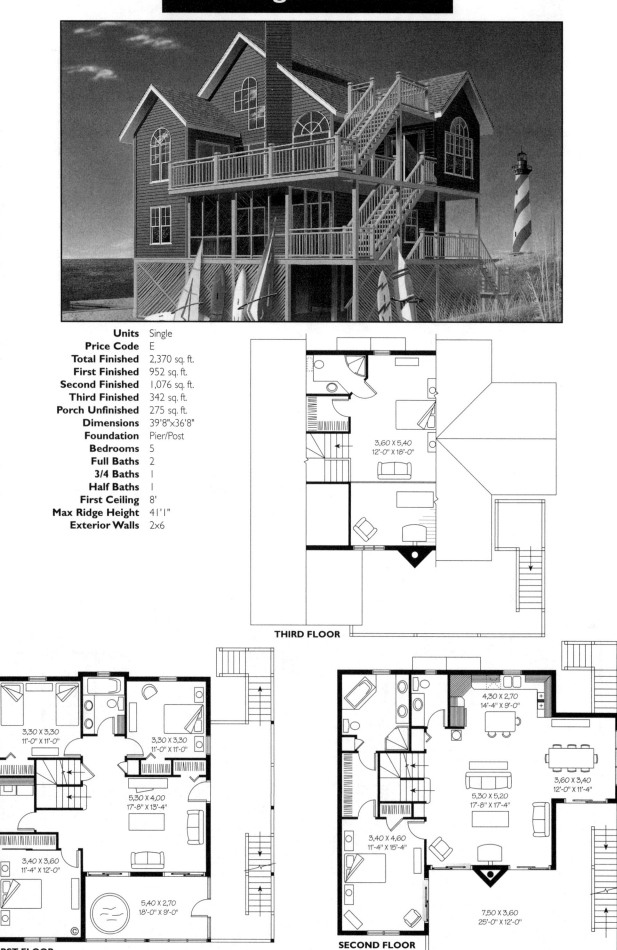

Units	Single
Price Code	E
Total Finished	2,370 sq. ft.
First Finished	952 sq. ft.
Second Finished	1,076 sq. ft.
Third Finished	342 sq. ft.
Porch Unfinished	275 sq. ft.
Dimensions	39'8"x36'8"
Foundation	Pier/Post
Bedrooms	5
Full Baths	2
3/4 Baths	1
Half Baths	1
First Ceiling	8'
Max Ridge Height	41'1"
Exterior Walls	2x6

THIRD FLOOR

3,60 X 5,40
12'-0" X 18'-0"

FIRST FLOOR

3,30 X 3,30
11'-0" X 11'-0"

3,30 X 3,30
11'-0" X 11'-0"

5,30 X 4,00
17'-8" X 13'-4"

3,40 X 3,60
11'-4" X 12'-0"

5,40 X 2,70
18'-0" X 9'-0"

SECOND FLOOR

4,30 X 2,70
14'-4" X 9'-0"

3,60 X 3,40
12'-0" X 11'-4"

5,30 X 5,20
17'-8" X 17'-4"

3,40 X 4,60
11'-4" X 15'-4"

7,50 X 3,60
25'-0" X 12'-0"

Design 94289

Units	Single
Price Code	H
Total Finished	2,374 sq. ft.
First Finished	1,510 sq. ft.
Second Finished	864 sq. ft.
Bonus Unfinished	1,290 sq. ft.
Deck Unfinished	275 sq. ft.
Porch Unfinished	275 sq. ft.
Dimensions	44'x49'
Foundation	Basement
Bedrooms	3
Full Baths	3
Half Baths	1
Max Ridge Height	43'4"
Roof Framing	Truss
Exterior Walls	2x6

* Alternate foundation options available at an additional charge.
Please call 1-800-235-5700 for more information.

SECOND FLOOR

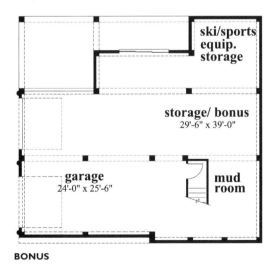

BONUS

FIRST FLOOR

Design 57022

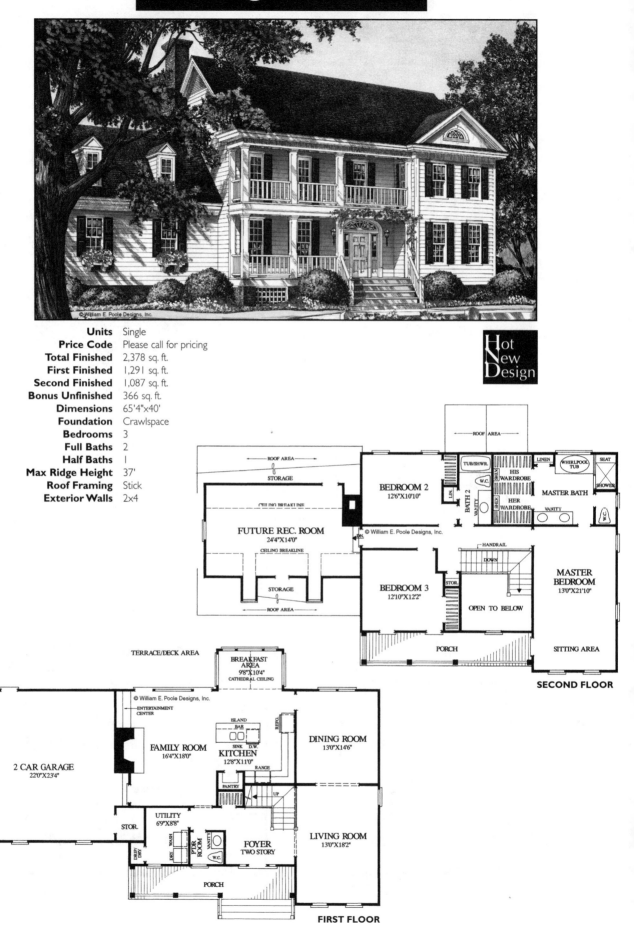

Units Single
Price Code Please call for pricing
Total Finished 2,378 sq. ft.
First Finished 1,291 sq. ft.
Second Finished 1,087 sq. ft.
Bonus Unfinished 366 sq. ft.
Dimensions 65'4"x40'
Foundation Crawlspace
Bedrooms 3
Full Baths 2
Half Baths 1
Max Ridge Height 37'
Roof Framing Stick
Exterior Walls 2x4

Hot New Design

© William E. Poole Designs, Inc.

ROOF AREA

ROOF AREA
STORAGE

CEILING BREAKLINE

FUTURE REC. ROOM
24'4"X14'0"

CEILING BREAKLINE

STORAGE

ROOF AREA

BEDROOM 2
12'6"X10'10"

LIN.
BATH 2
VANITY

TUB/SHWR.
W.C.

SHLV.
HIS WARDROBE
HER WARDROBE
SHLV.

LINEN
MASTER BATH
VANITY

WHIRLPOOL TUB
SEAT
SHOWER
W.C.

© William E. Poole Designs, Inc.

BEDROOM 3
12'10"X12'2"

STOR.

HANDRAIL
DOWN

OPEN TO BELOW

MASTER BEDROOM
13'0"X21'10"

PORCH

SITTING AREA

SECOND FLOOR

TERRACE/DECK AREA

BREAKFAST AREA
9'8"X10'4"
CATHEDRAL CEILING

ENTERTAINMENT CENTER

© William E. Poole Designs, Inc.

2 CAR GARAGE
22'0"X23'4"

FAMILY ROOM
16'4"X18'0"

ISLAND
BAR
SINK D.W.
KITCHEN
12'8"X11'0"
RANGE
PANTRY

REF.

DINING ROOM
13'0"X14'6"

UP

LIVING ROOM
13'0"X18'2"

UTILITY
6'9"X8'8"

STOR.

REF/DRY
WASH
DRY

PDR ROOM
W.C.
VANITY

FOYER
TWO STORY

PORCH

FIRST FLOOR

Design 57004

Units	Single
Price Code	Please call for pricing
Total Finished	2,380 sq. ft.
First Finished	1,712 sq. ft.
Second Finished	668 sq. ft.
Bonus Unfinished	573 sq. ft.
Dimensions	86'×50'2"
Foundation	Combo Basement/ Crawlspace
Bedrooms	3
Full Baths	2
Half Baths	1
First Ceiling	9'
Max Ridge Height	28'
Roof Framing	Stick
Exterior Walls	2x4

Hot New Design

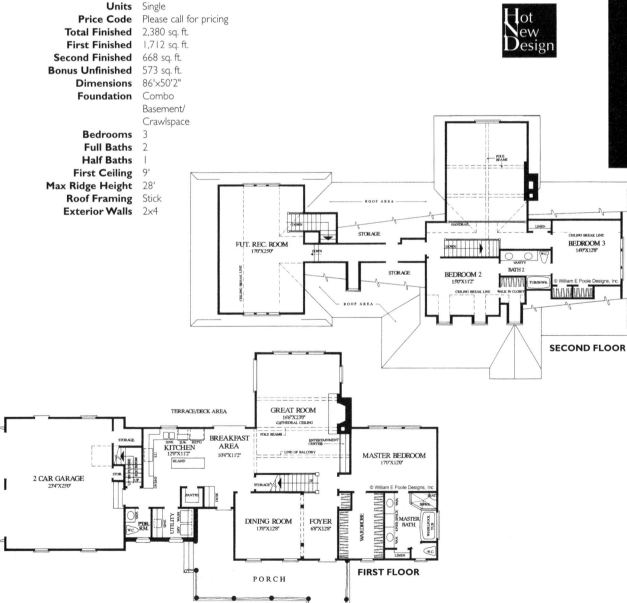

SECOND FLOOR

FIRST FLOOR

Design 57024

Units	Single
Price Code	Please call for pricing
Total Finished	2,410 sq. ft.
First Finished	1,627 sq. ft.
Second Finished	783 sq. ft.
Bonus Unfinished	418 sq. ft.
Dimensions	46'x58'
Foundation	Crawlspace
Bedrooms	4
Full Baths	2
Half Baths	1
First Ceiling	9'
Second Ceiling	8'
Max Ridge Height	30'
Roof Framing	Stick
Exterior Walls	2x4

Hot New Design

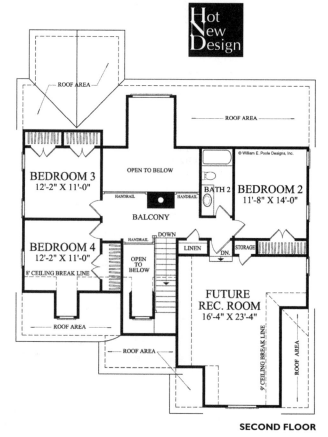

SECOND FLOOR

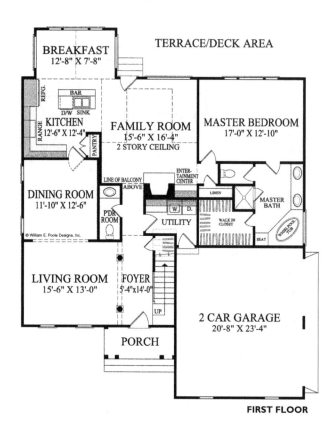

FIRST FLOOR

Design 57007

© William E Poole Designs, Inc.

Units	Single
Price Code	Please call for pricing
Total Finished	2,419 sq. ft.
First Finished	1,776 sq. ft.
Second Finished	643 sq. ft.
Bonus Unfinished	367 sq. ft.
Dimensions	61'8"x74'4"
Foundation	Combo Basement/ Crawlspace
Bedrooms	4
Full Baths	3
Max Ridge Height	29'
Roof Framing	Stick
Exterior Walls	2x4

Hot New Design

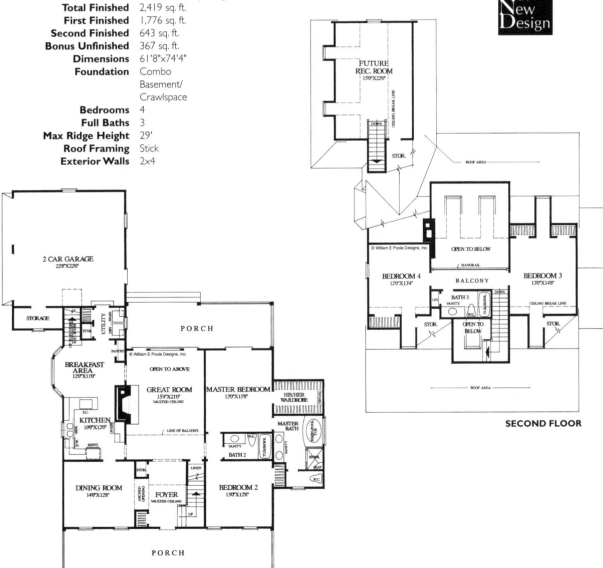

SECOND FLOOR

FIRST FLOOR

Design 20095

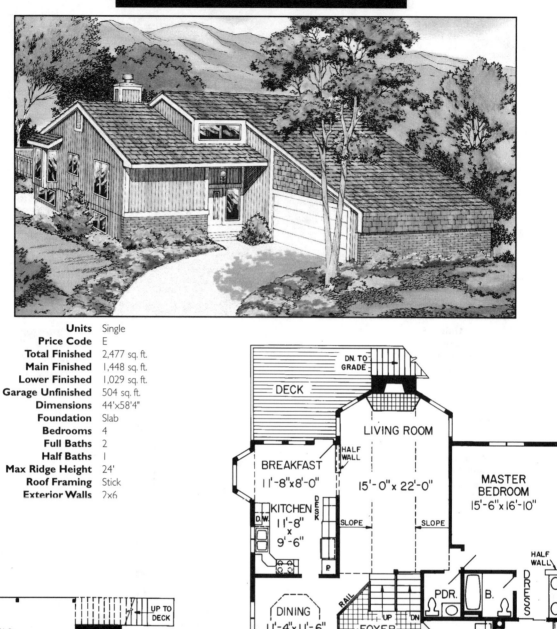

Units	Single
Price Code	E
Total Finished	2,477 sq. ft.
Main Finished	1,448 sq. ft.
Lower Finished	1,029 sq. ft.
Garage Unfinished	504 sq. ft.
Dimensions	44'x58'4"
Foundation	Slab
Bedrooms	4
Full Baths	2
Half Baths	1
Max Ridge Height	24'
Roof Framing	Stick
Exterior Walls	2x6

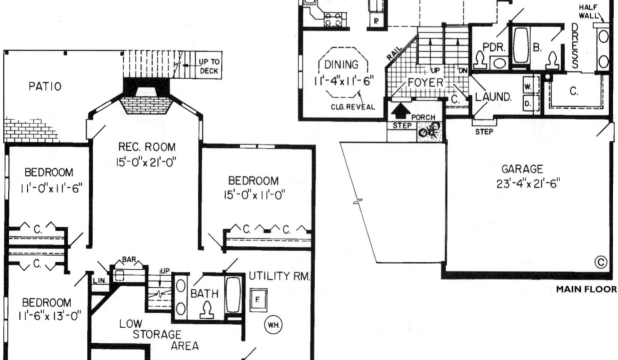

DECK

LIVING ROOM 15'-0" x 22'-0"

BREAKFAST 11'-8"x8'-0"

HALF WALL

MASTER BEDROOM 15'-6"x16'-10"

KITCHEN 11'-8" x 9'-6"

D.W. DESK SLOPE SLOPE P

HALF WALL

DINING 11'-4"x11'-6"

CLG. REVEAL

RAIL

PDR. B. DRESS

FOYER UP DN

W. D. C.

LAUND.

STEP PORCH

STEP

GARAGE 23'-4" x 21'-6"

©

MAIN FLOOR

PATIO

UP TO DECK

REC. ROOM 15'-0"x 21'-0"

BEDROOM 11'-0"x 11'-6"

C.

C.

BEDROOM 15'-0"x 11'-0"

C. C.

BAR

LIN. UP

BATH

UTILITY RM. F.

BEDROOM 11'-6"x 13'-0"

LOW STORAGE AREA

W.H.

LOWER FLOOR

Design 57011

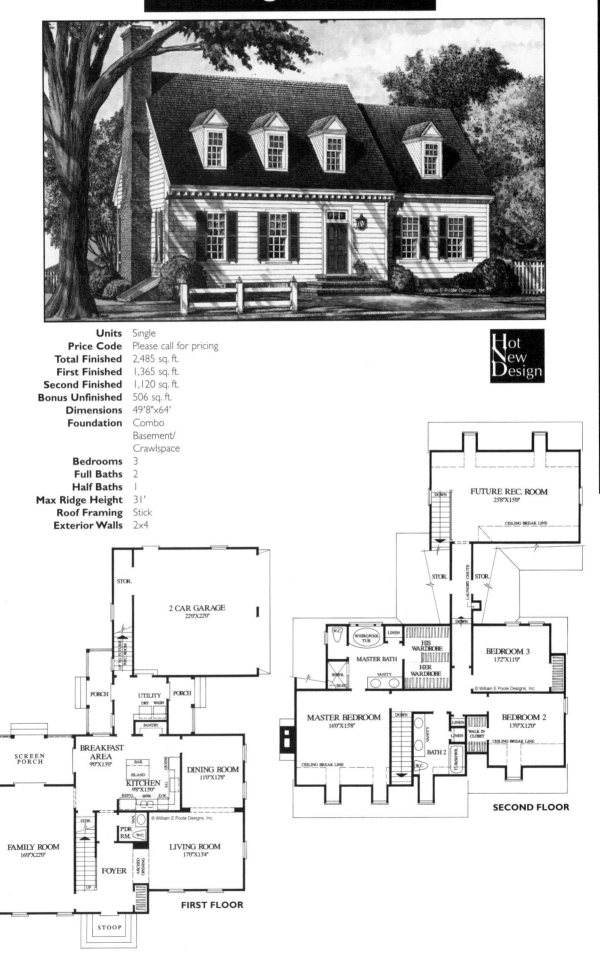

Hot New Design

Units	Single
Price Code	Please call for pricing
Total Finished	2,485 sq. ft.
First Finished	1,365 sq. ft.
Second Finished	1,120 sq. ft.
Bonus Unfinished	506 sq. ft.
Dimensions	49'8"x64'
Foundation	Combo Basement/ Crawlspace
Bedrooms	3
Full Baths	2
Half Baths	1
Max Ridge Height	31'
Roof Framing	Stick
Exterior Walls	2x4

FUTURE REC. ROOM
25'8"X15'0"

2 CAR GARAGE
22'0"X22'0"

MASTER BATH

BEDROOM 3
13'2"X11'0"

MASTER BEDROOM
16'0"X15'8"

BEDROOM 2
13'0"X12'0"

BATH 2

© William E Poole Designs, Inc.

SECOND FLOOR

SCREEN PORCH

BREAKFAST AREA
9'0"X13'0"

DINING ROOM
11'0"X12'8"

KITCHEN
9'8"X13'0"

FAMILY ROOM
16'0"X22'0"

LIVING ROOM
17'0"X13'4"

FOYER

STOOP

© William E Poole Designs, Inc.

FIRST FLOOR

Units	Single
Price Code	E
Total Finished	2,497 sq. ft.
First Finished	1,437 sq. ft.
Second Finished	1,060 sq. ft.
Basement Unfinished	1,437 sq. ft.
Garage Unfinished	438 sq. ft.
Deck Unfinished	256 sq. ft.
Porch Unfinished	96 sq. ft.
Dimensions	48'x60'
Foundation	Basement
Bedrooms	3
Full Baths	2
3/4 Baths	1
Half Baths	1
First Ceiling	9'
Second Ceiling	8'
Max Ridge Height	25'4"
Roof Framing	Truss
Exterior Walls	2x6

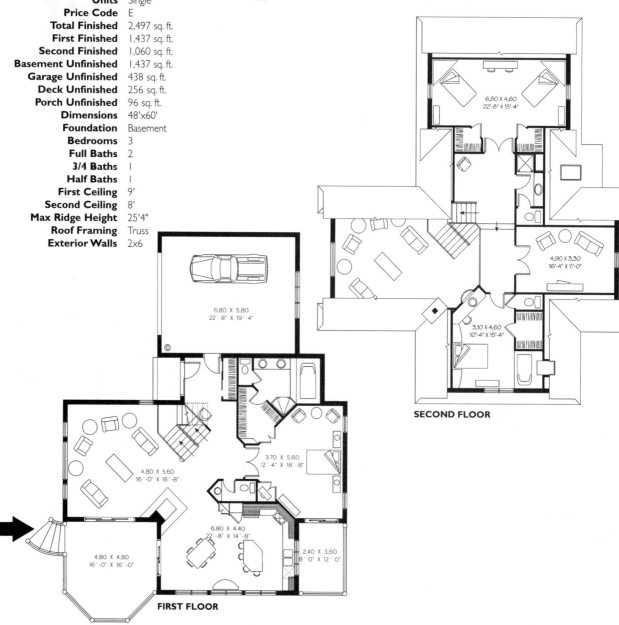

SECOND FLOOR

FIRST FLOOR

Design 64127

Units	Single
Price Code	H
Total Finished	2,502 sq. ft.
Main Finished	2,502 sq. ft.
Basement Unfinished	1,742 sq. ft.
Garage Unfinished	612 sq. ft.
Deck Unfinished	108 sq. ft.
Porch Unfinished	397 sq. ft.
Dimensions	70'x72'
Foundation	Basement
	Slab
Bedrooms	3
Full Baths	2
Max Ridge Height	27'4"
Exterior Walls	2x6
Roof Framing	Stick/Truss

* Alternate foundation options available at an additional charge.
Please call 1-800-235-5700 for more information.

OPTIONAL BASEMENT STAIR LOCATION

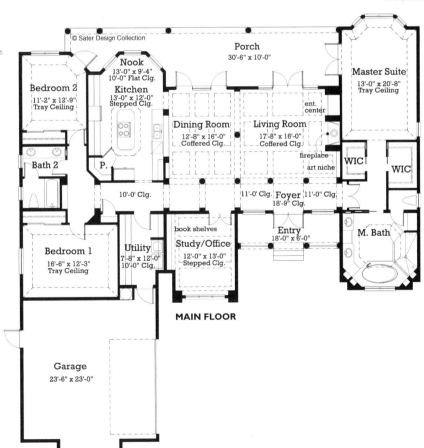

MAIN FLOOR

Design 32382

PHOTOGRAPHY: MICHAEL PARTENIO

Units	Single
Price Code	F
Total Finished	2,512 sq. ft.
First Finished	1,340 sq. ft.
Second Finished	1,172 sq. ft.
Basement Unfinished	733 sq. ft.
Garage Unfinished	607 sq. ft.
Porch Unfinished	520 sq. ft.
Dimensions	56'x42'
Foundation	Basement
Bedrooms	3
Full Baths	2
Half Baths	1
First Ceiling	8'
Second Ceiling	8'
Max Ridge Height	33'10
Roof Framing	Stick
Exterior Walls	2x6

Please note: The photographed home may have been modified to suit homeowner preferences. If you order plans, have a builder or design professional check them against the photograph to confirm actual construction details.

SECOND FLOOR

SECOND FLOOR: MASTER BEDROOM 13x16, OPEN TO GREAT-ROOM, BATH, CLOS, HALL, DN, BEDROOM 14x14, BEDROOM 14x14, OPEN

FIRST FLOOR: SCREEN PORCH 6x23, GREAT-ROOM 14x14, GREAT-ROOM 13x21, DINING 14x10, DEN 14x14, DN, KITCHEN 14x12, ENTRY, UP, W, D, PORCH

FIRST FLOOR

Design 94295

2,501-3,000 sq.ft. HOME PLANS

Units	Single
Price Code	I
Total Finished	2,513 sq. ft.
First Finished	1,542 sq. ft.
Second Finished	971 sq. ft.
Bonus Unfinished	747 sq. ft.
Garage Unfinished	663 sq. ft.
Deck Unfinished	264 sq. ft.
Porch Unfinished	330 sq. ft.
Dimensions	46'x51'
Foundation	Basement
Bedrooms	3
Full Baths	3
Max Ridge Height	39'4"
Roof Framing	Truss
Exterior Walls	2x6

** Alternate foundation options available at an additional charge.
Please call 1-800-235-5700 for more information.*

br. 3
11'-4" x 13'-0"
vaulted clg.

deck

open to below

sitting

overlook

**master
suite**
16'-0" x 14'-0"
vaulted clg.

dn

dn

open

master
bath

w.i.c.

SECOND FLOOR

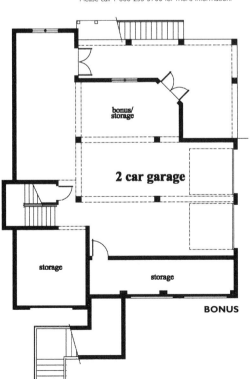

bonus/
storage

2 car garage

storage

storage

BONUS

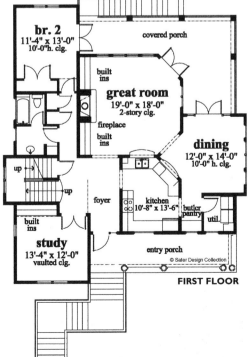

br. 2
11'-4" x 13'-0"
10'-0" h. clg.

covered porch

built
ins

great room
19'-0" x 18'-0"
2-story clg.

fireplace

built
ins

dining
12'-0" x 14'-0"
10'-0" h. clg.

up

up

foyer

kitchen
10'-8" x 13'-6"

butler
pantry

util.

built
ins

study
13'-4" x 12'-0"
vaulted clg.

entry porch

© Sater Design Collection

FIRST FLOOR

Units	Single
Price Code	F
Total Finished	2,520 sq. ft.
First Finished	1,305 sq. ft.
Second Finished	1,215 sq. ft.
Bonus Unfinished	935 sq. ft.
Garage Unfinished	480 sq. ft.
Deck Unfinished	717 sq. ft.
Porch Unfinished	1,434 sq. ft.
Dimensions	30'6"x72'2"
Foundation	Slab
	Pier/Post
Bedrooms	3
Full Baths	2
Half Baths	1
Max Ridge Height	39'6"
Roof Framing	Stick/Truss
Exterior Walls	2x6

* Alternate foundation options available at an additional charge.
Please call 1-800-235-5700 for more information.

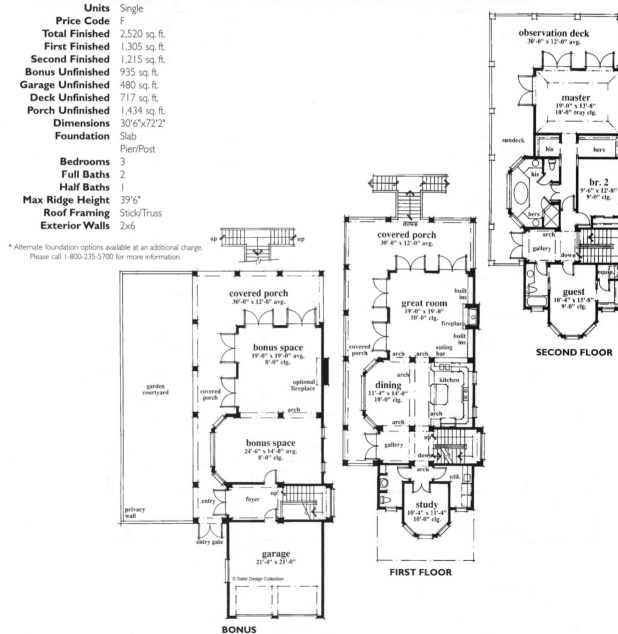

SECOND FLOOR

FIRST FLOOR

BONUS

© Sater Design Collection

Design 32188

Units	Single
Price Code	F
Total Finished	2,530 sq. ft.
First Finished	1,352 sq. ft.
Second Finished	1,178 sq. ft.
Basement Unfinished	1,352 sq. ft.
Garage Unfinished	480 sq. ft.
Dimensions	56'x72'4"
Foundation	Basement
Bedrooms	4
Full Baths	3
First Ceiling	8'9
Second Ceiling	8'
Max Ridge Height	32'
Roof Framing	Stick
Exterior Walls	2x6

Hot New Design

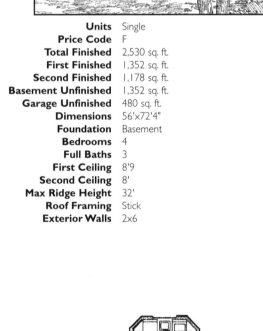

SECOND FLOOR

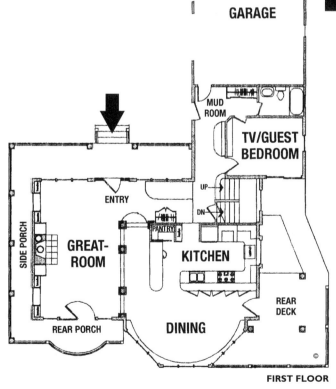

FIRST FLOOR

Design 97803

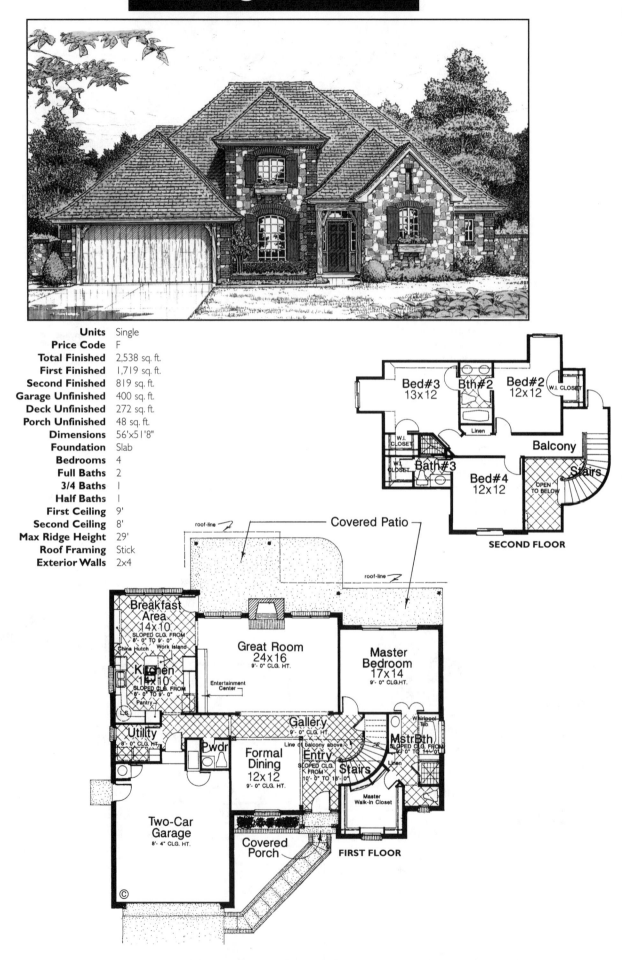

Units	Single
Price Code	F
Total Finished	2,538 sq. ft.
First Finished	1,719 sq. ft.
Second Finished	819 sq. ft.
Garage Unfinished	400 sq. ft.
Deck Unfinished	272 sq. ft.
Porch Unfinished	48 sq. ft.
Dimensions	56'x51'8"
Foundation	Slab
Bedrooms	4
Full Baths	2
3/4 Baths	1
Half Baths	1
First Ceiling	9'
Second Ceiling	8'
Max Ridge Height	29'
Roof Framing	Stick
Exterior Walls	2x4

SECOND FLOOR

Bed#3 13x12
Bth #2
Bed#2 12x12
W.I. CLOSET
Linen
Balcony
W.I. CLOSET
Bath#3
W.I. CLOSET
Bed#4 12x12
Stairs
OPEN TO BELOW

roof-line
Covered Patio
roof-line

Breakfast Area 14x10
SLOPED CLG. FROM 8'-0" TO 9'-0"
China Hutch
Work Island
Great Room 24x16
9'-0" CLG. HT.
Master Bedroom 17x14
9'-0" CLG.HT.
Kitchen 14x10
SLOPED CLG. FROM 8'-0" TO 9'-0"
Pantry
Entertainment Center
Whirlpool Tub
Utility
8'-0" CLG. HT.
Pwdr
Gallery 9'-0" CLG. HT.
Line of balcony above
MstrBth
SLOPED CLG. FROM 9'-0" TO 11'-0"
Formal Dining 12x12
9'-0" CLG. HT.
Entry
SLOPED CLG. FROM 10'-0" TO 18'-0"
Stairs
Linen
Master Walk-In Closet
Two-Car Garage
8'-4" CLG. HT.
Covered Porch

FIRST FLOOR

Design 64178

Units	Single
Price Code	H
Total Finished	2,555 sq. ft.
Main Finished	2,555 sq. ft.
Garage Unfinished	640 sq. ft.
Porch Unfinished	315 sq. ft.
Dimensions	70'x76'6"
Foundation	Crawlspace
Bedrooms	3
Full Baths	2
Half Baths	1
Max Ridge Height	28'4"
Exterior Walls	2x6
Roof Framing	Stick/Truss

* Alternate foundation options available at an additional charge.
Please call 1-800-235-5700 for more information.

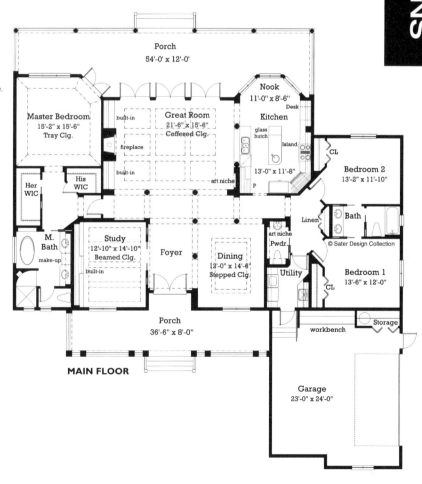

MAIN FLOOR

Design 57021

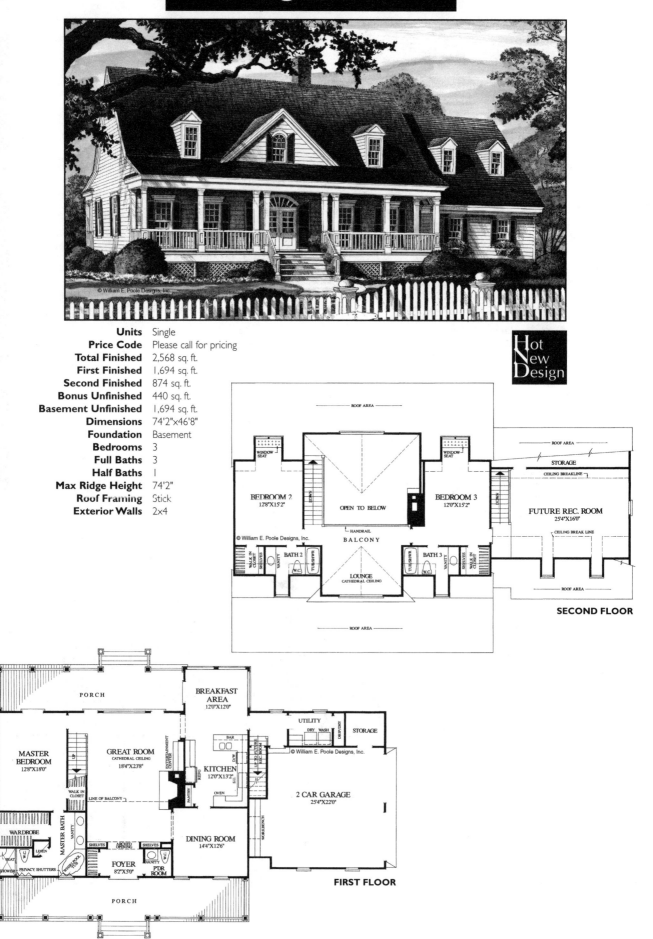

Units	Single
Price Code	Please call for pricing
Total Finished	2,568 sq. ft.
First Finished	1,694 sq. ft.
Second Finished	874 sq. ft.
Bonus Unfinished	440 sq. ft.
Basement Unfinished	1,694 sq. ft.
Dimensions	74'2"x46'8"
Foundation	Basement
Bedrooms	3
Full Baths	3
Half Baths	1
Max Ridge Height	74'2"
Roof Framing	Stick
Exterior Walls	2x4

Hot New Design

© William E. Poole Designs, Inc.

SECOND FLOOR

ROOF AREA

WINDOW SEAT

BEDROOM 2
12'8"X15'2"

OPEN TO BELOW

HANDRAIL

BALCONY

BATH 2
W.C.
TUB/SHWR

WALK IN CLOSET
SHELVES
VANITY

LOUNGE
CATHEDRAL CEILING

WINDOW SEAT

BEDROOM 3
12'0"X15'2"

BATH 3
TUB/SHWR
W.C.
VANITY
SHELVES
WALK IN CLOSET

ROOF AREA

STORAGE

CEILING BREAKLINE

FUTURE REC. ROOM
25'4"X16'0"

CEILING BREAK LINE

ROOF AREA

FIRST FLOOR

PORCH

BREAKFAST AREA
12'0"X12'0"

UTILITY
DRY WASH
DRIP/DRY
STORAGE

© William E. Poole Designs, Inc.

MASTER BEDROOM
12'8"X18'0"

GREAT ROOM
CATHEDRAL CEILING
18'4"X23'8"

UP

WALK IN CLOSET

LINE OF BALCONY

ENTERTAINMENT CENTER

BAR
KITCHEN
12'0"X13'2"
REFRIG
OVEN
DW

UP TO FUTURE REC. ROOM

2 CAR GARAGE
25'4"X22'0"

WARDROBE

MASTER BATH
VANITY
WHIRLPOOL

SEAT
SHOWER
LINEN
PRIVACY SHUTTERS

SHELVES
ARCHED OPENING
SHELVES

FOYER
8'2"X5'0"

PDR ROOM
VANITY

DINING ROOM
14'4"X12'6"

WORKBENCH

PANTRY

PORCH

Design 64142

Units	Single
Price Code	I
Total Finished	2,581 sq. ft.
First Finished	1,842 sq. ft.
Second Finished	739 sq. ft.
Bonus Unfinished	379 sq. ft.
Porch Unfinished	241 sq. ft.
Dimensions	79'×50'
Foundation	Crawlspace
Bedrooms	3
Full Baths	2
3/4 Baths	2
Half Baths	I
Max Ridge Height	22'4"
Exterior Walls	2×6

* Alternate foundation options available at an additional charge. Please call 1-800-235-5700 for more information.

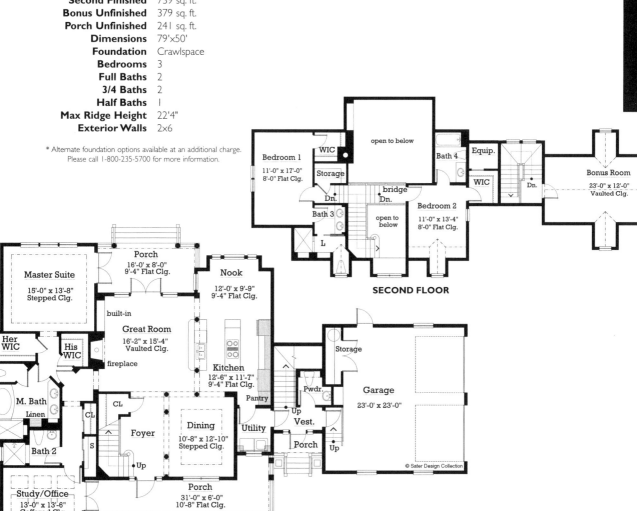

SECOND FLOOR

FIRST FLOOR

© Sater Design Collection

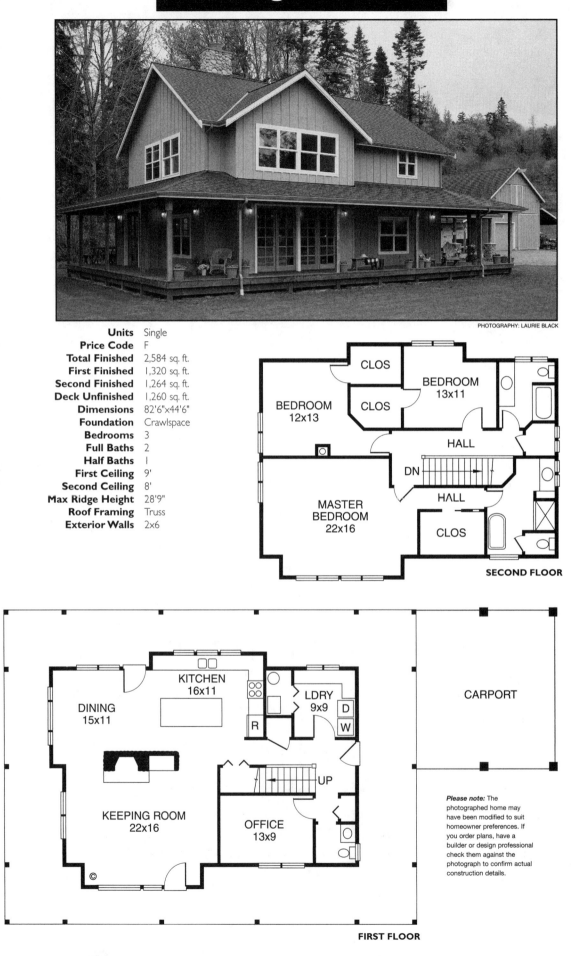

Design 32351

PHOTOGRAPHY: LAURIE BLACK

Units	Single
Price Code	F
Total Finished	2,584 sq. ft.
First Finished	1,320 sq. ft.
Second Finished	1,264 sq. ft.
Deck Unfinished	1,260 sq. ft.
Dimensions	82'6"x44'6"
Foundation	Crawlspace
Bedrooms	3
Full Baths	2
Half Baths	1
First Ceiling	9'
Second Ceiling	8'
Max Ridge Height	28'9"
Roof Framing	Truss
Exterior Walls	2x6

CLOS

BEDROOM
13x11

BEDROOM
12x13

CLOS

HALL

DN

MASTER
BEDROOM
22x16

HALL

CLOS

SECOND FLOOR

KITCHEN
16x11

LDRY
9x9

D

W

R

CARPORT

DINING
15x11

KEEPING ROOM
22x16

OFFICE
13x9

UP

Please note: The photographed home may have been modified to suit homeowner preferences. If you order plans, have a builder or design professional check them against the photograph to confirm actual construction details.

FIRST FLOOR

Design 65315

Units	Single
Price Code	F
Total Finished	2,590 sq. ft.
First Finished	1,352 sq. ft.
Second Finished	1,238 sq. ft.
Garage Unfinished	576 sq. ft.
Dimensions	62'x44'
Foundation	Basement
Bedrooms	3
Full Baths	2
Half Baths	1
First Ceiling	9'
Second Ceiling	8'
Max Ridge Height	31'8"
Roof Framing	Truss
Exterior Walls	2x6

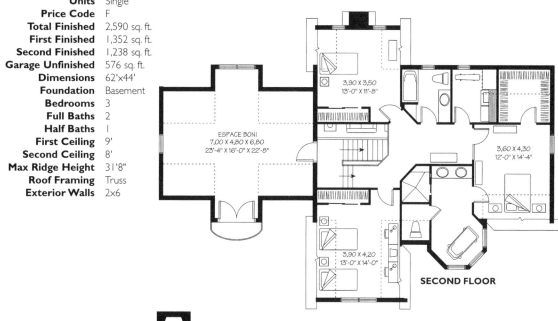

ESPACE BONI
7,00 X 4,80 X 6,80
23'-4" X 16'-0" X 22'-8"

3,90 X 3,50
13'-0" X 11'-8"

3,60 X 4,30
12'-0" X 14'-4"

3,90 X 4,20
13'-0" X 14'-0"

SECOND FLOOR

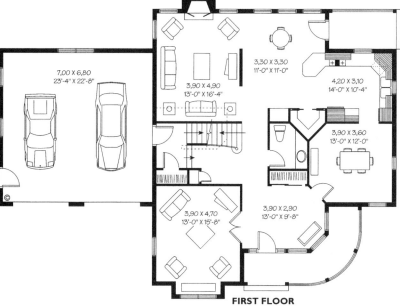

7,00 X 6,80
23'-4" X 22'-8"

3,90 X 4,90
13'-0" X 16'-4"

3,30 X 3,30
11'-0" X 11'-0"

4,20 X 3,10
14'-0" X 10'-4"

3,90 X 3,60
13'-0" X 12'-0"

3,90 X 4,70
13'-0" X 15'-8"

3,90 X 2,90
13'-0" X 9'-8"

FIRST FLOOR

Units	Single
Price Code	F
Total Finished	2,594 sq. ft.
First Finished	1,655 sq. ft.
Second Finished	939 sq. ft.
Bonus Unfinished	532 sq. ft.
Garage Unfinished	667 sq. ft.
Deck Unfinished	598 sq. ft.
Porch Unfinished	540 sq. ft.
Dimensions	50'x53'
Foundation	Pier/Post
Bedrooms	3
Full Baths	3
Half Baths	1
Roof Framing	Stick/Truss
Exterior Walls	2x6

* Alternate foundation options available at an additional charge.
Please call 1-800-235-5700 for more information.

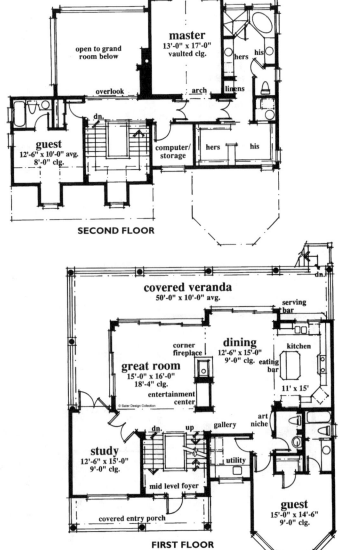

SECOND FLOOR

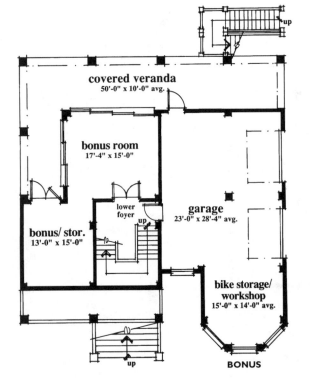

BONUS

FIRST FLOOR

Design 32090

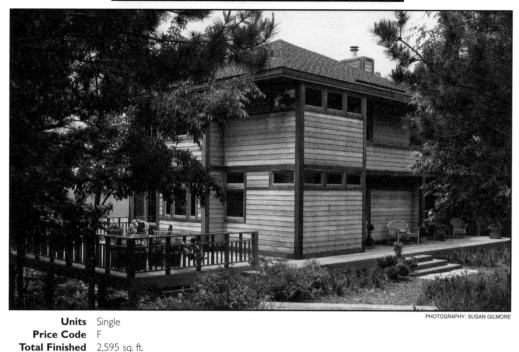

PHOTOGRAPHY: SUSAN GILMORE

Units	Single
Price Code	F
Total Finished	2,595 sq. ft.
First Finished	865 sq. ft.
Second Finished	865 sq. ft.
Lower Finished	865 sq. ft.
Dimensions	32'4"x45'8"
Foundation	Basement
Bedrooms	2
Full Baths	2
Half Baths	1
First Ceiling	10'
Second Ceiling	8'
Max Ridge Height	38'4"
Roof Framing	Stick
Exterior Walls	2x6

Please note: The photographed home may have been modified to suit homeowner preferences. If you order plans, have a builder or design professional check them against the photograph to confirm actual construction details.

LOWER FLOOR

FIRST FLOOR

SECOND FLOOR

Design 92156

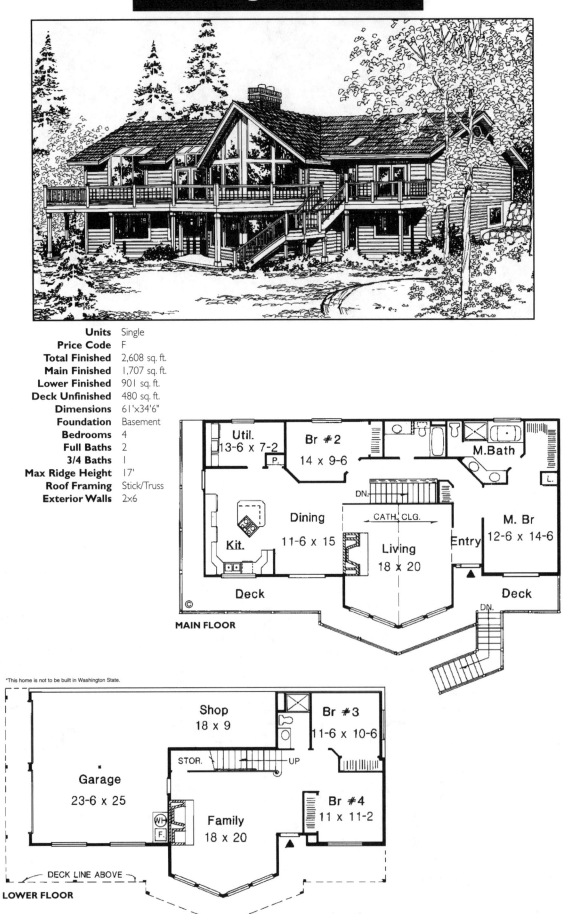

Units	Single
Price Code	F
Total Finished	2,608 sq. ft.
Main Finished	1,707 sq. ft.
Lower Finished	901 sq. ft.
Deck Unfinished	480 sq. ft.
Dimensions	61'x34'6"
Foundation	Basement
Bedrooms	4
Full Baths	2
3/4 Baths	1
Max Ridge Height	17'
Roof Framing	Stick/Truss
Exterior Walls	2x6

Util.
13-6 x 7-2

Br #2
14 x 9-6

M.Bath

DN.

Dining
11-6 x 15

Kit.

CATH. CLG.

Living
18 x 20

Entry

M. Br
12-6 x 14-6

Deck

Deck

DN.

MAIN FLOOR

*This home is not to be built in Washington State.

Shop
18 x 9

Br #3
11-6 x 10-6

STOR.

UP

Garage
23-6 x 25

WH

F.

Family
18 x 20

Br #4
11 x 11-2

DECK LINE ABOVE

LOWER FLOOR

Design 26870

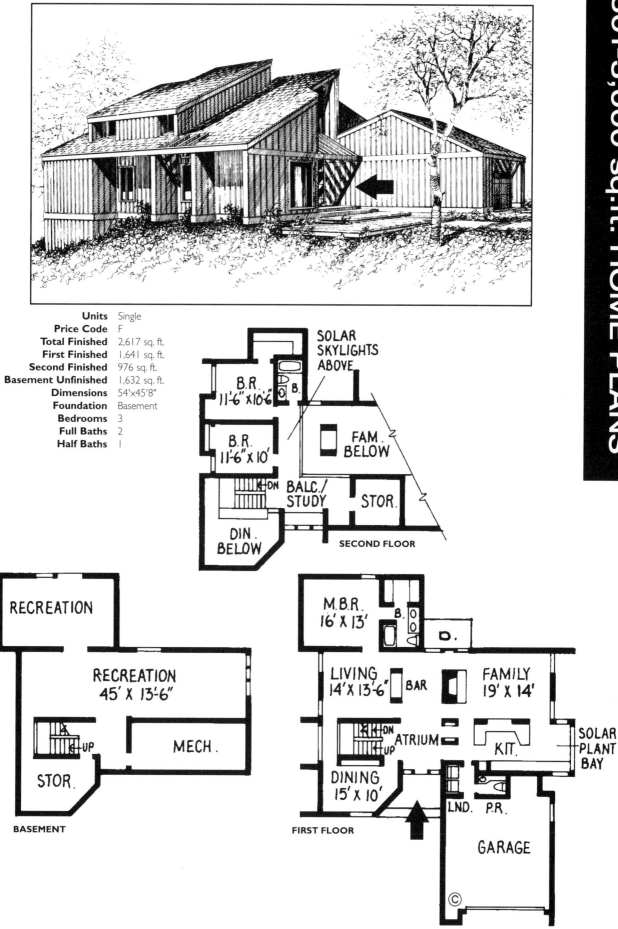

Units	Single
Price Code	F
Total Finished	2,617 sq. ft.
First Finished	1,641 sq. ft.
Second Finished	976 sq. ft.
Basement Unfinished	1,632 sq. ft.
Dimensions	54'x45'8"
Foundation	Basement
Bedrooms	3
Full Baths	2
Half Baths	1

SOLAR SKYLIGHTS ABOVE

B.R. 11'-6" X 10'-6" B.

FAM. BELOW

B.R. 11'-6" X 10'

BALC./ STUDY   STOR.

DIN. BELOW

SECOND FLOOR

RECREATION

RECREATION 45' X 13'-6"

MECH.

STOR.

BASEMENT

M.B.R. 16' X 13' B. D.

LIVING 14' X 13'-6" BAR   FAMILY 19' X 14'

ATRIUM   KIT.   SOLAR PLANT BAY

DINING 15' X 10'

LND. P.R.

GARAGE

FIRST FLOOR

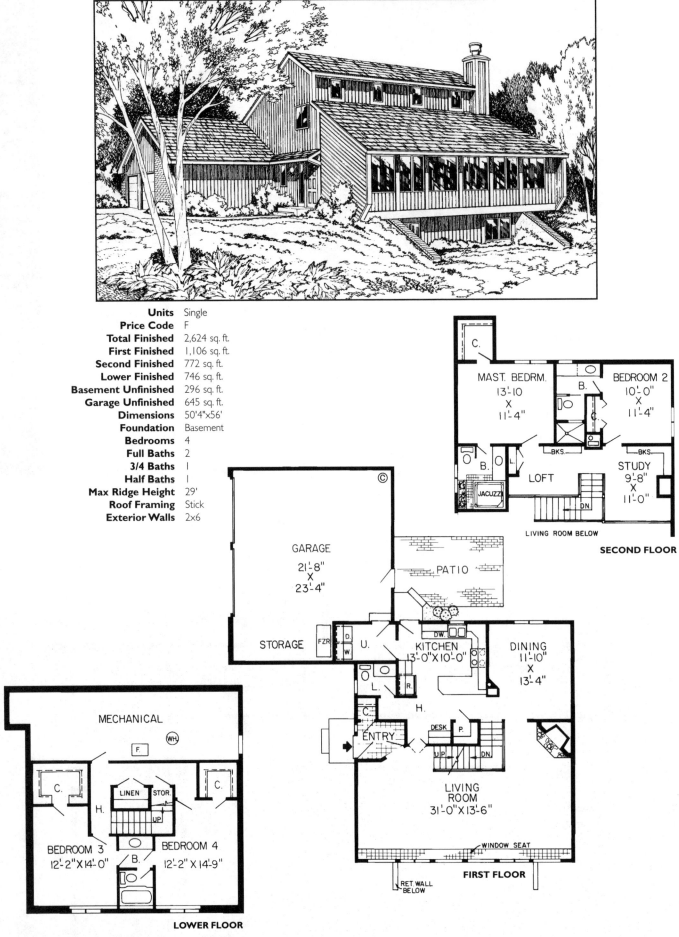

Units	Single
Price Code	F
Total Finished	2,624 sq. ft.
First Finished	1,106 sq. ft.
Second Finished	772 sq. ft.
Lower Finished	746 sq. ft.
Basement Unfinished	296 sq. ft.
Garage Unfinished	645 sq. ft.
Dimensions	50'4"×56'
Foundation	Basement
Bedrooms	4
Full Baths	2
3/4 Baths	1
Half Baths	1
Max Ridge Height	29'
Roof Framing	Stick
Exterior Walls	2x6

SECOND FLOOR

MAST. BEDRM.
13'-10 X 11'-4"

BEDROOM 2
10'-0" X 11'-4"

LOFT

STUDY
9'-8" X 11'-0"

JACUZZI

LIVING ROOM BELOW

GARAGE
21'-8" X 23'-4"

PATIO

STORAGE

KITCHEN
13'-0"X10'-0"

DINING
11'-10" X 13'-4"

ENTRY

DESK

LIVING ROOM
31'-0"X13'-6"

WINDOW SEAT

RET. WALL BELOW

FIRST FLOOR

MECHANICAL

LINEN   STOR.

BEDROOM 3
12'-2"X14'-0"

BEDROOM 4
12'-2" X 14'-9"

LOWER FLOOR

Design 66117

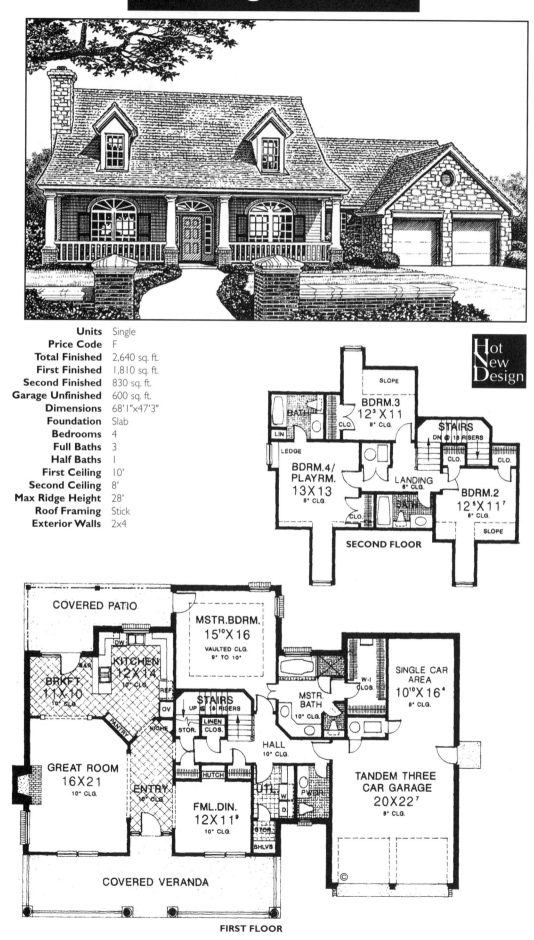

Units	Single
Price Code	F
Total Finished	2,640 sq. ft.
First Finished	1,810 sq. ft.
Second Finished	830 sq. ft.
Garage Unfinished	600 sq. ft.
Dimensions	68'1"x47'3"
Foundation	Slab
Bedrooms	4
Full Baths	3
Half Baths	1
First Ceiling	10'
Second Ceiling	8'
Max Ridge Height	28'
Roof Framing	Stick
Exterior Walls	2x4

Hot New Design

SECOND FLOOR

BDRM.3 12³ X 11 8' CLG.
BATH
LIN
LEDGE
STAIRS DN @ 18 RISERS
BDRM.4/ PLAYRM. 13 X 13 8' CLG.
LANDING 8' CLG.
BDRM.2 12⁵ X 11⁷ 8' CLG.
SLOPE

FIRST FLOOR

COVERED PATIO
MSTR.BDRM. 15¹⁰ X 16 VAULTED CLG. 9' TO 10'
KITCHEN 12 X 14 10' CLG.
BRKFT 11 X 10 10' CLG.
BAR
DW
PANTRY
REF
OV
NICHE
STAIRS UP @ 18 RISERS
STOR.
LINEN CLOS.
HUTCH
GREAT ROOM 16 X 21 10' CLG.
ENTRY 10' CLG.
FML.DIN. 12 X 11⁹ 10' CLG.
UTL
W
D
STOR.
SHLVS
HALL 10' CLG.
MSTR. BATH 10' CLG.
W-I CLOS.
PWR
SINGLE CAR AREA 10¹⁰ X 16⁴ 8' CLG.
TANDEM THREE CAR GARAGE 20 X 22⁷ 8' CLG.
COVERED VERANDA

Design 24403

Units	Single
Price Code	F
Total Finished	2,647 sq. ft.
First Finished	1,378 sq. ft.
Second Finished	1,269 sq. ft.
Basement Unfinished	1,378 sq. ft.
Garage Unfinished	717 sq. ft.
Dimensions	71'x45'
Foundation	Basement
	Crawlspace
	Slab
Bedrooms	4
Full Baths	2
3/4 Baths	1
First Ceiling	9'
Second Ceiling	8'
Max Ridge Height	29'
Roof Framing	Stick
Exterior Walls	2x4

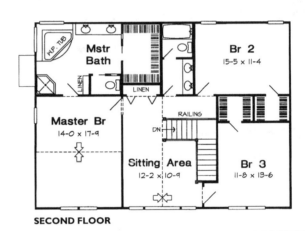

SECOND FLOOR

Mstr Bath

Br 2
15-5 x 11-4

Master Br
14-0 x 17-9

Sitting Area
12-2 x 10-9

Br 3
11-8 x 13-6

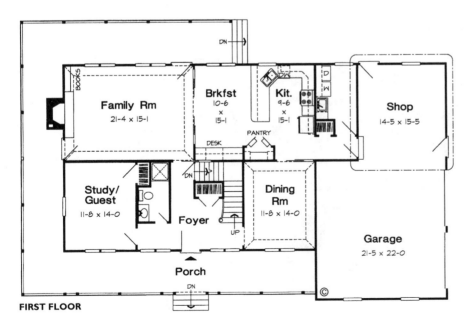

FIRST FLOOR

Family Rm
21-4 x 15-1

Brkfst
10-6 x 15-1

Kit.
9-6 x 15-1

Shop
14-5 x 15-5

Study/Guest
11-8 x 14-0

Foyer

Dining Rm
11-8 x 14-0

Garage
21-5 x 22-0

Porch

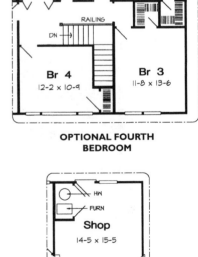

OPTIONAL FOURTH BEDROOM

Br 4
12-2 x 10-9

Br 3
11-8 x 13-6

Shop
14-5 x 15-5

OPTIONAL CRAWLSPACE/SLAB FOUNDATION

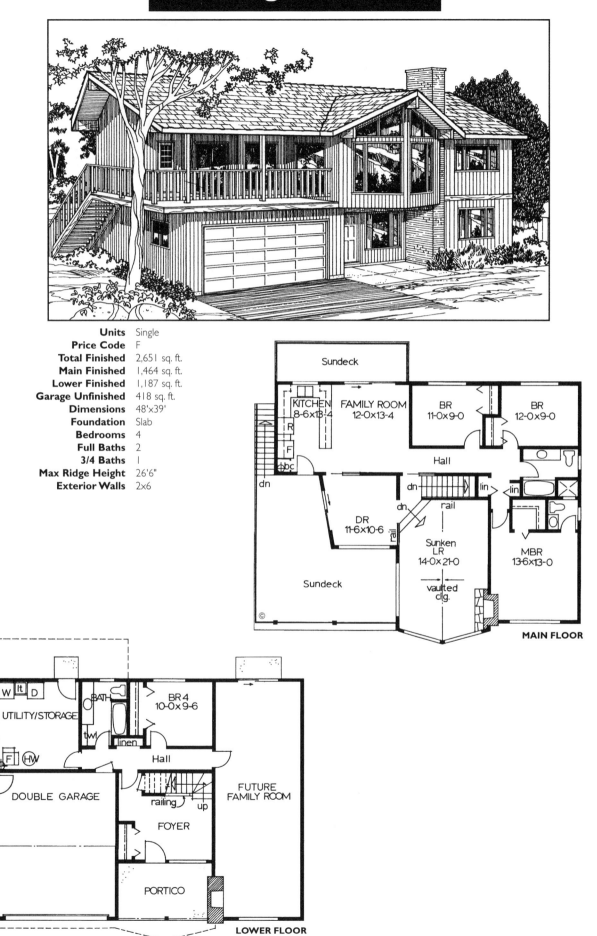

Design 90941

2,501-3,000 sq. ft. HOME PLANS

Units	Single
Price Code	F
Total Finished	2,651 sq. ft.
Main Finished	1,464 sq. ft.
Lower Finished	1,187 sq. ft.
Garage Unfinished	418 sq. ft.
Dimensions	48'x39'
Foundation	Slab
Bedrooms	4
Full Baths	2
3/4 Baths	1
Max Ridge Height	26'6"
Exterior Walls	2x6

Sundeck

KITCHEN 8-6x13-4

FAMILY ROOM 12-0x13-4

BR 11-0x9-0

BR 12-0x9-0

Hall

dn

DR 11-6x10-6

Sunken LR 14-0x 21-0

MBR 13-6x13-0

Sundeck

vaulted clg.

MAIN FLOOR

up

UTILITY/STORAGE

BATH

BR 4 10-0x 9-6

linen

Hall

DOUBLE GARAGE

FUTURE FAMILY ROOM

railing

up

FOYER

PORTICO

LOWER FLOOR

To order blueprints, call **800-235-5700** or visit us on the web, familyhomeplans.com   **353**

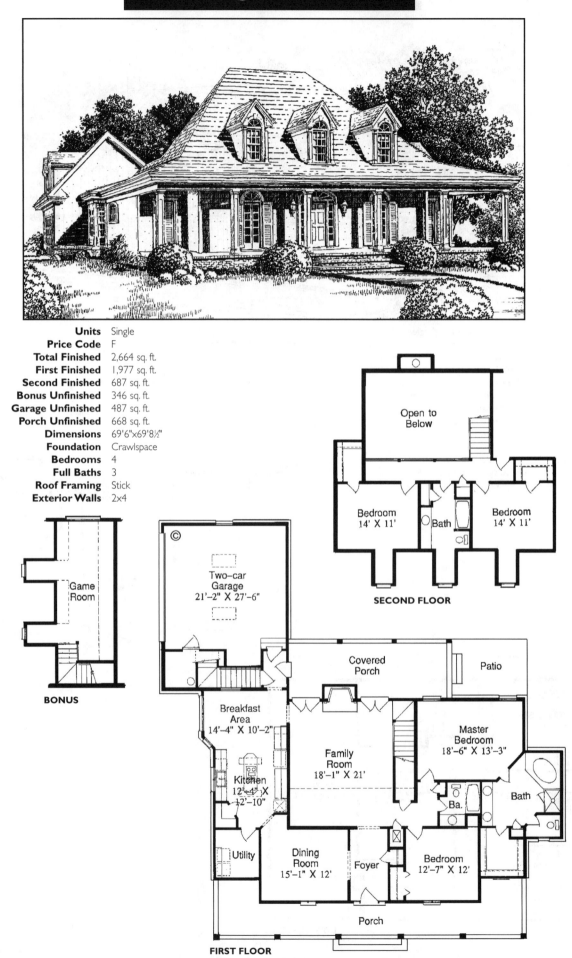

Units	Single
Price Code	F
Total Finished	2,664 sq. ft.
First Finished	1,977 sq. ft.
Second Finished	687 sq. ft.
Bonus Unfinished	346 sq. ft.
Garage Unfinished	487 sq. ft.
Porch Unfinished	668 sq. ft.
Dimensions	69'6"x69'8½"
Foundation	Crawlspace
Bedrooms	4
Full Baths	3
Roof Framing	Stick
Exterior Walls	2x4

Open to Below

Bedroom 14' X 11'

Bath

Bedroom 14' X 11'

SECOND FLOOR

Game Room

BONUS

Two-car Garage 21'-2" X 27'-6"

Breakfast Area 14'-4" X 10'-2"

Kitchen 12'-4" X 12'-10"

Family Room 18'-1" X 21'

Covered Porch

Patio

Master Bedroom 18'-6" X 13'-3"

Ba.

Bath

Utility

Dining Room 15'-1" X 12'

Foyer

Bedroom 12'-7" X 12'

Porch

FIRST FLOOR

Design 32220

PHOTOGRAPHY: JAMES SALOMON

Units	Single
Price Code	F
Total Finished	2,665 sq. ft.
First Finished	1,322 sq. ft.
Second Finished	619 sq. ft.
Lower Finished	724 sq. ft.
Basement Unfinished	483 sq. ft.
Garage Unfinished	440 sq. ft.
Deck Unfinished	232 sq. ft.
Porch Unfinished	187 sq. ft.
Dimensions	76'7"x57'8"
Foundation	Basement
Bedrooms	3
Full Baths	2
Half Baths	1
First Ceiling	8'
Second Ceiling	8'
Max Ridge Height	29'
Roof Framing	Stick
Exterior Walls	2x6

SECOND FLOOR

MASTER SUITE

DN BALCONY WIC

GARAGE

COVERED WALK

Please note: The photographed home may have been modified to suit homeowner preferences. If you order plans, have a builder or design professional check them against the photograph to confirm actual construction details.

STORAGE

UTILITY ROOM

FAMILY ROOM

BEDROOM #2

BEDROOM #3

LOWER COURT AREA

LOWER FLOOR

FRONT PORCH

CRAFT ROOM

LAUNDRY

LIBRARY

SIDE PORCH

KITCHEN

CABINET

GREAT-ROOM

DECK

FIRST FLOOR

Units	Single
Price Code	F
Total Finished	2,668 sq. ft.
First Finished	1,278 sq. ft.
Second Finished	1,390 sq. ft.
Garage Unfinished	491 sq. ft.
Dimensions	60'x44'
Foundation	Basement
Bedrooms	3
Full Baths	1
Half Baths	1

3,30 X 3,10
11'-0" X 10'-4"

3,00 X 3,60
10'-0" X 12'-0"

3,90 X 4,20
13'-0" X 14'-0"

SECOND FLOOR

5,50 X 2,70
18'-4" X 9'-0"

3,70 X 6,20
12'-4" X 20'-8"

3,90 X 3,30
13'-0" X 11'-0"

3,60 X 3,60
13'-0" X 13'-0"

FIRST FLOOR

Design 57023

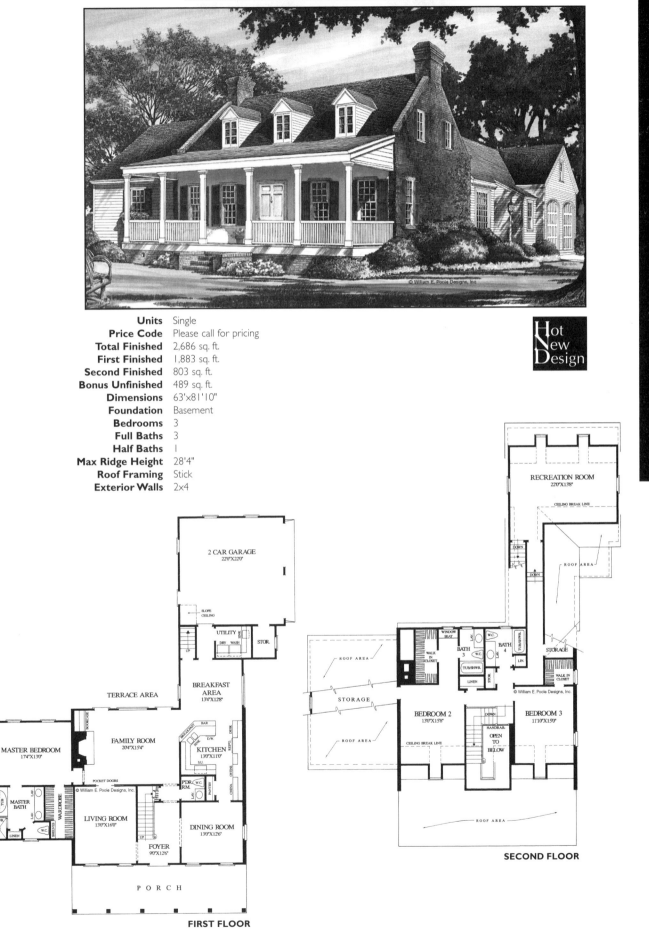

Hot New Design

Units	Single
Price Code	Please call for pricing
Total Finished	2,686 sq. ft.
First Finished	1,883 sq. ft.
Second Finished	803 sq. ft.
Bonus Unfinished	489 sq. ft.
Dimensions	63'x81'10"
Foundation	Basement
Bedrooms	3
Full Baths	3
Half Baths	1
Max Ridge Height	28'4"
Roof Framing	Stick
Exterior Walls	2x4

© William E. Poole Designs, Inc

FIRST FLOOR

SECOND FLOOR

Design 62006

Units	Single
Price Code	F
Total Finished	2,701 sq. ft.
First Finished	2,352 sq. ft.
Second Finished	349 sq. ft.
Garage Unfinished	697 sq. ft.
Porch Unfinished	724 sq. ft.
Dimensions	69'x69'10"
Foundation	Basement
	Crawlspace
	Slab
Bedrooms	3
Full Baths	2
3/4 Baths	2
Half Baths	1
First Ceiling	9'
Second Ceiling	8'
Roof Framing	Stick
Exterior Walls	2x4

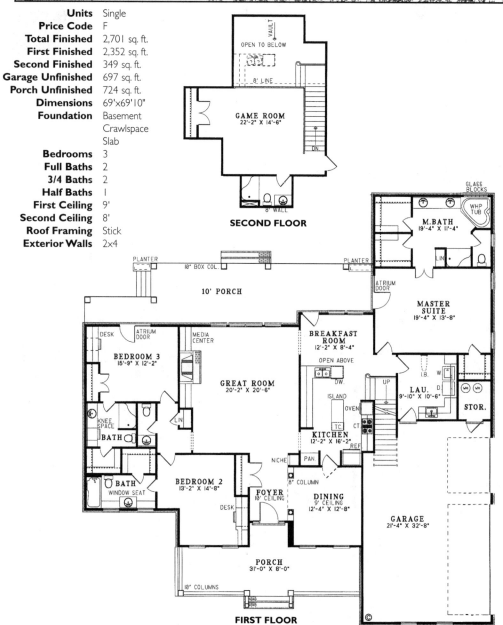

SECOND FLOOR

FIRST FLOOR

Design 57005

Units	Single
Price Code	Please call for pricing
Total Finished	2,753 sq. ft.
First Finished	1,809 sq. ft.
Second Finished	944 sq. ft.
Bonus Unfinished	440 sq. ft.
Dimensions	54'4"×59'
Foundation	Combo Basement/ Crawlspace
Bedrooms	4
Full Baths	3
Half Baths	1
Max Ridge Height	31'
Roof Framing	Stick
Exterior Walls	2x4

Hot New Design

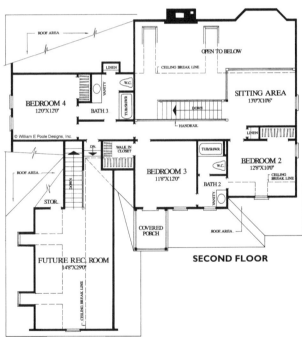

SECOND FLOOR

FIRST FLOOR

© William E Poole Designs, Inc.

Units	Single
Price Code	Please call for pricing
Total Finished	2,757 sq. ft.
First Finished	1,805 sq. ft.
Second Finished	952 sq. ft.
Bonus Unfinished	475 sq. ft.
Dimensions	48'10"x64'10"
Foundation	Combo Basement/ Crawlspace
Bedrooms	4
Full Baths	3
Half Baths	1
First Ceiling	9'
Max Ridge Height	35'8"
Roof Framing	Stick
Exterior Walls	2x4

Hot New Design

SECOND FLOOR

FIRST FLOOR

Design 98581

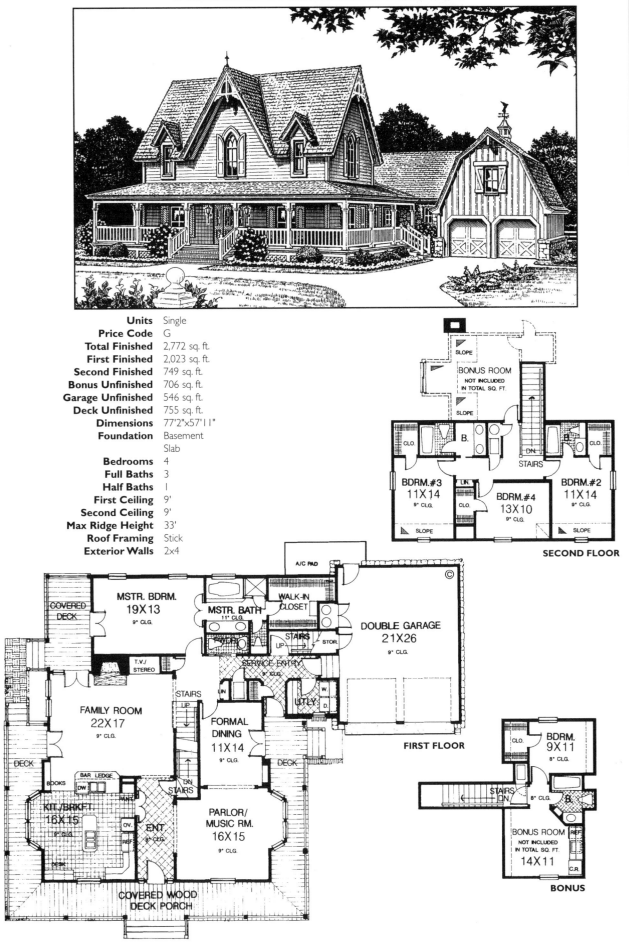

Units	Single
Price Code	G
Total Finished	2,772 sq. ft.
First Finished	2,023 sq. ft.
Second Finished	749 sq. ft.
Bonus Unfinished	706 sq. ft.
Garage Unfinished	546 sq. ft.
Deck Unfinished	755 sq. ft.
Dimensions	77'2"x57'11"
Foundation	Basement
	Slab
Bedrooms	4
Full Baths	3
Half Baths	1
First Ceiling	9'
Second Ceiling	9'
Max Ridge Height	33'
Roof Framing	Stick
Exterior Walls	2x4

SECOND FLOOR

BONUS ROOM — NOT INCLUDED IN TOTAL SQ. FT.

BDRM.#3 11X14 — 9" CLG.

BDRM.#4 13X10 — 9" CLG.

BDRM.#2 11X14 — 9" CLG.

STAIRS

FIRST FLOOR

MSTR. BDRM. 19X13 — 9" CLG.

MSTR. BATH — 11" CLG.

WALK-IN CLOSET

DOUBLE GARAGE 21X26 — 9" CLG.

COVERED DECK

T.V./ STEREO

FAMILY ROOM 22X17 — 9" CLG.

FORMAL DINING 11X14 — 9" CLG.

SERVICE ENTRY

UTLY.

DECK

KIT./BRKFT. 16X15 — 9" CLG.

BAR LEDGE

BOOKS

ENT — 9" CLG.

PARLOR/ MUSIC RM. 16X15 — 9" CLG.

COVERED WOOD DECK PORCH

A/C PAD

BONUS

BDRM. 9X11 — 8" CLG.

STAIRS DN.

BONUS ROOM — NOT INCLUDED IN TOTAL SQ. FT. — 14X11 — 8" CLG.

2,501–3,000 sq. ft. HOME PLANS

Units	Single
Price Code	G
Total Finished	2,772 sq. ft.
Main Finished	1,408 sq. ft.
Lower Finished	1,364 sq. ft.
Garage Unfinished	309 sq. ft.
Porch Unfinished	244 sq. ft.
Dimensions	52'x40'
Foundation	Basement
Bedrooms	3
Full Baths	2
3/4 Baths	1
First Ceiling	8'
Second Ceiling	8'
Max Ridge Height	31'3"
Roof Framing	Truss
Exterior Walls	2x6

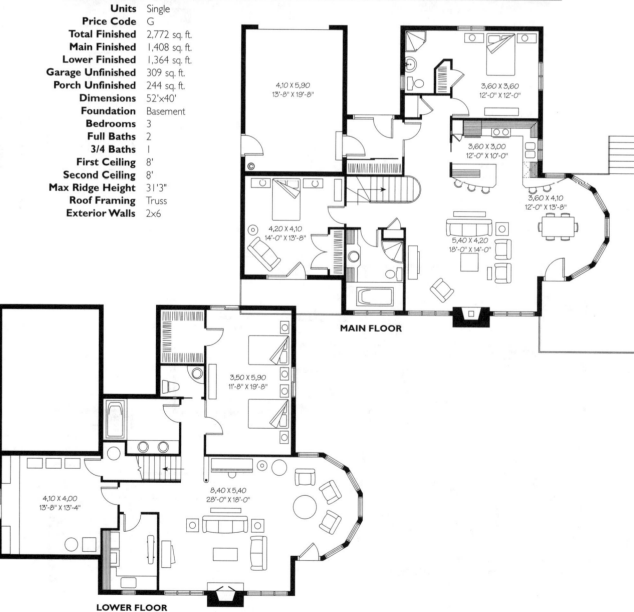

MAIN FLOOR

LOWER FLOOR

Design 98536

Units	Single
Price Code	I
Total Finished	2,787 sq. ft.
Main Finished	2,787 sq. ft.
Bonus Unfinished	636 sq. ft.
Garage Unfinished	832 sq. ft.
Deck Unfinished	152 sq. ft.
Porch Unfinished	212 sq. ft.
Dimensions	101'x58'8"
Foundation	Crawlspace
	Slab
Bedrooms	4
Full Baths	2
Half Baths	I
Main Ceiling	9'
Second Ceiling	7'-9'
Max Ridge Height	28'6"
Roof Framing	Stick
Exterior Walls	2x4

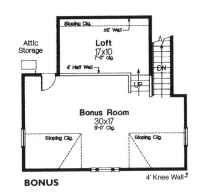

BONUS

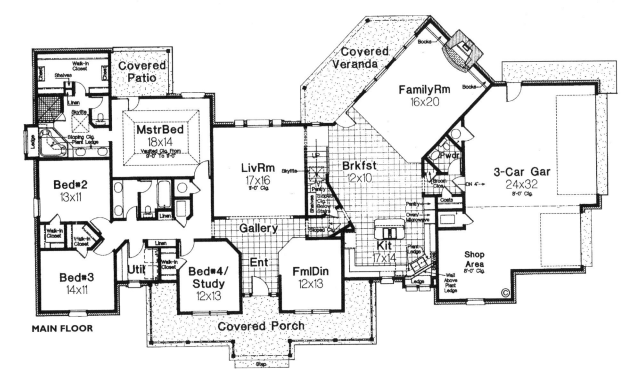

MAIN FLOOR

Design 94636

Units	Single
Price Code	G
Total Finished	2,801 sq. ft.
First Finished	1,651 sq. ft.
Second Finished	1,150 sq. ft.
Dimensions	46'4"x79'1"
Foundation	Crawlspace
	Slab
Bedrooms	5
Full Baths	3
First Ceiling	9'
Second Ceiling	8'
Roof Framing	Stick
Exterior Walls	2x4

SECOND FLOOR

Bedroom #3

Gameroom
17' X 10'–10"

Ba.

Bedroom #4
14'–4" X 13'

Bedroom #5
17' X 12'

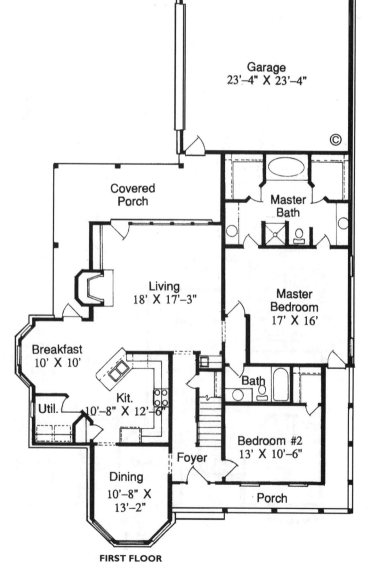

FIRST FLOOR

Garage
23'–4" X 23'–4"

Covered Porch

Master Bath

Living
18' X 17'–3"

Master Bedroom
17' X 16'

Breakfast
10' X 10'

Bath

Util.

Kit.
10'–8" X 12'–6"

Bedroom #2
13' X 10'–6"

Foyer

Dining
10'–8" X 13'–2"

Porch

Design 81026

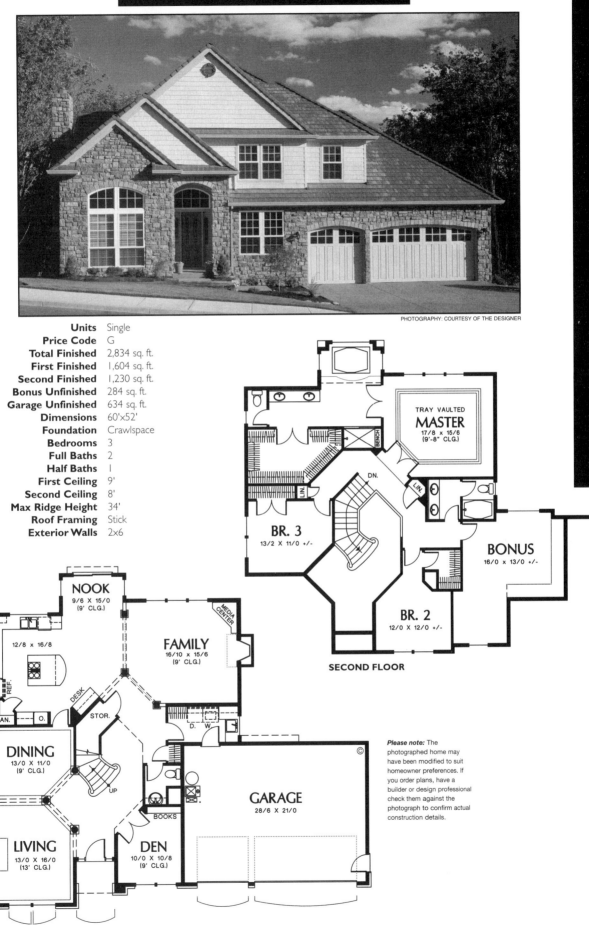

PHOTOGRAPHY: COURTESY OF THE DESIGNER

Units	Single
Price Code	G
Total Finished	2,834 sq. ft.
First Finished	1,604 sq. ft.
Second Finished	1,230 sq. ft.
Bonus Unfinished	284 sq. ft.
Garage Unfinished	634 sq. ft.
Dimensions	60'x52'
Foundation	Crawlspace
Bedrooms	3
Full Baths	2
Half Baths	1
First Ceiling	9'
Second Ceiling	8'
Max Ridge Height	34'
Roof Framing	Stick
Exterior Walls	2x6

SECOND FLOOR

TRAY VAULTED
MASTER
17/8 x 15/6
(9'-8" CLG.)

BR. 3
13/2 X 11/0 +/-

BONUS
16/0 x 13/0 +/-

BR. 2
12/0 X 12/0 +/-

FIRST FLOOR

NOOK
9/6 X 15/0
(9' CLG.)

12/8 x 16/8

MEDIA CENTER

FAMILY
16/10 x 15/6
(9' CLG.)

REF.

PAN.   O.

DESK

STOR.

D. W.

DINING
13/0 X 11/0
(9' CLG.)

UP

BOOKS

GARAGE
28/6 X 21/0

LIVING
13/0 X 16/0
(13' CLG.)

DEN
10/0 X 10/8
(9' CLG.)

Please note: The photographed home may have been modified to suit homeowner preferences. If you order plans, have a builder or design professional check them against the photograph to confirm actual construction details.

2,501-3,000 sq. ft. HOME PLANS

Design 26810

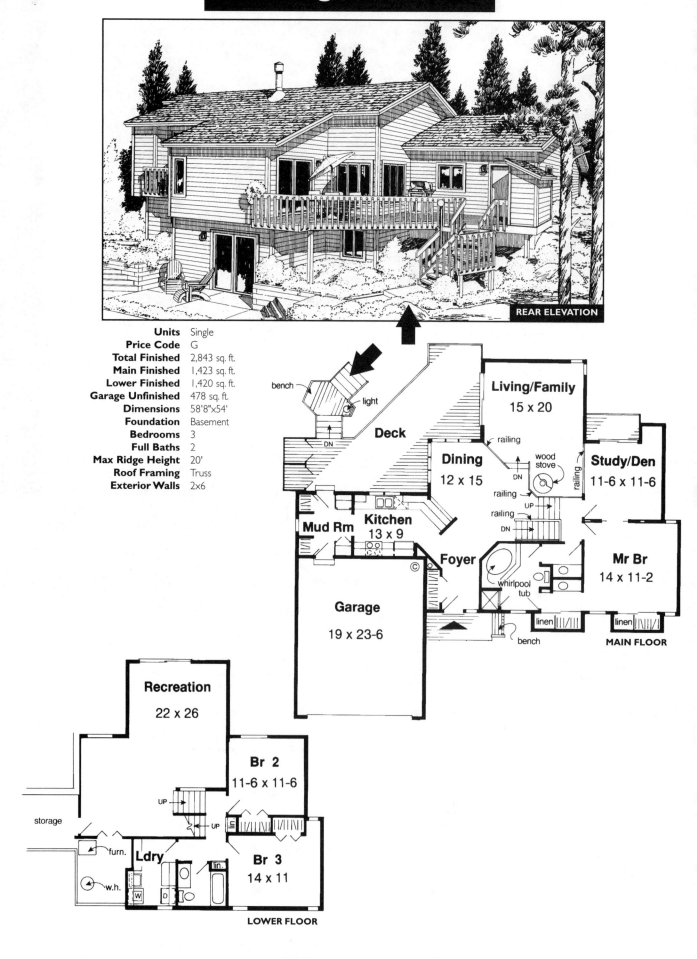

REAR ELEVATION

Units	Single
Price Code	G
Total Finished	2,843 sq. ft.
Main Finished	1,423 sq. ft.
Lower Finished	1,420 sq. ft.
Garage Unfinished	478 sq. ft.
Dimensions	58'8"x54'
Foundation	Basement
Bedrooms	3
Full Baths	2
Max Ridge Height	20'
Roof Framing	Truss
Exterior Walls	2x6

bench

light

Deck

DN

Living/Family
15 x 20

railing

wood
stove

DN

Study/Den
11-6 x 11-6

Dining
12 x 15

railing

UP

Mud Rm

Kitchen
13 x 9

railing

DN

Foyer

whirlpool
tub

Mr Br
14 x 11-2

Garage
19 x 23-6

bench

linen

linen

MAIN FLOOR

Recreation
22 x 26

Br 2
11-6 x 11-6

storage

UP

UP

lin.

furn.

Ldry

lin.

Br 3
14 x 11

w.h.

W

D

LOWER FLOOR

Design 97313

Units	Single
Price Code	G
Total Finished	2,875 sq. ft.
First Finished	2,079 sq. ft.
Second Finished	796 sq. ft.
Porch Unfinished	234 sq. ft.
Dimensions	63'x68'
Foundation	Basement
Bedrooms	4
Full Baths	2
Half Baths	1
First Ceiling	9'1⅛"
Second Ceiling	8'1⅛"
Max Ridge Height	33'2"
Roof Framing	Truss
Exterior Walls	2x6

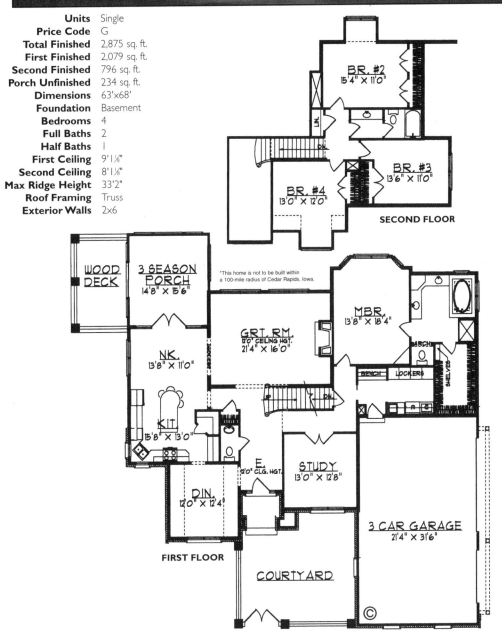

SECOND FLOOR

BR. #2
15'4" x 11'0"

BR. #3
13'6" x 11'0"

BR. #4
13'0" x 12'0"

WOOD DECK

3 SEASON PORCH
14'8" x 15'6"

*This home is not to be built within a 100-mile radius of Cedar Rapids, Iowa.

NK.
13'8" x 11'0"

GRT. RM.
12'0" CEILING HGT.
21'4" x 16'0"

MBR.
13'8" x 18'4"

KIT.
15'8" x 13'0"

DIN.
12'0" x 12'4"

E.
12'0" CLG. HGT.

STUDY
13'0" x 12'8"

3 CAR GARAGE
21'4" x 31'6"

FIRST FLOOR

COURTYARD

Design 94668

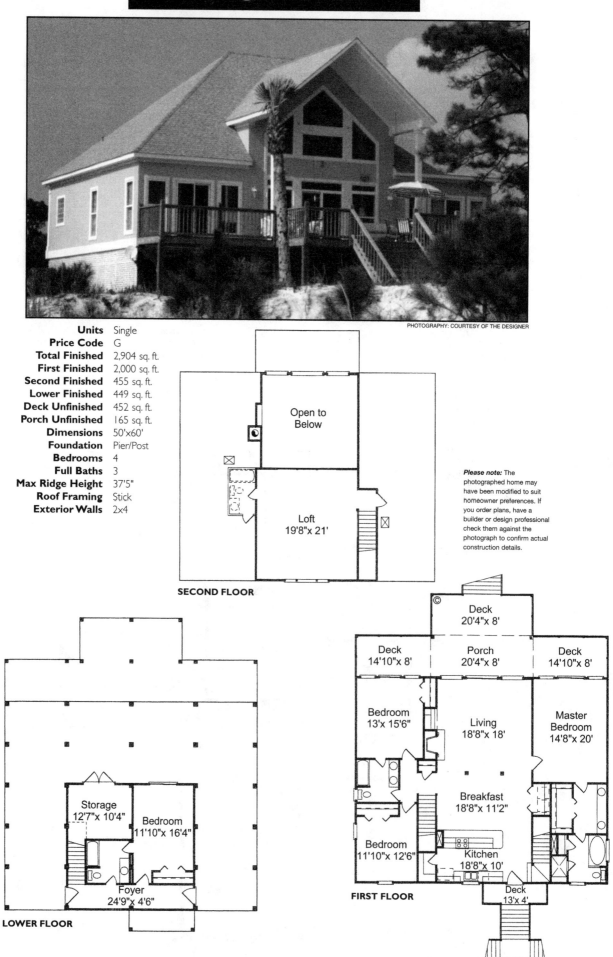

PHOTOGRAPHY: COURTESY OF THE DESIGNER

Units	Single
Price Code	G
Total Finished	2,904 sq. ft.
First Finished	2,000 sq. ft.
Second Finished	455 sq. ft.
Lower Finished	449 sq. ft.
Deck Unfinished	452 sq. ft.
Porch Unfinished	165 sq. ft.
Dimensions	50'x60'
Foundation	Pier/Post
Bedrooms	4
Full Baths	3
Max Ridge Height	37'5"
Roof Framing	Stick
Exterior Walls	2x4

Open to Below

Loft
19'8"x 21'

SECOND FLOOR

Please note: The photographed home may have been modified to suit homeowner preferences. If you order plans, have a builder or design professional check them against the photograph to confirm actual construction details.

Storage
12'7"x 10'4"

Bedroom
11'10"x 16'4"

Foyer
24'9"x 4'6"

LOWER FLOOR

Deck
20'4"x 8'

Deck
14'10"x 8'

Porch
20'4"x 8'

Deck
14'10"x 8'

Bedroom
13'x 15'6"

Living
18'8"x 18'

Master Bedroom
14'8"x 20'

Breakfast
18'8"x 11'2"

Bedroom
11'10"x 12'6"

Kitchen
18'8"x 10'

FIRST FLOOR

Deck
13'x 4'

To order blueprints, call **800-235-5700** or visit us on the web, **familyhomeplans.com**

Design 32514

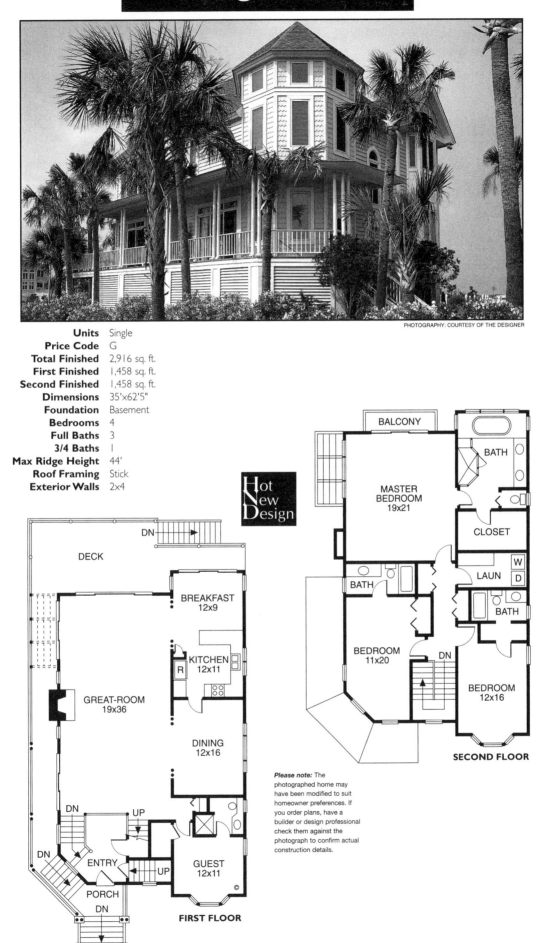

PHOTOGRAPHY: COURTESY OF THE DESIGNER

Units	Single
Price Code	G
Total Finished	2,916 sq. ft.
First Finished	1,458 sq. ft.
Second Finished	1,458 sq. ft.
Dimensions	35'x62'5"
Foundation	Basement
Bedrooms	4
Full Baths	3
3/4 Baths	I
Max Ridge Height	44'
Roof Framing	Stick
Exterior Walls	2x4

Hot New Design

DECK

DN

BREAKFAST
12x9

KITCHEN
12x11
R

GREAT-ROOM
19x36

DINING
12x16

DN UP

DN

ENTRY UP

GUEST
12x11

PORCH

DN

FIRST FLOOR

BALCONY

BATH

MASTER
BEDROOM
19x21

CLOSET

W
LAUN
D

BATH

BATH

BEDROOM
11x20

DN

BEDROOM
12x16

SECOND FLOOR

Please note: The photographed home may have been modified to suit homeowner preferences. If you order plans, have a builder or design professional check them against the photograph to confirm actual construction details.

Units	Single
Price Code	H
Total Finished	2,942 sq. ft.
First Finished	2,073 sq. ft.
Second Finished	869 sq. ft.
Garage Unfinished	528 sq. ft.
Dimensions	64'x76'2"
Foundation	Crawlspace
Bedrooms	3
Full Baths	2
Half Baths	1
Max Ridge Height	32'
Exterior Walls	2x6

* Alternate foundation options available at an additional charge. Please call 1-800-235-5700 for more information.

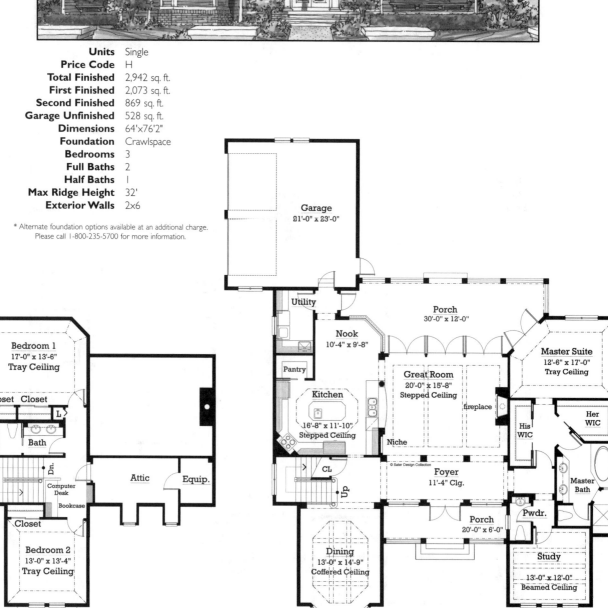

SECOND FLOOR

FIRST FLOOR

Design 94261

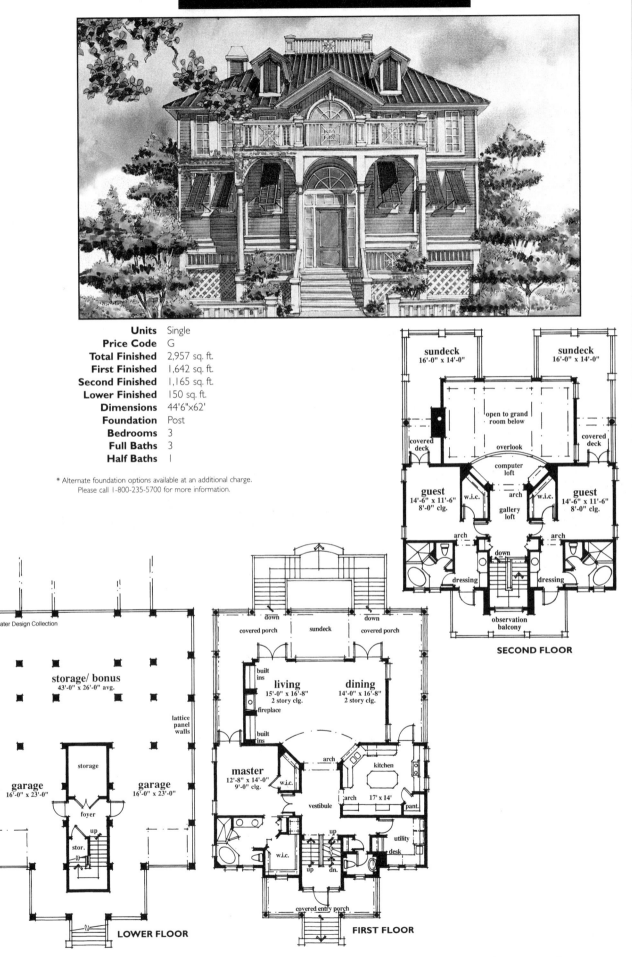

Units	Single
Price Code	G
Total Finished	2,957 sq. ft.
First Finished	1,642 sq. ft.
Second Finished	1,165 sq. ft.
Lower Finished	150 sq. ft.
Dimensions	44'6"x62'
Foundation	Post
Bedrooms	3
Full Baths	3
Half Baths	1

* Alternate foundation options available at an additional charge.
Please call 1-800-235-5700 for more information.

© Sater Design Collection

SECOND FLOOR

sundeck 16'-0" x 14'-0"

sundeck 16'-0" x 14'-0"

open to grand room below

covered deck

overlook

covered deck

computer loft

guest 14'-6" x 11'-6" 8'-0" clg.

w.i.c.

arch

w.i.c.

guest 14'-6" x 11'-6" 8'-0" clg.

gallery loft

arch

down

arch

dressing

dressing

observation balcony

LOWER FLOOR

storage/ bonus 43'-0" x 26'-0" avg.

lattice panel walls

storage

garage 16'-0" x 23'-0"

garage 16'-0" x 23'-0"

foyer

up

stor.

FIRST FLOOR

down

down

covered porch

sundeck

covered porch

built ins

living 15'-0" x 16'-8" 2 story clg.

dining 14'-0" x 16'-8" 2 story clg.

fireplace

built ins

arch

kitchen

master 12'-8" x 14'-0" 9'-0" clg.

w.i.c.

arch

17' x 14'

pant.

vestibule

utility

desk

w.i.c.

up

up

dn.

covered entry porch

Design 32353

PHOTOGRAPHY: LAURIE BLACK

Units	Single
Price Code	G
Total Finished	2,977 sq. ft.
First Finished	2,111 sq. ft.
Second Finished	866 sq. ft.
Garage Unfinished	912 sq. ft.
Deck Unfinished	948 sq. ft.
Dimensions	76'x93'
Foundation	Crawlspace
Bedrooms	3
Full Baths	1
3/4 Baths	1
Half Baths	1
First Ceiling	8'
Second Ceiling	8'
Vaulted Ceiling	23'2
Max Ridge Height	29'6
Roof Framing	Truss
Exterior Walls	2x6

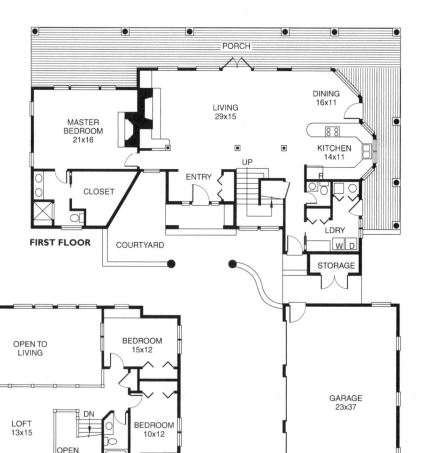

Please note: The photographed home may have been modified to suit homeowner preferences. If you order plans, have a builder or design professional check them against the photograph to confirm actual construction details.

Design 94242

Units	Single
Price Code	H
Total Finished	2,978 sq. ft.
Main Finished	2,978 sq. ft.
Garage Unfinished	702 sq. ft.
Dimensions	84'x90'
Foundation	Slab
Bedrooms	3
Full Baths	2
3/4 Baths	1
Half Baths	1
Max Ridge Height	36'6"
Roof Framing	Stick

* Alternate foundation options available at an additional charge.
  Please call 1-800-235-5700 for more information.

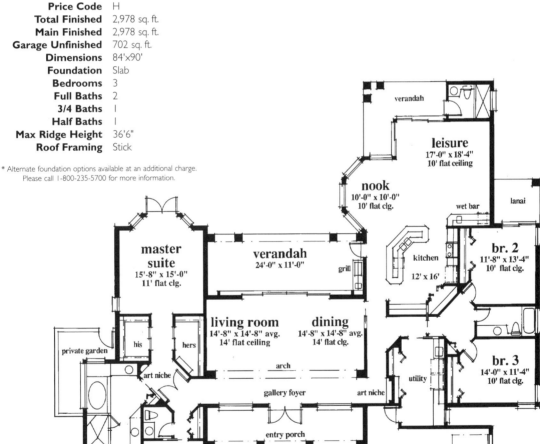

MAIN FLOOR

© Sater Design Collection

Design 81027

Units	Single
Price Code	G
Total Finished	2,986 sq. ft.
First Finished	2,162 sq. ft.
Second Finished	824 sq. ft.
Garage Unfinished	705 sq. ft.
Porch Unfinished	147 sq. ft.
Dimensions	67'x68'
Foundation	Crawlspace
Bedrooms	3
Full Baths	2
Half Baths	1
First Ceiling	9'
Second Ceiling	8'
Max Ridge Height	31'
Roof Framing	Stick
Exterior Walls	2x6

SECOND FLOOR

GREAT RM. BELOW

BR. 2
12/0 X 10/8 +

LIBRARY
12/6 X 8/8 +/-

LINEN

BR. 3
12/6 X 11/0

GAMES RM.
12/6 X 11/0

FIRST FLOOR

PATIO

NOOK
12/0 X 11/0
(9' CLG.)

MASTER
13/2 x 16/0
(10'-8" CLG.)

BUILT-IN

TWO STORY
GREAT RM.
19/0 X 19/8

REF.

DEN
14/2 X 12/0
(9'-10" CLG.)

BOOKCASE

NICHE

BUILT-IN

BUTLER'S PANTRY

PANTRY

D. W.

DN.

DINING
12/6 X 15/4
(9' CLG.)

GARAGE
22/0 X 29/0 +

Design 65008

Units	Single
Price Code	H
Total Finished	3,072 sq. ft.
Main Finished	1,635 sq. ft.
Lower Finished	1,437 sq. ft.
Garage Unfinished	474 sq. ft.
Dimensions	36'×62'
Foundation	Slab
Bedrooms	4
Full Baths	3
Main Ceiling	8'
Lower Ceiling	8'
Max Ridge Height	26'6"
Roof Framing	Truss
Exterior Walls	2x6

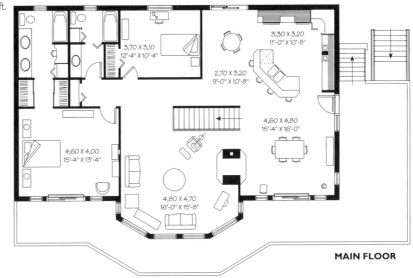

MAIN FLOOR

LOWER FLOOR

Units	Single
Price Code	J
Total Finished	3,098 sq. ft.
First Finished	2,146 sq. ft.
Second Finished	952 sq. ft.
Basement Unfinished	929 sq. ft.
Garage Unfinished	1,004 sq. ft.
Deck Unfinished	426 sq. ft.
Porch Unfinished	426 sq. ft.
Dimensions	52'x65'4"
Foundation	Crawlspace
Bedrooms	3
Full Baths	1
3/4 Baths	2
Half Baths	1
Max Ridge Height	39'
Exterior Walls	2x6

* Alternate foundation options available at an additional charge.
Please call 1-800-235-5700 for more information.

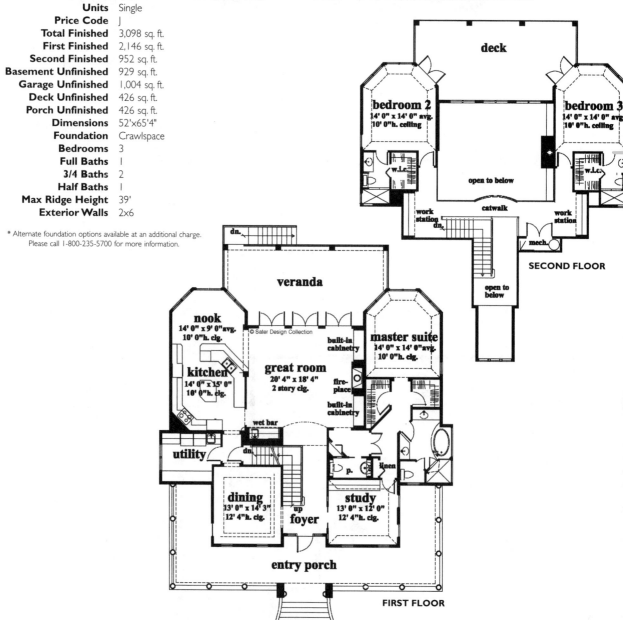

Design 57016

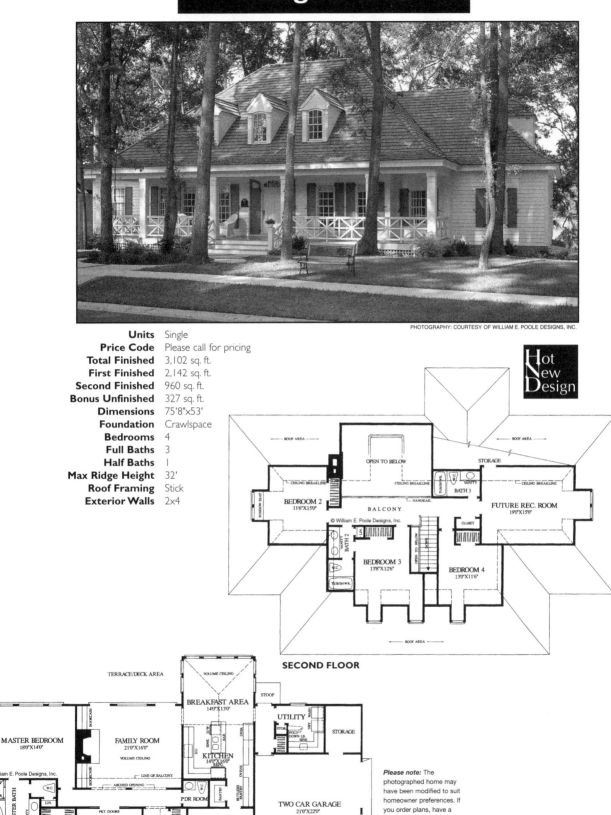

PHOTOGRAPHY: COURTESY OF WILLIAM E. POOLE DESIGNS, INC.

Hot New Design

Units	Single
Price Code	Please call for pricing
Total Finished	3,102 sq. ft.
First Finished	2,142 sq. ft.
Second Finished	960 sq. ft.
Bonus Unfinished	327 sq. ft.
Dimensions	75'8"x53'
Foundation	Crawlspace
Bedrooms	4
Full Baths	3
Half Baths	1
Max Ridge Height	32'
Roof Framing	Stick
Exterior Walls	2x4

SECOND FLOOR

ROOF AREA

ROOF AREA

OPEN TO BELOW

STORAGE

CEILING BREAKLINE

CEILING BREAKLINE

BATH 3

CEILING BREAKLINE

BEDROOM 2
11'6"X15'0"

BALCONY

HANDRAIL

FUTURE REC. ROOM
19'0"X15'0"

© William E. Poole Designs, Inc.

BATH 2

CLOSET

OPEN TO BELOW

BEDROOM 3
13'8"X12'6"

BEDROOM 4
13'0"X11'6"

ROOF AREA

FIRST FLOOR

TERRACE/DECK AREA

VOLUME CEILING

BREAKFAST AREA
14'0"X13'0"

STOOP

UTILITY

STORAGE

MASTER BEDROOM
18'0"X14'0"

FAMILY ROOM
21'0"X16'0"

VOLUME CEILING

KITCHEN
14'0"X16'0"

© William E. Poole Designs, Inc.

LINE OF BALCONY

MASTER BATH

ARCHED OPENING

P'DR ROOM

PANTRY

BUTLERS PANTRY

TWO CAR GARAGE
21'0"X22'0"

WHIRLPOOL TUB

VANITY

SHELVES

PKT. DOORS

LIVING ROOM
13'0"X15'0"

FOYER
8'8"X15'0"

DINING ROOM
13'0"X15'0"

HIS/HER WARDROBE

WINDOW SEAT

COVERED PORCH

Please note: The photographed home may have been modified to suit homeowner preferences. If you order plans, have a builder or design professional check them against the photograph to confirm actual construction details.

Design 32309

PHOTOGRAPHY: LAURIE BLACK

Units	Single
Price Code	H
Total Finished	3,109 sq. ft.
First Finished	2,340 sq. ft.
Second Finished	769 sq. ft.
Garage Unfinished	576 sq. ft.
Dimensions	52'x56'5"
Foundation	Crawlspace
Bedrooms	2
Full Baths	2
3/4 Baths	I
Half Baths	I
First Ceiling	9'
Vaulted Ceiling	13'6"
Roof Framing	Stick
Exterior Walls	2x6

Please note: The photographed home may have been modified to suit homeowner preferences. If you order plans, have a builder or design professional check them against the photograph to confirm actual construction details.

SECOND FLOOR

FIRST FLOOR

Design 57015

Units	Single
Price Code	Please call for pricing
Total Finished	3,137 sq. ft.
First Finished	2,092 sq. ft.
Second Finished	1,045 sq. ft.
Bonus Unfinished	546 sq. ft.
Dimensions	77'×56'4"
Foundation	Crawlspace
Bedrooms	4
Full Baths	3
Half Baths	1
Max Ridge Height	33'
Roof Framing	Stick
Exterior Walls	2×4

SECOND FLOOR

FIRST FLOOR

Design 19257

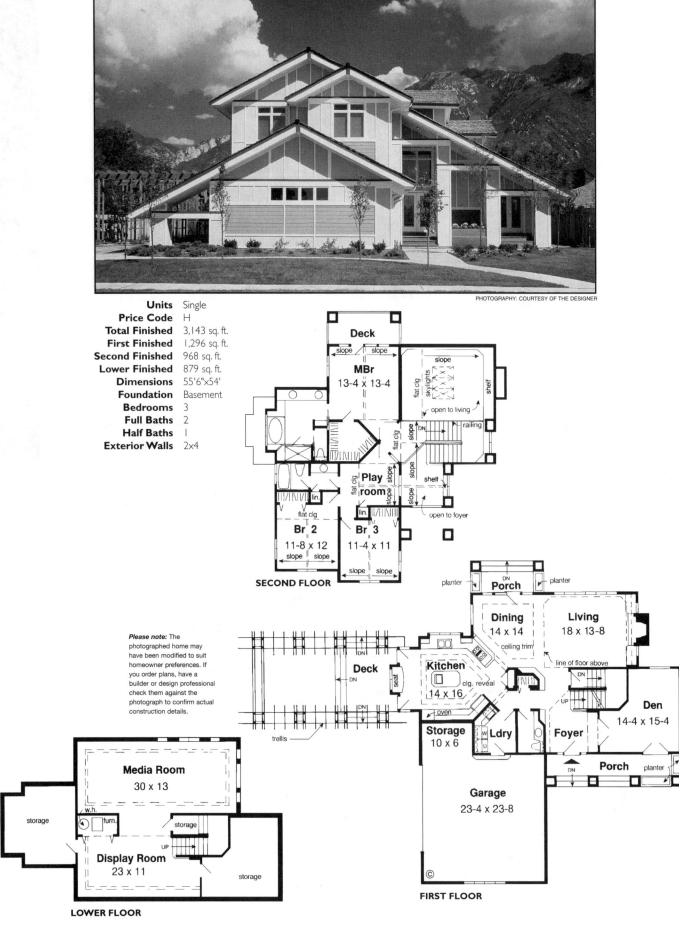

PHOTOGRAPHY: COURTESY OF THE DESIGNER

Units	Single
Price Code	H
Total Finished	3,143 sq. ft.
First Finished	1,296 sq. ft.
Second Finished	968 sq. ft.
Lower Finished	879 sq. ft.
Dimensions	55'6"x54'
Foundation	Basement
Bedrooms	3
Full Baths	2
Half Baths	1
Exterior Walls	2x4

Deck

MBr
13-4 x 13-4

open to living

railing

shelf

Play room

open to foyer

shelf

Br 2
11-8 x 12

Br 3
11-4 x 11

SECOND FLOOR

Please note: The photographed home may have been modified to suit homeowner preferences. If you order plans, have a builder or design professional check them against the photograph to confirm actual construction details.

Porch
planter   planter

Dining
14 x 14

ceiling trim

Living
18 x 13-8

line of floor above

Deck

Kitchen
14 x 16
clg. reveal

seat

oven

Den
14-4 x 15-4

Storage
10 x 6

Ldry
W
D

Foyer

Porch
planter

trellis

Garage
23-4 x 23-8

Media Room
30 x 13

storage

w.h.   furn.

storage

Display Room
23 x 11

storage

LOWER FLOOR

FIRST FLOOR

Design 91319

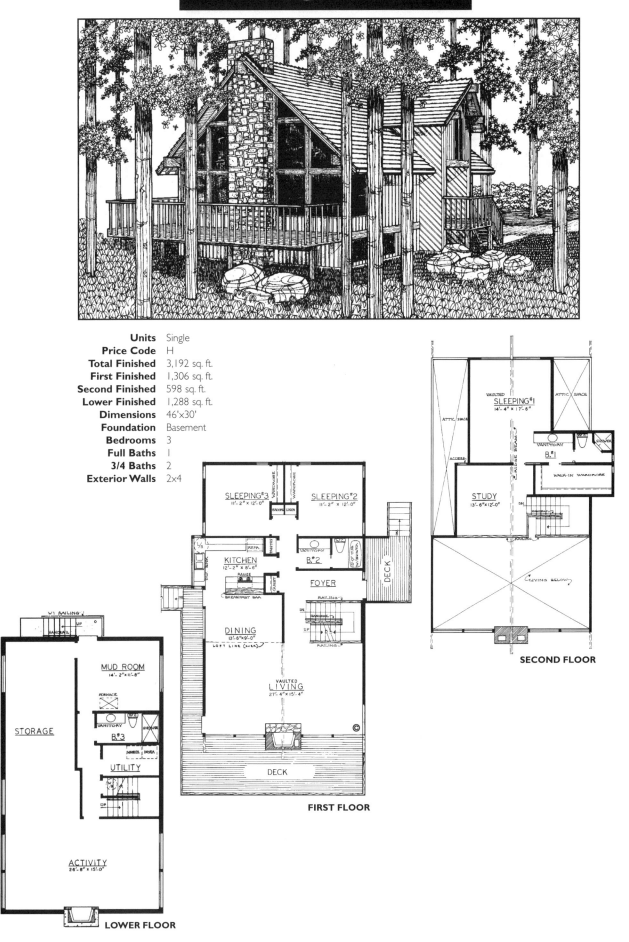

Units	Single
Price Code	H
Total Finished	3,192 sq. ft.
First Finished	1,306 sq. ft.
Second Finished	598 sq. ft.
Lower Finished	1,288 sq. ft.
Dimensions	46'x30'
Foundation	Basement
Bedrooms	3
Full Baths	1
3/4 Baths	2
Exterior Walls	2x4

SECOND FLOOR

FIRST FLOOR

LOWER FLOOR

Design 98588

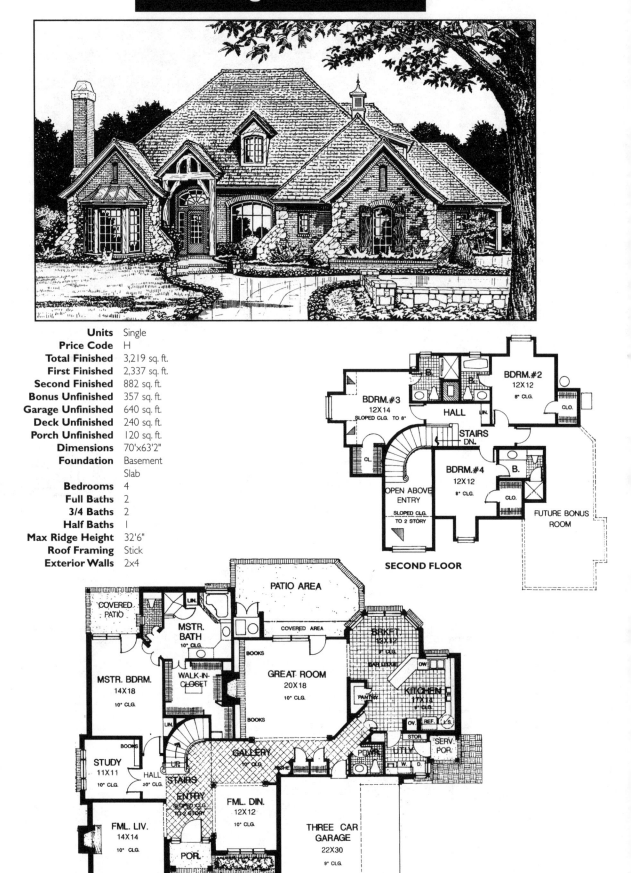

Units	Single
Price Code	H
Total Finished	3,219 sq. ft.
First Finished	2,337 sq. ft.
Second Finished	882 sq. ft.
Bonus Unfinished	357 sq. ft.
Garage Unfinished	640 sq. ft.
Deck Unfinished	240 sq. ft.
Porch Unfinished	120 sq. ft.
Dimensions	70'x63'2"
Foundation	Basement
	Slab
Bedrooms	4
Full Baths	2
3/4 Baths	2
Half Baths	I
Max Ridge Height	32'6"
Roof Framing	Stick
Exterior Walls	2×4

SECOND FLOOR

BDRM.#3 12X14 SLOPED CLG. TO 8'

BDRM.#2 12X12 8' CLG.

HALL

STAIRS DN.

BDRM.#4 12X12 8' CLG.

OPEN ABOVE ENTRY SLOPED CLG. TO 2 STORY

FUTURE BONUS ROOM

FIRST FLOOR

COVERED PATIO

MSTR. BATH 10' CLG.

PATIO AREA

COVERED AREA

BRKFST. 12X12

MSTR. BDRM. 14X18 10' CLG.

WALK-IN CLOSET

GREAT ROOM 20X18 10' CLG.

PANTRY

KITCHEN 17X14

STUDY 11X11 10' CLG.

HALL

STAIRS UP

GALLERY 10' CLG.

ENTRY SLOPED CLG. TO 2 STORY

PDWR.

UTLY.

SERV. POR.

FML. DIN. 12X12 10' CLG.

THREE CAR GARAGE 22X30 9' CLG.

FML. LIV. 14X14 10' CLG.

POR.

Design 94253

Units	Single
Price Code	I
Total Finished	3,285 sq. ft.
First Finished	2,747 sq. ft.
Second Finished	538 sq. ft.
Garage Unfinished	616 sq. ft.
Deck Unfinished	204 sq. ft.
Porch Unfinished	80 sq. ft.
Dimensions	66'x80'6"
Foundation	Slab
Bedrooms	5
Full Baths	3
Max Ridge Height	33'4"
Roof Framing	Truss

* Alternate foundation options available at an additional charge.
Please call 1-800-235-5700 for more information.

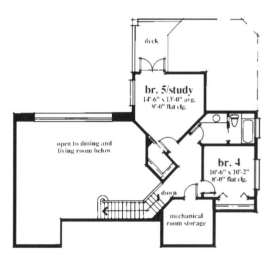

SECOND FLOOR

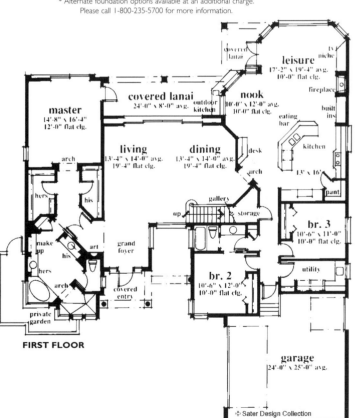

FIRST FLOOR

Units	Single
Price Code	I
Total Finished	3,308 sq. ft.
First Finished	1,719 sq. ft.
Second Finished	1,589 sq. ft.
Bonus Unfinished	515 sq. ft.
Garage Unfinished	720 sq. ft.
Porch Unfinished	302 sq. ft.
Dimensions	65'x52'
Foundation	Crawlspace
Bedrooms	4
Full Baths	3
3/4 Baths	I
First Ceiling	9'
Second Ceiling	9'
Max Ridge Height	33'5"
Roof Framing	Truss
Exterior Walls	2x6

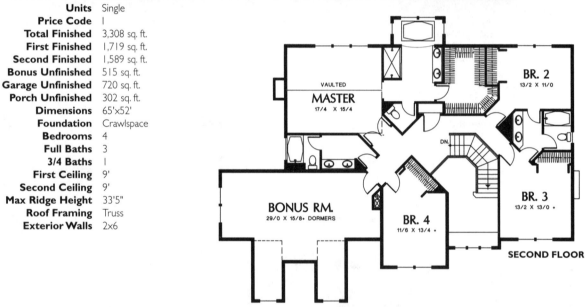

SECOND FLOOR

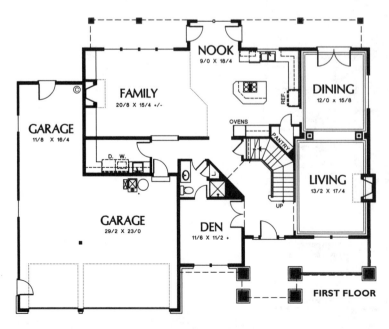

FIRST FLOOR

Design 65382

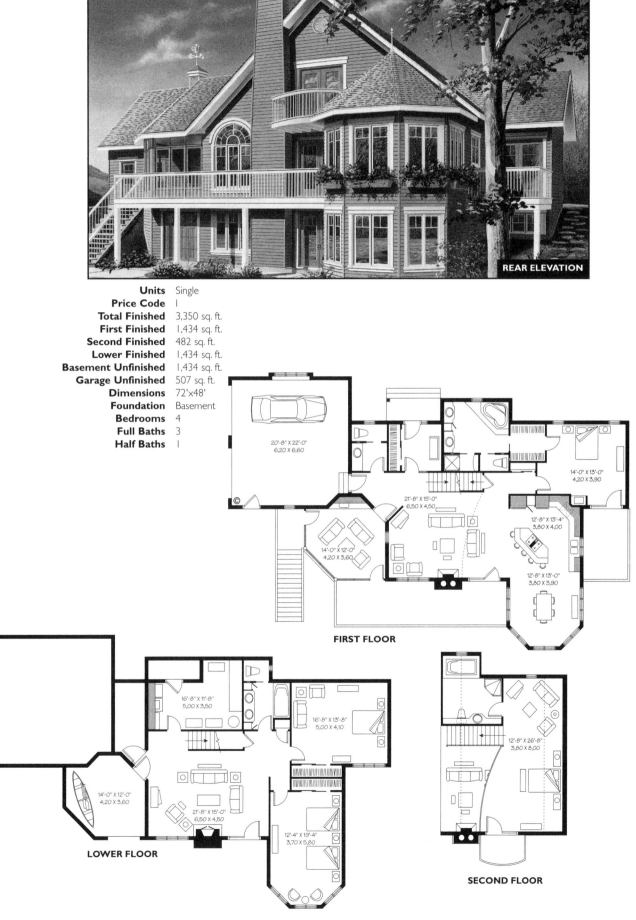

REAR ELEVATION

Units	Single
Price Code	I
Total Finished	3,350 sq. ft.
First Finished	1,434 sq. ft.
Second Finished	482 sq. ft.
Lower Finished	1,434 sq. ft.
Basement Unfinished	1,434 sq. ft.
Garage Unfinished	507 sq. ft.
Dimensions	72'x48'
Foundation	Basement
Bedrooms	4
Full Baths	3
Half Baths	I

FIRST FLOOR

LOWER FLOOR

SECOND FLOOR

Units	Single
Price Code	I
Total Finished	3,352 sq. ft.
Main Finished	3,352 sq. ft.
Garage Unfinished	672 sq. ft.
Deck Unfinished	462 sq. ft.
Porch Unfinished	60 sq. ft.
Dimensions	91'x71'9"
Foundation	Slab
Bedrooms	4
Full Baths	2
3/4 Baths	I
Half Baths	I
Main Ceiling	9'-11'
Max Ridge Height	28'2"
Roof Framing	Stick
Exterior Walls	2x4

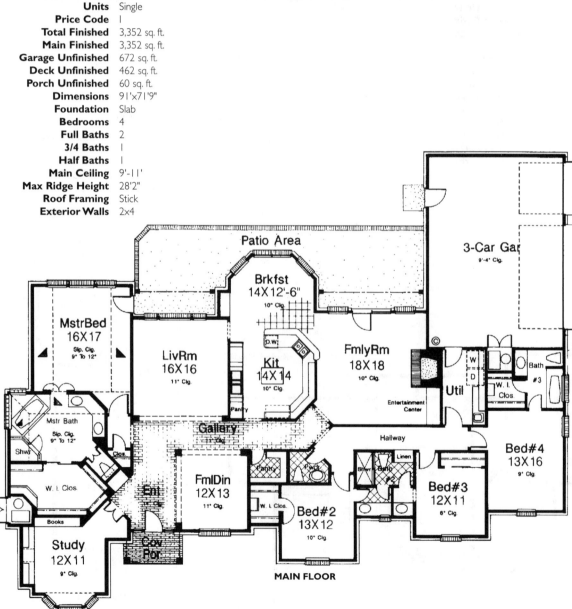

MAIN FLOOR

Design 81021

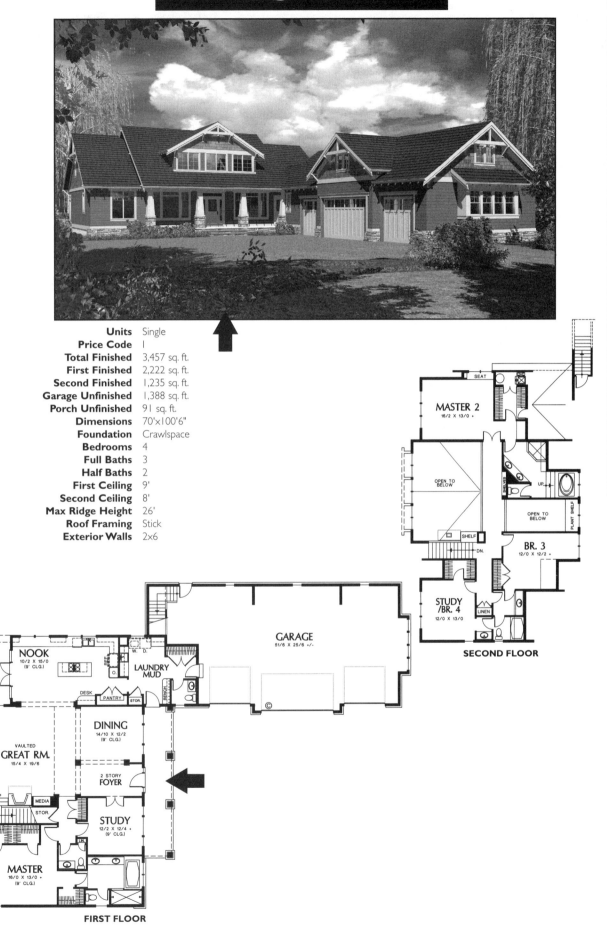

Units	Single
Price Code	I
Total Finished	3,457 sq. ft.
First Finished	2,222 sq. ft.
Second Finished	1,235 sq. ft.
Garage Unfinished	1,388 sq. ft.
Porch Unfinished	91 sq. ft.
Dimensions	70'x100'6"
Foundation	Crawlspace
Bedrooms	4
Full Baths	3
Half Baths	2
First Ceiling	9'
Second Ceiling	8'
Max Ridge Height	26'
Roof Framing	Stick
Exterior Walls	2x6

SECOND FLOOR

MASTER 2
16/2 X 13/0 +

OPEN TO BELOW

BR. 3
12/0 X 12/2

STUDY /BR. 4
12/0 X 13/0

OPEN TO BELOW

LINEN

FIRST FLOOR

GARAGE
51/6 X 25/6 +/-

NOOK
10/2 X 15/0
(9' CLG.)

VAULTED PORCH

LAUNDRY MUD

W. D.

DESK

PANTRY

STOR.

DINING
14/10 X 12/2
(9' CLG.)

VAULTED GREAT RM.
15/4 X 19/6

2 STORY FOYER

MEDIA

STOR.

STUDY
12/2 X 12/4
(9' CLG.)

MASTER
16/0 X 13/0 +
(9' CLG.)

PHOTOGRAPHY: LAURIE BLACK

Units	Single
Price Code	J
Total Finished	3,560 sq. ft.
First Finished	2,348 sq. ft.
Second Finished	1,212 sq. ft.
Garage Unfinished	608 sq. ft.
Porch Unfinished	140 sq. ft.
Dimensions	62'4"x82'
Foundation	Crawlspace
Bedrooms	3
Full Baths	2
Half Baths	1
First Ceiling	9'
Second Ceiling	9'
Max Ridge Height	24'8"
Roof Framing	Truss
Exterior Walls	2x6

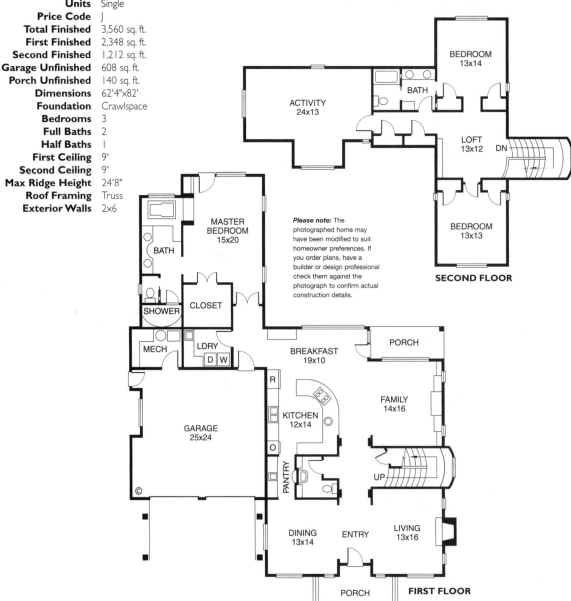

Please note: The photographed home may have been modified to suit homeowner preferences. If you order plans, have a builder or design professional check them against the photograph to confirm actual construction details.

SECOND FLOOR

FIRST FLOOR

Design 32438

PHOTOGRAPHY: EMILY J. FOLLOWILL

Units	Single
Price Code	J
Total Finished	3,574 sq. ft.
First Finished	2,524 sq. ft.
Second Finished	1,050 sq. ft.
Bonus Unfinished	720 sq. ft.
Basement Unfinished	2,524 sq. ft.
Garage Unfinished	845 sq. ft.
Porch Unfinished	826 sq. ft.
Dimensions	108'3"×58'6½"
Foundation	Basement
Bedrooms	4
Full Baths	4
Half Baths	1
First Ceiling	10'
Second Ceiling	8'4"
Vaulted Ceiling	24'4"
Max Ridge Height	44'2"
Roof Framing	Stick
Exterior Walls	2x4

Please note: The photographed home may have been modified to suit homeowner preferences. If you order plans, have a builder or design professional check them against the photograph to confirm actual construction details.

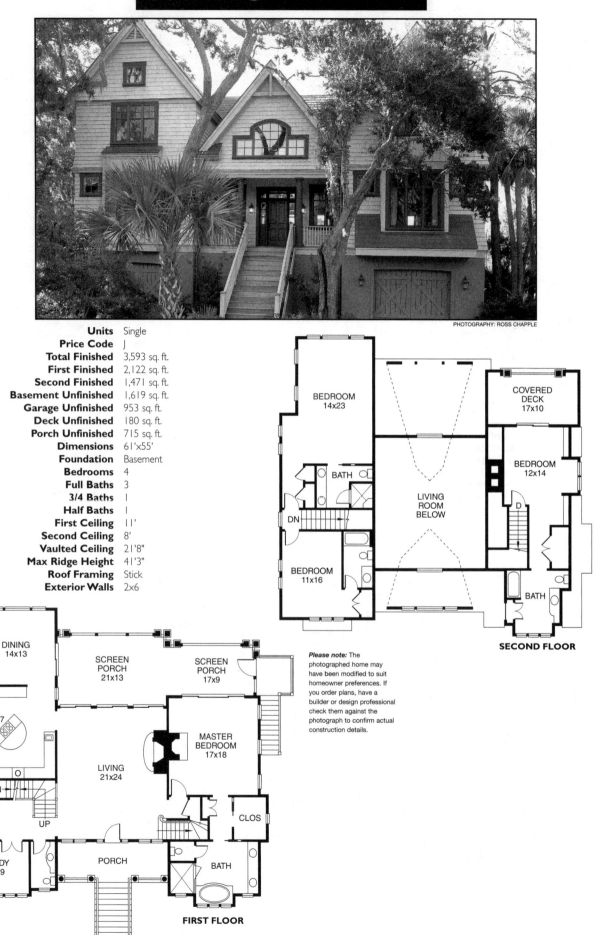

PHOTOGRAPHY: ROSS CHAPPLE

Units	Single
Price Code	J
Total Finished	3,593 sq. ft.
First Finished	2,122 sq. ft.
Second Finished	1,471 sq. ft.
Basement Unfinished	1,619 sq. ft.
Garage Unfinished	953 sq. ft.
Deck Unfinished	180 sq. ft.
Porch Unfinished	715 sq. ft.
Dimensions	61'x55'
Foundation	Basement
Bedrooms	4
Full Baths	3
3/4 Baths	1
Half Baths	1
First Ceiling	11'
Second Ceiling	8'
Vaulted Ceiling	21'8"
Max Ridge Height	41'3"
Roof Framing	Stick
Exterior Walls	2x6

SECOND FLOOR

BEDROOM 14x23

BATH

LIVING ROOM BELOW

COVERED DECK 17x10

BEDROOM 12x14

DN

BEDROOM 11x16

BATH

Please note: The photographed home may have been modified to suit homeowner preferences. If you order plans, have a builder or design professional check them against the photograph to confirm actual construction details.

FIRST FLOOR

DINING 14x13

SCREEN PORCH 21x13

SCREEN PORCH 17x9

KIT 17x17

MASTER BEDROOM 17x18

LIVING 21x24

R

O

DN

UP

W D

CLOS

STUDY 12x9

PORCH

BATH

Design 66034

Units	Single
Price Code	J
Total Finished	3,619 sq. ft.
First Finished	2,317 sq. ft.
Second Finished	1,302 sq. ft.
Garage Unfinished	672 sq. ft.
Deck Unfinished	166 sq. ft.
Porch Unfinished	78 sq. ft.
Dimensions	74'x56'
Foundation	Slab
Bedrooms	4
Full Baths	3
Half Baths	1
First Ceiling	10'
Second Ceiling	8'
Max Ridge Height	32'
Roof Framing	Stick
Exterior Walls	2x4

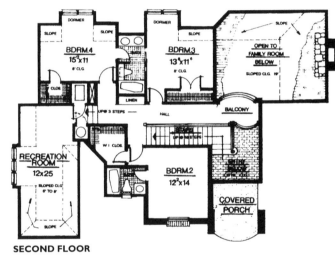

SECOND FLOOR

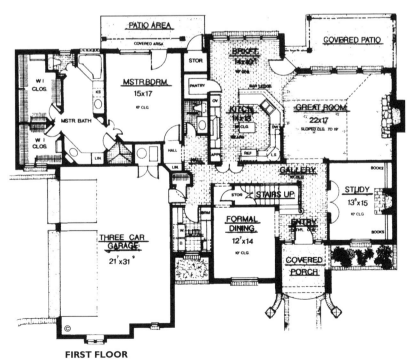

FIRST FLOOR

Design 32326

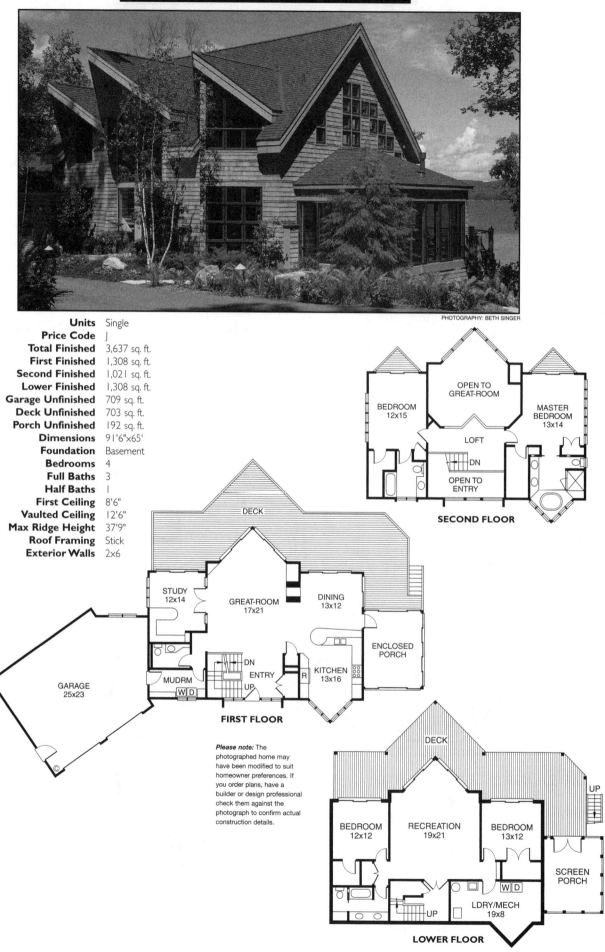

PHOTOGRAPHY: BETH SINGER

Units	Single
Price Code	J
Total Finished	3,637 sq. ft.
First Finished	1,308 sq. ft.
Second Finished	1,021 sq. ft.
Lower Finished	1,308 sq. ft.
Garage Unfinished	709 sq. ft.
Deck Unfinished	703 sq. ft.
Porch Unfinished	192 sq. ft.
Dimensions	91'6"×65'
Foundation	Basement
Bedrooms	4
Full Baths	3
Half Baths	I
First Ceiling	8'6"
Vaulted Ceiling	12'6"
Max Ridge Height	37'9"
Roof Framing	Stick
Exterior Walls	2x6

SECOND FLOOR

BEDROOM 12x15

OPEN TO GREAT-ROOM

MASTER BEDROOM 13x14

LOFT

DN

OPEN TO ENTRY

FIRST FLOOR

DECK

STUDY 12x14

GREAT-ROOM 17x21

DINING 13x12

ENCLOSED PORCH

DN

ENTRY

KITCHEN 13x16

MUDRM

W D

R

UP

GARAGE 25x23

Please note: The photographed home may have been modified to suit homeowner preferences. If you order plans, have a builder or design professional check them against the photograph to confirm actual construction details.

LOWER FLOOR

DECK

UP

BEDROOM 12x12

RECREATION 19x21

BEDROOM 13x12

SCREEN PORCH

W D

UP

LDRY/MECH 19x8

Units	Single
Price Code	J
Total Finished	3,663 sq. ft.
First Finished	3,298 sq. ft.
Second Finished	365 sq. ft.
Garage Unfinished	962 sq. ft.
Porch Unfinished	427 sq. ft.
Dimensions	100'x66'
Foundation	Crawlspace
Bedrooms	3
Full Baths	2
3/4 Baths	1
First Ceiling	10'
Second Ceiling	9'
Max Ridge Height	32'6"
Roof Framing	Stick
Exterior Walls	2x6

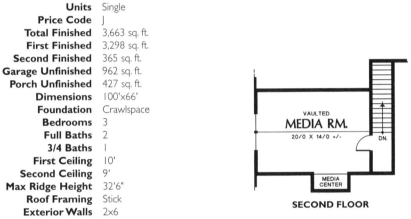

VAULTED
MEDIA RM.
20/0 x 14/0 +/-

DN.

MEDIA
CENTER

SECOND FLOOR

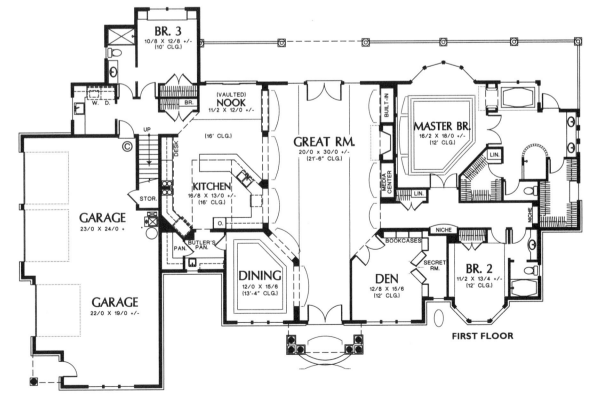

BR. 3
10/8 X 12/8 +/-
(10' CLG.)

W. D.

BR.

(VAULTED)
NOOK
11/2 X 12/0 +/-

(16' CLG.)

UP

DESK

GREAT RM.
20/0 X 30/0 +/-
(21'-6" CLG.)

BUILT-IN

MASTER BR.
16/2 X 18/0 +/-
(12' CLG.)

LIN.

MEDIA
CENTER

LIN.

KITCHEN
16/8 X 13/0 +/-
(16' CLG.)

STOR.

O.

NICHE

GARAGE
23/0 X 24/0 +

BUTLER'S
PAN.

PAN.

BOOKCASES

NICHE

GARAGE
22/0 X 19/0 +/-

DINING
12/0 X 15/6
(13'-4" CLG.)

DEN
12/8 X 15/6
(12' CLG.)

SECRET
RM.

BR. 2
11/2 X 13/4 +/-
(12' CLG.)

FIRST FLOOR

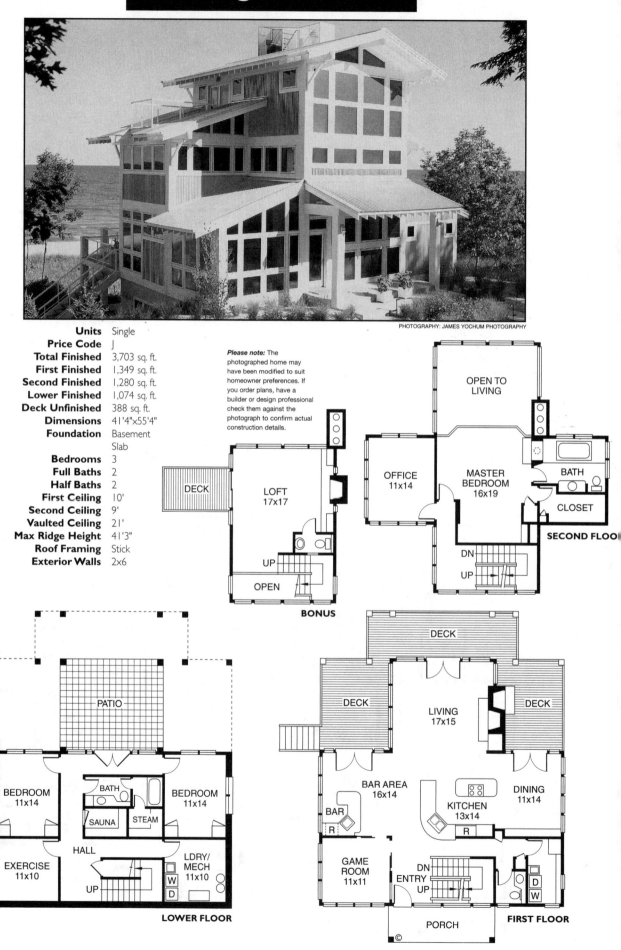

PHOTOGRAPHY: JAMES YOCHUM PHOTOGRAPHY

Units	Single
Price Code	J
Total Finished	3,703 sq. ft.
First Finished	1,349 sq. ft.
Second Finished	1,280 sq. ft.
Lower Finished	1,074 sq. ft.
Deck Unfinished	388 sq. ft.
Dimensions	41'4"x55'4"
Foundation	Basement
	Slab
Bedrooms	3
Full Baths	2
Half Baths	2
First Ceiling	10'
Second Ceiling	9'
Vaulted Ceiling	21'
Max Ridge Height	41'3"
Roof Framing	Stick
Exterior Walls	2x6

Please note: The photographed home may have been modified to suit homeowner preferences. If you order plans, have a builder or design professional check them against the photograph to confirm actual construction details.

DECK

LOFT
17x17

UP

OPEN

BONUS

OPEN TO LIVING

OFFICE
11x14

MASTER BEDROOM
16x19

BATH

CLOSET

DN

UP

SECOND FLOOR

PATIO

BEDROOM
11x14

BATH

SAUNA

STEAM

BEDROOM
11x14

HALL

EXERCISE
11x10

UP

LDRY/ MECH
11x10

W D

LOWER FLOOR

DECK

DECK

LIVING
17x15

DECK

BAR AREA
16x14

BAR

R

KITCHEN
13x14

R

DINING
11x14

GAME ROOM
11x11

DN ENTRY UP

D W

PORCH

FIRST FLOOR

Design 96934

PHOTOGRAPHY: COURTESY OF THE DESIGNER

Units	Single
Price Code	J
Total Finished	3,709 sq. ft.
First Finished	2,538 sq. ft.
Second Finished	1,171 sq. ft.
Basement Unfinished	2,621 sq. ft.
Garage Unfinished	779 sq. ft.
Dimensions	67'7"×85'1"
Foundation	Basement
Bedrooms	4
Full Baths	3
Half Baths	1
First Ceiling	10'
Second Ceiling	9'
Tray Ceiling	11'
Max Ridge Height	34'6"
Roof Framing	Stick
Exterior Walls	2x4

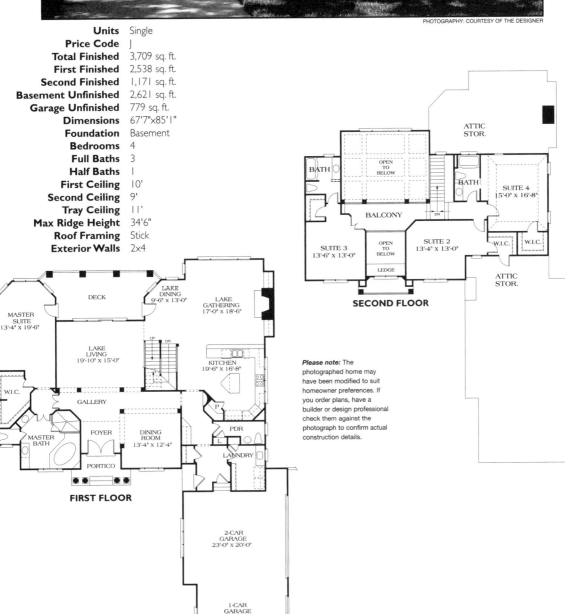

Please note: The photographed home may have been modified to suit homeowner preferences. If you order plans, have a builder or design professional check them against the photograph to confirm actual construction details.

Design 94252

Units	Single
Price Code	J
Total Finished	3,714 sq. ft.
Main Finished	3,714 sq. ft.
Dimensions	85'4"x91'0"
Foundation	Slab
Bedrooms	3
Full Baths	2
3/4 Baths	2
Half Baths	1
Max Ridge Height	29'10"
Roof Framing	Truss

* Alternate foundation options available at an additional charge.
Please call 1-800-235-5700 for more information.

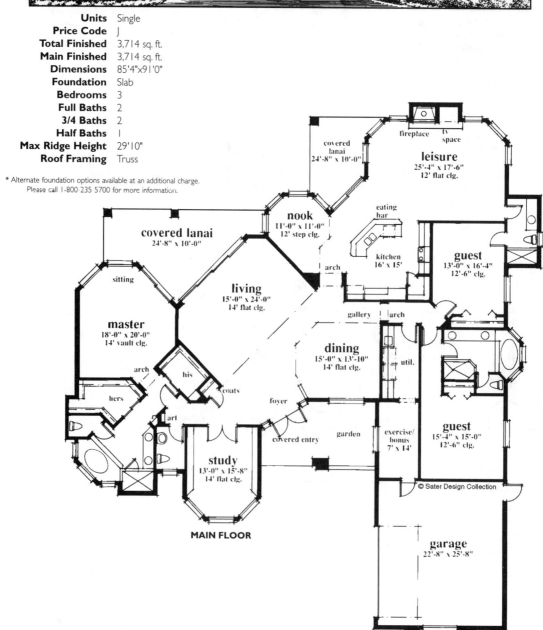

MAIN FLOOR

© Sater Design Collection

Design 32337

PHOTOGRAPHY: JAMES YOCHUM PHOTOGRAPHY

Units	Single
Price Code	E
Total Finished	3,756 sq. ft.
First Finished	2,038 sq. ft.
Second Finished	1,718 sq. ft.
Basement Unfinished	1,629 sq. ft.
Porch Unfinished	144 sq. ft.
Dimensions	52'x59'4"
Foundation	Basement
Bedrooms	4
Full Baths	2
Half Baths	2
First Ceiling	9'
Second Ceiling	8'
Vaulted Ceiling	18'
Max Ridge Height	34'6"
Roof Framing	Stick
Exterior Walls	2x4

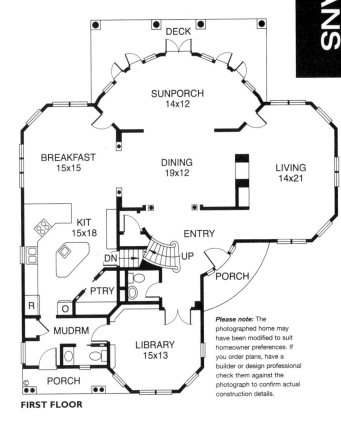

Please note: The photographed home may have been modified to suit homeowner preferences. If you order plans, have a builder or design professional check them against the photograph to confirm actual construction details.

FIRST FLOOR

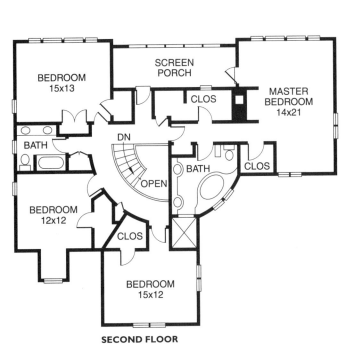

SECOND FLOOR

Design 10583

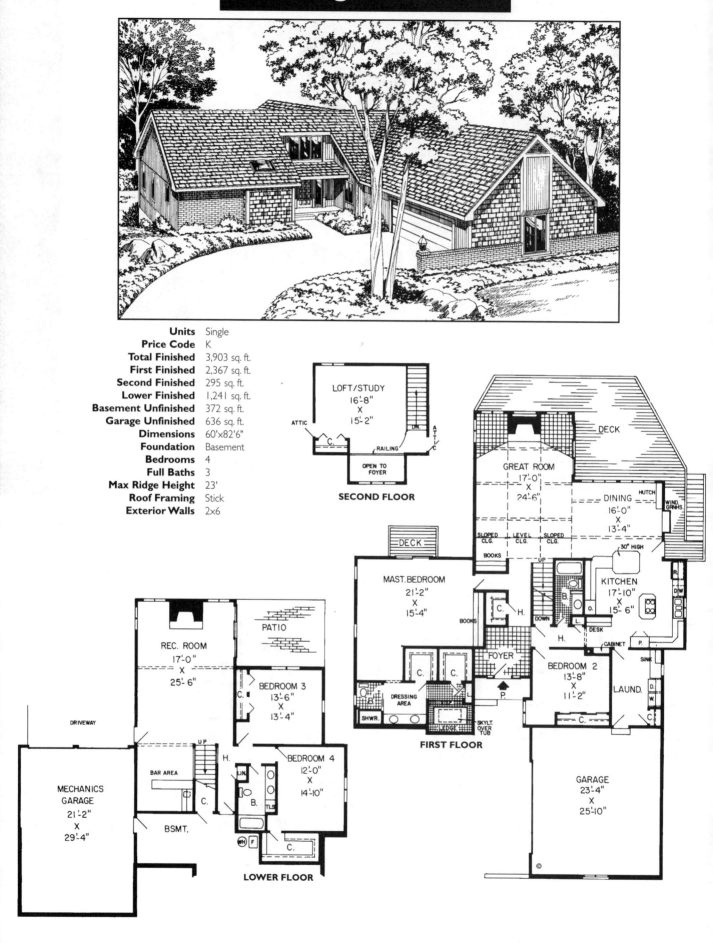

Units	Single
Price Code	K
Total Finished	3,903 sq. ft.
First Finished	2,367 sq. ft.
Second Finished	295 sq. ft.
Lower Finished	1,241 sq. ft.
Basement Unfinished	372 sq. ft.
Garage Unfinished	636 sq. ft.
Dimensions	60'x82'6"
Foundation	Basement
Bedrooms	4
Full Baths	3
Max Ridge Height	23'
Roof Framing	Stick
Exterior Walls	2x6

SECOND FLOOR

LOFT/STUDY
16'-8" X 15'-2"
ATTIC
OPEN TO FOYER
RAILING

FIRST FLOOR

DECK
GREAT ROOM 17'-0" X 24'-6"
DINING 16'-0" X 13'-4"
HUTCH
WIND. GRNHS.
KITCHEN 17'-10" X 15'-6"
SLOPED CLG. LEVEL CLG. SLOPED CLG.
BOOKS
30" HIGH
DECK
MAST. BEDROOM 21'-2" X 15'-4"
DOWN
DESK
BOOKS
FOYER
BEDROOM 2 13'-8" X 11'-2"
LAUND.
DRESSING AREA
SHWR.
LEDGE
SKYLT. OVER TUB
SINK
CABINET
GARAGE 23'-4" X 25'-10"

LOWER FLOOR

PATIO
REC. ROOM 17'-0" X 25'-6"
BEDROOM 3 13'-6" X 13'-4"
DRIVEWAY
BAR AREA
UP
MECHANICS GARAGE 21'-2" X 29'-4"
BSMT.
BEDROOM 4 12'-0" X 14'-10"
WH F
C.

Design 32374

Units	Single
Price Code	L
Total Finished	4,071 sq. ft.
First Finished	2,585 sq. ft.
Second Finished	1,486 sq. ft.
Basement Unfinished	2,009 sq. ft.
Garage Unfinished	576 sq. ft.
Deck Unfinished	506 sq. ft.
Porch Unfinished	507 sq. ft.
Dimensions	59'10"x52'4"
Foundation	Basement
Bedrooms	5
Full Baths	2
3/4 Baths	2
Half Baths	1
First Ceiling	9'
Second Ceiling	9'
Max Ridge Height	37'6"
Roof Framing	Stick
Exterior Walls	2x4

Hot New Design

Please note: The photographed home may have been modified to suit homeowner preferences. If you order plans, have a builder or design professional check them against the photograph to confirm actual construction details.

SECOND FLOOR

BEDROOM 13x20

BEDROOM 15x21

BEDROOM 16x14

BEDROOM 12x14

GALLERY

DN

OPEN TO ENTRY

BATH

DECK

PORCH

MASTER BEDROOM 18x16

SUNROOM 18x12

CLOSET

LIVING 22x27

DINING 15x15

BATH

DN UP

ENTRY

R

KITCHEN 15x18

STUDY 14x14

PORCH

LAUNDRY

D W

FIRST FLOOR

Design 32604

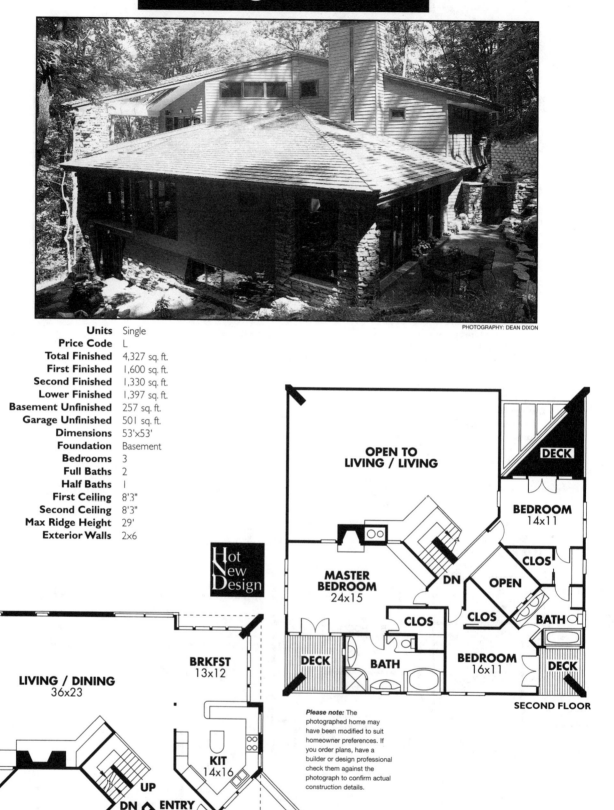

PHOTOGRAPHY: DEAN DIXON

Units	Single
Price Code	L
Total Finished	4,327 sq. ft.
First Finished	1,600 sq. ft.
Second Finished	1,330 sq. ft.
Lower Finished	1,397 sq. ft.
Basement Unfinished	257 sq. ft.
Garage Unfinished	501 sq. ft.
Dimensions	53'x53'
Foundation	Basement
Bedrooms	3
Full Baths	2
Half Baths	1
First Ceiling	8'3"
Second Ceiling	8'3"
Max Ridge Height	29'
Exterior Walls	2×6

Hot New Design

SECOND FLOOR

OPEN TO LIVING / LIVING

DECK

BEDROOM 14x11

MASTER BEDROOM 24x15

DN

OPEN

CLOS

BATH

CLOS

CLOS

BEDROOM 16x11

DECK

BATH

DECK

Please note: The photographed home may have been modified to suit homeowner preferences. If you order plans, have a builder or design professional check them against the photograph to confirm actual construction details.

FIRST FLOOR

LIVING / DINING 36x23

BRKFST 13x12

KIT 14x16

UP

DN ENTRY

GARAGE 18x23

PORCH

400 To order blueprints, call **800-235-5700** or visit us on the web, **familyhomeplans.com**

Design 19389

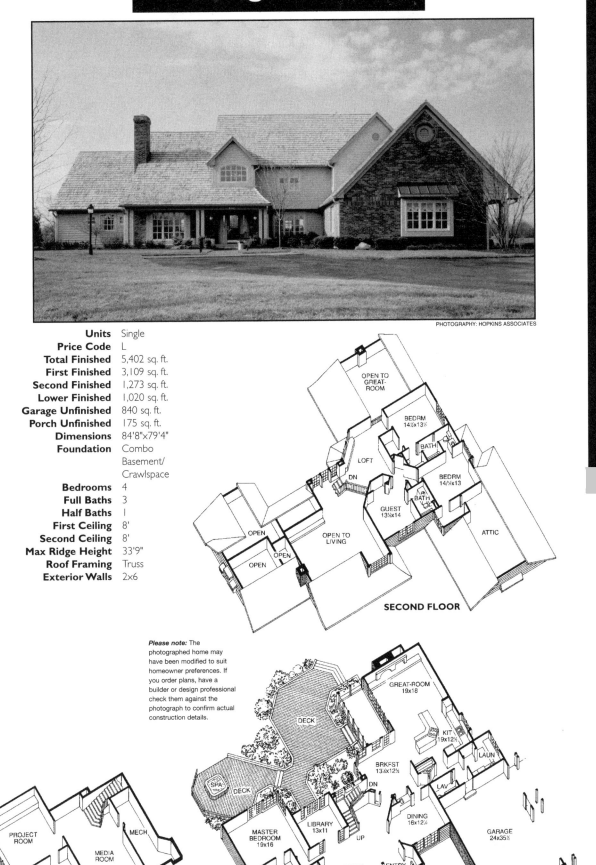

PHOTOGRAPHY: HOPKINS ASSOCIATES

Units	Single
Price Code	L
Total Finished	5,402 sq. ft.
First Finished	3,109 sq. ft.
Second Finished	1,273 sq. ft.
Lower Finished	1,020 sq. ft.
Garage Unfinished	840 sq. ft.
Porch Unfinished	175 sq. ft.
Dimensions	84'8"x79'4"
Foundation	Combo Basement/ Crawlspace
Bedrooms	4
Full Baths	3
Half Baths	1
First Ceiling	8'
Second Ceiling	8'
Max Ridge Height	33'9"
Roof Framing	Truss
Exterior Walls	2x6

Please note: The photographed home may have been modified to suit homeowner preferences. If you order plans, have a builder or design professional check them against the photograph to confirm actual construction details.

SECOND FLOOR

FIRST FLOOR

LOWER FLOOR

Design 19255

PHOTOGRAPHY: SUSAN GILMORE

Units	Single
Price Code	L
Total Finished	4,454 sq. ft.
First Finished	2,372 sq. ft.
Second Finished	1,031 sq. ft.
Lower Finished	1,051 sq. ft.
Bonus Unfinished	177 sq. ft.
Basement Unfinished	488 sq. ft.
Garage Unfinished	864 sq. ft.
Dimensions	82'5"×63'4"
Foundation	Basement
Bedrooms	4
Full Baths	2
Half Baths	1
First Ceiling	11'
Roof Framing	Truss
Exterior Walls	2x6

SECOND FLOOR

OPEN TO LIVING

BEDROOM 15x10

LOFT 10x11

DN

OPEN TO SUNROOM

BEDROOM 13x10

DN

BALCONY

BATH

BEDROOM 14x11

FUTURE EXPANSION 35x12

FIRST FLOOR

LIBRARY 8x13 UP

LIVING 15x18

MASTER BEDROOM 17x16

UP

UP

DINING 10x11

CLOSET

UP

SUNROOM 18x18

BATH

BRKFST 8x9

DN

Please note: The photographed home may have been modified to suit homeowner preferences. If you order plans, have a builder or design professional check them against the photograph to confirm actual construction details.

KITCHEN 17x12

R

D W

ENTRY

GARAGE 35x23

Design 91595

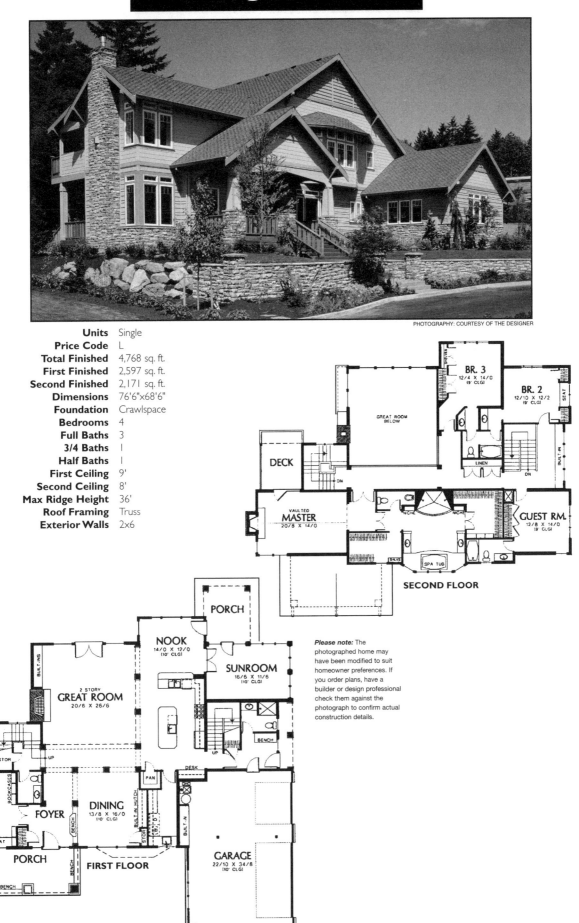

PHOTOGRAPHY: COURTESY OF THE DESIGNER

Units	Single
Price Code	L
Total Finished	4,768 sq. ft.
First Finished	2,597 sq. ft.
Second Finished	2,171 sq. ft.
Dimensions	76'6"x68'6"
Foundation	Crawlspace
Bedrooms	4
Full Baths	3
3/4 Baths	1
Half Baths	1
First Ceiling	9'
Second Ceiling	8'
Max Ridge Height	36'
Roof Framing	Truss
Exterior Walls	2x6

Please note: The photographed home may have been modified to suit homeowner preferences. If you order plans, have a builder or design professional check them against the photograph to confirm actual construction details.

Design 32200

PHOTOGRAPHY: JAMES SALOMON

Units	Single
Price Code	L
Total Finished	5,818 sq. ft.
First Finished	1,670 sq. ft.
Second Finished	2,683 sq. ft.
Lower Finished	1,465 sq. ft.
Garage Unfinished	996 sq. ft.
Deck Unfinished	249 sq. ft.
Porch Unfinished	1,152 sq. ft.
Dimensions	68'x58'8"
Foundation	Basement
Bedrooms	4
Full Baths	2
3/4 Baths	2
Half Baths	1
First Ceiling	8'
Second Ceiling	8'
Max Ridge Height	38'
Roof Framing	Stick
Exterior Walls	2x6

Hot New Design

BONUS

OFFICE 13x13
CEDAR CLOS
OPEN
DN
BEDROOM 14x15
ATTIC
OPEN TO ENTRY
PLANT LOFT
CLOSET
OPEN TO BATH

FIRST FLOOR

PORCH
FAMILY 23x15
DINING 13x13
BAR
LIVING 15x24
DN
UP
R
KIT/BRKFST 22x15
ENTRY
PORCH

SECOND FLOOR

DECK
BEDROOM 18x19
HALL
UP
MASTER BEDROOM 22x18
DN
BEDROOM 14x15
OPEN TO ENTRY
CLOSET

LOWER FLOOR

STORAGE
EXERCISE 17x16
BILLIARD ROOM 18x24
SAUNA
GARAGE 22X40
STOR/UTILITY 17x11
HALL
UP

Please note: The photographed home may have been modified to suit homeowner preferences. If you order plans, have a builder or design professional check them against the photograph to confirm actual construction details.

Exterior Elevations

These front, rear, and sides of the home include information pertaining to the exterior finish materials, roof pitches, and exterior height dimensions.

Cabinet Plans

These plans, or in some cases elevations, will detail the layout of the kitchen and bathroom cabinets at a larger scale. Available for most plans.

Typical Wall Section

This section will address insulation, roof components, and interior and exterior wall finishes. Your plans will be designed with either 2x4 or 2x6 exterior walls, but if you wish, most professional contractors can easily adapt the plans to the wall thickness you require.

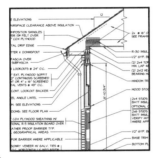

Fireplace Details

If the home you have chosen includes a fireplace, a fireplace detail will show typical methods of constructing the firebox, hearth, and flue chase for masonry units, or a wood frame chase for zero-clearance units. Available for most plans.

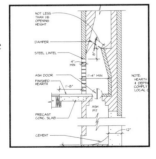

Foundation Plan

These plans will accurately show the dimensions of the footprint of your home, including load-bearing points and beam placement if applicable. The foundation style will vary from plan to plan. **(Please note: There may be an additional charge for optional foundation plan. Please call for details.)**

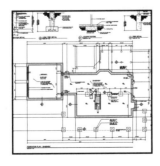

Roof Plan

The information necessary to construct the roof will be included with your home plans. Some plans will reference roof trusses, while many others contain schematic framing plans. These framing plans will indicate the lumber sizes necessary for the rafters and ridgeboards based on the designated roof loads.

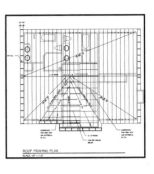

Typical Cross Section

A cut-away cross section through the entire home shows your building contractor the exact correlation of construction components at all levels of the house. It will help to clarify the load bearing points from the roof all the way down to the basement. Available for most plans.

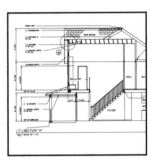

Detailed Floor Plans

The floor plans of your home accurately depict the dimensions of the positioning of all walls, doors, windows, stairs, and permanent fixtures. They will show you the relationship and dimensions of rooms, closets, and traffic patterns. The schematic of the electrical layout may be included in the plan.

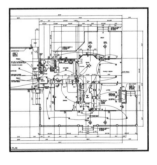

Stair Details

If the design you have chosen includes stairs, the plans will show the information that you need in order to build them—either through a stair cross section or on the floor plans.

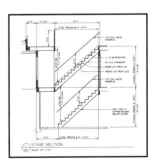

Garlinghouse Options & Extras

Reversed Plans can Make Your Dream Home Just Right!

You could have exactly the home you want by flipping it end-for-end. Simply order your plans "reversed." We'll send you one full set of mirror-image plans (with the writing backwards) as a master guide for you and your builder.

The remaining sets of your order will come as shown in this book so the dimensions and specifications are easily read on the job site. Most plans in our collection come stamped "reversed" so there is no construction confusion.

We can only send reversed plans with multiple-set orders. There is a $50 charge for this service.

Some plans in our collection are available in "Right Reading Reverse." Right Reading Reverse plans will show your home in reverse. This easy-to-read format will save you valuable time and money. Please contact our Sales Department at 800-235-5700 to check for Right Reading Reverse availability. There is a $135 charge for this service. **RRR**

Remember to Order Your Materials List

Available at a modest additional charge, the Materials List gives the quantity, dimensions, and specifications for the major materials needed to build your home. You will get faster, more accurate bids from your contractors and building suppliers—and avoid paying for unused materials and waste. **Materials Lists are available for all home plans except as otherwise indicated, but can only be ordered with a set of home plans.** Due to differences in regional requirements and homeowner or builder preferences, electrical, plumbing and heating/air conditioning equipment specifications are not designed specifically for each plan. **ML**

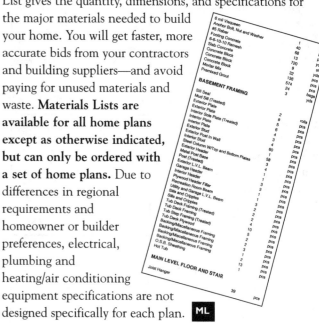

What Garlinghouse Offers

Home Plan Blueprint Package

By purchasing a multiple-set package of blueprints or a Vellum from Garlinghouse, you not only receive the physical blueprint documents necessary for construction, but you are also granted a license to build one (and only one) home. You can also make simple modifications, including minor non-structural changes and material substitutions, to our design as long as these changes are made directly on the blueprints purchased from Garlinghouse and no additional copies are made.

Home Plan Vellums

By purchasing Vellums for one of our home plans, you receive the same construction drawings found in the blueprints, but printed on vellum paper. Vellums can be erased and are perfect for making design changes. They are also semi-transparent, making them easy to duplicate. But most importantly, the purchase of home plan Vellums comes with a broader license that allows you to make changes to the design (i.e., create a hand drawn or CAD derivative work), to make copies of the plan, and to build one home from the plan.

License to Build Additional Homes

With the purchase of a blueprint package or Vellums, you automatically receive a license to build one home and only one home. If you want to build more homes than you are licensed to build through your purchase of a plan, then additional licenses must be purchased at reasonable costs from Garlinghouse. Inquire for more information.

Modifying Your Favorite Design Made Easy

#1 Modifying Your Garlinghouse Home Plan

Simple modifications to your dream home, including minor non-structural changes and material substitutions, can be made by you and your builder with the consent of your local building official, by marking the changes directly on your blueprints. However, if you are considering making significant changes to your chosen design, we recommend that you use the services of The Garlinghouse Design Staff. We will help take your ideas and turn them into a reality, just the way you want. Here's our procedure:

Call 800-235-5700 and order your modification estimate. The fee for this estimate is $50. We will review your plan changes and provide you with an estimate to draft your specific modifications before you purchase the vellums. *Please note: A vellum must be purchased to modify a home plan design.*

After you receive your estimate, if you decide to have Garlinghouse do the changes, the $50 estimate fee will be deducted from the cost of your modifications. If, however, you chose to use a different service, the $50 estimate fee is non-refundable. *(Note: Personal checks cannot be accepted for the estimate.)*

A 75% deposit is required before we begin making the actual modifications to your plans.

Once the design changes have been completed to your vellum plan, a representative will call to inform you that your modified vellum plan is complete and will be shipped as soon as the final payment has been made. For additional information, call us at 1-800-235-5700. Please refer to the Modification Pricing Guide for estimated modification costs.

#2 Reproducible Vellums for Local Modification Ease

If you decide not to use Garlinghouse for your modifications, we recommend that you follow our same procedure of purchasing vellums. You then have the option of using the services of the original designer of the plan, a local professional designer, or an architect to make the modifications.

With a vellum copy of our plans, a design professional can alter the drawings just the way you want, then you can print as many copies of the modified plans as you need to build your house. And, since you have already started with our complete detailed plans, the cost of those expensive professional services will be significantly less than starting from scratch. Refer to the price schedule for vellum costs.

Ignoring Copyright Laws Can Be A $100,000 MISTAKE

U.S. copyright laws allow for statutory penalties of up to $100,000 per incident for copyright infringement involving any of the copyrighted plans found in this publication. The law can be confusing. So, for your own protection, take the time to understand what you can and cannot do when it comes to home plans.

What You Can't Do

You Cannot Duplicate Home Plans

Purchasing a set of blueprints and making additional sets by reproducing the original is illegal. If you need more than one set of a particular home plan, you must purchase them.

You Cannot Copy Any Part of a Home Plan to Create Another

Creating your own plan by copying even part of a home design found in this publication without permission is called "creating a derivative work" and is illegal.

You Cannot Build a Home Without a License

You must have specific permission or a license to build a home from a copyrighted design, even if the finished home has been changed from the original plan. It is illegal to build one of the homes found in this publication without a license.

How to obtain a construction cost calculation based on labor rates and building material costs in your zip code area.

What will your dream home cost? ZIP QUOTE has the answer!

How does Zip Quote actually work? When you call to order, you must choose from the options available for your specific home in order for us to process your order. Once we receive your Zip Quote order, we process your specific home plan building materials list through our Home Cost Calculator which contains up-to-date rates for all residential labor trades and building material costs in your zip code area. The result? A calculated cost to build your dream home in your zip code area. This calculation will help you (as a consumer or a builder) evaluate your building budget.

All database information for our calculations is furnished by Marshall & Swift, L.P. For over 60 years, Marshall & Swift L.P. has been a leading provider of cost data to professionals in all aspects of the construction and remodeling industries.

Zip Quote can be purchased in two separate formats, either an itemized or a bottom-line format.

Option 1 The **Itemized Zip Quote** is a detailed building materials list. Each building materials list line item will separately state the labor cost, material cost, and equipment cost (if applicable) for the use of that building material in the construction process. This building materials list will be summarized by the individual building categories and will have additional columns where you can enter data from your contractor's estimates for a cost comparison between the different suppliers and contractors who will actually quote you their products and services.

Option 2 The **Bottom-Line Zip Quote** is a one line summarized total cost for the home plan of your choice. This cost calculation is also based on the labor cost, material cost, and equipment cost (if applicable) within your zip code area. Bottom-Line Zip Quote is available for most plans. Please call for availability.

Cost The price of your Itemized Zip Quote is based upon the pricing schedule of the plan you have selected, in addition to the price of the materials list. Please refer to the pricing schedule on our order form. The price of your initial Bottom-Line Zip Quote is $29.95. Each additional Bottom-Line Zip Quote ordered in conjunction with the initial order is only $14.95. A Bottom-Line Zip Quote may be purchased separately and does NOT have to be purchased in conjunction with a home plan order.

FYI An Itemized Zip Quote Home Cost Calculation can ONLY be purchased in conjunction with a Home Plan order. The Itemized Zip Quote can not be purchased separately. If you find within 60 days of your order date that you will be unable to build this home, then you may apply the price of the plans and the materials list towards the price of a new set of plans (see order info pages for plan exchange policy). The Itemized Zip Quote and the Bottom-Line Zip Quote are NOT returnable. The price of the initial Bottom-Line Zip Quote order can be credited toward the purchase of an Itemized Zip Quote order, only if available. Additional Bottom-Line Zip Quote orders, within the same order can not be credited. Please call our Sales Department for more information.

An Itemized Zip Quote is available for plans where you see this symbol. **ZIP**

A Bottom-Line Zip Quote is available for all plans under 4,000 sq. ft. or where you see this symbol. **BL** Please call for current availability.

Some More Information The Itemized and Bottom-Line Zip Quotes give you approximated costs for constructing the particular house in your area. These costs are not exact and are only intended to be used as a preliminary estimate to help determine the affordability of a new home and/or as a guide to evaluate the general competitiveness of actual price quotes obtained through local suppliers and contractors. **Land, landscaping, sewer systems, site work, contractor overhead and profit, and other expenses are not included in our building cost figures. Excluding land and landscaping, you may incur an additional 20% to 40% in costs from the original estimate.** Garlinghouse and Marshall & Swift L.P. cannot guarantee any level of data accuracy or correctness in a Zip Quote and disclaim all liability for loss with respect to the same, in excess of the original purchase price of the Zip Quote product. All Zip Quote calculations are based upon the actual blueprints and do not reflect any differences or options that may be shown on the published house renderings, floor plans, or photographs.

CAD Files Now Available

A CAD file is available for plans where you see this symbol.

Cad files are available in .dc5 or .dxf format or .dwg formats (R12, R13, R14, R2000). Please specify the file format at the time of your order. You will receive one bond set along with the CAD file when you place your order. **NOTE: CAD files are NOT returnable and can not be exchanged.**

Your Blueprints Can Be Sealed by A Registered Architect

We can have your home plan blueprints sealed by an architect that is registered in most states. Please call our Order Department for details. Although an architect's seal will not guarantee approval of your home plan blueprints, a seal is sometimes required by your state or local building department in order to get a building permit. Please talk to your local building officials, before you order your blueprints, to determine if a seal is needed in your area. You will need to provide the county and state of your building site when ordering an architect's seal on your blueprints, and please allow additional time to process your order (an additional five to fifteen working days, at least). Seals are available for plans numbered 0-15,999, 17,000-18,999, 20,000 - 31,999, and 34,000 - 34,999.

State Energy Certificates

A few states require that an energy certificate be prepared for your new home to their specifications before a building permit can be issued. Again, your local building official can tell you if one is required in your state. You will first need to fill out the energy certificate checklist available to you when your order is placed. This list contains questions about type of heating used, siding, windows, location of home, etc. This checklist provides all the information needed to prepare your state energy certificate. **Please note: energy certificates are only available on orders for blueprints with an architect's seal.** Certificates are available for plans numbered 0-15,999, 17,000-18,999, 20,000 - 31,999, and 34,000 - 34,999.

Specifications & Contract Form

We send this form to you free of charge with your home plan order. The form is designed to be filled in by you or your contractor with the exact materials to use in the construction of your new home. Once signed by you and your contractor it will provide you with peace of mind throughout the construction process.

Detail Plans
Valuable Information About Construction Techniques—Not Plan Specific

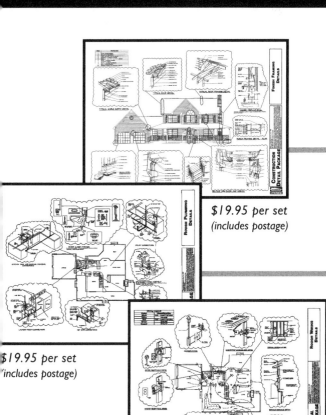

$19.95 per set
(includes postage)

$19.95 per set
(includes postage)

$19.95 per set
(includes postage)

PLEASE NOTE: The detail plans are not specific to any one home plan and should be used only as a general reference guide. Because local codes and requirements vary greatly, we recommend that you obtain drawings and bids from licensed contractors to do your mechanical plans. However, if you want to know more about techniques — and deal more confidently with subcontractors — we offer these remarkably useful detail sheets. These detail sheets will aid in your understanding of these technical subjects.

RESIDENTIAL CONSTRUCTION DETAILS

Ten sheets that cover the essentials of stick-built residential home construction. Details foundation options — poured concrete basement, concrete block, or monolithic concrete slab. Shows all aspects of floor, wall and roof framing. Provides details for roof dormers, overhangs, chimneys and skylights. Conforms to requirements of Uniform Building code or BOCA code. Includes a quick index and a glossary of terms.

RESIDENTIAL PLUMBING DETAILS

Eight sheets packed with information detailing pipe installation methods, fittings, and sized. Details plumbing hook-ups for toilets, sinks, washers, sump pumps, and septic system construction. Conforms to requirements of National Plumbing code. Color coded with a glossary of terms and quick index.

RESIDENTIAL ELECTRICAL DETAILS

Eight sheets that cover all aspects of residential wiring, from simple switch wiring to service entrance connections. Details distribution panel layout with outlet and switch schematics, circuit breaker and wiring installation methods, and ground fault interrupter specifications. Conforms to requirements of National Electrical Code. Color coded with a glossary of terms.

Questions?
Call our customer service number at 1-800-235-5700.

The Garlinghouse Company

BEST PLAN VALUE IN THE INDUSTRY!

Order Code No. **H4CCC**

Order Form

_____foundation

____ set(s) of blueprints for plan #_____ $_____

____ Vellum for plan #_____ $_____

____ Additional set(s) @ $50 each for plan #_____ $_____
(Not available for 1 set-study set)

____ Mirror Image Reverse @ $50 each $_____

____ Right Reading Reverse @ $135 each $_____

____ Materials list for plan #_____ $_____

____ Detail Plans (Not plan specific) @ $19.95 each

     ❏ Construction   ❏ Plumbing   ❏ Electrical $_____

____ Bottom-Line Zip Quote @ $29.95 for plan #_____ $_____

____ Additional Bottom-Line Zip Quotes

     @ $14.95 for plan(s) #_____ $_____

Zip code where building _____

____ Itemized Zip Quote for plan(s) #_____ $_____

Shipping $_____

Subtotal $_____

Sales Tax (VA residents add 4.5%. Not required for other states.) $_____

TOTAL AMOUNT ENCLOSED $_____

Send your check, money order, or credit card information to:
(No C.O.D.'s Please)

Please submit all United States & other nations orders to:

The Garlinghouse Co.
Attn: Order Fulfillment Dept.
4125 Lafayette Rd. Ste. 100
Chantilly, VA. 20151
CALL: (800) 235-5700

Please Submit all Canadian plan orders to:
Garlinghouse Company
102 Ellis Street
Penticton, BC V2A 4L5
CALL: (800) 361-7526   FAX: (250) 493-7526

ADDRESS INFORMATION:

NAME: _____

STREET: _____

CITY: _____

STATE: _____ ZIP: _____

DAYTIME PHONE: _____

E-MAIL ADDRESS: _____

Credit Card Information

Charge To: ❏ Visa   ❏ Mastercard

Card # | | | | | | | | | | | | | | | | | | |

Signature _____ Exp. ____/____

410

To order your plan on-line now
using our secure server, visit:
www.garlinghouse.com

CUSTOMER SERVICE	TO PLACE ORDERS
Questions on existing orders?	• To order your home plans • Questions about a plan
➡ **1-800-895-3715**	➡ **1-800-235-5700**

Privacy Statement (please read)

Dear Valued Garlinghouse Customer,

Your privacy is extremely important to us. We'd like to take a little of your time to explain our privacy policy.

As a service to you, we would like to provide your name to companies such as the following:

- Building material manufacturers that we are affiliated with, who would like to keep you current with their product line and specials.
- Building material retailers that would like to offer you competitive prices to help you save money.
- Financing companies that would like to offer you competitive mortgage rates.

In addition, as our valued customer, we would like to send you newsletters to assist in your building experience. *We* would also appreciate *your* feedback by filling out a customer service survey aimed to improve our operations.

You have total control over the use of your contact information. You let us know exactly how you want to be contacted. Please check all boxes that apply.
Thank you.

❏ Don't mail
❏ Don't call
❏ Don't E-mail
❏ Only send Garlinghouse newsletters
    and customer service surveys

In closing, we hope this shows Garlinghouse's firm commitment to providing superior customer service and protection of your privacy. We thank you for your time and consideration.

Sincerely,

The Garlinghouse Company

For Our **USA** Customers:
Order Toll Free: 1-800-235-5700
Monday-Friday 8:00 a.m. to 8:00 p.m. Eastern Time

CUSTOMER SERVICE	TO PLACE ORDERS
Questions on existing orders?	• To order your home plans • Questions about a plan
➡ 1-800-895-3715	➡ 1-800-235-5700

For Our **Canadian** Customers:
Order Toll Free: 1-800-361-7526
Monday-Friday 8:00 a.m. to 5:00 p.m. Pacific Time
or FAX your Credit Card order to 1-250-493-7526
Customer Service: 1-250-493-0942

Please have ready: **1. Your credit card number** **2. The plan number** **3. The order code number** ➡ **H4CCC**

Garlinghouse 2004 Blueprint Price Code Schedule
Prices subject to change without notice.

	1 Set Study Set	4 Sets	8 Sets	Vellums	ML	Bottom-Line ZIP Quote	CADD Files
A	$395	$435	$485	$600	$60	$29.95	$1,250
B	$425	$465	$515	$630	$60	$29.95	$1,300
C	$450	$490	$540	$665	$60	$29.95	$1,350
D	$490	$530	$580	$705	$60	$29.95	$1,400
E	$530	$570	$620	$750	$70	$29.95	$1,450
F	$585	$625	$675	$800	$70	$29.95	$1,500
G	$630	$670	$720	$850	$70	$29.95	$1,550
H	$675	$715	$765	$895	$70	$29.95	$1,600
I	$700	$740	$790	$940	$80	$29.95	$1,650
J	$740	$780	$830	$980	$80	$29.95	$1,700
K	$805	$845	$895	$1,020	$80	$29.95	$1,750
L	$825	$865	$915	$1,055	$80	$29.95	$1,800

Shipping — (Plans 1-35999)

	1-3 Sets	4-6 Sets	7+ & Vellums
Standard Delivery (UPS 2-Day)	$25.00	$30.00	$35.00
Overnight Delivery	$35.00	$40.00	$45.00

Shipping — (Plans 36000-99999)

	1-3 Sets	4-6 Sets	7+ & Vellums
Ground Delivery (7-10 Days)	$15.00	$20.00	$25.00
Express Delivery (3-5 Days)	$20.00	$25.00	$30.00

International Shipping & Handling

	1-3 Sets	4-6 Sets	7+ & Vellums
Regular Delivery Canada (10-14 Days)	$30.00	$35.00	$40.00
Express Delivery Canada (7-10 Days)	$60.00	$70.00	$80.00
Overseas Delivery Airmail (3-4 Weeks)	$50.00	$60.00	$65.00

Additional sets with original order $50

IMPORTANT INFORMATION TO READ BEFORE YOU PLACE YOUR ORDER

How Many Sets of Plans Will You Need?

The Standard 8-Set Construction Package

Our experience shows that you'll speed up every step of construction and avoid costly building errors by ordering enough sets to go around. Each tradesperson wants a set—the general contractor and all subcontractors: foundation, electrical, plumbing, heating/air conditioning, and framers. Don't forget your lending institution, building department, and, of course, a set for yourself. * Recommended For Construction *

The Minimum 4-Set Construction Package

If you're comfortable with arduous follow-up, this package can save you a few dollars by giving you the option of passing down plan sets as work progresses. You might have enough copies to go around if work goes exactly as scheduled and no plans are lost or damaged by subcontractors. But for only $60 more, the 8-set package eliminates these worries. * Recommended For Bidding *

The 1 Set-Study Set

We offer this set so you can study the blueprints to plan your dream home in detail. They are stamped "study set only—not for construction" and you cannot build a home from them. In pursuant to copyright laws, it is illegal to reproduce any blueprint. 1 set-study sets cannot be ordered in a reversed format.

To Reorder, Call 800-235-5700

If you find after your initial purchase that you require additional sets of plans, a materials list, or other items, you may purchase them from us at special reorder prices (please call for pricing details) provided that you reorder within six months of your original order date. There is a $28 reorder processing fee that is charged on all reorders. For more information on reordering plans, please contact our Sales Department.

Customer Service/Exchanges Call 800-895-3715

If for some reason you have a question about your existing order, please call 800-895-3715. Your plans are custom printed especially for you once you place your order. For that reason we cannot accept any returns. If for some reason you find that the plan you have purchased from us does not meet your needs, then you may exchange that plan for any other plan in our collection. We allow you 60 days from your original invoice date to make an exchange. At the time of the exchange, you will be charged a processing fee of 20% of the total amount of your original order, plus the difference in price between the plans (if applicable), plus the cost to ship the new plans to you. Call our Customer Service Department for more information. Please Note: Reproducible Vellums can only be exchanged if they are unopened.

Important Shipping Information

Please refer to the shipping charts on the order form for service availability for your specific plan number. Our delivery service must have a street address or Rural Route Box number—never a post office box. (PLEASE NOTE: Supplying a P.O. Box number will only will delay the shipping of your order.) Use a work address if no one is home during the day. Orders being shipped to APO or FPO must go via First Class Mail. Please include the proper postage.

For our International Customers, only Certified bank checks and money orders are accepted and must be payable in U.S. currency. For speed, we ship international orders Air Parcel Post. Please refer to the chart for the correct shipping cost.

Important Canadian Shipping Information

To our friends in Canada, we have a plan design affiliate in Penticton, BC. This relationship will help you avoid the delays and charges associated with shipments from the United States. Moreover, our affiliate is familiar with the building requirements in your community and country. We prefer payments in U.S. currency. If you however are sending Canadian funds, please add 45% to the prices of the plans and shipping fees.

An Important Note About Building Code Requirements

All plans are drawn to conform to one or more of the industry's major national building standards. However, due to the variety of local building regulations, your plan may need to be modified to comply with local requirements—snow loads, energy loads, seismic zones, etc. Do check them fully and consult your local building officials.

A few states require that all building plans used be drawn by an architect registered in that state. While having your plans reviewed and stamped by such an architect may be prudent, laws requiring non-conforming plans like ours to be completely redrawn forces you to unnecessarily pay very large fees. If your state has such a law, we strongly recommend you contact your state representative to protest.

The rendering, floor plans, and technical information contained within this publication are not guaranteed to be totally accurate. Consequently, no information from this publication should be used either as a guide to constructing a home or for estimating the cost of building a home. Complete blueprints must be purchased for such purposes.

Index

Index

Option Key

TOP SELLING
GARAGE PLANS

Save money by Doing-It-Yourself using our Easy-To-Follow plans. Whether you intend to build your own garage or contract it out to a building professional, the Garlinghouse garage plans provide you with everything you need to price out your project and get started. Put our 90+ years of experience to work for you. Order now!!

No. 06016C $24.95

Cape Cod Style Apartment Garage With One Bedroom

- 28' x 24' Overall Dimensions
- 544 Square Foot Apartment
- 12/12 Gable Roof with Dormers
- Slab or Stem Wall Foundation Options

No. 06015C $24.95

Apartment Garage With Two Bedrooms

- 28' x 26' Overall Dimensions
- 728 Square Foot Apartment
- 4/12 Pitch Gable Roof
- Slab or Stem Wall Foundation Options

No. 06012C $16.95

30' Deep Gable &/or Eave Entry Jumbo Garages

- 4/12 Pitch Gable Roof
- Available Options for Extra Tall Walls, Garage & Personnel Doors, Foundation, Window, & Sidings
- Package contains 4 Different Sizes
- 30' x 28'   • 30' x 32'   • 30' x 36'   • 30' x 40'

No. 06013C $16.95

Two-Car Eave Entry Garage With Mudroom/Breezeway

- Attaches to Any House
- 36' x 24' Eave Entry
- Available Options for Utility Room with Bath, Mudroom, Screened-In Breezeway, Roof, Foundation, Garage & Personnel Doors, Window, & Sidings

No. 06001C $14.95

12', 14' & 16' Wide-Gable Entry 1-Car Garages

- Available Options for Roof, Foundation, Window, Door, & Sidings
- Package contains 8 Different Sizes
- 12' x 20' Mini-Garage • 14' x 22' • 16' x 20' • 16' x 24'
- 14' x 20' • 14' x 24' • 16' x 22' • 16' x 26'

No. 06003C $14.95

24' Wide-Gable Entry 2-Car Garages

- Available Options for Side Shed, Roof, Foundation, Garage & Personnel Doors, Window, & Sidings
- Package contains 5 Different Sizes
- 24' x 22' • 24' x 28' • 24' x 36'
- 24' x 24' • 24' x 32'

No. 06007C $16.95

Gable 2-Car Gable Entry Gambrel Roof Garages

- Rear Stairs to Loft Workshop
- Front Loft Cargo Door With Pulley Lift
- Available Options for Foundation, Garage & Personnel Doors, Window, & Sidings
- Package contains 5 Different Sizes
- 22' x 26' • 22' x 28' • 24' x 28' • 24' x 30' • 24' x 32'

No. 06006C $16.95

22' & 24' Deep Eave Entry 2 & 3-Car Garages

- Can Be Built Stand-Alone or Attached to House
- Available Options for Roof, Foundation, Garage & Personnel Doors, Window, & Sidings
- Package contains 6 Different Sizes
- 22' x 28' • 22' x 32' • 24' x 32'
- 22' x 30' • 24' x 30' • 24' x 36'

No. 06002C $14.95

20' & 22' Wide-Gable Entry 2-Car Garages

- Available Options for Roof, Foundation, Garage & Personnel Doors, Window, & Sidings
- Package contains 7 Different Sizes
- 20' x 20' • 20' x 24' • 22' x 22' • 22' x 28'
- 20' x 22' • 20' x 28' • 22' x 24'

No. 06008C $16.95

Eave Entry 2 & 3-Car Clerestory Roof Garages

- Interior Side Stairs to Loft Workshop
- Available Options for Engine Lift, Foundation, Garage & Personnel Doors, Window, & Sidings
- Package contains 4 Different Sizes
- 24' x 26' • 24' x 28' • 24' x 32' • 24' x 36'

Order Code No: **H4CCC**

Garage Order Form

Please send me 1 complete set of the following GARAGE PLAN BLUEPRINTS:

Item no. & description _____	Price
	$ _____
Additional Sets	
(@ $10.00 EACH)	$ _____
Garage Vellum	
(@ $200.00 EACH)	$ _____

Shipping Charges: **UPS Ground (3-7 days within the US)** $ _____
  1-3 plans $7.95
  4-6 plans $9.95
  7-10 plans $11.95
  11 or more plans $17.95

Subtotal: $ _____

Resident sales tax: $ _____
(VA residents add 4.5%. Not required for other states.)

Total Enclosed: $ _____

My Billing Address is:

Name: _____

Address: _____

City: _____

State: _____ Zip: _____

Daytime Phone No. (_____) _____

My Shipping Address is:

Name: _____

Address: _____
        (UPS will not ship to P.O. Boxes)

City: _____

State: _____ Zip: _____

For Faster Service...Charge It!
U.S. & Canada Call
1(800)235-5700

MASTERCARD, VISA

Card # | | | | | | | | | | | | | | | |

Signature _____ Exp. ____ / ____

If paying by credit card, to avoid delays:
billing address must be as it appears on credit card statement

Here's What You Get

- One complete set of drawings for each plan ordered
- Detailed step-by-step instructions with easy-to-follow diagrams on how to build your garage (not available with apartment garages)
- For each garage style, a variety of size and garage door configuration options
- Variety of roof styles and/or pitch options for most garages
- Complete materials list
- Choice between three foundation options: Monolithic Slab, Concrete Stem Wall or Concrete Block Stem Wa
- Full framing plans, elevations and cross-sectionals fo each garage size and configuration

Garage Plan Blueprints

All blueprint garage plan orders contain one complete se of drawings with instructions and are priced as listed nex to the illustration. **These blueprint garage plans can no be modified.** Additional sets of plans may be obtained fo $10.00 each with your original order. UPS shipping i used unless otherwise requested. Please include th proper amount for shipping.

Garage Plan Vellums

By purchasing vellums for one of our garage plans, yo receive one vellum set of the same construction drawing found in the blueprints, but printed on vellum pape Vellums can be erased and are perfect for making desig changes. They are also semi-transparent making ther easy to duplicate. But most importantly, the purchase o garage plan vellums comes with a broader license tha allows you to make changes to the design (ie, create hand drawn or CAD derivative work), to make copies o the plan and to build one garage from the plan.

the Garlinghouse company

Send your order to:
(With check or money order payable in U.S. funds only)
The Garlinghouse Company
Attn: Order Fulfillment Dept.
4125 Lafayette Rd. Ste. 100
Chantilly, Va. 20151

No C.O.D. orders accepted; U.S. funds only. UPS will not ship to Post Office boxes, FPO boxes, APO boxes, Alaska or Hawaii.

Canadian orders:
UPS Ground (5-10 days within Canada)
  1-3 plans $15.95
  4-6 plans $17.95
  7-10 plans $19.95
  11 or more plans $24.95
Prices subject to change without notice.